# 1001 DAYS OUT

HISTORIC HOUSES, GARDENS AND PLACES TO VISIT

# 1001 DAYS OUT

## HISTORIC HOUSES, GARDENS AND PLACES TO VISIT

*p*

This is a Parragon Book
First Published in 2006

Parragon
Queen Street House
4 Queen Street
Bath BA1 1HE, UK

Copyright © Parragon Books Ltd 2006

All the information given in this book has come directly
from the attractions included and was correct at the time
of going to press. The Publishers will be grateful for any
information that will assist in keeping future editions up
to date. While every care has been taken in the preparation
of this book, neither the Compilers nor the Publishers
can accept any liability for any consequences arising from
the use thereof, or the information contained therein.
The prices, times and facilities given should be used as
a guide only as they will vary with time.

ISBN 1-40546-312-0

Designed by Butler and Tanner
Printed in Indonesia

*Front cover*
Stonehenge, courtesy of ©Britain on View

*Frontispiece*
Norwich Cathedral close, courtesy of ©Britain on View

*Right*
Lacock Abbey, courtesy of ©Britain on View

**IMPORTANT NOTE FOR THE READER**

We have made every effort to ensure the information in this
guide is accurate and up to date, but things do change very
quickly. Prices and opening times are sometimes altered at
short notice, and sadly some venues close unexpectedly. We
would therefore urge readers to telephone the venue before
setting out on a visit. This will ensure you are aware of any
changes in ticket prices or opening times, and will avoid
unexpected disappointments or problems.

The contents of this book are believed correct at the time of
printing. The Publisher cannot be held responsible for any errors,
omissions or changes in the information in this guide or for the
consequences of any reliance on the information provided.

# Contents

# Introduction

Britain is one of the most popular holiday destinations in the world. It's easy to see why. Major cities like London, Glasgow and York with their world-famous museums, palaces and stately architecture attract visitors all year round. There are also areas of outstanding natural beauty like the Lake District and the Peak District, the Brecon Beacons and the Gower Peninsula in Wales and the Highlands in Scotland – all with their own natural history and wildlife. There are mountains and moors, industrial landscapes, castles, gardens ... all surrounded by more than 3,000 miles of coastline. But with so many places to choose from, it's hard to know where to begin.

*1001 Days Out* will help you do just that. The book is packed with ideas to form the basis of a day out in Britain where you will discover the natural beauty, rich heritage and cultural attractions that England, Scotland and Wales have to offer. This practical guide offers a broad selection of attractions ranging from world-famous castles, stately homes and gardens to carefully restored windmills, ancient ruins and rediscovered gardens. But also included are many small and more unusual places to visit. With 1001 entries, all tastes are catered for.

Of course, at any one time, many attractions are closed for renovation or refurbishment. For this reason a few of the renowned and popular attractions you may be expecting to see may not in fact have been included in this edition: but as *1001 Days Out* is published annually, these attractions will be considered for inclusion next year.

## About this guide

This guide covers England, Scotland (including the Northern and Western Islands) and Wales and is arranged in regions, shown on the national map on page viii. The counties within each region, the towns within each county and the attractions within each town are all, as far as possible, arranged alphabetically. Each attraction also has a reference number and this is used to identify it on the regional map at the beginning of each section.

## Understanding the entries

Coloured bands at the top of each page indicate regions; the numbers in the top corners next to the regional name refer to the numbered range of attractions on the page. The nearest major town or village to the attraction is indicated above the name of the attraction.

### Quick-reference icons

an all-weather attraction

an attraction for sunny days only

the expected duration of your visit

when the attraction is open

### Description

Each entry has a brief description of the attraction and a flavour of what visitors may expect to find. Additional features are also highlighted beneath the description.

### Facilities

toilet facilities available

space available for you to eat your own food

restaurant, café or kiosk facilities available

good access for wheelchairs    restricted access

dogs allowed, but they may have to be kept on a lead

### Disabled visitors

Visitors with mobility difficulties should look for the wheelchair symbol showing that all or most of the attraction is accessible to wheelchair users. We strongly recommend that visitors telephone in advance of a visit to check exact details, including access to toilets and refreshment facilities. Assistance dogs are usually accepted unless stated otherwise. For the hard of hearing, please check that hearing induction loops are available by contacting the attraction itself.

## Location

These are simple directions, usually for motorists (though Underground directions are given for attractions in London) and have been provided by the attraction itself.

## Opening times

These times are inclusive, e.g. Apr–Oct indicates that the attraction will be open from the beginning of April to the end of October. Where an attraction has varied opening times, these are indicated; and if it is open seven days a week, this is simply referred to as 'Daily'. Bank Holiday opening is indicated where provided by the attraction. *If you are travelling a long way, please check with the attraction itself to ensure any unexpected circumstances are not going to prevent your entry.*

## Admission

Wherever possible, the charges quoted are for the 2005–6 season, but please note that prices are subject to change and are correct only at the time of going to print. If no price is quoted, it does not mean that a charge will not be made. Many places that do not charge admission may ask for a voluntary donation. In some instances discounts may be available to families, groups, local residents or members of certain organisations such as English Heritage and the National Trust.

## Contact details

We have given details of the administrative address and telephone number for each attraction. While these are usually those of the attraction itself, some properties are administered by an area office, in which case these details are given (several English Heritage properties fall into this category).

Telephone numbers, email and website addresses are also included wherever possible.

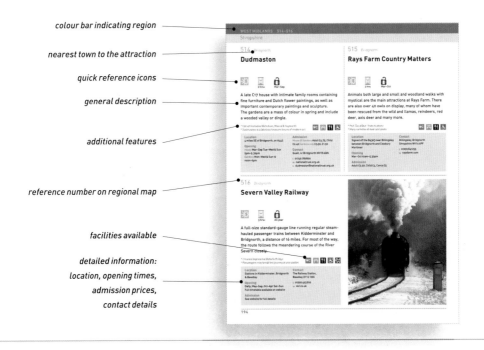

colour bar indicating region

nearest town to the attraction

quick reference icons

general description

additional features

reference number on regional map

facilities available

detailed information:
location, opening times,
admission prices,
contact details

**Regional colour key**

- South East
- South West
- Eastern
- East Midlands
- West Midlands
- Wales
- Yorkshire
- North West
- North East
- Scotland

Oast House, Doves Farm, Kent

# South East

Berkshire  Buckinghamshire  East Sussex
Hampshire and Isle of Wight  Kent  London
Oxfordshire  Surrey  West Sussex

331–332
366–367
Sudbury
Ipswich
410
Royston
Saffron
Walden
356
403
Felixstowe
Baldock
ESSEX
364
Halstead
Manningtree
Harwich
7
378
Braintree
359–362
STANSTED
368
Colchester
The Naze
ORDSHIRE
Bishop's Stortford
Witham
West
363
Clacton-on-Sea
wyn
M11
Mersea
en
Ware
Hertford
Harlow
Chelmsford
357–358
Maldon
Hatfield
–376
ddesdon
374
370
Burnham-
on-Crouch
arnet
M25
Enfield
Chigwell
Brentwood
Rayleigh
Foulness
Island
M11
093–128
M25
Basildon
365
Southend-on-Sea
ONDON
CITY
Canvey Island
369
Tilbury
Sheerness
Richmond
Woolwich
Isle of Sheppey
Margate
ingston
Dartford
Gravesend
Herne
069
on-Thames
Rochester
Whitstable
Bay
140
074
Swanley
Gillingham
Sittingbourne
Ramsgate
ton
M25
Chatham
073
Faversham
Canterbury
Sandwich
54
M20
084–085
070–072
Epsom
078–079
North Downs
Deal
Caterham
M26
Sevenoaks
M2
KENT
092
088
Maidstone
075–076
eigate Redhill
Oxted
M20
Dover
077
087
Tonbridge
Ashford
CHANNEL
TUNNEL
Folkestone
ATWICK
172
East
Tunbridge Wells
068
TERMINAL
vley
036
Grinstead
091
080–081
Cranbrook
M20
Hythe
083
089
Tenterden
Horsham
Crowborough
090
082
Haywards
041
Uckfield
New Romney
Heath
Heathfield
086
LYDD/ASHFORD
173–174
Rye
173–174
Hurstpierpoint
Battle
Dungeness
E. SSUSSEX
038–039
031
Hastings
outh
Hailsham
Lewes
Bexhill-on-Sea
Downs
040
Hove Brighton
Newhaven
ning
032–035
Seaford
037
Eastbourne
Beachy
Head

©MAPS IN MINUTES™ 2005. ©Crown Copyright, Ordnance Survey 2005.

## 001   Bracknell

# Go Ape!

2 hrs+   Mar–Oct

Go Ape! is the ultimate in adrenalin-fuelled adventure, high above the forest floor. Test your nerve exploring the network of rope bridges, trapezes and death slides that stretches for roughly a mile through the tree canopy.

* 115ft aerial walkway for May 2006
* Age limit is 10 & height restriction of 1.4m applies

**Location**
Follow signs for Go Ape on A322 S of Bracknell

**Opening**
Mar–Oct 9am–5pm
Nov weekends only
Closed Dec–Feb

**Admission**
Adult £2.80, Child £1.40, Concs £2.10

**Contact**
The Look Out, Nine Mile Ride
Swinley Forest, Bracknell RG12 7QW
t  0870 444 5562
w  goape.co.uk
e  info@goape.co.uk

## 002   Bracknell

# The Lookout Discovery Centre

2 hrs+   All year

A hands-on science exhibition with fun for the entire family. 'Pluck' the laser beams of the Light Harp to make a little light music or put all your energy into launching the Hydrogen Rocket. Explore the wonders of the human body or try the amazing puzzles.

* Children's play area
* 2,600 acres of woodlands

**Location**
Follow signs for Look Out Discovery Centre on A322 S Bracknell

**Opening**
Daily: 10am–5pm

**Admission**
Please phone for details

**Contact**
Nine Mile Ride, Bracknell RG12 7QW
t  01344 354400
w  bracknell-forest.gov.uk/lookout
e  thelookout@bracknell-forest.gov.uk

## 003   Maidenhead

# Cliveden

3 hrs   Mar–Dec

This spectacular estate overlooking the River Thames has a series of gardens, each with its own character, featuring topiary, statuary, water gardens, a formal parterre, informal vistas, woodland and riverside walks. It was once the home of Nancy, Lady Astor.

* Magnificent Italianate palace
* Winter parks & gardens

**Location**
2 miles N of Taplow, A404 to Marlow & follow brown signs

**Opening**
*House* Apr–Oct Thur & Sun
3pm–5.30pm
*Estate & Gardens* Daily: Mar–Oct
11am–6pm; Nov–Dec 11am–4pm

**Admission**
Adult £7, Child £3.50

**Contact**
Taplow, nr Maidenhead SL6 0JA
t  01628 605069
w  nationaltrust.org.uk
e  cliveden@nationaltrust.org.uk

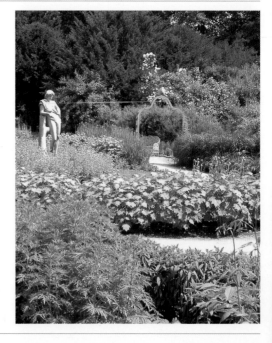

## 004 Newbury

# Ashdown House

1 hr   Apr–Oct

An extraordinary Dutch-style C17 house, famous for its association with Elizabeth of Bohemia, Charles I's sister, to whom the house was consecrated. The interior has a great staircase rising from hall to attic, and important paintings contemporary to the house.

* Spectacular views from the roof over the gardens
* Beautiful walks in neighbouring Ashdown Woods

**Location**
2 miles S of Ashbury, 3 miles N of Lambourn, on W side of B4000

**Opening**
*House & Gardens* Apr–Oct Wed & Sat 2pm–5pm
Tours begin at 2.15pm, 3.15pm & 4.15pm
*Woodland* All year, closed Fri

**Admission**
Adult £2.50, Child free

**Contact**
Lambourn, Newbury RG16 7RE
t 01488 72584
w nationaltrust.org.uk
e ashdownhouse@nationaltrust.org.uk

## 005 Newbury

# Desmoulin

½ hr+   All year

Desmoulin is housed in the granary on the wharf, in one of Newbury's finest old buildings. This contemporary gallery exhibits an ever-changing collection of quality art and artefacts – paintings, photographs, furniture, jewellery in silver and gold, glassware and ceramics.

* Café supplies light lunches, caters for vegetarians

**Location**
Town centre next to Tourist Information Centre

**Opening**
Mon–Sat 10am–5pm,
Sun by appointment

**Admission**
Free

**Contact**
The Granary, The Wharf, Newbury RG14 5AS
t 01635 35001
w desmoulin.co.uk
e snail@desmoulin.co.uk

## 006 Newbury

# Donnington Castle

½ hr+   All year

Constructed during the late C14, the striking twin-towered gatehouse of this castle survives amid some impressive earthworks. Originally built as a fortified residence, it was seized by Royalists at the beginning of the English Civil War.

* External viewing only

**Location**
1 mile N of Newbury off B4494

**Opening**
dawn–dusk

**Admission**
Free

**Contact**
Newbury RG14 8LT
t 0870 333 1182
w english-heritage.org.uk

## 007 Newbury

# Greenham & Crookham Common

2 hrs+   All year

After many years as a military site, the common has been restored and reopened to the public. Paths and marked walk routes allow you to explore the heathland and visit old bombsites and taxiways. Visitors can look across the cruise missile silo enclosure.

* The area is a Site of Special Scientific Interest (SSSI)
* Rare plant communities

**Location**
Car park at Bury's Bank Road, Greenham

**Opening**
Daily: *summer* 8am–8pm
*winter* 8am–4pm

**Admission**
Free

**Contact**
West Berkshire Council, Countryside & Environment, Council Offices, Faraday Road, Newbury RG14 2AF
t 01635 519808
w westberks.gov.uk
e tourism@westberks.gov.uk

## 008 Newbury

# Highclere Castle

1 hr    Jul–Aug

Highclere is probably the finest Victorian house in existence. The three men who made Highclere what it is today were the 3rd Earl of Carnarvon who built the new house, Sir Charles Barry who designed it and the 4th Earl of Carnarvon who finished the interiors.

* Georgian pleasure grounds laid out by Robert Herbert
* 5th Earl of Carnarvon found the tomb of Tutankhamun

**Location**
Off A34, 4½ miles S of Newbury

**Opening**
Jun–Aug Mon–Fri 11am–4pm;
all Bank Hols
last admission 1 hr before close

**Admission**
Adult £7.50, Child £4, Concs £6

**Contact**
Highclere, Newbury RG20 9RN

t  01635 253210
w  highclerecastle.co.uk
e  theoffice@highclerecastle.co.uk

## 009 Newbury

# The Living Rainforest

1 hr+    All year

Explore the rainforest and discover its wonders for yourself. This living rainforest aims to promote a sustainable future by providing education on the world's rainforests. It features a tropical rainforest-inspired ecological garden with free-roaming animals.

* Endangered Goeldi's monkeys leap among branches
* Birds, butterflies, lizards roam freely as you explore

**Location**
Clearly signed from junction 13 of M4

**Opening**
Daily: 10am–5.15pm (last admission 4.30pm)

**Admission**
Please phone for details or check the website

**Contact**
Hampstead Norreys RG18 0TN

t  01635 202444
w  livingrainforest.org
e  enquiries@livingrainforest.org

## 010 Reading

# Basildon Park

1 hr+    Mar–Oct

Fascinating and beautiful, this C18 Palladian mansion has an extraordinary history. It was used as a hospital during WWI, and as a base for American servicemen during WWII when it was left a near ruin. It has been lovingly restored by Lord and Lady Iliffe.

* Location for Netherfield in *Pride and Prejudice*
* Pleasure gardens & trails through woodland

**Location**
A329 between Pangbourne
& Streatley

**Opening**
26 Mar–29 Oct Wed–Sun & Bank Hols
*House* 1pm–5.30pm
*Grounds* 11am–5.30pm

**Admission**
Adult £5, Child £2.50

**Contact**
Lower Basildon, Reading RG8 9NR

t  0118 984 3040
w nationaltrust.org.uk
e  basildonpark@nationaltrust.org.uk

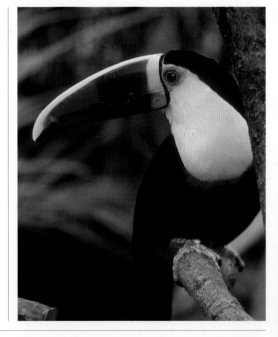

## 011 Reading

# Beale Park

4 hrs    All year

This unique RBST-approved charity is home to an amazing collection of birds including swans, owls, parrots and pheasants. It also boasts a narrow-gauge railway. There are boat trips in summer, acres of lawns and gardens for picnics, sculpture, ponds and fountains.

* The Trust breeds & rears endangered species
* New continental aviaries

**Location**
6 miles from Reading on A329
between Pangbourne & Streatley

**Opening**
Daily: 14 Apr–30 Sep 10am–6pm;
1 Oct–13 Apr 10am–5pm

**Admission**
Adult £6.50, Child £4.50, Concs £5.50

**Contact**
Lower Basildon,
Reading RG8 9NH

t  0870 777 7160
w  bealepark.co.uk
e  administration@bealepark.co.uk

---

## 012 Reading

# Museum of English Rural Life

1 hr    All year

Founded by the University of Reading in 1951, the museum reflects the changing face of farming and the countryside. It houses collections of national importance, including objects, archives, photographs, film and books.

* A programme of free fun family days
* Part of the University's Museum & Collections Service

**Location**
Adjacent to Royal Berkshire Hospital
on London Road

**Opening**
Tue–Fri 10am–4.30pm;
closed Christmas, New Year & Easter

**Admission**
Free

**Contact**
Redlands Road, Reading RG1 5EX

t  0118 378 8660
w  merl.org.uk
e  merl@reading.ac.uk

---

## 013 Thatcham

# Thatcham Nature Discovery Centre

2 hrs+    All year

An exciting place to learn about local wildlife. The wide range of hands-on exhibits in Discovery Hall are set against a dramatic backdrop of giant insect models, colourful banners and wildlife quilts. Visitors can enjoy a walk around the lake and visit the reed-bed bird hide.

* Gallery with changing exhibitions
* Bird hide

**Location**
Between Thatcham & Newbury signed
from A4

**Opening**
Mar–Oct Tue–Sun 11am–5pm;
Nov–Feb Tue–Sun 1pm–4pm

**Admission**
Free, donations appreciated

**Contact**
Muddy Lane, Lower Way,
Thatcham RG19 3FU

t  01635 874381
w  westberks.gov.uk
e  naturecentre@westberks.gov.uk

## 014 Windsor

# Windsor Castle

2 hrs+   All year

This is an official residence of the Queen and the largest occupied castle in the world. A fortress for more than 900 years, the castle remains a working palace today. Visit the state apartments – extensive suites of rooms at the heart of the working palace.

\* The magnificent & beautiful St George's Chapel
\* Apr–Jun, Changing of the Guard at 11am (not Sun)

**Location**
Follow brown signs to central Windsor

**Opening**
Daily: Mar–Oct 9.45am–5.15pm;
Nov–Feb 9.45am–4.15pm;

**Admission**
Please phone for details

**Contact**
Ticket Sales and Information Office,
The Official Residences of The Queen,
London SW1A 1AA
t 0207 766 7304
w royalcollection.org.uk
e information@royalcollection.org.uk

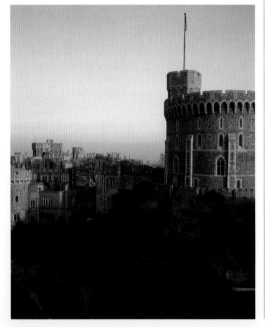

## 015 Aylesbury

# Buckinghamshire County Museum & Roald Dahl Gallery

1 hr+   All year

This award-winning museum is housed in beautifully restored buildings, some dating from the C15. It is a showcase for the county's heritage and runs a varied programme of exhibitions as well as interactive fun in the Roald Dahl Children's Gallery.

\* Regular Roald Dahl activities & events
\* Collections of British studio pottery, costume & lace

**Location**
Aylesbury town centre

**Opening**
*Museum* Mon–Sat 10am–5pm;
Sun 2pm–5pm
*Roald Dahl Gallery* Mon–Fri 3pm–5pm
(term time) 10am–5pm (hols);
Sat 10am–5pm, Sun 2pm–5pm

**Admission**
*Museum* **Free**
*Roald Dahl Gallery* **Adult £3.25,
Child £3.25**

**Contact**
Church Street, Aylesbury HP20 2QP
t 01296 331441
w buckscc.gov.uk/museum
e museum@buckscc.gov.uk

## 016 Aylesbury

# Buckinghamshire Railway Centre

2 hrs+   Apr–Oct

A working steam museum where you can experience the sights, sounds and smells of the golden age of steam. Ride behind a full-sized steam engine or aboard the miniature railway. The centre has a large collection of steam locomotives, carriages and wagons.

\* See the Royal Train of 1901
\* Santa Steaming the four weekends before Christmas

**Location**
Signed from A41 near Waddesdon
& A413 at Whitchurch

**Opening**
Apr–Oct Wed–Fri 10.30am–4.30pm;
weekends 10.30am–5.30pm

**Admission**
Adult £6, Child £4, Concs £5

**Contact**
Quainton Road Station, Quainton,
Aylesbury HP22 4BY
t 01296 655720
w bucksrailcentre.org
e abaker@bucksrailcentre.btopenworld.
com

# 017 Aylesbury

## The King's Head

2hrs     All year

Thought to be one of the oldest surviving courtyard inns in the country. Enclosed by the public area and the stable block, it provided services for the many horse-drawn carriages. Excavation has proved activity from the Bronze Age.

*Second hand bookshop in Great Hall 11am-3pm
* Large mullioned window contains pieces of C15 glass

| Location | Admission |
|---|---|
| At NW corner of Market Square in Aylesbury | Adult £2, Child £1 |
| Opening | Contact |
| *Trust* Mon-Fri 9am-6pm, Sat 10am-4pm | King's Head Passage, |
| *Bar* Mon-Sun 12-10.30pm; | Market Square, Aylesbury HP20 2RW |
| Sat 11am–11pm | t  01296 381501 |
| | w  nationaltrust.org.uk |
| | e  kingshead@ntrust.org.uk |

# 018 Aylesbury

## Tiggywinkles, The Wildlife Hospital Trust

1½ hrs+     All year

Since opening its doors, the Wildlife Hospital Trust has treated more than 100,000 patients. Watch and learn about a remarkable number of patients including hedgehogs, badgers, rabbits, deer, wild birds and snakes. Virtually all species of British wildlife feature.

* Hedgehog  history museum & baby bird sanctuary
* New children's play area & CCTV link to animal hospital

| Location | Contact |
|---|---|
| Signed off A418 from Aylesbury | Aston Road, Haddenham, |
| Opening | Aylesbury HP17 8AF |
| Easter–Sep Mon–Sun 10am–4pm; | t  01844 292292 |
| Oct–Easter Mon– Fri 10am–4pm | w  sttiggywinkles.com |
| Admission | e  mail@sttiggywinkles.org.uk |
| Adult £3.80, Child & Concs £2.80 | |

# 019 Aylesbury

## Waddesdon Manor

2 hrs+     All year

Created by Baron Ferdinand de Rothschild, this Renaissance-style chateau was built in the 1870s for his house parties. The house contains a unique collection of French C18 objects. The landscape gardens are famous for their spectacular views.

* Meissen exhibition
* Good example of C19 needlework window dressings

| Location | Admission |
|---|---|
| Via Waddesdon village, 6 miles NW of Aylesbury on A41 | *House* Adult £11, Child £8 |
| | *Grounds* Adult £4, Child £2 |
| Opening | Contact |
| *House* 23 Mar–30 Oct Wed–Sun & Bank Hols 11am–4pm; 17 Nov–23 Dec Wed–Sun 10am–5pm | Waddesdon, Aylesbury HP18 0JH |
| *Grounds* 3 Mar–31 Oct & 17 Nov–23 Dec Wed–Sun 10am–5pm; call for Jan–Mar | t  01296 653211/226 |
| | w  waddesdon.org.uk |

## 020 Brill

# Boarstall Tower

1 hr  Mar–Oct

Visit the C14 gatehouse and gardens of Boarstall House (demolished 1778). Built by John de Haudlo in 1312, and updated in 1615 for use as a banqueting pavilion or hunting lodge, the tower has retained its medieval belfry, crossloops and crenellations.

\* Many rooms remain virtually unchanged since 1615
\* Handsome oriel windows

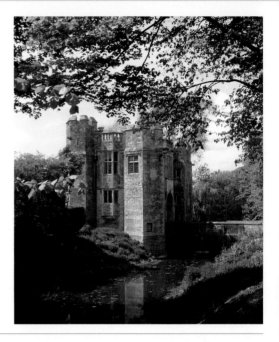

**Location**
Midway between Bicester and Thame, 2 miles W of Brill

**Opening**
27 Apr–30 Oct Wed 2pm–6pm,
Sat 11am–4pm
Bank Hol Mons 2pm-6pm

**Admission**
Adult £2.30, Child £1.10, Family £5.50

**Contact**
Boarstall, Aylesbury HP18 9UX

t 01844 239339
w boarstall.com
e boarstall@erros.co.uk

## 021 Buckingham

# The Old Gaol

½ hr+  All year

The Old Gaol is the landmark building in Buckingham town centre. Restored by the Buckingham Heritage Trust, it houses a fascinating museum that reflects the building's history via an audio-visual display and exhibits of Buckingham's past and military history.

\* Regular themed exhibitions
\* The ancient cells with their double doors still remain

**Location**
Buckingham town centre

**Opening**
Mon-Sat 10am–4pm

**Admission**
Adult £2, Child & Concs £1.50

**Contact**
Market Hill, Buckingham MK18 1JX

t 01280 823020
w mkheritage.co.uk
e old.gaol@lineone.net

## 022 Buckingham

# Stowe Landscape Gardens

2 hrs+  All year

This is one of the finest Georgian landscape gardens, comprising valleys, vistas, narrow lakes and rivers. You'll also find more than 40 temples and monuments designed by many of the leading architects of the C18. At the centre is Stowe House, now Stowe School.

\* Completed restoration of Corinthian art
\* Newly discovered C18 hermitage pathway

**Location**
3 miles NW of Buckingham via Stowe Avenue, off A422

**Opening**
Feb–Oct Wed–Sun 11am–5.30pm;
Nov–Feb Sat &Sun 10am–4pm

**Admission**
Adult £5.80, Child £2.90

**Contact**
Buckingham MK18 5EH

t 01280 822850
w nationaltrust.org.uk
e stowegarden@nationaltrust.org.uk

## 023 Chalfont St Giles

# Chiltern Open Air Museum

2 hrs+    Apr–Oct

This unusual museum contains more than 30 historic buildings, including a 1940s fully furnished prefab and a working Victorian farm and forge. Set in beautiful open parkland with a nature walk and seat-sculpture trail, the museum is a wonderful place for all ages to visit.

\* Explore more than 30 rescued historic buildings
\* Visit Skippings Barn, home to the Hawk & Owl Trust

**Location**
Signposted from A413 at Chalfont St Giles and Chalfont St Peter

**Opening**
Daily: Apr–Oct 10am–5pm

**Admission**
Adult £7, Child £4.50, Concs £5.50

**Contact**
Newland Park, Gorelands Lane, Chalfont St Giles HP8 4AB

t  01494 871117
w  coam.org.uk
e  coamuseum@netscape.net

## 024 Chalfont St Giles

# John Milton's Cottage

1 hr+    Mar–Oct

This picturesque late C16 Grade I-listed cottage, set in an attractive garden, is the only surviving building in which the famous writer and parliamentarian lived. It was bought by public subscription in 1887 to celebrate Queen Victoria's jubilee and to preserve it for visitors.

\* Milton came here in 1665 to escape the plague
\* He completed *Paradise Lost* here

**Location**
On A40 to Chalfont St Giles, cottage in centre of village

**Opening**
1 Mar–31 Oct 10am–1pm & 2pm–6pm; closed Mon, except Bank Hol Mon

**Admission**
Adult £3, Child £1

**Contact**
Chalfont St Giles HP8 4JH

t  01494 872313
w  miltonscottage.org
e  info@miltonscottage.org

## 025 High Wycombe

# Hellfire Caves

1 hr+    All year

These caves were originally excavated in the 1750s by Sir Francis Dashwood on the site of an ancient quarry. It is thought that his inspiration for the design of the caves came from his grand tour of Europe and the Ottoman Empire.

\* Sir Francis Dashwood founded the Hellfire Club
\* The caves are said to be haunted by Sir Paul Whitehead

**Location**
Approximately 3 miles from High Wycombe on A40 towards Oxford

**Opening**
Mar–Oct Mon–Fri 11am–5.30pm; weekends 11am–5.300m

**Admission**
Adult £4, Concs £3

**Contact**
High Wycombe HP14 3AJ

t  01494 533739
w  hellfirecaves.co.uk

## 026 High Wycombe

# Hughenden Manor

2 hrs+    Mar–Oct

The home of Victorian prime minister and statesman Benjamin Disraeli from 1848 until his death in 1881. Most of his furniture, books and pictures remain here – his private retreat from parliamentary life in London. There are beautiful walks through the surrounding park.

\* Certain rooms have low electric light – avoid dull days
\* Events throughout the house & park

**Location**
1 mile N of High Wycombe W of Great Missenden road (A4128)

**Opening**
*House* Mar Sat & Sun 1pm–5pm; Apr–Oct Wed–Sun 12noon–5pm
*Gardens* Mar Sat & Sun; Apr–Oct Wed–Sun

**Admission**
Please phone for details

**Contact**
High Wycombe HP14 4LA

t  01497 755565/573
w  nationaltrust.org.uk
e  hughenden@nationaltrust.org.uk

027 High Wycombe

# Wycombe Museum

1 hr+        All year

Trails and special activities combine with imaginative displays to make this a lively museum for visitors. Permanent exhibits, videos and sound recordings tell the story of High Wycombe and the local district.

* Superb collection of Windsor chairs
* Museum art on display

**Location**
Off A404 towards Amersham

**Opening**
Mon–Sat 10am–5pm, Sun 2pm–5pm;
closed Bank Hols

**Admission**
Free, donations appreciated

**Contact**
Priory Avenue,
High Wycombe HP13 6PX
t 01494 421895
w wycombe.gov.uk/museum
e museum@wycombe.gov.uk

028 High Wycombe

# Wycombe Summit Ski & Snowboard Centre

2 hrs        All year

This world-class ski and snowboard school is suitable for experts and beginners. It has a 300m main slope, 100m trainer slope and seven nursery areas with three lifts. Training available at all ability levels. The centre regularly hosts national race competitions.

* England's longest ski slope
* Special holiday programmes & children's camps

**Location**
Between junctions 3 & 4 of the
M40, just ½ hour from London

**Opening**
Daily: *summer* Mon–Fri 10am–10pm,
Sat & Sun 10am–6pm
*winter* 10am–10pm
Please phone for details

**Admission**
Please phone for details

**Contact**
Abbey Barn Lane
High Wycombe HP10 9QQ
t 01494 474711/439099
w wycombesummit.com
e info@wycombesummit.com

Buckinghamshire

East Sussex

029 Stoke Mandeville

# Obsidian Art

½ hr+    All year

This large art gallery houses more than 300 original paintings, drawings, sculptures and limited edition prints. The gallery exhibits a range of British art, from traditional to modern abstract.

* Regularly changing exhibitions & local artists
* Opportunity to purchase original artwork & gifts

**Location**
On A4010 S of Stoke Mandeville, follow signs for Goat Centre

**Opening**
Tue–Sun 10am–5pm

**Admission**
Free

**Contact**
Obsidian Art,
Old Risborough Road,
Stoke Mandeville HP22 5XJ

t 01296 612150
w obsidianart.co.uk
e info@obsidianart.co.uk

---

030 Wendover

# The Chiltern Brewery

1 hr    All year

Opened in 1980, this family-run establishment is now Buckinghamshire's oldest working brewery. The site offers tours and tastings.

* Five bespoke, award-winning beers are produced here
* Tours on Sat only, booking necessary

**Location**
On B4009, which joins A413
1 mile from Wendover

**Opening**
Mon–Sat 9am–5pm

**Admission**
Free Tours £3.95

**Contact**
Nash Lee Road, Terrick,
Aylesbury HP17 0TQ

t 01296 613647
w chilternbrewery.co.uk
e enquiries@chilternbrewery.co.uk

---

031 Battle

# Battle Abbey & Battlefield

1 hr+    All year

There is almost as much myth surrounding the Battle of Hastings as known fact. The two armies did not even fight at Hastings, but at a place south of the town now named Battle. Visit the ruins of the abbey that William the Conqueror built to commemorate his victory.

* Interactive audio tour recreates the sounds of battle
* Stand on the spot where defeated King Harold fell

**Location**
In Battle, at S end of high street. Battle is reached by turning off A21 on to A2100 10 mins from Battle station

**Opening**
Daily: Apr–Sep 10am–6pm;
Oct–Mar 10am–4pm

**Admission**
Adult £5.30, Child £2.70, Concs £4

**Contact**
High Street, Battle TN3 30AD

t 01424 773792
w english-heritage.org.uk

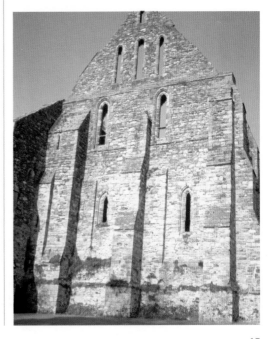

## 032 Brighton

# Brighton Museum & Art Gallery

2 hrs+   All year

The museum has a famous collection of Arts & Crafts, Art Nouveau and Art Deco; Salvador Dali's sofa in the shape of Mae West's lips and stunning gowns from Schiaparelli to Zandra Rhodes. Exhibits include intricate sculptures, decorated masks and beautiful textiles.

\* Paintings by Duncan Grant & Edward Lear
\* Regularly changing exhibits

**Location**
Brighton town centre

**Opening**
Tue 10am–7pm, Wed–Sat 10am–5pm,
Sun 2pm–5pm, Bank Hol Mons
10am–5pm

**Admission**
Free

**Contact**
Royal Pavilion Gardens,
Brighton
BN1 1EE
t  01273 290900
w  virtualmuseum.info
e  museums@brighton–hove.gov.uk

## 033 Brighton

# Brighton Sea Life Centre

2 hrs+   All year

Originally opened in 1872, the centre combines beautifully restored Victorian architecture with spectacular displays of marine life from shrimps to sharks. It is active in marine conservation projects and in raising awareness about threats to marine life.

\* One of the longest underwater tunnels in England
\* More than 30 modern marine & freshwater habitats

**Location**
Take the M23/A23 from London or
the A27 from Portsmouth & Lewes

**Opening**
Daily: from 10am; please phone for
details of winter opening times

**Admission**
Adult £9.50, Child £7.50, Concs £8.50

**Contact**
Marine Parade,
Brighton BN2 1TB
t  01273 604234
w  sealifeeurope.com
e  slcbrighton@merlinentertainment.biz

## 034 Brighton

# The Royal Pavilion

2 hrs+   All year

This former seaside residence of King George IV with its exotic Indian-style exterior boasts myriad domes and minarets. Admire magnificent decorations and furnishings in the Chinese style and gardens replanted to the original Regency scheme. Complete with a superb shop.

\* Tactile/Sennheiser tours for partially sighted/hearing
\* Wonderful Regency furniture & antiques

**Location**
Brighton town centre, 15 min walk
from Brighton station

**Opening**
Daily: Apr–Sep daily 9.30am–5.45pm
(last admissions 5pm);
Oct–Mar 10am–5.15pm
(last admissions 4.30pm)

**Admission**
Adult £6.10, Child £3.60, Concs £4.30

**Contact**
Brighton BN1 1EE
t  01273 290900
w  royalpavilion.org.uk
e  visitor.services@brightonhove.gov.uk

## 035 Brighton

# University of Brighton Gallery & Theatre

1 hr   All year

The presence of some of the country's most innovative artists and students makes this one of the most appealing gallery spaces in the South. The modern gallery presents exhibitions covering many aspects of the arts.

\* A frequently changing exhibition programme
\* Theatre has lectures & musical performances

**Location**
Grand Parade university campus, central Brighton

**Opening**
*Gallery* Mon–Sat 10am–5pm
*Theatre* Many evenings, please phone
for details

**Admission**
*Gallery* Free
*Theatre* Please phone for details

**Contact**
Grand Parade, Brighton BN2 0JY
t  01273 643012
w  brighton.ac.uk/gallery-theatre/
e  c.l.matthews@brighton.ac.uk

# 036 East Grinstead

## Ashdown Forest Llama Park

2 hrs    All year

See more than 100 llamas and alpacas! Watch them in the fields or get close to them in the barns. Enjoy farm walks, a museum, a picnic area, a coffee shop, an adventure play area and a lovely shop selling alpaca knitwear and South American crafts.

* Walking with llamas
* Angora & cashmere goats

**Location**
Located beside A22, 300 yrds S of junction with A275

**Opening**
Daily: 10am–5pm

**Admission**
Adult £5.50, Child & Concs £3.75

**Contact**
Wychross Forest Row RH18 5JN

t  01825 712040
w  llamapark.co.uk
e  info@llamapark.co.uk

# 037 Exceat

## Seven Sisters Country Park

4 hrs+   All year

Named after the famous Seven Sisters that form part of the Sussex chalk cliffs on Britain's heritage coastline. This site, situated in an Area of Outstanding Natural Beauty, is a popular location for outdoor activities including walking, cycling and canoeing.

* Shop selling leaflets, maps & souvenirs

**Location**
Off A259 between Eastbourne and Seaford or 712, 713 or 714 bus from Eastbourne

**Opening**
Daily: Easter–Oct;
Nov–Oct weekends only

**Admission**
Free

**Contact**
Exceat, Seaford BN25 4AD

t  01323 870280
w  www.sevensisters.org.uk
e  sevensisters@southdowns-aonb.
   gov.uk

# 038 Hailsham

## Herstmonceux Castle

2–4 hrs   Easter–Oct

Herstmonceux is renowned for its magnificent moated castle, beautiful parkland and Elizabethan gardens. Built originally as a country home in the mid-C15, the castle embodies the history of medieval England and the romance of Renaissance Europe.

* Castle is open only to guided tour parties
* Tours last for approximately 1 hour

**Location**
Off A27 on A22 towards Hailsham

**Opening**
Castle Phone in advance for details
Gardens Daily: Easter–Sep 10am–6pm;
Sep–Oct 10am–5pm

**Admission**
Gardens Adult £4.50, Child £3,
Concs £3.50 Castle £2.50, £1, £2.50

**Contact**
Hailsham BN27 1RN

t  01323 833816
w  herstmonceux-castle.com
e  c_dennett@isc.queensu.ac.uk

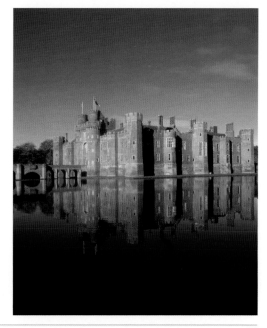

## 039 Hailsham

# Michelham Priory

4hrs+   Mar–Oct

England's longest medieval water-filled moat, guarded by a C14 gatehouse, encloses the remains of an Augustinian priory that incorporates a Tudor mansion. There are 7 acres of picturesque gardens, enhanced by a working watermill and Elizabethan Great Barn.

\* House dates back to 1229
\* Regular art exhibitions

| Location | Admission |
|----------|-----------|
| 2 miles W of Hailsham, follow signs from A22 or A27 | Adult £5.60, Child £2.90, Concs £4.70 |
| | Contact |
| Opening | Upper Dicker, nr Hailsham, |
| Mar–Oct; Tue–Sun from 10.30am; | East Sussex BN27 3QS |
| daily during August; | |
| (also open on Bank Hols) | t 01323 844224 |
| | w sussexpast.co.uk |
| | e adminmich@sussexpast.co.uk |

## 040 Pevensey

# Pevensey Castle

1 hr   All year

The ruins of this medieval castle stand in one corner of a Roman fort, on what was once a peninsula surrounded by the sea and salt marshes. The Roman fort, named Anderida, was built in about AD290. It is one of the largest surviving examples in Britain.

\* Britons massacred here by Anglo-Saxons in 491
\* William the Conqueror landed his army here in 1066

| Location | Contact |
|----------|---------|
| In Pevensey off A259 | High Street, Pevensey BN24 5LE |
| Opening | t 01323 762604 |
| Daily: Apr–Sep 10am–6pm | w english-heritage.org.uk |
| Oct–Mar Sat & Sun 10am–4pm | |
| Admission | |
| Adult £3.70, Child £1.90, | |
| Concs £2.80 | |

## 041 Sheffield Green

# Bluebell Railway

1 hr+   All year

This is the UK's first preserved standard gauge railway, which runs along the Lewes to East Grinstead line of the old London, Brighton and South Coast Railway. It serves to preserve this country branch line, its steam locomotives, coaches and signalling systems.

\* Famous Terrier class engines, Stepney & Fenchurch
\* Featured in the film *The Railway Children*

| Location | Contact |
|----------|---------|
| Sheffield Park Station | Sheffield Park Station TN22 3QL |
| Opening | t 01825 720800 |
| Daily: Apr–Oct 11am–4pm; | w bluebell-railway.co.uk |
| Oct–Apr Sat & Sun 11am–4pm | e info@bluebell-railway.co.uk |
| Admission | |
| Adult £9.50, Child £4.70 Concs £7 | |

042  Alton

# Jane Austen's House

1 hr+    All year

Jane Austen's house is a pleasant C17 house in the pretty village of Chawton, not far from her birthplace of Steventon. The museum houses an attractive collection of items connected with Jane Austen and her family including the table at which she wrote her novels.

* Pretty garden with varieties of C18 plants & herbs
* Examples of Austen's jewellery & needlework skills

**Location**
In the village of Chawton, 2 miles SW of Alton

**Opening**
Daily: Mar–Nov 11am–4pm;
Dec–Feb Sat–Sun only

**Admission**
Adult £4.50, Child £1, Concs £3.50

**Contact**
Chawton, Alton GU34 1SD

t  01420 83262
w  jane-austens-house-museum.org.uk
e  enquiries@jahmusm.org.uk

043  Bishop's Waltham

# Bishop's Waltham Palace

1 hr    Apr–Sep

The last Bishop of Winchester to live at Bishop's Waltham left in a dung cart, disguised as a farm labourer! He was escaping from Oliver Cromwell's troops after unsuccessfully defending his palace. Much of what can be seen today dates from the C12 and C14.

* Exhibition on the powerful bishops of Winchester
* Decorative & furnished Victorian farmhouse

   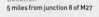

**Location**
5 miles from junction 8 of M27

**Opening**
Apr–Sep 10am–6pm, closed Sat

**Admission**
Free Mon–Fri;
Sun exhibition Adult £2.50,
Child £1.30, Concs £1.90

**Contact**
Winchester Road,
Bishop's Waltham SO32 1DH

t  01489 892460
w  english-heritage.org.uk
e  customer@english-heritage.org.uk

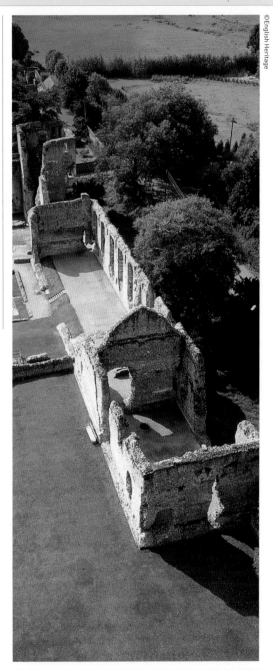

© English Heritage

044 Brockenhurst

# Beaulieu Abbey & National Motor Museum

3 hrs+    All year

Visit the C13 Beaulieu Abbey, Palace House and grounds, and the National Motor Museum. Few car museums in the world can match the unique collection here at Beaulieu, with legendary world record breakers like *Bluebird* and *Golden Arrow*.

\* Exhibition of James Bond vehicles & props
\* In 2004 the abbey celebrated its 800-year anniversary

**Location**
Going W on M27 take A326. Signed Beaulieu or National Motor Museum

**Opening**
Daily: May–Sep 10am–6pm; Oct–Apr 10am–5pm; closed 25 Dec

**Admission**
Adult £14, Child £7.25, Concs £13

**Contact**
Brockenhurst SO42 7ZN
t  01590 612345
w  beaulieu.co.uk
e  info@beaulieu.co.uk

©English Heritage

045 East Cowes

# Osborne House

3 hrs+    Apr–Sep

Queen Victoria's favourite country home captures the spirit of a world unchanged since the country's longest-reigning monarch died here 100 years ago. Queen Victoria and Prince Albert rebuilt the original Osborne House in 1845 as a 'modest country home'.

\* Indian Durbar Room, Queen Victoria's gifts from India
\* Glorious gardens & Swiss cottage

**Location**
1 mile SE of East Cowes

**Opening**
Daily: Apr–Sep 10am–5pm

**Admission**
Please phone for details

**Contact**
East Cowes PO32 6JY
t  01983 200022
w  english-heritage.org.uk
e  customer@english-heritage.org.uk

Fareham

# Titchfield Abbey

½ hr    All year

An abbey was first founded at Titchfield in the C13 by the Bishop of Winchester. Its history was uneventful until the Dissolution when drastic alterations were made to convert the abbey into a mansion known as Place House. Now a ruin, the remains are magnificent.

\* Residents were the Earls of Southampton
\* The 3rd Earl was closely connected to Shakespeare

| Location | Contact |
|---|---|
| ½ mile N of Titchfield off A27 | Mill Lane, Titchfield, Fareham PO15 5RA |
| Opening | |
| Daily: Apr–Sep 10am–6pm; | t 01329 842133 |
| Oct 10am–5pm; Nov–Mar 10am–4pm | w english-heritage.org.uk |
| Admission | |
| Free | |

Fordingbridge

# Braemore House & Museum

3 hrs    Apr–Sep

This is a large Elizabethan house, set in beautiful parkland, with a Saxon church near by. Former kitchen gardens house a major countryside museum, village workshops and a reconstructed cottage. Pleasant walks lead to an ancient maze on the Downs.

\* Fine collection of pictures & C17 furniture
\* Visitors can see displays of how villages were self-sufficient

| Location | Admission |
|---|---|
| 3 miles N of Fordingbridge, off A338 | Adult £7, Child £4.50, Concs £6 |
| Opening | Contact |
| *House* 2pm–5.30pm | nr Fordingbridge SP6 2DF |
| Dates vary please phone for details | |
| *Museum* 1pm–5.30pm (last tour | t 01725 512233 |
| 4.15pm) Dates vary please phone for | w braemorehouse.com |
| details | e braemore@ukonline.co.uk |

Gosport

# Explosion! The Museum of Naval Firepower

2 hrs+    All year

An award-winning visitor experience on the shores of Portsmouth Harbour, Explosion! tells the story of naval warfare from the day of gunpowder to the Exocet. A hands-on, interactive museum set in the historic buildings of the Navy's former armaments depot.

\* See Old Bill's Locker–supplied the Navy C18-C20
\* Trafalgar Gunpowder Trail in main museum

| Location | Admission |
|---|---|
| M27 to junction 11. Follow A32 to | Adult £5.50, Child £3.50, Concs £4.50 |
| Gosport & brown tourist signs | |
| | Contact |
| Opening | Priddy's Hard, Gosport PO12 4LE |
| Daily: Apr–Oct 10am–5.30pm; | |
| Nov–Mar Thu, Sat & Sun | t 02392 505600 |
| 10am–4.30pm | w explosion.org.uk |
| | e info@explosion.org.uk |

## 049  Lymington

# Hurst Castle

3 hrs+        Apr–Oct

Hurst Castle was built by Henry VIII as one of a chain of coastal fortresses and it was completed in 1544. The location was perfect to defend the western approach to the Solent. Charles I was imprisoned here in 1648 before being taken to London for his trial and execution.

\* Modernised during the Napoleonic wars
\* Two huge 38 ton guns

**Location**
By ferry from Keyhaven or on foot from Milford-on-Sea

**Opening**
Daily: Apr–Sep 10.30am–5.30pm; Oct 10.30am–4pm

**Admission**
Adult £3, Child £1.80, Concs £2.70

**Contact**
Hurst Spit, Keyhaven, Lymington SO41 0QU

t  01590 642500
w  hurst-castle.co.uk
e  info@hurst-castle.co.uk

## 050  Newport

# Carisbrooke Castle

1 hrs+        All year

Built more than 1,000 years ago, this castle has a rich and varied history. Since time immemorial, whoever controlled Carisbrooke controlled the Isle of Wight. The castle has been a feature of the island since its foundation as a Saxon camp during the C18.

\* Remnants of a Saxon wall & a Norman keep
\* Interactive museum

**Location**
1 mile SW of Newport on B3323

**Opening**
Daily: Apr–Sep 10am–5pm,
Oct 10am–5pm; Nov–Mar 10am–4pm;

**Admission**
Adult £5.30, Child £2.70, Concs £4

**Contact**
Carisbrooke, Newport, Isle of Wight

t  01983 522107
w  english-heritage.org.uk

## 051  Newport

# Classic Boat Museum

2 hrs+        Mar–Nov

A great indoor collection of lovingly restored sailing and motorised classic boats, from the C19 on. Highlights include the ultimate sailing classic, a Dragon, WWII airborne lifeboats, and a fragile folding canoe. Also on display are engines, equipment and memorabilia.

\* Displays & boats change annually
\* Items from *Gypsy Moth IV* on view

**Location**
On the harbour, free parking

**Opening**
Daily: Mar–Nov 10am–4.30pm

**Admission**
Adult £3, Child £1, Concs £2

**Contact**
The Quay, Newport Harbour, Newport, Isle of Wight PO30 2EF

t  01983 533493
w  netguides.co.uk/wight/boatmus
e  cbmiow@fsmail.net

## 052  Petersfield

# Queen Elizabeth Country Park

3 hrs+        All year

This park forms part of the landscape of the South Downs and falls in the East Hampshire Area of Outstanding Natural Beauty. There are 1,400 acres of open access woodland and downland. The site features trackways, barrows, lynchets and the remains of a Roman farmstead.

\* Visitor centre
\* National nature reserve

**Location**
In SE Hampshire, 4 miles S of Petersfield

**Opening**
Daily: Please phone for details

**Admission**
Car park £1 per day Mon–Sat;
  £1.50 per day Sun & Bank Hols

**Contact**
Gravel Hill, Horndean Hampshire PO8 0QE

t  02392 595040
w  hants.gov.uk/countryside/qecp
e  info.centres@hants.gov.uk

053 Portsmouth

# Charles Dickens' Birthplace Museum

½ hr+    Apr–Oct

Charles Dickens was born in this modest house in Portsmouth in 1812. The house has survived and is now preserved as a museum furnished in the style of 1809, the year in which Dickens' parents John and Elizabeth began their married life together.

\* Regency-style furniture & household objects
\* Charles Dickens & Portsmouth exhibition   WC

| Location | Contact |
|---|---|
| Just off A3 heading S towards city centre | 393 Old Commercial Road, Portsmouth PO1 4QL |
| **Opening** | t 02392 827261 |
| Daily: Apr–Sep 10am–5.30pm; Oct 10am–5pm | w portsmouthmuseums.co.uk |
| | e david.evans@portsmouthcc.gov.uk |
| **Admission** | |
| Adult £2.50, Child £1.50, Concs £1.80 | |

054 Portsmouth

# Portsmouth Historic Dockyard

2–4 hrs+    All year

This is the home of the Tudor warship *Mary Rose*, Admiral Lord Nelson's flagship HMS *Victory*, the mighty iron-hulled HMS *Warrior* (1860), the Royal Naval Museum and the attraction Action Stations. Together they make Portsmouth Historic Dockyard an essential stopping place.

\* Frigates, destroyers, mine warfare ships & more
\* Harbour boat tour  

| Location | Contact |
|---|---|
| Follow Historic Waterfront & Historic Dockyard signs from junction 12 of M27 | Visitor Centre, College Road, HM Naval Base. Portsmouth PO1 3LJ |
| **Opening** | t 02392 861533 |
| Daily: Apr–Oct 9.45am–5.30pm; Nov–March 10am–5pm | w historicdockyard.co.uk |
| | e enquiries@historicdockyard.co.uk |
| **Admission** | |
| Adult £15.50, Child £12.50, Concs £12.50 | |

055 Portsmouth

# Royal Garrison Church

½ hr+    Apr–Sep

This church was constructed around 1212 as a hostel for pilgrims. It was also used as a store for weapons and ammunition before becoming a garrison church in the 1560s. The church was badly damaged in 1941 and modern windows tell the story of the building.

\* Charles II married Catherine of Braganza here in 1662
\* Once known as Cathedral Church of the British Army  

| Location | Contact |
|---|---|
| On Grand Parade S of Portsmouth high street | Grand Parade, Old Portsmouth |
| **Opening** | t 02392 823973 |
| Apr–Sep Mon–Sat 11am–4pm | w english-heritage.org.uk |
| **Admission** | |
| Free | |

056  Portsmouth

# Spinnaker Tower

1 hr    All year

A new contemporary, national icon on the South coast, providing a unique 'window on the sea'. The Spinnaker Tower is a striking new seamark, soaring 170 metres above Portsmouth Harbour, offering visitors spectacular views from a great height.

* Lift to upper levels
* Cross Europe's largest glass floor on Level 1

**Location**
Come in to Portsmouth on M275 and follow the brown signs to Historic Waterfront, and then Spinnaker Tower

**Opening**
Daily: Mon–Wed 10am–6pm;
Thu–Sat 10am–8pm; Sun 11am–5pm

**Admission**
Adult £4.95, Child £4, Concs £4.50

**Contact**
Gunwharf Quays,
Portsmouth PO1 3TT
t  02392 857520
w  spinnakertower.co.uk
e  info@spinnakertower.co.uk

057  Romsey

# Mottisfont Abbey

2 hrs+    Mar–Oct

This C12 Augustinian priory boasts sweeping lawns and magnificent old trees, set amid glorious countryside. Medieval monastic remains include a cellarium and original stonework revealed through cut-away sections of the building.

* Unusual *trompe-l'oeil* painting by Rex Whistler
* National Collection of old-fashioned roses

**Location**
4½ miles NW of Romsey,
1 mile W of A3057

**Opening**
Mar–May & Sep–Oct 11am–6pm,
closed Thu & Fri;
Daily: Jun 11.30am–8.30pm;
July & Aug 11am–6pm, closed Fri

**Admission**
Adult £7, Child £3.50

**Contact**
Mottisfont, nr Romsey SO51 0LP
t  01794 340757
w  nationaltrust.org.uk
e  mottisfontabbey@nationaltrust.co.org.uk

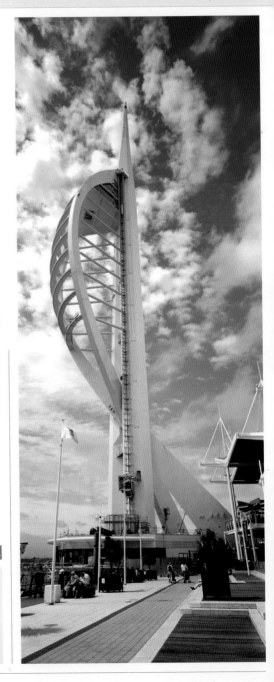

## 058 Romsey
# Sir Harold Hillier Gardens

3 hrs+    All year

These gardens, which were formerly known as the Hillier Arboretum, hold the greatest collection of hardy trees and shrubs in the world. Started by the late Sir Harold Hillier in 1953, the gardens now extend to 180 acres.

* Gurkha memorial garden
* Largest winter garden of its kind in Europe

**Location**
Between Ampfield & Braishfield,
3 miles NE of Romsey

**Opening**
Daily: 10.30am–6pm

**Admission**
Adult £7, Child free, Concs £6

**Contact**
Jermyns House, Jermyns Lane,
Ampfield, Romsey SO51 0QA

t 01794 368787
w hilliergardens.org.uk
e info@hilliergardens.org.uk

## 059 Shanklin
# Shanklin Chine

1 hr    Easter–Oct

This historic gorge has formed over the past 10,000 years and boasts a unique collection of flora and fauna, many extremely rare. There is a designated trail with numbered stopping places. The Chine drops 105ft to sea level and covers an area of approximately 3 acres.

* More than 150 varieties of wild plants
* 45-ft waterfall

**Location**
Enter via old village, off A3055 or through W of Shanklin Esplanade, off Chine Hill

**Opening**
31 March–25 May 10am–5pm;
26 May–10 Sep 10am–10pm;
11 Sep–29 Oct 10am–5pm

**Admission**
Adult £3.75, Child £2, Concs £2.75

**Contact**
12 Ponona Road, Shanklin,
Isle of Wight PO37 6PF

t 01983 866432
w shanklinchine.co.uk
e jill@shanklinchine.co.uk

## 060 Southampton
# Maritime Museum

1 hr+    All year

Originally a warehouse for Southampton's wool trade, this building was used to house hundreds of prisoners of war 200 years ago; more recently it was an aircraft factory. Now the museum tells the history of the port from the building of the first docks to the present day.

* Titanic Voices exhibition
* Regularly changing temporary exhibitions

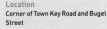

**Location**
Corner of Town Key Road and Bugel Street

**Opening**
Tue–Fri 10am–5pm,
Sat 10am–4pm, Sun 2pm–5pm

**Admission**
Free

**Contact**
Wool House, Town Quay,
Southampton SO14 2AR

t 02380 635904
w southampton.gov.uk/heritage
e museums@southampton.gov.uk

## 061 Southampton
# Southampton City Art Gallery

2 hrs+    All year

This gallery is internationally renowned for its impressive collection of contemporary works by British artists. A fine selection of works by the Camden Town Group, plus paintings by Sir Stanley Spencer, Matthew Smith and Philip Wilson Steer are brought together.

* Pre-Raphaelite work by Sir Coley-Burn-Jones
* Regular exhibitions throughout the year

**Location**
Central Southampton

**Opening**
Tue–Sat 10am–5pm, Sun 1pm–4pm
closed 21 Dec–2 Jan & Good Friday

**Admission**
Free

**Contact**
Civic Centre, Commercial Road,
Southampton SO14 7LP

t 02380 832277
w southampton.gov.uk/art
e art.gallery@southampton.gov.uk

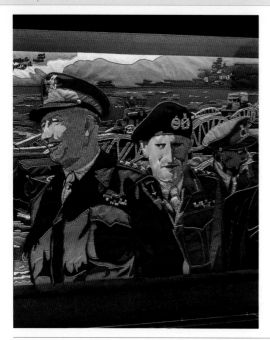

# The D-Day Museum & Overlord Embroidery

1 hr+    All year

This museum was established in 1984 to tell the story of Operation Overlord from its origins in the dark days of 1940 to victory in Normandy in 1944. The museum's centrepiece is the Overlord embroidery.

\* Audio-visual theatre
\* Dawn-to-dusk reconstruction of the Allied landings

| Location | Contact |
|---|---|
| On seafront, 2 miles from town centre | Clarence Esplanade, Southsea PO5 3NT |
| **Opening** | |
| Daily: Apr–Sep 10am–5.30pm; Oct–Mar 10am–5pm | t 02392 827261 |
| | w ddaymuseum.co.uk |
| **Admission** | e enquiries@ddaymuseum.co.uk |
| Adult £5.50, Child £3.30, Concs £4 | |

# Museum of Army Flying

2 hrs+    All year

Celebrating more than 100 years of army aviation, this award-winning museum houses one of the country's finest collections of military kites, gliders, aeroplanes and helicopters. Trace the development of army flying from the Royal Flying Corps to the present day.

\* Children's science & education centre
\* Viewing gallery overlooking airfield

| Location | Admission |
|---|---|
| A343 6 miles from Andover & 12 miles from Salisbury. Accessible from A30, A303 & M3 | Adult £5, Child £3.50, Concs £4 |
| | **Contact** |
| | Middle Wallop, Stockbridge SO20 8DY |
| **Opening** | |
| Daily: 10am–4pm | t 01980 674421 |
| | w flying-museum.org.uk |
| | e enquiries@flying-museum.org.uk |

# Ventnor Botanic Garden

2 hrs+    All year

This is one of the youngest botanic gardens in Britain. The southern edge of the garden comprises clifftop grassland and cliffs, and the eastern end is backed by a cliff face to the north. Enjoy the large number of British native flowers.

\* Japanese plant collection & visitor centre
\* Southern hemisphere plant collection

| Location | Contact |
|---|---|
| Southern tip of Isle of Wight | Undercliff Drive, Ventnor Isle of Wight PO38 1UL |
| **Opening** | |
| Daily: *summer* 10am–5pm, except July–Aug 10am–6pm | t 01983 855397 |
| *winter* weekends only 10am–6pm | w botanic.co.uk |
| **Admission** | e simon.goodenough@iow.gov.uk |
| Free | |

## 065 Winchester

# INTECH-Hands-on Science & Technology Centre

2 hrs+    All year

This unique hands-on interactive science and technology centre houses more than 100 exhibits designed to amuse and enthuse. Here you will understand how to bend light, create your own tornado spout and vortex and work out how much energy it takes to power a lightbulb.

* Regularly changing exhibitions
* Gift-shop with unusual & educational items

| Location | Contact |
|---|---|
| Junction 9 off the M3, take B3404 towards Alton | INTECH, Telegraph Way Morn Hill, Winchester SO21 1HX |
| Opening | t 01962 86379 |
| Daily: 10am–4pm | w intech-uk.com |
| | e htcf@intech-uk.com |
| Admission | |
| Adult £5.95, Child £3.90, Concs £4.50 | |

## 066 Winchester

# Winchester Cathedral

1 hr+    All year

Visit this 900-year-old cathedral and see the memorials of Jane Austen and Isaac Walton, and a unique collection of chantry chapels and hear the story of the diver, William Walker, who saved the cathedral in 1906. The crypt boasts the Anthony Gormley Sound II sculpture.

* The longest medieval cathedral
* The Winchester Bible – finest of the great C12 bibles

| Location | Contact |
|---|---|
| Winchester town centre | Cathedral Office, 1 The Close, Winchester SO23 9LS |
| Opening | |
| Daily: Mon–Sat 8.30am–6pm, Sun 8.30am–5pm | t 01962 857200 |
| | w winchester-cathedral.org.uk |
| Admission | e cathedral.office@ |
| Adult £4, Concs £3 donations appreciated | winchester-cathedral.org.uk |

## 067 Wroxall

# Appuldurcombe House Owl & Falconry Centre

2 hrs+    Feb–Dec

Visit the ruin of Appuldurcombe, designed by Capability Brown and once the grandest house on the Isle of Wight. A display of prints and photographs depicts the house and its history. The former servants' quarters now house the owl and falconry centre.

* Old brew house used for indoor bird flying
* Horseback falconry flying

| Location | Contact |
|---|---|
| In Wroxall off the B3327 to Ventnor | Wroxall, Isle of Wight PO38 3EW |
| Opening | t 01983 852484 |
| Daily: Apr, Sep & Oct 10am–4pm; Feb–Mar, May–Aug, Nov–Dec 10am–5pm | w appuldurcombe.co.uk |
| | e enquiries@appuldurcombe.co.uk |
| Admission | |
| Please phone for details | |

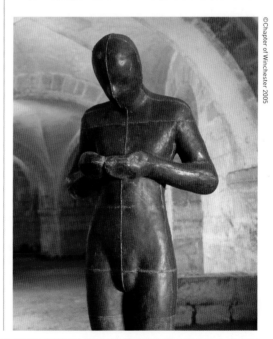

## 068 Ashford

# Godinton House & Gardens

1 hr+    Mar–Oct

Built in the C14, Godinton House is one of the most fascinating homes in Kent whose history, from its medieval origins to the present day, is revealed through the variety of its style, taste and furnishings. Set in glorious gardens.

\* Collection of porcelain, pictures & furniture
\* Three stunning delphinium borders best mid Jun–Jul

| Location | Admission |
|---|---|
| Junction 9 off M20, for Maidstone A20 | *House & Gardens* £6, Child free |
| | *Gardens* Adult £3, Child free |
| **Opening** | |
| *House* 7 Apr–8 Oct Fri–Sun | **Contact** |
| 2pm–5.30pm (last tour at 4.30pm) | Godinton Lane, Ashford TN23 3BP |
| *Gardens* 25 Mar–29 Oct Thu–Mon | t  01233 620 773 |
| 2pm–5.30pm | w  godinton-house-gardens.co.uk |
| | e  ghpt@godinton.fsnet.co.uk |

## 069 Broadstairs

# Dickens' House Museum

½ hr+    All year

Once the home of Miss Mary Pearson Strong, on whom Charles Dickens based the character of Miss Betsey Trotwood in his novel *David Copperfield*, this building has been adapted as a museum to commemorate the novelist's association with the town of Broadstairs.

\* Some of the author's own letters & memorabilia
\* Collection of costumes & Victoriana

| Location | Contact |
|---|---|
| On main seafront at Broadstairs | 2 Victoria Parade, |
| | Broadstairs CT10 1QS |
| **Opening** | |
| Daily: 10am–5pm (last admission 4pm) | t  01843 861232 |
| | w  dickenshouse.co.uk |
| **Admission** | e  aleeault@aol.com |
| Adult £2.50, Child £1.20 | |

## 070 Canterbury

# Canterbury Cathedral

1 hr+    All year

Founded in AD597 by St Augustine, a missionary from Rome, the cathedral has been the home of Christianity in England for 1,400 years and has attracted thousands of pilgrims each year since the murder of Archbishop Thomas à Becket in 1170.

\* Site of the murder of Archbishop Thomas à Becket
\* Stained-glass windows from the C12

| Location | Contact |
|---|---|
| City centre, off high street | Cathedral House, 11 The Precinct, |
| | Canterbury CT1 2EH |
| **Opening** | |
| Daily: *summer* 9am–6.30pm | t  01227 762862 |
| *winter* 9am–5.30pm | w  canterbury-cathedral.org |
| | e  enquiries@canterbury-cathedral.org |
| **Admission** | |
| Adult £5, Concs £4 | |

## 071 Canterbury

# The Canterbury Tales

1 hr+    Mar–Jan

This fascinating audio-visual experience, sited in the centre of Canterbury, is one of the town's most popular visitor attractions. Step back in time to experience the sights, sounds and smells of the Middle Ages in this stunning reconstruction of C14 England.

\* Uses headsets with earphones
\* Recreates the pilgrimages of Chaucerian England

| Location | Contact |
|---|---|
| City centre, off high street | St Margaret's Street, |
| | Canterbury CT1 2TG |
| **Opening** | |
| Daily: Mar–Jun 10am–5pm; Jul–Aug | t  01227 479227 |
| 9.30am–5pm; Sep–Oct 10am–5pm; | w  canterburytales.org.uk |
| Nov–Jan 10am–4.30pm | e  info@canterburytales.org.uk |
| **Admission** | |
| Adult £6.95, Child £5.25, Concs £5.95 | |

## 072 Canterbury

# Roman Museum

1 hr     All year

This underground museum is an exciting mix of excavated real objects, authentic reconstructions and remains of a Roman town house with mosaics. Reconstructions include a Roman market place, with a shoemaker's workshop plus fruit and vegetable stall.

* Computer reconstruction shows the Roman house
* Touch-screen computer game on Roman technology

| Location | Contact |
| --- | --- |
| Butchery Lane, close to cathedral | Longmarket, Butchery Lane, Canterbury CT1 2JE |
| **Opening** | t 01227 785575 |
| Mon–Sat 10am–5pm (last admission 4pm); Jun–Oct also open Sun 1.30pm–5pm | w canterburymuseums.co.uk |
| | e museums@canterbury.gov.uk |
| **Admission** | |
| Adult £2.90, Child & Concs £1.80 | |

## 073 Chatham

# The Historic Dockyard Chatham

4 hrs+    Feb–Nov

Housed in wonderful Victorian and Georgian buildings, the dockyard complex brings 400 years of naval history to life. Attractions include historic warships and the Wooden Walls exhibition that recreates the sights, sounds and smells of the dockyard in 1758.

* Royal dockyard from 1613 to 1984
* Nelson's flagship HMS *Victory* was built here

| Location | Admission |
| --- | --- |
| Leave M2 at junction 1, 3 or 4 & follow the signs | Adult £10, Child £6.50, Concs £7.50 |
| **Opening** | **Contact** |
| Daily: 11 Feb–25 Mar 10am–4pm; 26 Mar 29 Oct 10am–6pm (last admission 4pm); Nov weekends only 10am–4pm | Chatham ME4 4TZ |
| | t 01634 823800 |
| | w thedockyard.co.uk |
| | e info@chdt.org.uk |

## 074 Chislehurst

# Chislehurst Caves

1 hr     All year

Grab a lantern and get ready for an amazing adventure! Visit the caves and the whole family can travel back in time and explore the maze of passageways deep beneath Chislehurst. During a 45-minute guided tour, visit the Caves Church, Druid altar, Haunted Pool and more.

* Lamp-lit tours
* Original WWII air-raid shelter

| Location | Admission |
| --- | --- |
| Take the A222 between the A20 & A21. At railway bridge turn into Station Road then right again to Caveside Close | Adult £4, Child £2, Concs £2 |
| | **Contact** |
| | Old Hill, Chislehurst BR7 5NB |
| **Opening** | t 020 8467 3264 |
| School hols daily 10am–4pm (except Christmas). Rest of year Wed–Sun 10am–4pm | w chislehurstcaves.co.uk |
| | e enquiries@chislehurstcaves.co.uk |

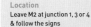

## 075 Dover

# Dover Castle

4 hrs+    All year

Commanding the shortest Channel sea crossing, this site has been the UK's most important defence against invasion since the Iron Age. It was built in the C12 and reinforced by Henry VIII in the 1530s. Underneath the nearby White Cliffs is a series of underground tunnels.

\* Reconstruction of Henry VIII's visit in 1539
\* Visit the Dunkirk command room

**Location**
Clearly signed to E of city, on the white cliffs

**Opening**
Mar–Sep daily 10am–6pm; Oct daily 10am–5pm; Nov–Jan Thu–Mon 10am–4pm; Feb–Mar daily 10am–4pm

**Admission**
Please phone for details

**Contact**
Dover CT16 1HU

t 01304 211067
w english-heritage.org.uk

## 076 Dover

# South Foreland Lighthouse

½ hr    Mar–Oct

Built in 1843, this distinctive landmark on the White Cliffs was the first lighthouse to use electricity and the first to display an electrically powered signal. It was used by Marconi for his first successful international radio transmission.

\* Original 3500 watt lamp on display
\* Leaflets on local walks available

**Location**
2½ miles NE along coast from Dover
2 mile walk from NT car park

**Opening**
*Guided tour* Mar–Oct Thu–Mon 11am–5pm; weekends 11am–5.30pm; school hols daily

**Admission**
Adult £3.60, Child £1.80

**Contact**
The Front, St Margaret's Bay, Dover CT15 6HP

t 01304 852463
w nationaltrust.org.uk
e southforeland@nationaltrust.org.uk

## 077 Edenbridge

# Hever Castle & Gardens

4 hrs    Mar–Nov

This romantic C13 castle was the childhood home of Anne Boleyn. It is set in magnificent gardens, which include a formal Italian garden, a lake and a Sunday walk. There is a water maze on Sixteen Acre Island and the yew maze challenge.

\* Costumed figure exhibition
\* Historic instruments of execution & torture

**Location**
3 miles SE of Edenbridge off B2026 between Sevenoaks & East Grinstead

**Opening**
Daily: Mar–Nov
*Castle* 12noon–6pm (last admission 5pm); Mar & Nov 11am–4pm
*Gardens* 11am–6pm

**Admission**
*Castle & Gardens* Adult £9.20, Child £5, Concs £7.20
*Gardens* £7.30, £4.80, £6.30

**Contact**
Edenbridge TN8 7NG

t 01732 865224
w hevercastle.co.uk
e ampedley@hevercastle.co.uk

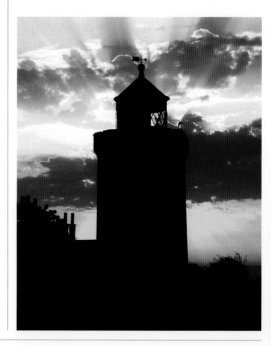

## 078 Eynsford

# Eagle Heights
# Bird of Prey Centre

4 hrs+     Jan–Nov

With more than 100 birds in indoor and outdoor aviaries, the centre gives visitors the opportunity to see birds of prey in action during flying displays, promoting conservation through education. It also provides sanctuary for injured and unwanted animals.

* Five-day falconry courses available
* Now housing otters

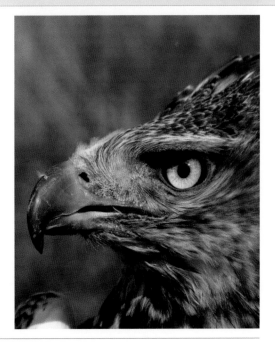

**Location**
Off M25 at junction 3 onto A20, or M20 at junction 1

**Opening**
Daily Mar–Oct 10.30am–5pm;
Nov–Feb weekends 11am–4pm

**Admission**
Adult £6.60, Child £4.60, Concs £5.60

**Contact**
Lullingstone Lane,
Eynsford DA4 0JB

t  01322 866466
w  eagleheights.co.uk
e  office@eagleheights.co.uk

---

## 079 Eynsford

# Lullingstone Roman Villa

1 hr+     All year

One of the best-preserved Roman villas in England, Lullingstone was built in AD75 and rediscovered in 1949. It is now housed in a modern two-storey building. Renowned for its mosaics, it also features a fresco and a bathing complex.

* Free audio tour
* Gift shop

**Location**
Off M25 at junction 3, just outside
Eynsford on A225

**Opening**
Please phone for details

**Admission**
Please phone for details

**Contact**
Lullingstone Lane,
Eynsford DA4 0JA

t  01322 863467
w  english–heritage.org.uk
e  customers@english-heritage.org.uk

---

## 080 Goudhurst

# Bedgebury Pinetum

 3 hrs     All year

These wooded valleys, with the finest collection of conifers in the world, will delight visitors who come to appreciate their beauty and tranquillity. This unique attraction nestles quietly among lakes and valleys in the Kentish countryside.

* Special events & tours
* Pinetum Pantry provides light refreshments

**Location**
On B2079 from Goudhurst,
signed from A21 before Flimwell

**Opening**
Daily: Apr–Oct 10am–5pm;
Sep–Mar 10am–4pm

**Admission**
Please phone for details

**Contact**
Park Lane, Goudhurst TN17 2SL

t  01580 211781
w  bedgeburypinetum.org.uk
e  bedgebury@forestry.gov.uk

## 081  Goudhurst

# Finchcocks Living Museum of Music

3 hrs    Mar–Oct

This Georgian manor house in the Kent countryside has a huge collection of historical keyboard musical instruments, and contains the world's largest collection of playing instruments. The house is noted for its dramatic brickwork and its beautiful and tranquil garden.

* Annual music festival & special events in Sep
* All openings include a demonstration concert

**Location**
Take A262, Goudhurst turning, from A21, follow signs

**Opening**
Mar–Oct Sun 2pm–6pm; Mon–Sat by appointment
Aug Wed & Thu 2pm–6pm;
Bank Hols 2pm–6pm

**Admission**
*House & Gardens* Adult £7.80, Child £4
*Gardens only* £2.50

**Contact**
Finchcocks, Goudhurst TN17 1HH
t  01580 211702
w  finchcocks.co.uk
e  katrina@finchcocks.co.uk

## 082  Hamstreet

# South of England Rare Breeds Centre

3 hrs    All year

Here's a chance to meet and pet all your favourite friendly farm animals as you wander around a farm trail. The centre is also home to many endangered and rare British animals. Set in acres of beautiful woodland, there are plenty of places to picnic while the kids play.

* Woodland activity quiz trail
* Piglet racing in season & trailer rides

**Location**
Leave M20 at junction 10, follow signs to Brenzett and Hamstreet. Situated between Hamstreet & Woodchurch

**Opening**
Daily: Apr–Sep 10.30am–5.30pm;
Oct–Mar Tue–Sun 10.30am–4.30pm

**Admission**
Adult £6, Child £6, Concs £5

**Contact**
Woodchurch, Ashford TN26 3RJ
t  01233 861493
w  rarebreeds.org.uk
e  visit@rarebreeds.org.uk

## 083  Lamberhurst

# Bewl Water

1 hr+    All year

This reservoir is the largest area of open water in the South East. Set in an Area of Outstanding Natural Beauty, Bewl is home to a huge variety of wildlife. There are many exciting outdoor pursuits here, including windsurfing, fishing, cycling and walking.

* Water-efficient garden
* Interactive exhibition

**Location**
1 mile S of Lamberhurst, signed from A21

**Opening**
Daily: Mar–Oct 9am–sunset;
*winter* 9am–4pm

**Admission**
car park Apr–Oct £5, Nov–Mar £2.50

**Contact**
Bewl Water Reservoir,
nr Lamberhurst TN3 8JH
t  01892 890661
w  bewl.co.uk
e  bewl@southernwater.co.uk

## 084 Maidstone

# Leeds Castle

3 hrs    All year

This medieval castle, situated on two islands in a lake set in 500 acres of parkland, is a popular attraction. Once a Norman stronghold, the castle has since been residence for six of England's medieval queens, a palace for Henry VIII and a retreat for the powerful.

* Open-air concert programme
* Grand Firework spectacular

**Location**
Leave M20 at junction 8, castle is 7 miles E of Maidstone

**Opening**
Daily: Apr-Oct 10am-5.30pm; Nov-Mar 10am-3pm

**Admission**
Adult £13, Child £9, Concs £11
*Gardens & attractions* £10.50, £6.50, £8.50

**Contact**
Maidstone ME17 1PL
t 01622 765400
w leeds-castle.com
e enquiries@leeds-castle.co.uk

## 085 Maidstone

# Museum of Kent Life

2 hrs+    Feb-Nov

A unique open-air living museum that celebrates 300 years of Kentish history. Traditional crafts are shown on a working farm. One of the only places in England where hops are grown, harvested, dried and packed by hand, using time-honoured techniques.

* Calendar of events throughout the year
* Hop-picking festival in September

**Location**
Off M20 at junction 6. Follow signs

**Opening**
Daily: Feb-Nov 10am-5pm

**Admission**
Adult £6.50, Child £4.50, Concs £5

**Contact**
Cobtree, Lock Lane, Sandling, Maidstone ME14 3AU
t 01622 763936
w museum-kentlife.co.uk
e enquiries@museum-kentlife.co.uk

## 086 New Romney

# Romney, Hythe & Dymchurch Railway

2 hrs    All year

This was the world's smallest public railway when it opened in July 1927. It now runs passenger services covering a distance of 13½ miles from the picturesque Cinque Port of Hythe, near the Channel Tunnel, to the fishermen's cottages and lighthouses at Dungeness.

* Thomas the Tank Engine & Santa specials
* Dining-train specials

**Location**
The stations at New Romney, Dungeness and Hythe are all on or near A259 trunk road

**Opening**
Trains run daily Apr-Sep & weekends Oct-Mar. Please phone or see the website for timetable

**Admission**
Adult £5-£11, Child half fare

**Contact**
New Romney TN28 8PL
t 01797 362353
w rhdr.org.uk
e info@rhdr.org.uk

## Kent

### 087 Penshurst

# Penshurst Place & Gardens

3 hrs+    Mar–Oct

This medieval manor house was built in 1341. The Great Hall, with its 60ft-high, chestnut-beamed roof and trestle tables, is regarded as one of the world's grandest rooms. Much of the house and the gardens remain unchanged since the days when Elizabeth I made her visits here.

* Includes a fabulous toy museum
* A Family Home for 450 Years exhibition

**Location**
Leave M25 at junction 5 or M20/M26 at junction 2a, follow A21 to Hildenborough, then signed

**Opening**
Daily: Mar–Oct *House* 12noon–5pm; *Gardens* 10.30am–6pm

**Admission**
*House & Gardens* Adult £7, Child £5, Concs £6.50 *Gardens* £5.50, £4.50, £5

**Contact**
Penshurst TN11 8DG

t  01892 870307
w  penshurstplace.com
e  enquiries@penshurstplace.com

### 088 Sevenoaks

# Knole

2 hrs+    Mar–Oct

This great house is set in a magnificent deer park. The original C15 house was enlarged and embellished in 1603 and has remained largely unaltered since then. State rooms house a superb collection of furniture, tapestries and paintings.

* Virtual-reality tour of state rooms
* Children's period costume events

**Location**
Sevenoaks town centre, off A225

**Opening**
*House* 25 Mar–29 Oct Wed–Sun 12am–4pm
*Gardens* Please phone for details

**Admission**
*House* Adult £7.50, Child £3.75
*Gardens* £2, £1

**Contact**
Sevenoaks TN15 0RP

t  01732 462100
w  nationaltrust.org.uk/knole
e  knole@nationaltrust.org.uk

### 089 Sissinghurst

# Sissinghurst Castle Garden

2 hrs+    Mar–Oct

This is one of the world's most celebrated gardens, created by Vita Sackville-West and her husband Sir Harold Nicolson, in the ruins of a large Elizabethan house. The library and tower, which are open to the public, include Vita's writing room.

* History of the house & the making of the garden
* Restaurant uses local recipes & produce

**Location**
1 mile E of Sissinghurst on A262

**Opening**
19 Mar–30 Oct Mon, Tue, Sat & Sun 10am–6pm (last admission 30 mins before close)
*Woodland walks* Open all year

**Admission**
Phone for details. *Woodland* free

**Contact**
Sissinghurst, nr Cranbrook TN17 2AB

t  01580 710701/710700
w  nationaltrust.org.uk/places/sissinghurst
e  sissinghurst@nationaltrust.org.uk

## 090 Tenterden

# The Chapel Down Winery

2 hrs+    All year

This 25-acre vineyard is at the forefront of the English wine making industry. Visitors are free to wander around the winery, vineyard and herb garden. Guided tours explain the wine-making process in more detail. A free wine tasting follows each tour.

\* Café, wine & gift shop
\* Guided tours available during the summer months

**Location**
From Tenterden (A28), turn on to B2082 to Wittersham & Rye. Vineyard is 2 miles on the right at Small Hythe

**Opening**
Daily: 10am–5pm

**Admission**
Free
*Tours* Adult £5, 12–17 yrs £1, Child free

**Contact**
Small Hythe, Tenterden TN30 7NG

t  01580 766111
w  englishwinesgroup.com
e  tourism@englishwinesgroup.com

---

## 091 Tunbridge Wells

# Groombridge Place Gardens & The Enchanted Forest

4 hrs+    Apr–Nov

Groombridge Place's history dates back to medieval times. Flanked by a deep moat, and with a classical C17 manor as its backdrop, the formal gardens boast a rich variety of lawns and flower displays. High above the walled gardens and vineyard lies the Enchanted Forest.

\* Bird of prey raptor centre
\* Maze

**Location**
A26 towards Tunbridge Wells, turn right on to B2176 towards Penshurst. 3 miles past Penshurst village, turn left at T junction with A264. Follow signs

**Opening**
Daily Apr–Nov 9.30am–6pm

**Admission**
Adult £8.70, Child & Concs £7.20

**Contact**
The Estate Office, Groombridge Place, Groombridge,
Royal Tunbridge Wells  TN3 9QG

t  01892 863999/861444
w  groombridge.co.uk
e  office@groombridge.co.uk

---

## 092 Westerham

# Chartwell

2 hrs+    Apr–Oct

The home of Winston Churchill for more than 40 years, Chartwell remains as it was in his day. With many personal possessions and reminders of the man voted greatest Briton of all time, the house captures the mood of a key period in British history.

\* Exhibition of sound recordings
\* Collection of Churchill's paintings

**Location**
2 miles S of Westerham, turn off A25 on to B2026. Follow signs

**Opening**
Apr–Oct Wed–Sun 11am–5pm;
July–Aug Tue & Bank Hols as well

**Admission**
Adult £10, Child £5

**Contact**
Chartwell, Mapleton Road,
Westerham TN16 1PS

t  01732 866368
w  nationaltrust.org.uk/places/
chartwell
e  chartwell@nationaltrust.org.uk

## 093 Bloomsbury

# The British Museum

2 hrs+    All year

The British Museum is home to a collection of art and antiquities from ancient and living cultures. Housed in one of Britain's architectural landmarks, the collection is one of the finest in existence, spanning two million years of human history.

\* Spectacular covered courtyard

| Location | Contact |
|----------|---------|
| *Underground* Tottenham Court Road | Great Russell Street, London WC1B 3DG |
| Opening | |
| Daily: Sat–Wed 10am–5.30pm; Thu–Fri 10am–8.30pm (selected galleries 5.30pm–8.30pm) | t 020 7323 8299 w thebritishmuseum.ac.uk e information@thebritishmuseum. ac.uk |
| Admission | |
| Free, exhibitions may charge | |

## 094 Bloomsbury

# The Charles Dickens Museum

1 hr    All year

Charles Dickens lived in this house between 1837 and 1839 and wrote several of his most famous novels during that time. The house is now the world's foremost repository of Dickens-related material and the headquarters of the Dickens Fellowship.

\* Celebrating an 80th anniversary
\* Collection of letters, first editions & portraits

| Location | Contact |
|----------|---------|
| *Underground* Russell Square | 48 Doughty Street, London WC1N 2LX |
| Opening | |
| Mon–Sat 10am–5pm; Sun 11am–5pm | t 020 7405 2127 w dickensmuseum.com e info@dickensmuseum.com |
| Admission | |
| Adult £5, Child £3, Concs £4 | |

## 095 Chelsea

# Chelsea Physic Garden

2 hrs+    Apr–Oct

Founded in 1673 by the Worshipful Society of Apothecaries, this is one of Europe's oldest botanic gardens. Its 3.8 acres hold a garden showing the history of medicinal plants, a pharmaceutical garden, glasshouses and many rare plants.

\* Historical walk
\* One of the oldest rock gardens in Europe (1773)

| Location | Contact |
|----------|---------|
| *Underground* Sloane Square | 66 Royal Hospital Road, Chelsea, London SW3 4HS |
| Opening | |
| Apr–Oct Wed 12noon–5pm, Sun 2pm–6pm | t 020 7352 5646 w chelseaphysicgarden.co.uk e enquiries@chelseaphysicgarden. co.uk |
| Admission | |
| Adult £6, Child £3.50 | |

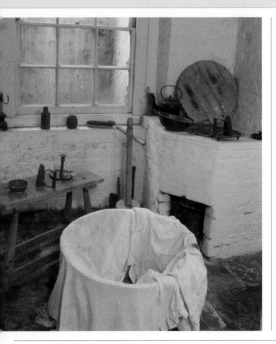

## 096 City

# Museum of London

2 hrs+  All year

The Museum of London is the world's largest urban museum and presents a quarter of a million years of history. Its collections include more than a million items relating to one of the finest cities in the world.

\* Covers the history of the city since it began
\* Photographic exhibition of the Route to Reckoning

| Location | Contact |
|---|---|
| *Underground* Barbican, St Paul's | London Wall, London EC2Y 5HN |
| Opening | |
| Mon–Sat 10am–5.50pm, | t 0870 444 3852 |
| Sun 12noon–5.50pm | w museumoflondon.org.uk |
| | e info@museumoflondon.org.uk |
| Admission | |
| Free | |

## 097 City

# St Paul's Cathedral

1 hr+  All year

The distinctive dome of Sir Christopher Wren's magnificent cathedral is prominent in London's skyline. Its monumental interior, sacred tombs and atmospheric crypt ensure it remains one of London's major tourist attractions.

\* Newly restored interior
\* Try out the Whispering Gallery

| Location | Admission |
|---|---|
| The top of Ludgate Hill | Free *Guided tours* Adult £8, Child |
| *Underground* St Paul's | £3.50, Concs £7 |
| Opening | Contact |
| Mon–Sat 8.30am–4pm | The Chapter House, St Paul's |
| Special services and events may close | Churchyard, London EC4M 8AD |
| all or part of the cathedral | t 020 7236 4128 |
| | w stpauls.co.uk |
| | e chapter@stpaulscathedral.org.uk |

## 098 City

# The Streets of London

2 hrs  All year

The Streets of London invites you to sample the many faces of this great and fascinating city. Journey through 2,000 years of history on walks that will inform, excite and stimulate your curiosity.

\* Programme of fascinating walks all over the city
\* Each walk lasts approximately two hours

| Location | Contact |
|---|---|
| Walks start at different Tube stations | Please phone for details |
| every day of the week | t 020 8906 8657 |
| Opening | w thestreetsoflondon.co.uk |
| Please phone for details | e contactstreetsol@hotmail.com |
| Admission | |
| Adult £6, accompanied under-12s | |
| free | |

## 099 County Hall

# London Aquarium

2 hrs    All year

The London Aquarium is for everyone who appreciates the stunning and fascinating natural world. Let your imagination take you on a voyage under the sea, from the beautiful coral reefs and Indian Ocean to the secret depths of the Pacific and Atlantic Oceans.

\* Late-night opening times in summer
\* Themed activity weeks

**Location**
Inside County Hall on South Bank of the Thames by Westminster Bridge
*Underground* **Westminster**

**Opening**
Daily: 10am–6pm (7pm on selected summer evenings)

**Admission**
Please phone for details

**Contact**
County Hall, Westminster Bridge Road, London SE1 7PB

t  020 7967 8000
w  londonaquarium.co.uk
e  info@londonaquarium.co.uk

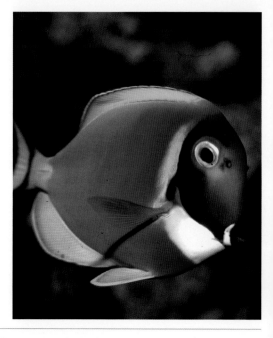

## 100 County Hall

# London Eye

½ hr    All year

This is the most popular tourist attraction in London. The 443ft (135m) big wheel provides the most spectacular views of one of the biggest cities in the world. On a clear day you can see 25 miles in every direction from a safe and comfortable capsule.

\* More than 15,000 people a day travel on the Eye
\* Views are breathtaking in all conditions

**Location**
On the South Bank of the Thames by County Hall
*Underground* **Waterloo**

**Opening**
Daily: May, Jun & Sep 9.30am–9pm;
Jul–Aug 9.30am–10pm; Jan–Apr &
Oct–Dec 9.30am–8pm

**Admission**
Adult £12.50, Child £6.50, Concs £10

**Contact**
BA London Eye, Riverside Building, County Hall, London SE1 7PB

t  0870 5000 600
w  ba-londoneye.com
e  customer.services@ba-londoneye.com

## 101 Green Park

# Buckingham Palace

1 hr+    Jul–Sep

The official London residence of Her Majesty The Queen. The state rooms are used extensively to entertain guests on state, ceremonial and official occasions but are open to the public during August and September when the Queen makes her annual visit to Scotland.

\* The state rooms form the heart of the working palace
\* Furnished with treasures from the Royal Collection

**Location**
*Mainline* **Victoria**
*Underground* **Victoria, Green Park & Hyde Park Corner**

**Opening**
23 Jul–27 Sep daily 9.30am–6pm

**Admission**
Adult £13.50, Child £7, Concs £11.50

**Contact**
Ticket Sales and Information Office,
The Official Residences of The Queen,
London SW1A 1AA

t  020 7766 7300
w  royalcollection.org.uk
e  bookinginfo@royalcollection.org.uk

## 102 Greenwich

# The *Cutty Sark*

1 hr    Jan–Sep

It's 1880 and the *Cutty Sark's* Captain has just jumped overboard, you're 1,000 miles from home and there is a 100ft wave in front of you! Actually, you're in Maritime Greenwich overlooking the River Thames, holding the wheel of the fastest tea clipper ever built.

\* Experience life on board one of the world's most famous ships
\* Visit now before the £25m conservation programme begins in October 2006

**Location**
*Mainline* Docklands Light Railway Cutty Sark Station
*Underground* Canary Wharf
By boat from Westminster Pier

**Opening**
Daily: 10am–5pm (last admission 4.30pm)

**Admission**
Adult £4.50, Child £3.25, Concs £3.75

**Contact**
King William Walk, Greenwich, London SE10 9HT

t  020 8858 3445
w  cuttysark.org.uk
e  enquiries@cuttysark.org.uk

## 103 Greenwich

# National Maritime Museum

2 hrs+    All year

This is part of a World Heritage site comprising the National Maritime Museum, Royal Observatory and the Queen's House. It houses important items on the history of Britain at sea, including maritime art, ship models, plans, navigational instruments and time keeping.

\* Three marvellous museums in close proximity
\* Planetarium shows at the Observatory, daily 2.30pm

**Location**
*Mainline* Greenwich or Maze Hill, *Docklands Light Railway* Cutty Sark station. Boat from Embankment or Westminster

**Opening**
Daily: *summer* 10am–6pm *winter* 10am–5pm

**Admission**
Free, exhibitions may charge

**Contact**
Park Row, Greenwich SE10 9NF

t  020 8312 6565
   020 8858 4422
w  nmm.ac.uk

## 104 Kensington

# Natural History Museum

2 hrs+    All year

The Natural History Museum has hundreds of exciting, interactive exhibits. Highlights include Dinosaurs, Creepy-Crawlies, Human Biology, the must-see exhibition about ourselves, and Mammals, with its unforgettable huge blue whale.

\* Investigate the wildlife garden
\*Special exhibitions throughout the year

**Location**
*Underground* South Kensington

**Opening**
Mon–Sat & Bank Hols 10am–5.50pm,
Sun 11am–5.50pm
(last admission 5.30pm);
closed 24, 25, 26 Dec

**Admission**
Free

**Contact**
Cromwell Road, London SW7 5BD

t  020 7942 5000
w  nhm.ac.uk
e  info@nhm.ac.uk

## 105 Kensington

# Science Museum

3 hrs+    All year

This museum presents a record of scientific, technological and medical change since the C18. Originally funded by profits from the Great Exhibition of 1851, the museum was intended to improve scientific and technical education, and has done so for 150 years.

\* Range of interactive exhibits, including new Energy Gallery
\* IMAX cinema

**Location**
*Underground* South Kensington

**Opening**
Daily: 10am–6pm

**Admission**
Free, donations welcomed,
exhibitions may charge

**Contact**
Exhibition Road, South Kensington,
London SW7 2DD

t  0870 870 4868
w  sciencemuseum.org.uk
e  sciencemuseum@nmsi.ac.uk

106 Kensington

# Victoria & Albert Museum

2–6 hrs    All year

The V&A is widely regarded as the world's greatest museum of art and design. Home to amazing artefacts from the world's richest cultures, the V&A's unsurpassable collection has inspired and informed for more than 150 years.

\* A wide choice of special events, exhibitions & activities
\* Spend time wandering the seven miles of corridors

| Location | Contact |
| --- | --- |
| *Underground* South Kensington | Cromwell Road, South Kensington, London SW7 2RL |
| Opening | |
| Daily: 10am–5.45pm, Weds 10am–10pm, last Fri of month 10am–10pm | t  020 7942 2000 |
| | w  vam.ac.uk |
| | e  vanda@vam.ac.uk |
| Admission | |
| Free, exhibitions may charge | |

107 Lambeth

# Imperial War Museum

3 hrs+    All year

This is the national museum of C20 conflict. It illustrates and records all aspects of modern war and of the individual's experience of it, whether allied or enemy, service or civilian, military or political. Its role embraces the causes, course and consequences of conflict.

\* Special Holocaust exhibition
\* Cinema shows museum's collection of film & video

| Location | Admission |
| --- | --- |
| *Mainline* Waterloo, Elephant & Castle | Free, exhibitions may charge |
| *Underground* Lambeth North 5 min walk | Contact |
| | Lambeth Road, London SE1 6HZ |
| Opening | |
| Daily: 10am–6pm | t  020 7416 5320 |
| | w  iwm.org.uk |
| | e  mail@iwm.org.uk |

## 108 Liverpool Street

# Bank of England Museum

1 hr+    All year

This fascinating collection charts the history of the bank from its earliest days to the present. Discover how banknotes are made, take an audio tour, lift a genuine gold bar, and view bank notes (real and forged), coins, books, furniture and pictures.

* Try to lift a real gold bar
* Special events & activities

**Location**
*Underground* **Bank & Liverpool Street**

**Opening**
Weekdays 10am–5pm; also open on day of Lord Mayor's Show; closed Sat, Sun & Bank Hols

**Admission**
Free

**Contact**
Threadneedle Street,
London EC2R 8AH

t  020 7601 5491
w  bankofengland.co.uk/museum
e  museum@bankofengland.co.uk

## 109 London Bridge

# London Dungeon

1 hr+    All year

Deep in the heart of London, buried beneath the paving stones of historic Southwark, lies the world's most chillingly famous horror attraction. The London Dungeon brings more than 2,000 years of gruesomely authentic history vividly back to life ... and death.

* Great Plague exhibition & Judgement Day boat ride
* The terrible truth about Jack the Ripper

**Location**
*Underground* **London Bridge**

**Opening**
Daily: 10am–5.30pm

**Admission**
Adult £15.50, Child £10.95, Concs £12.25

**Contact**
28–34 Tooley Street,
London SE1 2SZ

t  020 7403 7221
w  thedungeons.com
e  londondungeon@
merlinentertainments.biz

## 110 Marylebone

# Madame Tussaud's

2 hrs+    All year

Not only can you see all the famous people from pop idols to politicians, you can also try out for the England team, be snapped by the paparazzi, be scared witless by serial killers, and even explore the furthest depths of the universe.

* Updated & revamped Chamber of Horrors
* New online ticket booking allows timed ticketing

**Location**
*Underground* **Baker Street**

**Opening**
Weekdays 9.30am–5.30pm;
Weekends 9am–6pm

**Admission**
Adult from £19.99, Child from £15.99,
Concs from £17.99

**Contact**
Marylebone Road, London NW1 5LR

t  0870 400 3000
w  madame-tussauds.com
e  csc@madame-tussauds.com

# 111 Marylebone

# Wallace Collection

2 hrs+  All year

This is both a national museum and the finest private collection of art ever assembled by one family. It is displayed against the opulent backdrop of Hertford House. The collection is best known for its magnificent C18 French paintings, furniture and porcelain.

* Paintings by Titian, Rembrandt & Frans Hals
* Superb new restaurant

 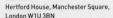

**Location**
*Underground* **Bond Street**

**Opening**
Daily: 10am–5pm

**Admission**
Free

**Contact**
Hertford House, Manchester Square,
London W1U 3BN

t  020 7563 9500
w  wallacecollection.org

# 112 Regent's Park

# London Zoo

4 hrs  All year

Come face to face with some of the hairiest, scariest, tallest and smallest animals on the planet. See the Animals in Action presentation and watch some of the finest flying, leaping and climbing animals showing off their skills. Don't miss a visit to B.U.G.S!

* Regular programme of feeding times & special shows
* New komodo dragon, a very impressive predator

**Location**
At NE corner of Regent's Park
on Outer Circle
*Underground* **Camden Town**

**Opening**
Daily: 7 Mar–23 Oct 10am–5.30pm;
24 Oct–31 Oct 10am–4.30pm; Nov–Feb
10am–4pm

**Admission**
Adult £14, Child £10.75, Concs £12

**Contact**
Regent's Park, London NW1 4RY

t  020 7722 3333
w  zsl.org

## 113 Shepherd's Bush

# BBC Television Centre Tours

2 hrs   All year

Tours of the most famous television centre in the world last up to two hours. You'll see behind the scenes and into studios, visit BBC News, play in the interactive studio and be shown around by well-informed, entertaining guides. No two tours are the same.

* Winner of the 2003 Group Travel Awards
* Also new CBBC tours

**Location**
*Underground* **White City**

**Opening**
Tours run 6 times a day Mon–Sat; booking essential

**Admission**
Adult £8.95,  Child £6.50

**Contact**
BBC Television Centre, Wood Lane, London W12 7RJ

t  0870 603 0304 (bookings)
w  bbc.co.uk/tours
e  bbctours@bbc.co.uk

## 114 St John's Wood

# Lord's Tour & MCC Museum

2 hrs   All year

The Lord's Tour is an enjoyable and informative visit to the world-famous home of cricket. The tour includes the Pavilion, Long Room, dressing room and MCC Museum, which houses cricketing memorabilia including bats, balls, paintings and much more.

* Don Bradman's cricket kit
* Home of the Ashes urn, regained by England in 2005

**Location**
*Underground* **St John's Wood**

**Opening**
Daily: Apr–Sep tours at 10am, 12noon & 2pm; Oct–Mar 12noon & 2pm;

**Admission**
Adult £8, Child £5, Concs £6

**Contact**
Lord's Cricket Ground, St John's Wood, London NW8 8QN

t  020 7616 8595 / 8596
w  lords.org
e  tours@mcc.org.uk

## 115 South Bank

# Clink Prison Museum

½ hr +   All year

On the site of the original Clink prison, this fascinating exhibition examines some of London's unsavoury past. From the C12 until its destruction in 1780; its inmates have ranged from priests to prostitutes.

* Possibly the oldest men's prison in London
* Whipping post, torture chair, foot crusher & more

**Location**
*Underground* **London Bridge**

**Opening**
Daily: 10am–7.30pm; summer & Sat–Sun 10am–9pm

**Admission**
Adult £5, Child & Concs £3.50

**Contact**
1 Clink Street, South Bank, London SE1 9DG

t  020 7378 1558
w  clink.co.uk
e  museum@clink.co.uk

*© Tate Modern: Turbine Hall Photocredit: Tate Photography*

## 116 South Bank

# Globe Theatre

1–3 hrs     All year

The Globe Theatre is a reconstruction of the open-air playhouse, designed in 1599, where Shakespeare worked and for which he wrote many of his greatest plays. You can see a performance or visit the Globe Exhibition, for an introduction to the theatre of Shakespeare's time.

\* Annual programme of Shakespeare's plays
\* Permanent exhibition & theatre tours

**Location**
*Mainline* London Bridge, Waterloo
*Underground* Southwark

**Opening**
Daily: May–Sep *Theatre* 10am–7.30pm
*Exhibition* 9am–5pm Oct–Apr *Exhibition*
10am–5pm (tours available)

**Admission**
*Exhibition* Adult £9, Child £6.50,
Concs £7.50

**Contact**
21 New Globe Walk, London SE1 9DT
t  *Enquiries* 020 7902 1400
   *Box office* 020 7401 9919
w  shakespeares-globe.org
e  info@shakespearesglobe.com

## 117 South Bank

# Tate Modern

2 hrs+     All year

This spectacular gallery of modern and contemporary art is housed in the old Bankside Power Station on the south side of the river Thames. It is one of the world's most popular modern art galleries, featuring a permanent collection alongside temporary exhibits.

\* Superb shop at gallery entrance
\* Marvelous river views from restaurant on level seven

**Location**
Opposite St Paul's Cathedral
*Underground* Southwark, Blackfriars
Boat from Tate Britain to Tate Modern

**Opening**
Daily: Sun–Thu 10am–6pm,
Fri & Sat 10am–10pm

**Admission**
Free, donations welcomed,
exhibitions may charge

**Contact**
Bankside, London SE1 9TG

t  020 7887 8000
w  tate.org.uk
e  info@tate.org.uk

## 118 Tower Bridge

# Design Museum

1 hr+     All year

The Design Museum is the world's leading museum of industrial design, fashion and architecture. A programme of critically acclaimed exhibitions captures the excitement of design's evolution, ingenuity and inspiration through the C20 and C21.

\* Rolling schedule of temporary exhibitions
\* Full range of talks, courses & kids' activities

**Location**
*Underground* Tower Hill, 10 min walk
over Tower Bridge
*Docklands Light Railway* Tower
Gateway

**Opening**
Daily: 10am–5.45pm;
*summer* Fri 10am–9pm

**Admission**
Adult £6, Child £4, Concs £4

**Contact**
Shad Thames, London SE1 2YD

t  0870 8339955
w  designmuseum.org
e  info@designmuseum.org

119 Tower Bridge

# HMS *Belfast*

1 hr+    All year

HMS *Belfast* was launched in 1938 and served throughout WWII, playing a leading part in the destruction of the German battle cruiser *Scharnhorst* and in the Normandy landings in 1944. In 1971 she was saved as a unique reminder of Britain's naval heritage.

\* Experience what life was like for the crew
\* Complete tours of this huge & complex warship

**Location**
*Underground* London Bridge

**Opening**
Daily: Mar–Oct 10am–6pm;
Nov–Feb 10am–5 pm;
(last admission 45 mins before close)

**Admission**
Adult £8, Child free, Concs £6

**Contact**
Morgan's Lane, Tooley Street,
London SE1 2JH

t  0207 940 6300
w  iwm.org.uk/belfast
e  hmsbelfast@iwm.org.uk

---

120 Tower Bridge

# Tower Bridge Exhibition

1 hr    All year

This is one of the world's most famous bridges. Visitors can go inside the Gothic towers to discover its history and see the original Victorian engine rooms. From the high-level walkways you can look out across the modern city skyline.

\* New interactive computer displays
\* Special ticket rate for Tower Bridge & Monument

**Location**
*Underground* Tower Hill and London Bridge
Boat from Tower Pier

**Opening**
Daily: 10am–6.30pm (last admission 5.30pm)

**Admission**
Adult £5.50, Child £3, Concs £4.25

**Contact**
Tower Bridge, London SE1 2UP

t  020 7403 3761
w  towerbridge.org.uk
e  enquiries@towerbridge.org.uk

---

121 Tower Hill

# Tower of London

3 hrs    All year

Founded by William the Conqueror and modified by successive sovereigns, the Tower of London is one of the world's most famous and spectacular fortresses. Discover its 900-year history as a palace, fortress, prison, mint, arsenal, menagerie and jewel house.

\* Ceremony of the Keys (please apply in writing)
\* Constant calendar of special events

**Location**
*Underground* Tower Hill

**Opening**
Mar–Oct Tues–Sat 9am–6pm,
Sun & Mon 10am–6pm;
Nov–Feb Tue–Sat 9am–5pm,
Sun & Mon 10am–5pm
(last admission 1 hr before close)

**Admission**
Adult £14.50, Child £9.50 , Concs £11

**Contact**
Tower Hill, London EC3N 4AB

t  0870 756 6060
w  tower-of-london.org.uk

122 Trafalgar Square

# National Gallery

1 hr+    All year

This gallery houses one of the greatest collections of European painting in the world. The permanent collection spans the period from 1250 to 1900 and includes paintings by artists Leonardo da Vinci, Michelangelo, J M W Turner and Vincent van Gogh.

\* Selection of courses & lectures available
\* Weekend & school holiday family events

**Location**
Trafalgar Square
*Underground* Leicester Square, Charing Cross

**Opening**
Daily: 10am–6pm; Wed 10am–9pm

**Admission**
Free, donations welcome, exhibitions may charge

**Contact**
Trafalgar Square, London WC2N 5DN
t 020 7747 2885
w nationalgallery.org.uk
e information@ng–london.org.uk

123 Trafalgar Square

# National Portrait Gallery

2 hrs    All year

Founded in 1856 to collect the likenesses of famous British men and women, the gallery aimed to be about history not art, and this remains its criterion today. The collection is the most comprehensive of its kind in the world.

\* Daytime & evening lectures & events
\* Roof-top restaurant that boasts stunning views

**Location**
*Underground* Charing Cross, Leicester Square

**Opening**
Daily: 10am–6pm, Thu & Fri 10am–9pm

**Admission**
Free, exhibitions may charge

**Contact**
St Martin's Place, London WC2H 0HE
t 020 7306 0055 / 020 7312 2463
w npg.org.uk

124 Twickenham

# Museum of Rugby

2 hrs    All year

More than just a collection of interesting artefacts, this museum is an inspirational journey through the development of this historic team game. Innovative, interactive exhibits bring to life some of the great moments of the international game.

\* Finest collection of rugby memorabilia
\* Action-packed films show footage of matches

**Location**
*Mainline* Twickenham (from Waterloo)

**Opening**
Tue–Sat 10am–5pm; Sun 11am–5pm

**Admission**
Adult £9, Child & Concs £6

**Contact**
Rugby Road, Twickenham, London TW1 1DZ
t 020 8892 8877
w rfu.com
e museum@rfu.com

## 125  Westminster

# Churchill Museum & Cabinet War Rooms

1 hr        All year

Learn about the man who inspired Britain's finest hour at the interactive and innovative Churchill Museum, the world's first major museum dedicated to the life of the greatest Briton. Discover the secret underground HQ that was the nerve centre of Britain's war effort in WWII.

\* New Winston Churchill museum opened 2005

| Location | Contact |
|---|---|
| *Underground* **Westminster** or St James's Park | King Charles Street, London SW1A 2AQ |
| *Mainline* **Charing Cross** or Victoria | t  020 7930 6961 |
| **Opening** | w  iwm.org.uk |
| Daily: 9.30am–6pm | e  cwr@iwm.org.uk |
| **Admission** | |
| Adult £10, Child free, Concs £8 | |

## 126  Westminster

# Houses of Parliament

2 hrs       July–Oct

The House of Commons and House of Lords meet in the Palace of Westminster, next to the River Thames in London. Parliament has met in the Palace of Westminster since around 1550. UK residents and overseas visitors must book tours in advance.

\* See & hear debates

| Location | Contact |
|---|---|
| *Underground* **Westminster** | House of Commons Information Office, Westminster, London SW1A 0AA |
| **Opening** | |
| Tours available during summer recess end Jul–early Oct | t  020 7219 4272 |
| Please phone for details | w  parliament.uk |
| **Admission** | e  hcinfo@parliament.uk |
| Please phone for details | |

## 127  Westminster

# Westminster Abbey

1 hr+       All year

An architectural masterpiece of the C13 to C16, Westminster Abbey presents a unique pageant of British history. It has been the setting for most coronations since 1066 and for numerous royal occasions. Today it is still a church dedicated to regular worship and events.

\* The tombs of kings & queens
\* Tomb of the Unknown Warrior

| Location | Admission |
|---|---|
| Next to Parliament Square, opposite Houses of Parliament | Adult £8, Child £6, Concs £6 |
| *Underground* **St James's Park** and Westminster | **Contact** |
| **Opening** | 20 Deans Yard, London SW1 P3PA |
| Mon–Fri 9.30am–3.45pm, Wed 9.30am–7pm, Sat 9.30am–1.45pm, Sun worship only | t  020 7654 4900 |
| | w  westminster-abbey.org |
| | e  press@westminster-abbey.org |

## 128  Wimbledon

# Wimbledon Lawn Tennis Museum

1 hr+       All year

This museum, on the site of the world's most famous lawn tennis tournament, offers a glimpse of both the Centre Court and the original trophies. Discover how the original medieval real tennis has become a multi million pound professional sport.

\*Audio-visual presentation of great players in action
\*New museum opening at the start of April

| Location | Contact |
|---|---|
| *Underground* **Southfields** | The All England Lawn Tennis Club, Church Road, Wimbledon, London SW19 5AE |
| **Opening** | |
| Daily: 10.30am–5pm | t  020 8946 6131 |
| **Admission** | w  wimbledon.org/museum |
| Adult £7.50, Child £4.75, Concs £6.25 | e  museum@aeltc.com |
| *Museum & Tour* £14.50, £11, £13.50, | |

## 129  Banbury

# Broughton Castle

1 hr+    May–Sep

This historic C14 moated castle was enlarged in C16. Home of the family of Lord Saye and Sele for 600 years. It has Civil War connections, fine walled gardens, old roses and herbaceous borders. There is also a large area of open parkland.

* Location for the film *Shakespeare In Love*
* Medieval manor house enlarged in 1600

**Location**
2 miles W of Banbury Cross on the B4035 Shipston-on-Stour road

**Opening**
1 May–11 Sep Wed & Sun 2pm–5pm;
Jul & Aug Wed, Thur & Sun 2pm–5pm;
Bank Hol Sun & Mon 2pm–5pm

**Admission**
Adult £6, Child £2.50, Concs £5

**Contact**
Broughton, Banbury OX15 5EB
t  01295 722 547/276070
w  broughtoncastle.demon.co.uk
e  admin@broughtoncastle.demon.co.uk

---

## 131  Chipping Norton

# The Rollright Stones

1 hr    All year

The Rollright Stones is an ancient site that consists of three main elements. The King's Men stone circle, the King Stone and the Whispering Knights. The name is believed to derive from 'Hrolla–landriht', the land of Hrolla.

* Discover the folklore of kings, witches & fairies
* 5,000-year-old burial chamber of a Neolithic barrow

**Location**
N of Chipping Norton

**Opening**
Sunrise–sunset

**Admission**
Adult 50p, Child 25p

**Contact**
The Friends of the Rollright Stones
PO Box 203,
Aberystwyth SY23 4WZ
w  rollrightstones.co.uk

---

## 130  Burford

# Cotswold Wildlife Park & Gardens

3 hrs+    All year

The park, which is set in 160 acres of parkland and gardens around a listed Victorian manor house, has been open to the public since 1970. It is home to a collection of mammals, birds, reptiles and invertebrates, from ants to white rhinos and bats to big cats.

* Insect & reptile houses
* Birds of prey flying demos at weekends in summer

**Location**
On A361, 2 miles S of Burford

**Opening**
Daily: Mar–Sep 10am–4.30pm;
Oct–Feb 10am–3.30pm

**Admission**
Adult £8, Child £5.50, Concs £5.50

**Contact**
Burford OX18 4JW
t  01993 823006
w  cotswoldwildlifepark.co.uk

132   Henley-on-Thames

# Greys Court

1 hr+        Apr–Sep

This intriguing Tudor house is set beside the ruins of C14 fortifications and one surviving tower dating from 1347. It has an interesting history involving Jacobean court intrigue. The outbuildings include a wheelhouse, a donkey wheel, an ice house and a maze.

\* Wisteria walk & ornamental vegetable garden
\* Intimate rooms contain beautiful C18 plasterwork

**Location**
From Henley take A4130 to Oxford.
At Nettlebed roundabout take B481

**Opening**
Apr–Sep *House* Wed–Fri 2pm–5pm;
Aug Wed–Sun 12.30–5pm
*Gardens* Tue–Sat 2pm–5pm

**Admission**
*House* Adult £5.40, Child £3.70
*Gardens* £3.90, £1.70

**Contact**
Rotherfield Greys,
Henley-on-Thames RG9 4PG

t   01491 628529
w  nationaltrust.org.uk
e  greyscourt@ntrust.org.uk

133   Henley-on-Thames

# River and Rowing Museum

2 hrs        All year

The museum has three main galleries devoted to the River Thames, the international sport of rowing and the town of Henley. Be magically transported into the world of Ratty, Mole, Badger and the irrepressible Toad from Kenneth Grahame's tale *The Wind in the Willows*.

\* Exhibits from 400BC to the Sydney 2000 Olympic Games
\* Theatrical & audio-visual techniques, models, lighting & sound

**Location**
Signed from centre of Henley

**Opening**
Daily: *summer* 10am–5.30pm
*winter* 10am–5pm

**Admission**
Adult £6, Child £4, Concs £5

**Contact**
Mill Meadows,
Henley-on-Thames RG9 1BF

t   01491 415600
w  rrm.co.uk
e  museum@rrm.co.uk

## 134 Oxford

# The Ashmolean Museum of Art & Archaeology

2 hrs+    All year

This is a museum of the University of Oxford. Founded in 1683, it is one of the oldest public museums in the world. The collections are divided between five curatorial departments: Antiquities, Cast Gallery, Eastern Art, Heberden Coin Room and Western Art.

**Location**
On Beaumont Street, opposite
Randolph Hotel, Oxford

**Opening**
Tue–Sat 10am–5pm,
Sun 12noon–5pm;
Bank Hol Mon 10am –5pm

**Admission**
Free

**Contact**
Beaumont Street, Oxford OX1 2PH UK

t 01865 278000
w ashmol.ox.ac.uk

## 135 Oxford

# Modern Art Oxford

1 hr    All year

One of the UK's leading centres for the presentation of modern and contemporary art. Recent exhibitions have included Tracey Emin, Jake and Dinos Chapman, Jim Lambie, Mike Nelson, Jannis Kounellis and Cecily Brown.

* A regular & changing programme of events
* Talks & tours, chidren's events & music evenings

**Location**
Town centre, 10 mins from train
station

**Opening**
Tue–Sat 10–5pm, Sun 12noon–5pm
Please phone for details

**Admission**
Free

**Contact**
30 Pembroke Street,
Oxford OX1 1BP

t 01865 722733
w modernartoxford.org.uk
e foh@modernartoxford.
org.uk

## 136 Oxford

# The Oxford University Museum of Natural History

1 hr+    All year

This museum houses Oxford University's extensive natural history collection in a high-Victorian Gothic building. Exhibits include the remains of the dodo, immortalised in *Alice in Wonderland* and extinct since 1680 and fossil dinosaur materials.

* The Oxford dinosaurs & other Mesozoic reptiles
* Historic material donated by scientists including Darwin

**Location**
In Parks Road facing Keble College,
signed

**Opening**
Daily: 12noon–5pm

**Admission**
Free, donations appreciated

**Contact**
Parks Road, Oxford OX1 3PW

t 01865 272950
w oum.ox.ac.uk
e info@oum.ox.ac.uk

## 137 Oxford

# University of Oxford Botanic Garden

1 hr+   All year

This garden holds a National Collection and has more than 8,000 different types of plant – the most compact yet diverse collection in the world. There is more biological diversity here than in tropical rainforests.

* Water garden, rock garden & Grade I walled garden
* Innovative black border & autumn borders

| Location | Admission |
|---|---|
| Opposite Magdalen College in centre of Oxford | Adult £2.60, Child free, Concs £2 |
| Opening | Contact |
| Daily: Mar, Apr, Sep & Oct 9am–5pm; May–Aug 9am–6pm; Nov–Feb 9am–4.30pm | Rose Lane, Oxford OX1 4AZ |
| | t 01865 286690 |
| | w botanic-garden.ox.ac.uk |
| | e postmaster@obg.ox.ac.uk |

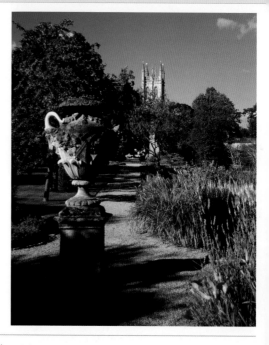

## 138 Wantage

# The Vale & Downland Museum

2 hr+   All year

This museum is housed in a converted C17 cloth merchant's house – a fine example of local vernacular architecture. The collections held at the museum contain geological, archaeological and contemporary objects. An important record of both natural and social history.

* The story of Victorian Rural Life in the Vale
* 3D, graphic design & audio-visual presentations

| Location | Admission |
|---|---|
| Well signed from Wantage town centre | Adult £2.50, Child £1, Concs £2 |
| Opening | Contact |
| Mon–Sat 10am–4.30pm; Sun 2.30pm–5pm Bank Hol Mon 2.30pm–5pm | Church Street, Wantage OX12 8BL |
| | t 01235 771447 |
| | w wantage.com/museum |
| | e museum@wantage.com |

## 139 Woodstock

# Blenheim Palace

4 hrs   Feb–Dec

This beautiful palace was built for John Churchill, 1st Duke of Marlborough, in 1705. Designed by Sir John Vanbrugh, it is one of the largest private houses in the country and contains a superb collection of tapestries, paintings, sculptures and furniture.

* The birthplace of Sir Winston Churchill
* Paintings include works by Reynolds & Van Dyck

| Location | Admission |
|---|---|
| Approaching Oxford on M40, exit at junction 9 & follow signs to Blenheim Palace | Adult £12.50, Child £7, Concs £10 Please phone for details |
| Opening | Contact |
| Palace Daily: mid Feb–mid Dec 10.30am–4.45pm; Nov–Dec closed Mon–Tue Park Daily: 9am–4.45pm | Woodstock OX20 1PX |
| | t 08700 602080 |
| | w www.blenheimpalace.com |
| | e administrator@blenheimpalace.com |

## 140 Cheam

# Whitehall

1 hr+    All year

A timber-framed Tudor house with additions over the centuries. There is a new virtual computer tour allowing 'access' to the upper floors situated on the ground floor. Collections include Syntax ware, Nonsuch pottery and Victorian schoolmaster's room.

\* Timber-framed construction
\* Audio tour available & touch-screen information system

**Location**
Off Broadway, centre of Cheam

**Opening**
Wed–Fri 2pm–5pm;
Sat 10am–5pm Sun & Bank Hols
2pm–5pm;
closed 21 Dec–1 Jan

**Admission**
Adult £1.25, Child 60p

**Contact**
1 Malden Road, Cheam SM3 8QD

t  020 8643 1236
w  sutton.gov.uk
e  curators@whitehallcheam.fsnet.
   co.uk

## 141 Chertsey

# Chertsey Museum

1 hr+    All year

Reopened in 2003 after a major redevelopment. Chertsey is famous as the site of a medieval abbey and has some of the best-preserved Georgian architecture in the county. The museum explores the history of the area and includes many items of national interest.

\* Hands-on exhibits in Grade II Regency town house
\* Nationally famous Olive Matthews costume collection

**Location**
Chertsey town centre

**Opening**
Tue–Fri 12.30–4.30pm, Sat 11am–4pm

**Admission**
Free

**Contact**
The Cedars, 33 Windsor Street,
Chertsey KT16 8AT

t  01932 565764
w  chertseymuseum.org.uk
e  enquiries@chertseymuseum.org.uk

## 142 Cobham

# Painshill Park

2 hrs+    All year

Within its 160 acres created by Charles Hamilton as a series of subtle and surprising vistas, its landscapes include authentic C18 plantings, working vineyard, Gothic Temple, Chinese Bridge, Crystal Grotto, Turkish Tent, newly restored Hermitage and Gothic Tower.

\* One of the most important C18 parks in Europe
\* 14-acre lake fed by a spectacular waterwheel

**Location**
Off A3 & A245 at Cobham

**Opening**
Mar–Oct 10.30am–6pm, closed Mon;
Nov–Feb 11am–4pm or dusk,
closed Mon & Tue

**Admission**
Adult £6, Child £3.50, Concs £5.25

**Contact**
Portsmouth Road, Cobham KT11 1JE

t  01932 868113
w  painshill.co.uk
e  info@painshill.co.uk

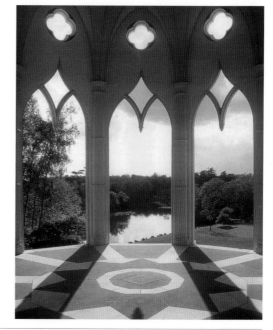

## 143 Churt

# Pride of the Valley Sculpture Park

2 hrs+    All year

Adjoining Frensham Country Park at the foot of Devil's Jumps with the finest views of the county. Some 100 renowned sculptors exhibit works of art in a woodland setting. There are acres of hills, valleys, arboretum and wildfowl-inhabited water gardens.

* Frensham Country Park provides extensive walks

**Location**
Jumps Road is off A287 S of Farnham

**Opening**
Tue–Sun 10am–5pm; closed Mon except Bank Hols

**Admission**
Adult £4.50, Child £2, Concs £2–£3

**Contact**
Jumps Road, Churt, nr Farnham GU10 2LE

t 01428 605453
w thesculpturepark.com
e eddiepowell@thesculpturepark.co.uk

## 144 East Molesey

# Hampton Court Palace

3 hrs+    All year

With 500 years of royal history, Hampton Court is one of England's finest attractions. It is a magnificent palace with diverse rooms such as Tudor kitchens and the sumptuous State Apartments. The palace is complemented by 60 acres of riverside gardens.

* Horse-drawn carriages through gardens in summer
* World-famous maze in which to get lost

**Location**
From M25, junction 10 to A307 or junction 12 to A308

**Opening**
Daily: 26 Mar–28 Oct 10am–6pm; 29 Oct–25 Mar 10am–4.30pm

**Admission**
Adult £12, Child £7.80, Concs £9

**Contact**
East Molesey KT8 9AU

t 0870 752 7777
w hamptoncourtpalace.org.uk
e hamptoncourt@hrp.org.uk

## 145 Esher

# Claremont Landscape Garden

  1hr+  All year

Claremont's creation and development involved some of the great names in garden history. Begun c.1715, it became famous throughout Europe. Restoration began in 1975 after years of neglect. The many features include a lake, grotto and great views.

* Design by Capability Brown & Sir John Vanbrugh
* Turf amphitheatre & island with pavilion

| Location | Admission |
|---|---|
| 1 mile outside Esher on Cobham road, (A307) | Adult £5, Child £2.50 |
| | **Contact** |
| **Opening** | Portsmouth Road, Esher KT10 9JG |
| Daily: Apr–Oct 10am–6pm; | t 01372 467806 |
| Sat, Sun & Bank Hols 10am–7pm; | w nationaltrust.org.uk/claremont |
| Nov–Mar Tue–Sun 10am–5pm | e claremont@nationaltrust.org.uk |

## 146 Farnham

# Farnham Castle Keep

    1 hr Apr–Sep

From the C12 until 1920, Farnham Castle was the seat of the Bishop of Winchester. Kings and Queens were entertained here and hunted in the nearby park. Damage was caused during the Civil War, though the medieval shell was maintained.

* Inclusive audio tour available
* Motte & bailey castle design

| Location | Contact |
|---|---|
| ½ mile N of Farnham on A287 | Castle Street, Farnham GU9 0AG |
| **Opening** | t 01252 713393 |
| Apr–Sep Fri–Sun & Bank Hol Mons 12noon–5pm (last admission 4.30pm) | w english-heritage.org.uk |
| **Admission** | |
| Adult £2.60, Child £1.30, Concs £2 | |

## 147 Farnham

# Rural Life Centre

  2 hrs+  All year

The Rural Life Centre is a museum of past village life covering the years from 1750 to 1960. It is set in more than 10 acres of garden and woodland and housed in purpose-built and reconstructed buildings including a chapel, village hall, cricket pavilion and school room.

* Displays show village crafts & trades
* Arboretum with more than 100 species of trees

| Location | Contact |
|---|---|
| Off A287, 3 miles S of Farnham | Old Kiln Museum, Reeds Road Tilford, Farnham GU10 2DL |
| **Opening** | t 01252 795 571 |
| Mar–Oct Wed–Sun & Bank Hol Mon 10am–5pm; | w rural-life.org.uk |
| Nov–Feb Wed & Sun 11am–4pm | e rural.life@lineone.net |
| **Admission** | |
| Adult £6, Child £4, Concs £5 | |

## 148 Godalming

# Winkworth Arboretum

   2 hrs All year

A hillside woodland, created in the C20 and now containing more than 1,300 different rare shrubs and trees. Impressive displays of magnolias, bluebells and azaleas in spring and stunning colours in autumn. There is a lake and wetland area with wildlife in abundance.

* Trees include Japanese maples & tupelos from USA
* Cool, peaceful walks through woodland

| Location | Contact |
|---|---|
| 2 miles SE of Godalming, off E side of B2130 | Hascombe Road, Godalming GU8 4AD |
| **Opening** | t 01483 208477 |
| Daily: dawn–dusk Wed–Sun | w nationaltrust.org.uk |
| **Admission** | e winkwortharboretum@national trust.org.uk |
| Adult £4.50, Child £2 | |

## 149 Guildford

# Clandon Park

2 hrs+     Mar–Oct

Built in 1730, this grand Palladian mansion is notable for its magnificent two-storeyed marble hall. The house has a superb collection of C18 furniture and porcelain. The attractive gardens contain a parterre, grotto and Maori meeting house with a fascinating history.

* Home of Queen's Royal Surrey Regiment Museum
* Designed by Venetian architect Giacomo Leoni

**Location**
Off A247 NE of Guildford

**Opening**
26 Mar–Oct Tue–Thu & Sun 11am–5pm; museum 12noon–5pm

**Admission**
Adult £6, Child £3

**Contact**
West Clandon, Guildford GU4 7RQ

t 01483 222 482
w nationaltrust.org.uk/clandonpark
e clandonpark@nationaltrust.org.uk

## 150 Guildford

# Guildford House Gallery

1 hr+     All year

Guildford House is a fascinating C17 town house that now contains the council's art gallery showing selections from the borough's collection and varied temporary exhibitions. The house has magnificent plaster ceilings, original panelling and period furniture.

* Constantly changing programme of exhibitions
* Spectacular carved oak staircase

**Location**
Guildford high street

**Opening**
Tue–Sat 10am–4.45pm; closed 25–27, 31 Dec & Good Friday

**Admission**
Free

**Contact**
155 Upper High Street, Guildford GU1 3AJ

t 01483 444740
w guildfordhouse.co.uk
e guildfordhouse@guilford.gov.uk

## 151 Guildford

# Hatchlands

2 hrs+     Apr–Oct

Set in the 430-acre Repton Park, Hatchlands is noted for its nautically themed interiors designed by Robert Adam. It is also home to the Cobbe Collection, the world's largest group of keyboard instruments, many associated with famous composers.

* Paintings by Van Dyck & Gainsborough
* Park offers variety of woodland walks

**Location**
N of A246 Guildford–Leatherhead road

**Opening**
*House* Apr–Jun & Sep–Oct Tue–Thu & Sun 2pm–5.30pm, Aug Tue–Fri & Sun Open Bank Hols
*Park* Daily 11am–6pm

**Admission**
Adult £6, Child £3

**Contact**
East Clandon, Guildford GU4 7RT

t 01483 222 482
w nationaltrust.org.uk
e hatchlands@nationaltrust.org.uk

## 152 Guildford

# Loseley Park

3 hrs+     May–Sep

Built in 1562, Loseley House is a fine example of Elizabethan architecture, set in acres of peaceful gardens and parklands. Highlights include an award-winning rose garden, a vine walk and an area of native wild flowers. Relax in the serene 'white garden'.

* Herb garden has six areas devoted to specific purposes

**Location**
A3 SW from Guildford on B3000

**Opening**
*House* May–Aug, Tue–Thurs & Sun 1pm–5pm; Bank Hols 11am–5pm
*Gardens* May–Sep Tue–Sun 11am–5pm

**Admission**
*House* Adult £6, Child £3, Concs £5
*Gardens* £3, £1.50, £2.50

**Contact**
Guildford GU3 1HS

t 01483 304440
w loseley-park.com
e enquiries@loseley-park.com

## 153  Guildford

# River Wey & Godalming Navigations & Dapdune Wharf

2 hrs+     Mar–Oct

The Wey was one of the first British rivers to be made navigable (1653). This 15-mile waterway linked Guildford to Weybridge on the River Thames. The visitor centre at Dapdune Wharf in Guildford tells the story of the people who lived and worked on the waterway.

\* Boat trips available
\* The entire 19-mile towpath is open to walkers

**Location**
Wharf Road is behind Surrey County Cricket Ground, off Woodbridge Road

**Opening**
End Mar–end Oct, Mon & Thu–Sun 11am–5pm

**Admission**
Adult £3.50, Child £2

**Contact**
Wharf Road, Guildford GU1 4RR
t  01483 561389
w  nationaltrust.org.uk
e  riverwey@nationaltrust.org.uk

## 154  Morden

# Morden Hall Park

2 hrs+     All year

This oasis in the heart of suburbia covers more than 125 acres of parkland with the River Wandle meandering through. The historic mill is now used as an environmental centre. The park has a hay meadow and there is an impressive rose garden with more than 2,000 roses.

\* Planned walks & monthly programme of events
\* Variety of bridges across the river

**Location**
Off Morden Hall Road

**Opening**
Daily: 8am–6pm

**Admission**
Free

**Contact**
Morden Hall Road, Morden SM4 5JD
t  020 8545 6850
w  nationaltrust.org.uk/places/mordenhallpark
e  mordenhallpark@nationaltrust.org.uk

## 155 Ockley

# The Hannah Peschar Sculpture Garden

2 hrs+     All year

A stunning woodland water-garden is the setting for this specialist exhibition of contemporary sculpture. Hannah Peschar and Anthony Paul are in the vanguard of a C21 revolution in garden design that uses predominantly sculpture and water.

**Location**
A29 to Ockley, near Oakwood Church

**Opening**
May–Oct, Fri–Sat 11am–6pm;
Sun & Bank Hols 2pm–5pm;
Nov–Apr Tue & Thu by appointment

**Admission**
Adult £8, Child £5, Concs £6

**Contact**
Black and White Cottage,
Standon Lane, Ockley RH5 5QR
t 01306 627269
w hannahpescharsculpture.com
e hpeschar@easynet.co.uk

## 156 Richmond

# Ham House & Gardens

2 hrs+     Mar–Oct

This outstanding Stuart house, built in 1610, is famous for its lavish interiors and spectacular collections of fine furniture, textiles and paintings. Restoration of the C17 formal gardens over the last 30 years has influenced similar projects in the great gardens of Europe.

* C18 dairy
* Reinstated C17 statuary in wilderness garden

**Location**
Off A307 W of Richmond

**Opening**
*House* 25 Mar–29 Oct Sat–Wed
1pm–5pm
*Gardens* Sat–Wed 11am–6pm or dusk

**Admission**
*House & Gardens* Adult £8, Child £4
*Gardens* Adult £4, Child £2

**Contact**
Ham Street, Richmond TW10 7RS
t 020 8940 1950
w nationaltrust.org.uk/hamhouse
e hamhouse@nationaltrust.org.uk

## 157 Richmond

# Royal Botanic Gardens Kew

3 hrs+     All year

Established in 1759, Kew has developed into 300 acres of garden containing a collection of more than 40,000 varieties of plant. Also see seven spectacular glasshouses and two art galleries, Japanese and rock gardens and regular exhibitions in the restored museum.

* One of England's top 100 attractions
* Inscribed as a World Heritage site in 2003

**Location**
Off A307 at Kew
*Underground* Kew Gardens

**Opening**
Daily: 9.30am–sunset

**Admission**
Adult £10, Child free, Concs £7

**Contact**
Kew, Richmond TW9 3AB
t 020 8332 5655
w kew.org
e info@kew.org

## 158 Weybridge

# Brooklands Museum

3 hrs+     All year

Constructed in 1907, Brooklands was the first purpose-built motor racing circuit in the world. Not only the birthplace of British motorsport but also of British aviation. The track and original buildings have been restored, and a motor and aircraft museum added.

* Concorde in pieces ready to assemble for display
* Large display of cars, bikes & aircraft

**Location**
Off B374, A3 to A245. Follow signs

**Opening**
Daily: *summer* 10am–5pm
*winter* 10am–4pm

**Admission**
Adult £7, Child £5, Concs £6

**Contact**
Brooklands Road,
Weybridge KT13 0QN
t 01932 857381
w brooklandsmuseum.com
e info@brooklandsmuseum.com

## 159 Windsor

# Runnymede

2 hrs+    All year

These historic meads on the banks of the River Thames are where the Magna Carta was sealed by King John in June 1215. A network of footpaths links the Magna Carta memorial with two others: one to John F Kennedy and one to the 20,000 Royal Air Force airmen killed in WWII.

\* Fairhaven Lodges, designed by Lutyens
\* Boat trips along the Thames available

**Location**
6 miles E of Windsor on S side of A308
M25 junction 13

**Opening**
Daily: *summer* 9am–7pm
*winter* 9am–5pm

**Admission**
Charges for parking, fishing & mooring

**Contact**
North Lodge, Windsor Road,
Old Windsor SL4 2JL

t  01784 432891
w  nationaltrust.org.uk/runnymede
e  runnymede@nationaltrust.org.uk

## 160 Woking

# RHS Garden Wisley

3 hrs+    All year

Wisley is Britain's best-loved garden with 240 acres offering a fascinating blend of beautiful and practical plants plus innovative design and cultivation techniques. It features richly planted borders, luscious rose gardens and the exotica of the glasshouses.

\* New plant varieties continuously developed
\* Extensive events & educational programmes

**Location**
Just S of junction 10 of M25

**Opening**
Mar–Oct Mon–Fri 10am–6pm
Sat & Sun 9am–6pm;
Nov–Feb Mon–Fri 10am–4.30pm
Sat & Sun 9am–4.30pm

**Admission**
Adult £7.50, Child £2, Concs £5.50

**Contact**
Woking GU23 6QB

t  01483 224234
w  rhs.org.uk

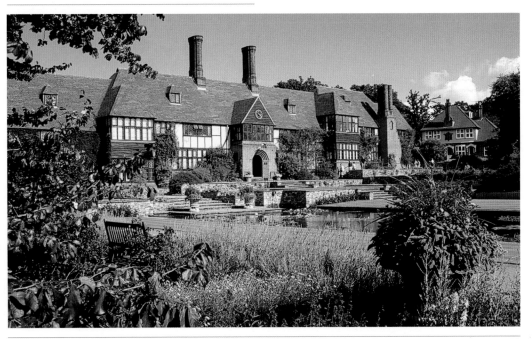

## 161 Arundel

# Amberley Working Museum

3 hrs+    Mar–Nov

Amberley is a 36-acre open-air museum set in the South Downs. With its historic buildings, working exhibits and demonstrations, the museum aims to show how science, technology and industry have affected people's lives.

* Variety of crafts demonstrated daily
* Trips on vintage bus & narrow gauge railway

| Location | Contact |
|---|---|
| Off B2139 between Arundel & Storrington | Amberley, Arundel BN18 9LT |
| **Opening** | t 01798 831370 |
| Mar–Nov Wed–Sun 10am–5.30pm | w amberleymuseum.co.uk |
| **Admission** | e office@amberleymuseum.co.uk |
| Adult £7.80, Child £4.50, Concs £6.80 | |

## 162 Arundel

# Arundel Castle

1 hr+    Mar–Oct

Originally built in the C11 by the Earl of Arundel, this centre has 1,000 years of fascinating history. There are fabulous displays of furniture, artefacts and paintings by Gainsborough, Reynolds and Van Dyck. The original motte, constructed in 1068, is more than 100ft (30m) high.

* Situated in magnificent grounds overlooking River Arun
* Seat of the Dukes of Norfolk for more than 850 years

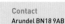

| Location | Contact |
|---|---|
| At Arundel on A27 | Arundel BN18 9AB |
| **Opening** | t 01903 882173 |
| 25 Mar–21 Oct Sun–Fri 11am–5pm; closed Sat & Good Friday | w arundelcastle.org |
| | e info@arundelcastle.org |
| **Admission** | |
| Adult £11, Child £7.50, Concs £9 | |

## 163 Arundel

# Denmans Garden

2 hrs+    All year

A beautiful garden designed for year-round interest; through the use of forms, colour and texture. Nearly 4 acres in size and the home of John Brookes MBE, renowned garden designer and writer, it is a garden full of ideas to be interpreted in smaller garden spaces.

* Large greenhouse provides shelter to tender plants
* Natural-looking lake is home to moorhens

| Location | Admission |
|---|---|
| Off A27 W between Chichester & Arundel, adjacent to Fontwell Racecourse | Adult £3.75, Child £1.95, Concs £3.25 |
| | **Contact** |
| **Opening** | Fontwell, Arundel BN18 0SU |
| *Gardens* 9am–5pm (Nov–Feb 9am–dusk) | t 01243 542808 |
| *Plant Centre* 9am–5pm | w denmans-garden.co.uk |
| *Garden Café* 10am–5pm | e denmans@denmans-garden.co.uk |

164 Arundel

# WWT Arundel

2 hrs+    All year

Surrounded by ancient woodland and overlooked by the town's historic castle, the wetlands at Arundel are home to many rare species of wetland wildlife. Many of the hundreds of birds you will see are tame enough to eat from your hand.

* Many rare birds regularly sighted
* Eye of the Wind  wildlife art gallery

**Location**
Close to A27 & A29, follow brown duck signs on approaching Arundel

**Opening**
Daily: 9.30am–5.30pm; 4.30pm in winter

**Admission**
Adult £5.95, Child £3.75, Concs £4.75

**Contact**
Mill Road, Arundel BN18 9PB

t  01903 883355
w  wwt.org.uk/visit/arundel
e  enquiries@wwt.org.uk

165 Ashington

# Holly Gate Cactus Garden

1 hr+    All year

This fascinating garden houses a world-renowned collection of more than 30,000 exotic plants. Rare plants from the arid areas of the world such as USA, Mexico, South America and Africa are represented, as well as cacti from the Central and South American jungles.

* 10,000ft$^2$ of glasshouses
* Many plants in flower throughout the year

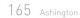

**Location**
Off A24 between Horsham & Worthing

**Opening**
Daily: Feb–Oct 9am–5pm
Nov–Jan 9am–4pm

**Admission**
Adult £2.50, Child & Concs £2

**Contact**
Billingshurst Road, Ashington RH20 3BB

t  01903 892930
w  hollygatecactus.co.uk
e  info@hollygatecactus.co.uk

## 166 Chichester

# Chichester Cathedral

1 hr    All year

For 900 years Chichester Cathedral has been a landmark from land and sea. Famous for its modern art, it boasts a stunning Chagall window. Its more ancient treasures include the Arundel Tomb that inspired Philip Larkin's poem.

\* C12 sculpture depicting Lazarus
\* Newly commissioned icon of St Richard

| Location | Contact |
|---|---|
| City centre | The Royal Chantry, Cathedral Cloisters, Chichester PO19 1PX |
| Opening | |
| Daily: subject to services | t 01243 782595 |
| | w chichestercathedral.org.uk |
| Admission | e reception@chichestercathedral. |
| Free, donations requested | org.uk |

## 167 Chichester

# Fishbourne Roman Palace & Gardens

2 hrs+    All year

This late C1 palace, discovered in 1960, is the largest Roman residence found to date in Britain. Its treasures include the country's finest collection of Roman mosaic floors and hypocausts. Finds are displayed, while an audio-visual presentation brings the site to life.

\* The remains of more than 20 mosaics are on display
\* Roman garden has been replanted to its original plan

| Location | Admission |
|---|---|
| N of A259 off A27 1½ mile W of Chichester | Adult £6.50, Child £3.40, Concs £5.50 |
| Opening | Contact |
| 1 Feb–15 Dec daily from 10am; | Salthill Road, Fishbourne, Chichester PO19 3QR |
| 16 Dec–31 Jan Sat & Sun only 10am–4pm | t 01243 785859 |
| | w sussexpast.co.uk |
| | e adminfish@sussexpast.co.uk |

## 168 Chichester

# Goodwood House

2 hrs    Mar–Oct

Goodwood House is home to one of the most significant private art collections in the country. The state apartments have been richly refurbished to their original Regency elegance and there is an Egyptian state dining room and magnificent ballroom.

\* Curator of the collection is author Rosemary Baird
\* Fine art collection includes Reynolds, Stubbs & Canaletto

| Location | Contact |
|---|---|
| 3 miles NE of Chichester of A27 | Goodwood, Chichester PO18 0PX |
| Opening | t 01243 755 040 |
| Mar–Oct Sun & Mon 1pm–5pm; | w goodwood.co.uk |
| 3–30 Aug Sun–Thu 1pm–5pm | e housevisiting@goodwood.co.uk |
| Please phone in advance | |
| Admission | |
| Adult £7, Child £3, Concs £6 | |

## 169 Chichester

# Military Aviation Museum

4 hrs+    Feb–Nov

Established in 1982, the museum tells the story of military flying from the earliest days, with emphasis on the RAF at Tangmere, and the air war over southern England from 1939 to 1945. Displays include the world speed record-breaking *Meteor* and *Hunter*.

\* Opportunity to 'fly' a fighter simulator
\* Direct bus service from Chichester to museum, No.55

| Location | Contact |
|---|---|
| 3 miles E of Chichester off A27 | Military Aviation Museum, Tangmere, Chichester PO20 6ES |
| Opening | t 01243 775223 |
| Daily: Feb & Nov 10am–4.30pm; | w tangmere–museum.org.uk |
| Mar–Oct 10am–5.30pm | e tangmeretrust@aol.com |
| Admission | |
| Adult £5, Child £1.50, Concs £4 | |

## 170 Chichester

# Weald & Downland Open-Air Museum

2 hrs+    All year

This museum in 50 acres of beautiful Sussex countryside offers a chance to wander through a fascinating collection of historic buildings dating from the C13 to the C19. Many have period gardens and farm animals. There are also woodland walks and a picturesque lake.

* The leading museum of historic buildings in England
* See food prepared in the working Tudor kitchen

**Location**
Situated 7 miles N of Chichester on the A286

**Opening**
Daily: Apr–Oct 10.30am–6pm;
Nov–3 Jan 10.30am–4pm;
4 Jan–12 Feb Wed, Sat & Sun 10.30am–4pm; 13 Feb–31 Mar 10.30am–4pm

**Admission**
Adult £7.70, Child £4, Concs £6.70

**Contact**
Singleton, Chichester PO18 0EU

t 01243 811363/811348
w wealddown.co.uk
e office@wealddown.co.uk

## 171 Chichester

# West Dean Gardens

3 hrs+    All year

These Edwardian gardens include 35 acres of ornamental grounds, a 100-yard pergola and herbaceous borders. A two-mile park walk, walled kitchen and fruit gardens, 16 restored greenhouses and a 45-acre arboretum are additional features.

* Christie's Garden of the Year 2002
* Licensed bar & gift shop at the visitor centre

**Location**
6 miles N of Chichester on A286

**Opening**
Daily: May–Sep 10.30am–5pm;
Oct, Mar & Apr 11am–5pm;
Nov–Feb Wed–Sun 10am–4.30pm

**Admission**
Adult £5.50, Child £2.50, Concs £5

**Contact**
West Dean, Chichester PO18 0QZ

t 01243 818210
w westdean.org.uk
e gardens@westdean.org.uk

# Standen

2 hrs+    Mar–Dec

Standen shows off pure Victorian style under the influence of the Arts & Crafts Movement. It's extensively decorated with William Morris carpets, fabrics and wallpaper, and externally finished in sandstone, weatherboards and brick.

* 12-acre garden with fine views over the countryside
* Custom-made furniture from Heal's & Morris

| Location | Contact |
|---|---|
| 2 miles S of East Grinstead off B2110 | West Hoathly Road, East Grinstead RH19 4NE |
| **Opening** | |
| *House* 25 Mar–29 Oct 11am–5pm | t 01342 323029 |
| *Gardens* 25 Mar–29 Oct 11am–6pm; | w nationaltrust.org.uk/standen |
| 5 Nov–18 Dec Fri–Sun 11am–3pm | e standen@nationaltrust.org.uk |
| **Admission** | |
| *House & Gardens:* Adult £6.75, Child £3.50 | |

# Borde Hill Gardens

2 hrs+    All year

Borde Hill is set in 200 acres of traditional country estate. The garden was established from 1,900 plants gathered from the Himalayas, China, Burma and Tasmania. Today Borde Hill has one of the most comprehensive collections of trees and shrubs in England.

* Magnificent rhododendrons, azaleas & camellias
* Winner of the Garden of the Year Award 2004 HHA

| Location | Contact |
|---|---|
| 1½ miles N of Haywards Heath | Balcombe Road, Haywards Heath RH16 1XP |
| **Opening** | |
| Daily: 10am–6pm | t 01444 450326 |
| | w bordehill.co.uk |
| **Admission** | e info@bordehill.co.uk |
| *summer* Adult £6, Child £3.50, Concs £5 | |
| *winter* £4, £2.50, £4 | |

# Nymans Gardens

2 hrs    All year

Nymans is one of the great gardens of the Sussex Weald and is internationally famous for its collection of rare plants. Created by three generations of the Messel family over a period of more than a hundred years, Nymans was one of the first gardens given to the National Trust (1953).

* Huge replanting programme followed 1987 storm
* Garden has individually characterised sections

| Location | Admission |
|---|---|
| On B2114 at Handcross, 4½ miles S of Crawley, just off M23/A23 | Adult £7, Child £3.50 |
| **Opening** | **Contact** |
| *House* 22 Mar–29 Oct 11.30am–5pm | Nymans Gardens, Handcross, nr Haywards Heath RH17 6EB |
| *Gardens* 15 Feb–29 Oct Wed–Sun 11am–6pm; 4 Nov–12 Feb Sat & Sun 11am–4pm | t 01444 400321 |
| | w nationaltrust.org.uk/nymans |
| | e nymans@nationaltrust.org.uk |

## 175 Horsham

# Leonardslee Lakes & Gardens

3 hrs+    Apr–Oct

A woodland garden set in a 240-acre valley with seven lakes. Leonardslee has many features including a rock garden and Alpine House, as well as deer and wallabies roaming in the parkland. It also houses a collection of Victorian motor cars (1889–1900).

* Accolade for most beautiful garden in Europe in May
* Behind the Doll's House exhibition

| Location | Contact |
|---|---|
| On the junction on A281 & B2110 in Lower Beeding | Lower Beeding, Horsham RH13 6PP |
| **Opening** | t 01403 891212 |
| Daily: 1 Apr–31 Oct 9.30am–6pm | w leonardslee.com |
| | e gardens@leonardslee.com |
| **Admission** | |
| Apr& Jun–Oct Adult £6, Child £4 | |
| May weekdays £8, £4 | |
| May weekends £10, £4 | |

## 176 Littlehampton

# Look and Sea!

1 hr+    All year

Explore the geology, geography and history of Littlehampton, finishing in the stunning glass-walled viewing tower with fantastic views across the River Arun out to sea and to Arundel. The attractions include an interactive maritime exhibition and a variety of displays.

* Newly opened riverside walks
* Café overlooking the river

| Location | Contact |
|---|---|
| By the river, 300 yrds from railway station | 63 Surrey Street Littlehampton BN17 5AW |
| **Opening** | t 01903 718984 |
| Daily: 9am–5pm | w lookandsea.co.uk |
| | e info@lookandsea.co.uk |
| **Admission** | |
| Adult £2.95, Child & Concs £2.50 | |

## 177 Petersfield

# Uppark

3 hrs    Apr–Oct

A late C17 house set high on the South Downs with magnificent sweeping views to the sea. It was rescued from a fire in 1989 and the restored Georgian interior houses a famous Grand Tour collection that includes paintings, furniture and ceramics.

* H G Wells's mother was a housekeeper
* A C18 doll's house is a star of the collection

| Location | Contact |
|---|---|
| 5 miles SE of Petersfield off B2146 | South Harting, Petersfield GU31 5QR |
| **Opening** | t 01730 825415 |
| *House* 2 Apr–26 Oct 12.30pm–4.30pm; | w nationaltrust.org.uk/uppark |
| 3–27 Oct Sun–Thur 1–4pm | e uppark@nationaltrust.org.uk |
| *Grounds* 2 Apr–26 Oct 11.30am–5pm | |
| **Admission** | |
| Adult £6.50, Child £3.25 | |

## 178  Petworth

# Petworth House & Park

3 hrs+          All year

A magnificent late C17 mansion set in a park landscaped by Capability Brown and immortalised in Turner's paintings. The house contains the National Trust's finest and largest collection of pictures, with numerous works by Turner, Van Dyck, Reynolds and Blake.

\* Ancient & neo classical sculpture
\* Fine furniture & carvings by Grinling Gibbons

**Location**
5½ miles E of Midhurst on A272

**Opening**
Mar–Oct Wed–Sat 11am–5pm;
park open all year

**Admission**
Adult £7.50, Child £4

**Contact**
Petworth GU28 0AE

t  01798 342207
w  nationaltrust.org.uk/petworth
e  petworth@nationaltrust.org.uk

## 179  Pulborough

# Bignor Roman Villa

1 hr+          Mar–Oct

Discovered in 1811, the site, which probably dates from the C3, comprises 50 living quarters in the main complex and nine outbuildings. They include a bath house, with one of the best-preserved Roman mosaics in England, and a summer and a winter dining room.

\* Spectacular mosaics depicting Venus & Medusa
\* One of the largest Roman villas in Britain

**Location**
6 miles N of Arundel, signed from A29 (Bignor-Billingshurst) and A285 (Chichester–Petworth)

**Opening**
Mar–Apr, Tues–Sun & Bank Hols 10am–5pm;
Daily: May & Oct 10am–5pm;
Jun–Sep 10am–6pm

**Admission**
Adult £4.20, Child £1.80, Concs £3

**Contact**
Bignor Lane,
Pulborough RH20 1PH

t  01798 869259
w  pyrrha.demon.co.uk
e  bignorromanvilla@care4free.net

## 180  Pulborough

# Parham House & Gardens

2 hrs+          Easter–Sept

In the Middle Ages Parham House was owned by Westminster Abbey. In 1601 it was sold to Thomas Bysshop and it remained in the family until bought in 1922 by Clive Pearson. He purchased many of the paintings, and added his own objets d'art and English furniture.

\* Award-winning four-acre walled garden
\* Idyllically sited in the heart of an ancient deer park

**Location**
Off A283 Pulborough–Storrington road

**Opening**
House 2–5pm;
Gardens Easter Sun–Sep 12noon–6pm;
Wed, Thu, Sun & Bank Hol Mon (also Tue & Fri in Aug)

**Admission**
House & Gardens Adult £6.50,
Child £2.50, Concs £5.50
Gardens only £5, £1, £4.50

**Contact**
Parham Park, nr Pulborough RH20 4HS

t  01903 742021
w  parhaminsussex.co.uk
e  enquiries@parhaminsussex.co.uk

# South West

Bristol Cornwall Devon Dorset
Gloucestershire Somerset Wiltshire

Fishguard

Newcastle
Emlyn

St David's

**PEMBROKESHIRE**    **CARMARTHEN**

Carmarthen

Haverfordwest    Narberth    St Clears    **660**

Milford
Haven    Neyland    **664**    Kidwelly

Pembroke    **667–668**    Burry    Llanelli
Dock    Tenby    Port    M4

Pembroke    **SWANSEA**    Swa

*Caldey
Island*

*St Govan's
Head*    Port
Einon    Mun

Ilfracombe

**215–21**
Ba

*Hartland
Point*    Bideford

Great
Torrington

**228–229**

Bude    **DE**

Holsworthy

Okehampton    **231**

**213**
Tintagel    Launceston

**195**    **202**    Do

Trevose Head    **205**    **194**    *Bodmin
Moor*    Tavistock

Padstow    Wadebridge    **CORNWALL**    **233**

NEWQUAY    Bodmin    Bu
✈    **191–193**    PLYMOUT

Newquay    Liskeard    Saltash    **PLYMOU**

St Austell    Fowey    Looe    Plyn

**210–211**    Torpoint    **234–235**

Truro    **214**    *Dodman
Point*

St Ives    Camborne    Redruth

**212**    **196–197**    St Mawes

St Just    Penzance    **204**    Falmouth

Sennen    **206–207**    **203**    **199–200**

*Land's End*    **208–209**    Helston

**198**

Lizard

*Lizard
Point*

**201**

*Isles of Scilly*

## 181 Brislington

# Bristol Blue Glass

1 hr   All year

Glass blowing in Bristol was fully established by the mid-C17 when the city was fêted as a centre of excellence for glass making and porcelain. See freeblown, handmade glass and watch glass blowing demonstrations from the public viewing gallery.

* Glass available to puchase in gift shop
* Join in with exciting hands-on activities

| Location | Contact |
|---|---|
| From M32 junction 3 and follow signs to A4 | Unit 7, Whitby Road, Brislington, Bristol BS4 3QF |
| **Opening** | |
| Daily: Mon–Sat 9am–5pm, Sun 11am–4pm | t  0117 972 0818 |
| | w  bristol-glass.co.uk |
| **Admission** | e  info@bristol-glass.co.uk |
| Adult £3, Child £1, Concs £2 | |

## 182 City Centre

# @Bristol

3 hrs+   All year

This is a unique destination bringing science, nature and art to life. It is a place of discovery and home to three attractions: Wildwalk, a living rainforest in the heart of the city; Explore, a C21 science centre; and a giant IMAX® Theatre with digital surround sound.

* Tropical forest with free flying birds & butterflies
* Planetarium – Bristol's very own planetarium

| Location | Contact |
|---|---|
| Off Anchor Road in central Bristol | Harbourside, Bristol BS1 5DB |
| **Opening** | |
| Daily: 10am–6pm | t  0845 345 1235 |
| | w  at-bristol.org.uk |
| **Admission** | e  information@at-bristol.org.uk |
| *Explore* | |
| Adult £8, Child £5.50, Concs £6.50 | |
| *Wildwalk & IMAX®* £6.50, £4.50, £5.50 | |

## 183 City Centre

# Bristol Cathedral

1 hr   All year

This fascinating building is a centre for Bristol's history, civic life and culture. Founded as an abbey in 1140, it became a cathedral in 1542 and developed architecturally through the ages. It is one of the finest examples of a 'hall church' anywhere in the world.

* Beautiful examples of Saxon stone carvings
* Expressionist window designed by Keith New in 1965

| Location | Contact |
|---|---|
| Central Bristol on College Green | College Green, Bristol BS1 5TJ |
| **Opening** | |
| Daily: 8am–6pm | t  0117 926 4879 |
| | w  bristol-cathedral.co.uk |
| **Admission** | e  reception@bristol-cathedral.co.uk |
| Donations appreciated, £2.50 per person | |

© Alan Russell

184 City Centre

# Bristol Ferry Boat Company

2–4 hrs    All year

Enjoy the exciting world of Bristol's historic harbour – for a round trip tour or just by visiting one of the many attractions. The journey takes in the Pump House, the Millennium Square and the SS *Great Britain*.

* River trips & pub ferry can be arranged
* Unique view of Bristol past & present

| Location | Contact |
|---|---|
| Bristol Harbour | MB *Tempora*, Welsh Back, Bristol BS1 4SP |
| **Opening** | t 0117 9273 416 |
| Daily: please phone for details | w bristolferryboat.co.uk |
| **Admission** | e enquiries@bristolferryboat.co.uk |
| Multistop Day Ticket: | |
| Adult £5, Child & Concs £3 | |

185 City Centre

# City Museum & Art Gallery

2 hrs+    All year

Bristol's premier museum and art gallery. This magnificent building houses important collections of minerals and fossils, natural history, Eastern art, world wildlife, Egyptology, archaeology, seven galleries of fine and applied art and ever-changing temporary exhibitions.

* World Wildlife Gallery
* Eastern art

| Location | Contact |
|---|---|
| In Clifton, follow brown signs from town centre | Queen's Road, Bristol BS8 1RL |
| **Opening** | t 0117 922 3571 |
| Daily: 10am–5pm | w bristol-city.gov.uk/museums |
| **Admission** | e general_museum@bristol-city. gov.uk |
| Free | |

## 186 City Centre

# The British Empire & Commonwealth Museum

2 hrs+    Feb–Dec

This award-winning national museum presents the dramatic 500-year history of the rise and fall of Britain's overseas empire. It is located in Isambard Kingdom Brunel's historic old Bristol station at Temple Meads.

\* 16 permanent & interactive galleries
\* Special half-term & holiday activities for families

| Location | Contact |
|---|---|
| Located right next to Temple Meads, Bristol's main railway station | Station Approach, Temple Meads, Bristol BS1 6QH |
| **Opening** | t 0117 925 4980 |
| Daily: 10am–5pm; Closed Jan Please phone for details | w empiremuseum.co.uk |
| | e admin@empiremuseum.co.uk |
| **Admission** | |
| Adult £6.50, Child £3.95, Concs £5.50 | |

## 187 City Centre

# CREATE Centre

1 hr    All year

CREATE is a showcase of environmental excellence. Bristol's ecological centre is a fount of information on environmental initiatives. Visit the Ecohome, a green home of the future, and learn about meeting the challenge of waste in the recycling exhibition.

\* A hands-on journey through waste & recycling
\* Themed events throughout the year

| Location | Contact |
|---|---|
| Cumberland Basin lies at far end of docks. CREATE is in a redbrick warehouse | Smeaton Road, Bristol BS1 6XN |
| | t 0117 925 0505 |
| **Opening** | w createcentre.co.uk |
| Mon–Fri 9am–5pm | e create@bristol–city.gov.uk |
| **Admission** | |
| Free | |

## 188 City Centre

# The Georgian House

1 hr    All year

This lovely house is an example of Bristol's C18 heritage illustrating how the city profited from being one of England's premier trading ports. Originally home to John Pinney, a West Indies merchant, the house is displayed as it might have looked in its heyday.

\* Home to the slave Pero
\* Illustrating life above & below stairs

| Location | Contact |
|---|---|
| Just off Park Street, near Cabot Tower | 7 Great George Street, Bristol BS1 5RR |
| **Opening** | t 0117 921 1362 |
| Sat–Wed 10am–5pm | w bristol–city.gov.uk |
| **Admission** | e general_museum@bristol–city.gov.uk |
| Free | |

## 189  City Centre

# SS *Great Britain*

2 hrs   All year

The world's first great ocean liner, the SS *Great Britain* is a unique surviving engineering masterpiece from Victorian times. Docked in the original Great Western Dock, this grand passenger liner has been the forerunner of all modern cruise ships.

* Designed by Isambard Kingdom Brunel
* The largest ship of her day

**Location**
Follow anchor signs in Bristol Historic Dockyard

**Opening**
Daily: Apr–Oct 10am–5.30pm;
Nov–Mar 10am–4.30pm

**Admission**
Adult £7.50, Child £4.50, Concs £6.50

**Contact**
Great Western Dockyard,
Gas Ferry Road, Bristol BS1 6TY

t  0117 926 0680
w  ssgreatbritain.org
e  admin@ss-great-britain.com

## 190  Whitchurch

# HorseWorld

3 hrs+   All year

The South West's leading horse welfare charity. In beautiful Mendip stone farm buildings, dating back to the early C19, meet more than 40 of the 300 rescued horses, ponies and donkeys. From Shetland ponies to shire horses, each has a different story to tell.

* Twice daily presentations
* Pony rides

**Location**
Take A37 from Bristol. Through
Whitchurch – HorseWorld is on left

**Opening**
Daily: Mar–Sep 10am–5pm (4pm in winter); Sep–Mar closed Mon

**Admission**
Please phone for details

**Contact**
Staunton Manor Farm,
Staunton Lane, Whitchurch,
Bristol BS14 0QJ

t  01275 540173
w  horseworld.org.uk
e  visitorcentre@horseworld.org.uk

## 191  Bodmin

# Lanhydrock House

3 hrs+   Apr–Oct

Largely rebuilt in 1881 after a fire, this fascinating C19 home captures the atmosphere and trappings of a high Victorian country house. 'Below stairs' has a huge kitchen, larder, dairy and bake house. The garden is set in 900 acres on the River Fowey.

* Magnificent gallery with moulded plaster ceiling

**Location**
2 miles E of Bodmin, follow signs off either A30 or A38

**Opening**
Apr–Oct Tue–Sun & Bank Hol Mons
11am–5.30pm (5pm in Oct)

**Admission**
Please phone for details

**Contact**
Lanhydrock, Bodmin PL30 5AD

t  01208 265950
w  nationaltrust.org.uk
e  lanhydrock@nationaltrust.org.uk

## 192 Bodmin

# Military Museum Bodmin

1 hr+   All year

More than 300 years of regimental history on the Duke of Cornwall Light Infantry is displayed at the Museum. The former barracks now houses the regimental museum with uniforms, pictures and medals including one of the country's finest small arms collections.

* General George Washington's bible, captured 1777
* Events from the capture of Gibraltar in 1704 to WWII

**Location**
Outskirts of Bodmin

**Opening**
Mon–Fri 9am–5pm (Sun in Jul–Aug)

**Admission**
Adult £2.50, Child 50p

**Contact**
The Keep, Bodmin PL31 1EG

t 01208 72810
e dclimus@talk21.com

## 193 Bodmin

# Pencarrow

3 hrs+   Apr–Oct

Pencarrow houses a superb collection of pictures, furniture, porcelain and antique dolls. The house sits in 50 acres of Grade II listed gardens and woodland with a lake, an ice house and a Victorian rockery. There are marked walks through the woodland and gardens.

* Grade II listed garden & Dogs Trust national award
* Sir Arthur Sullivan composed *Iolanthe* music here

**Location**
Follow signs off A389, 4 miles NW of Bodmin

**Opening**
*House, Restaurant, Shop* 2 Apr–26 Oct
Sun–Thu 9.30am–5.30pm
*Gardens* Daily: 1 Mar–31 Oct 9am–6pm

**Admission**
*House & Gardens* Adult £8, Child £4
*Gardens* £4, £1

**Contact**
Bodmin PL30 3AG

t 01208 841369
w pencarrow.co.uk
e pencarrow@aol.com

## 194 Bolventor

# Colliford Lake Park

3 hrs+    Easter–Oct

Acres of indoor and outdoor adventure and fun with a 'Beast of Bodmin Moor' theme. Colliford Lake Park is a farm-based attraction with 8 acres of woodland and 30 acres of farm stock with sheep, goats, red deer and other animals.

\* Extensive indoor & outdoor play areas
\* Nature trails around Colliford Lake

**Location**
500 yards off A30 between Launceston & Bodmin

**Opening**
Daily: Easter–Oct 11am–6pm

**Admission**
Adult £5.50, Child £4.50, Concs £4

**Contact**
Bolventor, Bodmin Moor PL14 6PZ
t 01208 821469
w collifordlakepark.com
e info@collifordlakepark.com

## 195 Camelford

# British Cycling Museum

1 hr+    All year

An excellent display of cycling history from 1818 to the present day. There are more than 400 machines on display and a large exhibition of cycling memorabilia including the first cycle oil lamps as well as candle lamps. Plus cycling medals, fobs and badges.

\* Extensive library of cycling books
\* Gallery of cycling pictures

**Location**
1 mile N of Camelford on B3266

**Opening**
Sun–Thu 10am–5pm

**Admission**
Adult £2.90, Child £1.90

**Contact**
The Old Station, Camelford PL32 9TZ
t 01840 212811
w chycor.co.uk/britishcycling-museum

## 196 Falmouth

# National Maritime Museum Cornwall

2 hrs    All year

Enjoy breathtaking views from the 29m tower, one of only three natural underwater viewing locations in the world, hands-on interactives, audio-visual immersive experiences, talks, special exhibitions and the opportunity to get out on to the water.

\* Cimb to the top of the tower for views over the harbour
\* Display of Cornish maritime heritage

**Location**
SE end of harbourside. Or follow signs from A39 for Park & Float

**Opening**
Daily: 10am–5pm

**Admission**
Adult £6.50, Child & Concs £4.30

**Contact**
Discovery Quay, Falmouth TR11 3QY
t 01326 313388
w nmmc.co.uk
e enquiries@nmmc.co.uk

## 197 Falmouth

# Pendennis Castle

2 hrs    All year

A Cornish fortress, ready for military action since the C16. Pendennis and its sister, St Mawes Castle, face each other across the mouth of the River Fal. Constructed c. 1540, they are the Cornish end of a chain of castles built by Henry VIII along the south coast.

**Location**
Pendennis Head, 1 mile S of Falmouth

**Opening**
Daily: 29 Mar–30 Jun & Sep 10am–5pm;
1Jul–31 Aug 10am –6pm;
Oct–Feb 10am–4pm;
every Sat 10am–4pm

**Admission**
Adult £4.60, Child £2.30, Concs £3.50

**Contact**
Pendennis Head,
Falmouth TR11 4LP
t 01326 316594
w english–heritage.org.uk
e jane.kessell@english–heritage.org.uk

## 198  Goonhilly

# Goonhilly Satellite Earth Station

2 hrs+   All year

One of the most striking attractions in Cornwall, on the Lizard Peninsula. Visit Goonhilly, the largest satellite station on earth, to learn about space and modern communications through the multimedia visitor centre, interactive exhibits and film shows with tour guides.

* 3D virtual head-creation & touch-screen Internet terminals
* See yourself in space & move a satellite

**Location**
Follow B3293 Helston to St Keverne road

**Opening**
Daily from 10am; closing times vary from 4pm to 6pm. Please phone for details. Closed Mon & Fri

**Admission**
Adult £6, Child £4, Concs £4.50

**Contact**
Goonhilly TR12 6LQ

t  0800 679593
w  goonhilly.bt.com
e  goonhilly.visitorscentre@bt.com

## 199  Helston

# Godolphin House & Garden

2 hrs   Apr–Sep

This historic landscape includes Godolphin Hill with its wonderful views over west Cornwall. The house has fine C16 and C17 English oak furniture and equine paintings including Wotton's painting of Godolphin Arabian – one of three ancestors to all British bloodstock.

* The estate has more than 400 archaeological features
* House dates from C15

**Location**
B3303 turn left to Godolphin Cross. Through Godolphin Cross village & house is on left with brown signs

**Opening**
Thu–Sat & Bank Hol Mon 11am–5pm, Sun 2am–5pm

**Admission**
Adult £6–£7, Child £1.50, Concs £5–£6

**Contact**
Godolphin Cross, Helston TR13 9RE

t  01736 763194
w  godolphinhouse.com
e  info@godolphinhouse.com

## 200  Helston

# Poldark Mine & Heritage Complex

3 hrs   All year

This Cornish tin mine has several underground routes with tunnels and stairs and is believed to be Europe's most complete mine workings open to the public. Some machines and waterpumping engines are on display around the garden.

* Entry to the site itself is free
* Family attractions in addition to mine

**Location**
2 miles from Helston on B3297

**Opening**
Please phone for details

**Admission**
*Underground tour* Adult £6.80, Child £4.40

**Contact**
Wendron, Helston TR13 0ES

t  01326 573173
w  poldark-mine.co.uk
e  info@poldark-mine.co.uk

## 201  Isles of Scilly

# Isles of Scilly Museum

1½ hrs   All year

The museum was established following severe gales in the winter of 1962, which yielded up some remarkable Romano-British finds. It now houses an extremely diverse collection including material from wrecks, as well as the original Romano-British artefacts.

**Location**
10 min walk from Hugh Town harbour

**Opening**
Easter–Sep Mon–Sat 10am–4pm; Oct–Easter Mon–Sat 10am–4pm

**Admission**
Adult £2.50, Child 50p, Concs £1.50

**Contact**
Church Street, St Mary's, Isles of Scilly TR21 0JT

t  01720 422337
w  iosmuseum.org
e  info@iosmuseum.org

## 202 Launceston

# Launceston Castle

1 hr        Apr–Oct

Set on the high motte of a stronghold built soon after the Norman Conquest, this strategically important building controlled the road and river crossing in and out of Cornwall. As the venue for the county assizes and jail, the castle witnessed many trials and hangings.

* Built first as earthwork after Norman Conquest
* Administrative centre for the Earls of Cornwall

**Location**
Centre of Launceston

**Opening**
Daily: Apr–June 10am–5pm;
July–Aug 10am–6pm;
Sep 10am–5pm;
Oct 10am–4pm

**Admission**
Adult £2.30, Child £1.20, Concs £1.70

**Contact**
Launceston PL15 7DR

t  01566 772365
w  english-heritage.org.uk
e  launceston.castle@english-heritage.
   org.uk

## 203 Marazion

# St Michael's Mount

2 hrs        All year

This former Benedictine priory and castle is one of Britain's most visited properties. It is linked to the mainland when the tide is out by a 500-yard causeway. Beautiful gardens contain many rare plants that are not often found growing out of doors in Britain.

* Once an important harbour & home to 300 people
* Castle is full of history including garrison & armoury

**Location**
Off coast of Marazion on A394

**Opening**
26 Mar–29 Oct Sun–Fri
10.30am–5.30pm, (last admission 4.45
pm on the island); Nov–end Mar open
when tides & weather favourable
*Gardens* May & Jun Mon–Fri; Jul–Oct
Thu & Fri

**Admission**
Adult £6, Child £3
*Gardens* £3

**Contact**
Marazion TR17 0HT

t  01736 710507
w  stmichaelsmount.co.uk
e  godolphin@manor-office.co.uk

## 204 Mawnan Smith

# Trebah Gardens

3 hrs    All year

This lovely sub-tropical ravine paradise winds through huge plantations of 100-year-old giant tree ferns, rhododendrons, magnolias, camellias, palms and 2 acres of massed hydrangeas to a private beach on the Helford River.

\* Part of the Eden Trail
\* Unique collection of rare plants & trees

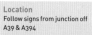

| Location | Contact |
|---|---|
| Follow signs from junction off A39 & A394 | Mawnan Smith, Falmouth TR11 5JZ |
| **Opening** | t 01326 250448 |
| Daily: 10.30am–6pm (last admission 5pm) | w trebah–garden.co.uk |
| | e mail@trebah–garden.co.uk |
| **Admission** | |
| *Mar–Oct* **Adult £5.80, Child £3, Concs £5** | |
| *Nov–Feb* £2.60, £1.40, £2.40 | |

## 205 Padstow

# Prideaux Place

2 hrs    Apr–Oct

Explore 40 acres of landscaped grounds with terraced walks, a formal garden, a temple, Roman antiquities and the C9 Cornish Cross. An ancient deer park overlooks the estuary of the River Camel. Also see the Elizabethan plastered ceiling in the Great Chamber.

\* Treasures include the Prideaux porcelain collection
\* Guided tours of house available

| Location | Contact |
|---|---|
| Off B3276, Padstow to Newquay road | Padstow PL28 8RP |
| **Opening** | t 01841 532411 |
| 16 Apr–20 Apr & 14 May–5 Oct | w prideauxplace.co.uk |
| Sun–Thur *House:* 1.30pm–4pm | e office@prideauxplace.co.uk |
| *Grounds:* 12.30pm–5pm | |
| **Admission** | |
| Adult £6.50, Child £2 | |
| *Grounds:* £2, £1 | |

## 206 Penzance

# Geevor Tin Mine

2 hrs    All year

The last working mine in West Penwith and now a mining museum and the largest preserved mining site in the UK, extending a mile inland. Some areas of the mine are 200 years old. A museum provides insight into the history of this traditional Cornish industry.

\* Expert guides conduct underground tours
\* Display of original mining machinery

| Location | Contact |
|---|---|
| On B3306 St Ives–Land's End road | Pendeen, Penzance TR19 7EW |
| **Opening** | t 01736 788662 |
| Daily: Apr–Oct 10am–5pm; | w geevor.com |
| Nov–Mar 10am–4pm, closed Sat | e info@geevor.com |
| **Admission** | |
| Adult £7, Child £4.30, Concs £6.50 | |

## 207 Penzance

# Land's End Visitor Centre

2 hrs+    All year

Set on the most westerly point of mainland Britain, this privately owned centre offers a range of facilities, including six pay-as-you-go exhibitions, restaurants, shops and a three-star hotel overlooking the sea. On a clear day you can see the Isles of Scilly, 23 miles away.

\* Land's End sweet factory
\* Stunning scenery

**Location**
At end of A30, 12 miles from Penzance

**Opening**
Daily: *summer* 10am–4pm
*winter* 10am–3pm

**Admission**
Adult £12.95, Child £6.95, Concs £8.95

**Contact**
Land's End, Sennen, Penzance TR19 7AA

t 01736 871501
w landsend-landmark.co.uk
e info@landsend.landmark.co.uk

## 208 Porthcurno

# Minack Theatre

2 hrs+    All year

This has to be one of the world's most spectacular theatres – an open-air auditorium carved into the cliffs high above Porthcurno's sandy cove. Founded and largely built by Rowena Cade in the 1930s, its remarkable story is now told in the visitor centre.

\* Full programme of performances through summer
\* Fantastic views from visitor centre

**Location**
3 miles from Land's End off A30

**Opening**
Daily: Apr–Sep 9.30am–5.30pm
Oct–Mar 10am–4pm

**Admission**
Seasonal charges; please phone for details

**Contact**
Porthcurno, Penzance TR19 6JU

t 01736 810181
w minack.com
e info@minack.com

209  Porthcurno

# Porthcurno Telegraph Museum

2 hrs        All year

This award-winning industrial heritage museum explains
the development of international telegraphy at the site
of the first underground cables that linked Britain to the
rest of the world (1870). It is housed in an underground
station built for protection during WWII.

\* Staff on hand to show how instruments work
\* Adjacent to stunning Minack Theatre

| Location | Contact |
|---|---|
| 3 miles from Land's End off A30 | Porthcurno, Penzance TR19 6JX |
| Opening | t  01736 810966 |
| Easter–Oct Fri–Mon 10am–5pm; | w  porthcurno.org.uk |
| Nov–Easter Sun & Mon 10am–5pm | e  mary.godwin@cw.com |
| Admission | |
| Adult £4.50, Child £2.50, Concs £3–£4 | |

210  St Austell

# The Eden Project

3 hrs+       All year

The Eden Project is dominated by two huge biomes –
effectively the largest greenhouses in the world. The
Humid Tropics Biome recreates the conditions and plant
life of a lush rainforest while the Warm Temperate Biome
has a Mediterranean climate.

\* Project has two million visitors a year
\* See coffee plants, palm trees & pineapples

| Location | Contact |
|---|---|
| Follow signs from A390 at St Austell | Bodelva, St Austell PL24 2SG |
| & A30 Bodmin bypass | t  01726 811900 |
| Opening | w  edenproject.com |
| Daily: summer 9.30am–6pm | e  info@edenproject.com |
| winter 10am–4.30pm | |
| Admission | |
| Adult £12.50, Child £5, Concs £9.50 | |

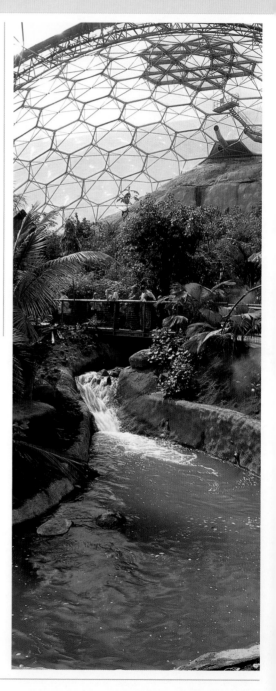

## 211 St Austell

# Lost Gardens of Heligan

4 hrs+    All year

These world-renowned gardens comprise 80 acres of pleasure grounds plus a complex of walled gardens. Many spectacular sub tropical species thrive in this frost-free Cornish valley. Heligan has undergone one of the largest restoration projects of its kind in Europe.

\* Stunning collection of plants from all over the world
\* Featured in a major Channel Four series

| Location | Contact |
|---|---|
| From St Austell, take Mevagissey road (B3273) & follow brown tourist signs | Pentewan, St Austell PL26 6EN |
| **Opening** Mar–Oct 10am–6pm; Nov–Feb 10am–5pm | t 01726 845100 w heligan.com e info@heligan.com |
| **Admission** Adult £7.50, Child £4, Concs £7 | |

## 212 St Ives

# Tate St Ives

2 hrs    All year

St Ives has been famous as an artists' colony since the early C20 and the opening of Tate St Ives in 1993 provided the opportunity to view modern art in the surroundings and atmosphere that inspired them. The gallery also manages the Hepworth Museum and Sculpture Garden.

\* Spectacular coastal setting
\* Visit Barbara Hepworth's home

| Location | Contact |
|---|---|
| Near Porthmeor Beach | Porthmeor Beach, St Ives TR26 1TG |
| **Opening** Mar–Oct daily 10am–5.30pm; Nov–Feb Tue–Sun 10am–4.30pm (last admission 30 mins before close) | t 01736 796226 w tate.org.uk/stives e tatestivesinfo@tate.org.uk |
| **Admission** Adult £5.50, Child free, Concs £2.75 | |

## 213 Tintagel

# Tintagel Castle

1 hr+    All year

This is the legendary home of King Arthur and Merlin, and its awesome setting with the crashing waves on three sides adds fuel to the story. The ruins that stand today are the remnants of a castle built by Earl Richard of Cornwall, brother of Henry III.

\* Short film about the castle
\* Put your foot in 'Arthur's Footprint'

| Location | Admission |
|---|---|
| Take ½ mile track from village, no vehicles beyond village | Adult £3.90, Child £2, Concs £2.90 |
| **Opening** Daily: Apr–Sep 10am–6pm; Oct 10am–5pm; Nov–Mar 10am–4pm | **Contact** Tintagel PL34 0HE t 01840 770328 w english-heritage.org.uk/membership e tintagel.castle@english-heritage.org.uk |

 © Tate St Ives

## 214 Truro

# Royal Cornwall Museum

2 hrs     All year

Cornwall's oldest and most prestigious museum, famed for its important collections. See a myriad of minerals, view our naked mummy and discover Cornwall's unique culture. The museum presents an exciting range of changing exhibitions from textiles to contemporary art.

* Diverse range of temporary exhibitions
* Pacific-Rim Restaurant *Stingi Lulu's*

| Location | Contact |
|---|---|
| Truro town centre | River Street, Truro TR1 2SJ |
| Opening | t  01872 272205 |
| Mon–Sat 10am–5pm; | w  royalcornwallmuseum.org.uk |
| closed Sun & Bank Hols | e  enquiries@royalcornwallmuseum. |
| Admission | org.uk |
| Free | |

## 215 Barnstaple

# Arlington Court

3 hrs+     Easter–Oct

Arlington Court houses the treasures amassed during the travels of Miss Rosalie Chichester. These include model ships, tapestries, pewter and shells. The stable block contains a magnificent collection of horse-drawn vehicles that offer carriage rides around the grounds.

* 'Batcam' films bat colony May–September
* Spectacular gardens & extensive parkland

| Location | Admission |
|---|---|
| Follow signs off A39, 8 miles N of Barnstaple | Adult £6.50, Child £3.25 |
| | Contact |
| Opening | Arlington, Barnstaple EX31 4LP |
| *House* Easter–Oct 11am–5.30pm; closed Sat | t  01271 850296 |
| *Gardens* daily; Jul–Aug 10.30am–5.30pm | w  nationaltrust.org.uk |
| | e  arlingtoncourt@nationaltrust.org.uk |

## 216 Barnstaple

# Marwood Hill Gardens

2 hrs+     All Year

Marwood Hill Gardens covers 20 acres and has year round interest. Camellias and rhododendrons are planted on the walk along the north side of the walled garden, including three borders of herbaceous peonies.The Lower Garden has a series of small lakes.

* Bog garden houses a National Collection of astilbes
* Walk between gardens passes plantings of bamboo

| Location | Contact |
|---|---|
| 4 miles N of Barnstaple | Barnstaple EX31 4EB |
| Opening | t  01271 342528 |
| Daily: 10am–5pm | w  marwoodhillgarden.co.uk |
| Admission | e  marwoodhillgarden@netbreeze. |
| Adult £4, Child free | co.uk |

## 217  Beer

# Pecorama Millennium Garden

3 hrs+    Easter–Oct

This unusual garden is one of a number of attractions on this hillside site overlooking Beer. Stunning designs include a roof garden enclosed by a ruined tower, a moat garden, a rainbow garden and stunning stonework – all with appropriately coloured plants and foliage.

\* Miniature railway with steam & diesel locomotives
\* Fully restored Pullman carriage from 1950s

| Location | Admission |
|---|---|
| Follow signs from Beer turning on A3052 | Please phone for details |
| **Opening** | **Contact** |
| 10 Apr–28 Oct Mon–Fri 10am–5.30pm Sat 10–1pm; 30 May–5 Sep 10am–5.30pm; open Easter Sun | Beer, nr Seaton EX12 3NA
t  01297 20580
w  peco-uk.com
e  pecorama@btconnect.com |

## 218  Bovey Tracey

# Devon Guild of Craftsmen

2 hrs    All year

This is the South West's leading gallery and craft showrooms with work selected from some 240 makers, many with national and international reputations. Riverside Mill, the Guild's showcase, features frequently changing exhibitions.

\* Newly refurbished gallery, extended craft shop
\* Riverside Mill dates from 1850

| Location | Contact |
|---|---|
| Follow signs for Bovey Tracey, 2 miles from A38 | Riverside Mill, Bovey Tracey TQ13 9AF
t  01626 832223
w  crafts.org.uk
e  devonguild@crafts.org.uk |
| **Opening** | |
| Daily: 10am–5.30pm; Fri & Sat 10am–8pm | |
| **Admission** | |
| Free, donations welcomed | |

## 219  Buckfastleigh

# Buckfast Abbey

3 hrs+    All year

Buckfast Abbey is the only English medieval monastery to have been restored after the Dissolution and used again for its original purpose. This active Benedictine community provides an insight into monastic life and remarkable church architecture in a peaceful setting.

\* Impressive marble flooring
\* Original building dates from 1018

| Location | Contact |
|---|---|
| Off A38, follow signs on A384 | Buckfastleigh TQ11 0EE
t  01364 645500
w  buckfast.org.uk
e  enquiries@buckfast.org.uk |
| **Opening** | |
| Daily: *summer* 9am–5.30pm *winter* 9am–5pm | |
| **Admission** | |
| Free | |

## 220 Buckfastleigh

# Buckfast Butterfly Farm & Dartmoor Otter Sanctuary

2 hrs    Easter–Oct

This unusual attraction offers an educational experience for animal lovers. See free-flying moths and butterflies from around the world in the indoor tropical garden. Otters swim in large glass enclosures to ensure marvellous underwater views.

\* Butterfly habitat constructed to maximise viewing
\* British, Asian & North American otters on show

| Location | Contact |
|---|---|
| Follow signs from A38 at A384 to Buckfastleigh | Buckfastleigh TQ11 0DZ |
| | t 01364 642916 |
| Opening | w ottersandbutterflies.co.uk |
| Easter–Oct 10am–5.30pm | e info@ottersandbutterflies.co.uk |
| Admission | |
| Adult £5.95, Child £4.50, Concs £5.50 | |

## 221 Budleigh Salterton

# Bicton Park Botanical Gardens

3 hrs+    All year

Bicton has sweeping lawns, water features, English borders and a formal Italian garden that survived the Capability Brown period. Its palm house is one of the world's most beautiful garden buildings. The museum contains an enormous collection of rural memorabilia.

\* Exhibition of traction engines & vintage machinery
\* Children's play area & narrow-gauge railway

| Location | Contact |
|---|---|
| Off M5 at junction 30, follow signs via Newton Poppleford | East Budleigh, Budleigh Salterton EX9 7BJ |
| | t 01395 568465 |
| Opening | w bictongardens.co.uk |
| Daily: *summer* 10am–6pm | e info@bictongardens.co.uk |
| *winter* 10am–5pm | |
| Admission | |
| Adult £5.95, Child & Concs £4.95 | |

## 222 Cullompton

# Coldharbour Mill & Working Wool Museum

4 hrs+    All year

This 200-year-old waterside mill houses working spinning and weaving machines, and steam engines restored to their former glory. There are regular exhibitions throughout the year.

\* Guided tours available
\* Steam engines can be seen running at special events

| Location | Contact |
|---|---|
| 2 miles off junction 27 of M5. Follow signs to Willand and the museum | Uffculme, Cullompton EX15 3EE |
| | t 01884 840960 |
| Opening | w coldharbourmill.org.uk |
| Daily: Mar–Sep 10.30am–5pm | e info@coldharbourmill.org.uk |
| Oct–Feb 11am–4pm | |
| Admission | |
| Adult £5.95, Child £2.95 Concs £5.50 | |

## 223 Dartmouth

# Blackpool Sands

1 hr+    Apr–Oct

This award-winning beach offers superb swimming conditions in clean clear water with a lifeguard on duty during the summer. Facilities include restaurants, a shop selling beach clothes and games, kayak, boogie boards, wetsuit and snorkel hire.

\* European Blue-Flag beach
\* Dogs allowed 1 Nov–1 Mar only

| Location | Contact |
|---|---|
| On A379, 3 miles from Dartmouth | Blackpool, Dartmouth TQ6 0RG |
| Opening | t 01803 770606 |
| Daily: Apr–Oct 9am–7pm | w blackpoolsands.co.uk |
| Admission | e info@blackpoolsands.co.uk |
| Free | |
| Car park charges apply Apr–Oct £2–£5 | |

224 Dartmouth

# Dartmouth Castle

1 hr          All year

Built by C14 merchants (led by mayor John Hawley) to protect themselves from invasion, this brilliantly positioned castle juts out into the narrow entrance to the Dart Estuary. It is said that Hawley was the inspiration for Chaucer's Shipman in *The Canterbury Tales*.

\* Hands-on exhibition brings 600 years of history to life
\* Complete Victorian gun battery

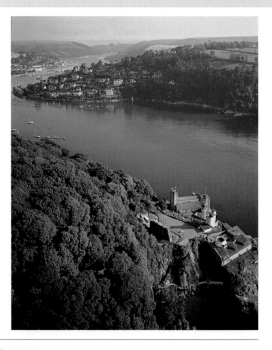

**Location**
1 mile SE of Dartmouth on B3025

**Opening**
Daily: Apr–Jun 10am–5pm
Jul–Aug 10am–6pm; Sep 10am–5pm;
Oct 10am–4pm; Nov–Mar Sat & Sun
10am–4pm

**Admission**
Adult £3.60, Child £1.80, Concs £2.70

**Contact**
Castle Road, Dartmouth TQ6 0JN

t  01803 833588
w english-heritage.org.uk
e dartmouth@english-heritage.org.uk

---

225 Exeter

# Exeter Cathedral

½ hr          All year

This magnificent Gothic cathedral was largely rebuilt in the C13, though the imposing towers remain from the earlier Norman structure. The cathedral has played an important historical role through the ages, particularly in the C17.

\* Elaborately carved choir stalls of particular note
\* Visited by William the Conqueror

**Location**
Just off high street in city centre

**Opening**
Daily: guided tours Apr–Oct

**Admission**
Free, donations encouraged,
Charge for group visits

**Contact**
The Cloisters, Exeter EX1 1HS

t  01392 285983
w exeter-cathedral.org.uk
e visitors@exeter-cathedral.org.uk

---

226 Exeter

# Killerton House

2 hrs+          Mar–Oct

An elegant C18 house in a hillside garden. The house has many treasures including the famous Killerton costume collection. The garden features a Victorian rock garden and an interesting ice house. There are fine views across the Devon countryside from the lawns.

\* Costume collection extends to over 9,000 items
\* Costume display changes every year

**Location**
6 miles from Exeter off B3181

**Opening**
15 Mar–29 Oct 11am–5pm, closed Tue
(& Mon in Aug); Aug daily

**Admission**
*House & Gardens*
Adult £6.50, Child £3

**Contact**
Broadclyst, Exeter EX5 3LE

t  01392 881345
w nationaltrust.org.uk

## 227 Exeter

# Powderham Castle

3 hrs+    Easter–Oct

Built in 1390 the Courtenay family home is occupied by the 18th Earl of Devon. It has rich history and architecture (music room by Wyatt), fine views of the deer park and Exe estuary and animals in the Secret Garden, a miniature train and tractor/trailer rides.

* Fantastic grand staircase once part of medieval hall
* Miniature railway & children's secret garden

**Location**
8 miles from Exeter on A379 to Dawlish

**Opening**
Easter–Oct Sun–Fri 10am–5.30pm

**Admission**
Adult £7.45, Child £4.10

**Contact**
Kenton, Exeter EX6 8JQ
t 01626 890243
w powderham.co.uk
e castle@powderham.co.uk

## 228 Great Torrington

# Dartington Crystal

3 hrs+    All year

Internationally known for handmade contemporary glassware. Discover the history of glass and the Dartington company in the visitor centre, and watch craftsmen at work in the factory. The factory shop is thought to be the biggest glass shop in the world.

* See Dartington's innovative glass designs
* Have your hand or foot cast

**Location**
In centre of Torrington off A386

**Opening**
Daily: Mon–Fri 9am–5pm, Sat 10am–5pm, Sun 10am–4pm (last tour 3.15pm); no factory tour at weekends

**Admission**
Please phone for details

**Contact**
Great Torrington EX38 7AN
t 01805 626242
w dartington.co.uk
e sfrench@dartington.co.uk

## 229 Great Torrington

# RHS Garden Rosemoor

3 hrs+    All year

RHS Garden Rosemoor is a garden of great importance. To the huge range of plants collected by its former owner, the RHS has added features such as the formal garden; herbaceous borders; herb, fruit, vegetable and cottage gardens, and Mediterranean and winter gardens.

* Extensive rose garden is most popular feature
* Extensive stream & lakeside planting

**Location**
Junction 27 of M5, A361 to South Molton. Follow signs

**Opening**
Daily: Apr–Sep 10am–6pm; Oct–Mar 10am–5pm

**Admission**
Adult £5.50, Child £1.50

**Contact**
Great Torrington EX38 8PH
t 01805 624067
w rhs.org.uk/rosemoor
e rosemooradmin@rhs.org.uk

## 230 Newton Abbott

# Tuckers Maltings

2 hrs+    Easter–Oct

Britain's only working malt house open to the public, making malt from barley for beer. With its working Victorian machinery, Tuckers Maltings is an education for all ages with video and audio. See and taste real ale from the in house brewery.

* Guided tours last one hour
* Speciality beer shop open all year

**Location**
3 min walk from Newton Abbot railway station

**Opening**
Easter–Oct 10am–5pm, closed Sun;
Please phone for tour times

**Admission**
Adult £5.45, Child £3.45, Concs £4.95

**Contact**
Teign Road,
Newton Abbott TQ12 4AA

t 01626 334734
w tuckersmaltings.com
e info@tuckersmaltings.com

## 231 Okehampton

# Okehampton Castle

3 hrs+    Apr–Sep

The impressive ruins of the largest castle in Devon stand on the banks of a river in the foothills of Dartmoor. The central keep is still impressive atop its motte, and there are excellent walks through the woodlands surrounding the castle.

* Free audio-tape tour available
* Beautiful picnic grounds

**Location**
1 mile SW of town centre

**Opening**
Daily: Apr–Jun & Sep 10am–5pm
Jun–Aug 10am–6pm

**Admission**
Adult £3, Child £1.50, Concs £2.30

**Contact**
Castle Lodge,
Okehampton EX20 1JB

t 01837 52844
w english-heritage.org.uk
e okehampton@english-heritage.org.uk

## 232 Paignton

# Paignton Zoo Environmental Park

3 hrs+    All year

Home to some of the world's most endangered plants and animals, the zoo has hundreds of different animals and birds, including tigers, rhinoceros and giant tortoises. They are grouped into different climate zones that reflect the world's major habitats.

* 1,500 different plants from around the world
* Starred in the BBC *Zoo Keepers* programme

**Location**
Situated on A3022 Totnes road,
1 mile from Paignton town centre

**Opening**
*summer* 10am–6pm
*winter* 10am–dusk

**Admission**
Please phone for details

**Contact**
Totnes Road, Paignton TQ4 7EU

t 01803 697500
w paigntonzoo.org.uk
e info@paigntonzoo.org.uk

## 233 Tavistock

# Morwellham Quay

4 hrs+    Easter–Oct

Despite being 23 miles from the sea, Morwellham Quay was the Empire's greatest copper port in the time of Queen Victoria. Today the 1860s are recreated with a Tamar ketch moored at the quay, shops, cottages and costumed staff to act as guides.

* Take a tram underground to explore a copper mine
* Explore the farm, wildlife reserve & parkland

**Location**
4 miles from Tavistock
on River Tamar

**Opening**
Daily: Easter–Oct 10am–6pm

**Admission**
Adult £8.90, Child £6, Concs £7.80

**Contact**
Morwellham, Tavistock PL19 8JL

t 01822 832766
w morwellham-quay.co.uk
e info@morwellham-quay.co.uk

## 234  Plymouth

# Plymouth Dome

2 hrs  All year

More than 400 years of Plymouth's great history is brought to life in this high-tech visitor centre. Walk through an Elizabethan street, find out about Drake, Cook and the *Mayflower*, link up a satellite and study weather patterns.

* Walk the gun deck of a galleon
* See the devastation of the Blitz

**Location**
Follow signs from city centre for Hoe

**Opening**
Apr–Oct daily 10am–5pm;
Nov–Mar Tues–Sat 10am–4pm

**Admission**
Adult £4.75, Child £3.25, Concs £3.75

**Contact**
The Hoe, Plymouth PL1 2NZ

t  01752 603300
w  plymouthdome.info
e  plymouthdome@plymouth.gov.uk

## 235  Plymouth

# Royal Albert Memorial Museum

2 hrs  All year

This outstanding collection of local and national importance ranges from local archaeological finds to natural history displays from around the world as well as works of art. The impact of geology on Devon and its people is explored in the Geology at Work Gallery.

* Fascinating building to commemorate Prince Albert
* Display of clocks, watches & timekeeping

**Location**
Queen Street is just off high street in city centre

**Opening**
Daily: 10am–5pm; closed Sun & Bank Hols

**Admission**
Free

**Contact**
Queen Street,
Exeter EX4 3RX

t  01392 665858
w  exeter.gov.uk/museums
e  ramm@exeter.gov.uk

## 236  Tiverton

# Tiverton Castle

1 hr  Easter–Oct

Originally built in 1106 as the home of the Earl of Devon, the building now exhibits aspects of architecture from medieval to modern. Visitors can climb to the roof for views of the town and surrounding hillside, try on some English Civil War armour, and stroll round the gardens.

* Celebrating 900th anniversary
* Superb holiday accommodation, please phone for details

**Location**
A361 to Tiverton, follow signs

**Opening**
Easter–Oct Sun, Thu & Bank Hols
2.30–5.30pm

**Admission**
Adult £5, Child £2

**Contact**
Park Hill,
Tiverton EX16 6RP

t  01884 253200
w  tivertoncastle.com
e  tiverton.castle@ukf.net

## 237  Torquay

# Bygones

2 hrs+  All year

This life-size Victorian street with shops and period rooms also features a giant model railway and railwayana collection, an interactive and illuminated children's fantasy land, a multi sensory WWI trench with militaria collection and a real Anderson shelter.

* Housed in a former cinema
* Christmas is a winter wonderland in a Victorian street

**Location**
Town centre, towards St Mary Church

**Opening**
Daily: Apr–Jun & Sep 10am–6pm;
Nov–Mar 10am–5pm;
Jul & Aug Sun–Thu 10am–9.30pm, Fri & Sat 10am–6pm

**Admission**
Adult £4.95, Child £3.50, Concs £4.50

**Contact**
Fore Street, St Mary Church
Torquay TQ1 4PR

t  01803 326108
w  bygones.co.uk

238 Torquay

# Living Coasts

2 hrs+   All year

A unique aquatic visitor attraction, focusing on the conservation of coastal and marine life around the globe. The spacious interior of the meshed aviary allows free flight for the birds and access for visitors, enabling an intimacy unusual in seabird exhibits in this country.

\* Adopt an animal & underwater viewing
\* Special events throughout the year

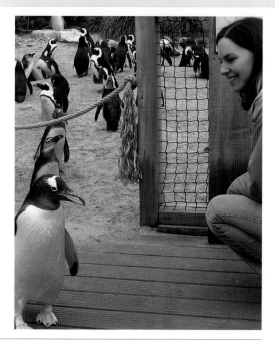

| Location | Contact |
|---|---|
| Situated in centre of Torquay, on the harbourside | Torquay Harbourside, Beacon Quay Torquay TQ1 2BG |
| **Opening** Mar–Sep 10am–6pm; Oct–Feb 10am–5.30pm | t 01803 202470 w livingcoasts.org.uk e info@livingcoasts.org.uk |
| **Admission** Adult £5.90, Child £4.10, Concs £4.60 | |

---

239 Torquay

# Torquay Museum

1 hr   All year

Devon's oldest museum (1845) holds an impressive collection of natural history – both local and from across the world. There are also displays of Torquay pottery, pictorial archives, the story of Agatha Christie's life and a model of an old Devon farmhouse.

\* A fragment of jaw bone from Britain's first human
\* More than 300,000 natural history specimens in store

| Location | Contact |
|---|---|
| Near Torquay harbour, a short walk from clocktower | 529 Babbacombe Road, Torquay TQ1 1HG |
| **Opening** Mon–Sat 9.30am–5pm; Sun & mid-Jul–Sep 1.30pm–5pm | t 01803 293975 w torquaymuseum.org |
| **Admission** Adult £3, Child £1.50, Concs £2 | |

240 Totnes

# Totnes Castle

1 hr   Apr–Oct

Totnes Castle sits high on a hill above the town, commanding the approaches from three valleys. One of the best surviving examples of a Norman motte and bailey castle, its C11 wood structure was replaced by a stone keep in the C13 and C14.

\* The keep has survived in excellent condition
\* Keep surrounded by a curtain wall, now crumbling

| Location | Contact |
|---|---|
| On a hill overlooking Totnes | Castle Street, Totnes TQ9 5NU |
| **Opening** Daily: Apr–Jun & Sep 10am–5pm; Jul–Aug 10am–6pm; Oct 10am–4pm | t 01803 864406 w english-heritage.org.uk |
| **Admission** Adult £2.30, Child £1.20, Concs £1.70 | |

## 241 Beaminster

# Mapperton Gardens

1 hr+    Mar–Oct

These terraced valley gardens surround a delightful Tudor/Jacobean manor house, stable blocks, dovecote and All Saints Church. They featured in Jane Austen's *Emma*, *Restoration* and *Tom Jones*. There is also a shop with plants, pots and gift items, and a charming café.

 * Spring plant sale

**Location**
15 mins from Crewkerne via A303 to Beaminster on the B3163

**Opening**
*House* 26 Jun–4 Aug 11am–5pm weekdays
*Gardens* Daily: Mar–Oct 11am–5pm

**Admission**
Please phone for details

**Contact**
Mapperton,
Beaminster DT8 3NR
t 01308 862645
w mapperton.com
e office@mapperton.com

## 242 Blandford

# Hall & Woodhouse Brewery

1 hr    All year

The brewery visitor centre tells the story of Hall & Woodhouse through the ages. Devise your own beer recipes, enjoy a virtual tour of the brewery, read the guide to beer tasting and view a personal collection of brewery artefacts and old advertising materials.

* Fascinating insight into this 225-year-old brewery
* Beer can be bought at the brewery shop

**Location**
Follow signs from centre of Blandford

**Opening**
*Visitor centre* Mon–Sat
10.30am–5.30pm, Sun 11am–2.30pm
*Brewery tours* Please phone for details

**Admission**
Free to visitor centre, charge for tour

**Contact**
Blandford,
St Mary DT11 9LS
t 01258 452141
w hall-woodhouse.co.uk
e enquiries@hall-woodhouse.co.uk

## 243 Bournemouth

# *Dorset Belle* Cruises

1 hr+    All year

Take a glorious coastal and harbour cruise on a number of routes linking Bournemouth, Swanage and Poole Quay as well as Brownsea Island and the Isle of Wight. Specialist cruises are also available along this stunning coastline.

* ½-hour cruise around the bay
* Fireworks & magnificent sunset cruises

**Location**
Boats depart from Bournemouth pier,
Swanage or Poole

**Opening**
Daily: Apr–Oct 7am–6pm;
Nov–Mar 10.30am–6pm

**Admission**
*From* Adult £5, Child £2.50

**Contact**
Pier Approach,
Bournemouth BH2 5AA
t 01202 558550
w dorsetbelles.co.uk
e info@dorsetbelles.co.uk

244 Bournemouth

# Oceanarium Bournemouth

2 hrs    All year

A visit to the aquarium provides an encounter with marine life from across the globe. This is a fully interactive experience with feeding demos and talks, a walk-through underwater tunnel and exhibits to help you discover more about this fascinating underwater world.

* Gift shop & café

| Location | Contact |
|---|---|
| Follow signs to Bournemouth beaches & piers | Pier Approach, Bournemouth BH2 5AA |
| Opening | t 01202 311993 |
| Please phone for details | w oceanarium.co.uk |
| Admission | e info@oceanarium.co.uk |
| Adult £6.50, Child £4.50, Concs £5.50 | |

---

245 Bovington

# Tank Museum

3 hrs+    All year

There are few places in the world where you can touch a WWII tank. There are even fewer that have tanks that are in fully restored, running condition. Here are examples of tanks from both world wars to the modern day, along with a good deal of post-war equipment.

* Indoor collection of 150 vehicles from 26 countries
* Vehicle rides & live demonstrations

| Location | Contact |
|---|---|
| Off A352, between Dorchester & Wareham, near Wool. Follow signs from Bere Regis | Bovington BH20 6JG |
| | t 01929 405096 |
| Opening | w tankmuseum.co.uk |
| Daily: 10am–5pm | e info@tankmuseum.co.uk |
| Admission | |
| Adult £8.50, Child £6, Concs £7.50 | |

---

246 Dorchester

# Dorset County Museum

1 hr+    All year

Visit Dorset's main general museum with 16 display rooms exploring aspects of local history, literature, geology, archaeology, fine art and natural science. Winner of the Best Museum of Social History category in the 1998 Museum of the Year awards.

* Interactive audio guide
* Exhibition of Trafalgar

| Location | Contact |
|---|---|
| Town centre, follow museum signs | High West Street, Dorchester DT1 1XA |
| Opening | |
| Oct–Jun Mon–Sat 10am–5pm; Jul–Sep daily 10am–5pm | t 01305 262735 |
| | w dorsetcountymuseum.org |
| Admission | e secretary@dor-mus.demon.co.uk |
| Adult £5, Child £1, Concs £4 | |

## 247 Dorchester

# The Dinosaur Museum

1 hr+   All year

Dedicated to dinosaurs, this award-winning museum is a treat. Audio-visual displays portray the earth millions of years ago. One fascinating exhibit explores the question of what life would be like today if the dinosaurs had not become extinct.

\* Winner of the Dorset Family Attraction Award
\* Top 10 Hands-on Museum in Britain

| Location | Contact |
|---|---|
| Centre of Dorchester | Icen Way, |
| | Dorchester DT1 1EW |
| **Opening** | |
| Daily: Easter–Oct 9.30am–5.30pm | t 01305 269880 |
| Nov–Mar 10am–4.30pm | w thedinosaurmuseum.com |
| | e info@thedinosaurmuseum.com |
| **Admission** | |
| Adult £6, Child £4.50, Concs £5.25 | |

## 248 Dorchester

# The Keep Military Museum of Devon & Dorset

1 hr+   All year

Learn stories of courage, tradition and sacrifice of those who served in the regiments of Devon and Dorset over 300 years. Experience spectacular views from the battlements of Dorchester and surrounding countryside, brought to life by the novels of Thomas Hardy.

\* Modern interactive & creative displays

| Location | Admission |
|---|---|
| On A35 Bridport road on W edge of | Adult £3.50, Child £2.50, Concs £2 |
| Dorchester | **Contact** |
| **Opening** | Bridport Road, Dorchester DT1 1RN |
| Apr–Sep Mon–Sat 9.30am–5pm; | |
| July & Aug Sun 10am–4pm; | t 01305 264066 |
| Oct–Mar Tue–Sat 9am–5pm | w keepmilitarymuseum.org |
| | e curator@keepmilitarymuseum.org |

## 249 Dorchester

# Kingston Maurward Gardens

2 hrs+   All year

Kingston Maurward Gardens are set deep in Hardy's Dorset and are listed on the English Heritage register of gardens. The 35 acres of Georgian and Edwardian parkland and lawns sweep majestically down to the lake from the Georgian house.

\* National Collections of penstemons & salvias
\* Edwardian formal & walled demonstration gardens

| Location | Contact |
|---|---|
| 1 mile E of Dorchester off A35 | Dorchester DT2 8PY |
| **Opening** | t 01305 215003 |
| Daily: 5 Jan–19 Dec 10am–5.30pm or | w kmc.ac.uk |
| dusk if earlier | e administration@kmc.ac.uk |
| **Admission** | |
| Adult £5, Child £3 | |

## 250 Dorchester

# The Tutankhamun Exhibition

1 hr    All year

This exhibition recreates the original Tutankhamun artefacts found when the pharaoh's tomb was reopened. The artefacts are displayed in a model of the tomb chamber as it looked in 1922 when local archaeologist Howard Carter unearthed it.

* A permanent exhibition of the World Heritage Organisation
* Death of Tutankhamun exhibition

**Location**
3 min walk from Dorchester centre

**Opening**
Daily: Easter–Oct 9.30am–5.30pm;
Nov–Easter Mon–Fri 9.30am–5pm,
Sat–Sun 10am–5pm

**Admission**
Adult £6, Child £4.50, Concs £5.25

**Contact**
High West Street,
Dorchester DT1 1UW

t  01305 269571
w  tutankhamun-exhibition.co.uk
e  info@tutankhamun-exhibition.co.uk

## 251 Poole

# Brownsea Island National Trust

3 hrs+    Mar–Oct

Just a short boat journey (not National Trust) from Poole or Sandbanks, the island offers glorious views, a peaceful setting for walks and picnics, a rich variety of habitats for wildlife including the rare red squirrel, and a varied and colourful history.

* Birthplace of Scout & Guide movement
* Dorset Wildlife Trust Reserve (Adult £2, Child £1)

**Location**
By boat from Poole, Sandbanks,
Bournemouth or Swanage

**Opening**
24 Mar–29 Oct 2006 from 10am;
closing time varies

**Admission**
Adult £4.20, Child £2

**Contact**
Poole Harbour, BH13 7EE

t  01202 707744
w  nationaltrust.org.uk/brownsea
e  brownseaisland@nationaltrust.
   org.uk

## 252 Portland

# Portland Castle

1 hr+    Apr–Oct

Portland Castle was built by Henry VIII as part of his ambitious scheme of coastal defences against the French and Spanish. It has survived largely unaltered since the C16, making it one of the best-preserved examples of Henry's castles.

* Audio guides around the castle
* 70% of the attraction now has disabled access

**Location**
Royal Naval Dockyard at Portland

**Opening**
Daily: Apr–Jun & Sep 10am–5pm;
Jul–Aug 10am–6pm; Oct 10am–4pm

**Admission**
Adult £3.60, Child £1.80, Concs £2.70

**Contact**
Castletown, Portland Harbour,
Weymouth DT5 1AZ

t  01305 820539
w  english-heritage.org.uk/portland
e  customers@english-
   heritage.org.uk

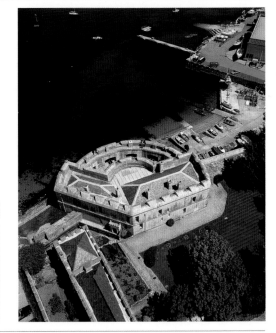

## 253 Sherborne

# Sherborne Abbey

1 hr+        All year

This former cathedral is home to a flourishing community of Benedictine monks. It was the monks who carried out a major rebuilding in the C15 and gave the abbey one of its chief glories, the earliest great fan-vaulted roof in Europe.

* Sherborne School is part of the abbey complex

**Location**
Centre of Sherborne

**Opening**
summer 8am–6pm
winter 8am–4pm

**Admission**
Free, donations encouraged
Guided tour free

**Contact**
Abbey Close, Sherborne DT9 3LQ

t  01935 812 452
w  sherborneabbey.com
e  abbey@sherborneabbey.com

## 254 Sherborne

# Sherborne Castle

2 hrs+        Apr–Oct

Built by Sir Walter Raleigh in 1594 and set in 30 acres of beautiful landscaped gardens around a 50-acre lake, Sherborne Castle has been home to the Digby family since 1617 and contains a fine collection of pictures, porcelain, furniture and decorative arts.

* Capability Brown lake

**Location**
1 mile E of Sherborne, follow signs from A30

**Opening**
Apr–Oct 11am–4.30pm, closed Mon & Fri; House Sat 2.30pm–4.30pm

**Admission**
Adult £7.50, Child free, Concs £7

**Contact**
Sherborne Castle Estates,
Cheap Street,
Sherborne DT9 3PY

t  01935 813182
w  sherbornecastle.com
e  enquiries@sherbornecastle.com

## 255 St Leonards

# Avon Heath Country Park

4 hrs+        All year

Dorset's largest country park has nearly 600 acres of heathland with stands of pine trees and birch woodland. Special events include pond dipping, Easter egg trails, bug hunts, den building, orienteering, animal tracks and signs, and dawn-chorus walks.

* Barbecue hire available
* Birthday parties and school visits

**Location**
On A31, 2 miles W of Ringwood

**Opening**
Park Daily: Apr–Sep 8am–7.30pm;
Oct–Mar 8.30am–5.30pm
Visitor centre Daily: 11am–4pm

**Admission**
Free. Car park charge

**Contact**
Brocks Pine, St Leonards
Ringwood BH24 2DA

t  01425 478470

## 256 Studland

# Studland Beach
# & Nature Reserve

3 hrs+        All year

Fine sandy beaches stretch for 3 miles from South Haven Point to the chalk cliffs of Handfast Point and Old Harry Rocks. Along the way are Shell Bay and a designated naturist area. The heathland behind the beach is a National Nature Reserve.

* Restrictions apply to dogs in summer months

**Location**
Across Bournemouth & Swanage motor road ferry or via Corfe Castle on B3351

**Opening**
Daily; Please phone for details

**Admission**
Parking charges vary through seasons, please phone for details

**Contact**
Countryside Office, Studland,
Swanage BH19 3AX

t  01929 450259
w  nationaltrust.org.uk
e  studlandbeach@nationaltrust.org.uk

## 257 Swanage

# Swanage Railway

2 hrs+          All year

This award-winning railway currently operates on the 6-mile track between Swanage and Norden, through the beautiful Isle of Purbeck, passing the magnificent ruins of Corfe Castle. At present there is extension work taking place to the north of Norden.

* Special events programme
* Train-driving lessons

**Location**
Station is in centre of Swanage, a few mins walk from the beach

**Opening**
Trains daily Apr–Oct. Weekends only rest of the year. Daily 26–31 Dec

**Admission**
Adult £7.50, Child & Concs £5.50

**Contact**
Station House, Swanage BH19 1HB
t  01929 425800
w  swanagerailway.co.uk
e  general@swanrail.freeserve.co.uk

## 258 Tolpuddle

# The Tolpuddle Martyrs Museum

1 hr          All year

Explore the harrowing tale of the Martyrs' arrest, trial and punishment, leading to the foundation of modern-day trade unionism. The museum has a modern, informative, and educational exhibition, using interactive touch-screen displays telling the story in text and images.

* Tolpuddle Martyrs Festival  third Sun in July
* Souvenir shop

**Location**
On edge of Tolpuddle in W of village

**Opening**
Please phone for details

**Admission**
Free

**Contact**
TUC Memorial Cottages, Tolpuddle, Dorchester DT2 7EH
t  01305 848237
w  tolpuddlemartyrs.org.uk
e  tolpuddle@tuc.org.uk

## 259 Wareham

# Corfe Castle

1 hr+    All year

One of Britain's more majestic ruins, this castle once controlled the gateway through the Purbeck Hills and in its time served as a fortress, prison and home. Many fine Norman and early English features remain.

\* Special events including historical re enactments
\* Guided tours available

**Location**
On A352 Wareham–Swanage road

**Opening**
Daily: Mar & Oct 10am–5pm; Apr–Sep 10am–6pm; Nov–Feb 10am–4pm

**Admission**
Adult £5, Child £2.50

**Contact**
The National Trust, The Square, Corfe Castle, Wareham BH20 5EZ
t 01929 481294
w nationaltrust.org.uk
e corfecastle@nationaltrust.org.uk

## 260 Wareham

# Lulworth Castle

3 hrs+    All year

Lulworth Castle was built between 1608 and 1610 but caught fire in 1929 and was all but ruined. In the 1970s careful restoration work began and the exterior is now as it was before the fire. This is a unique building with a rich history to discover.

\* Open-air theatre & concerts
\* Jousting shows throughout August

**Location**
3 miles SW of Wareham. Follow signs

**Opening**
*summer* Sun–Fri 10am–6pm
*winter* Sun–Fri 10.30am–4pm
Closed Sat

**Admission**
Adult £7, Child £4, Concs £6

**Contact**
East Lulworth, Wareham BH20 5QS
t 01929 400352
w lulworth.com
e estate.office@lulworth.com

## 261 Wareham

# Monkey World

2 hrs+    All year

Monkey World is a sanctuary for more than 160 rescued primates from all over the world. Living at the park is the largest group of chimpanzees outside Africa. Orang-utans, gibbons and many more primates inhabit spacious enclosures in a natural woodland setting.

\* Adoption scheme
\* The South's largest adventure playground

**Location**
Between Bere Regis and Wool, 1 mile from Wool station

**Opening**
Daily: 10am–5pm (6pm inJul & Aug)

**Admission**
Adult £9, Child & Concs £6.50

**Contact**
Longthorns, Wareham BH20 6HH
t 01929 462537
w monkeyworld.org
e apes@monkeyworld.org

## 262 Weymouth

# Brewers Quay

3 hrs+        All year

This redeveloped Victorian brewery is at the heart of Weymouth's Old Harbour, offering speciality shopping, entertainment and eating out. Step back in time at the 'Timewalk and Brewery Days' attraction.

**Location**
On harbour, 5 mins from town centre

**Opening**
Daily 10am–4.30pm

**Admission**
Free entry to complex
*Timewalk attraction* Adult £5.40,
Child £3.25, Concs £4

**Contact**
Hope Square, Weymouth DT4 8TR

t 01305 777 622
w brewers-quay.co.uk
e brewersquay@yahoo.co.uk

## 263 Weymouth

# Deep Sea Adventure

3 hrs        All year

Experience the exciting world of underwater exploration from the C17 to the high-tech equipment used today. Children of all ages will love to swing, slide and climb all four floors of this fantastic fun-filled play warehouse.

* Sharkey's Play & Party Warehouse for children up to 11 yrs
* Lazer shoot-out nights available

**Location**
A35 into Weymouth, follow signs

**Opening**
Daily: 9.30am (Please phone for closing times)

**Admission**
Adult £3.95, Child £2.95, Concs £3.45

**Contact**
9 Custom House Quay, Old Harbour, Weymouth DT4 8BG

t 0871 222 5760
w deepsea-adventure.co.uk
e enquiries@deepsea-adventure.co.uk

## 264 Wimborne

# Kingston Lacy House

3 hrs+        Mar–Nov

Kingston Lacy was home to the Bankes family for more than 300 years. All four floors are open to visitors and contain lavish interiors. The Edwardian laundry gives a fascinating insight into life below stairs 100 years ago. Formal gardens and parkland surround the house.

* Special snowdrop days in January
* Events throughout the year

**Location**
1½ miles from Wimborne on B3082

**Opening**
*House* Mar–Nov Wed–Sun & Bank Hols 11am–5pm
*Gardens* Daily: Mar–Nov 10.30am–6pm;
5 Nov–19 Dec Fri, Sat & Sun 10.30am–4pm

**Admission**
*House* Adult £9, Child £4.50
*Gardens* £4.50, £2.25

**Contact**
Wimborne BH214EA

t 01202 883402
w nationaltrust.org.uk
e kingstonlacy@nationaltrust.org.uk

## 265 Berkeley

# Edward Jenner Museum

1 hr+   Mar–Oct

This was the beautiful Georgian home of Edward Jenner (1749–1823), who discovered the smallpox vaccine and also studied birds, fossils and balloons. There is an exhibition of modern immunology with the aim of promoting wider public understanding.

* Explore the science of Jenner's work
* See how smallpox has been eradicated

**Location**
1½ miles W of A38 midway between Bristol & Gloucester

**Opening**
Mar–Oct Tue–Sat & Bank Hol Mon 12.30pm–5.30pm, Sun 1pm–5.30pm; Oct Sun only 1pm–5.30pm

**Admission**
Adult £3.50, Child £2, Concs £2.80

**Contact**
Church Lane, Berkeley GL13 9BN

t 01453 810631
w jennermuseum.com
e manager@jennermuseum.com

## 266 Bourton-on-the-Water

# Cotswold Motor Museum & Toy Collection

½ hr   Feb–Nov

A veritable treasure of yesteryear. Although the main focus is on motoring with a fine collection of classic cars, motorcycles and caravans, the museum has its very own toy collection including teddy bears and aeroplanes plus a rare collection of pedal cars.

* Large collection of historic motoring signs
* Home to the children's TV character Brum

**Location**
Bourton town centre at junction with Sherbourne Street

**Opening**
Daily: Feb–Nov 10am–6pm

**Admission**
Adult £3.25, Child £2.15

**Contact**
The Old Mill, Sherbourne Street, Bourton-on-the-Water, Cheltenham GL54 2BY

t 01451 821255
w cotswold-motor-museum.com
e motormuseum@csma-netlink.co.uk

## 267 Cheltenham

# Chedworth Roman Villa

2 hrs   Mar–Nov

The site comprises over a mile of walls, several fine mosaics, two bath houses, hypocausts, a water-shrine and latrine. Set in a wooded Cotswold combe, the site was excavated in 1864 and still has a Victorian atmosphere. The museum houses objects found on site.

* National Trust property
* One of the largest Roman villas in the country

**Location**
3 miles NW of Fossebridge on the Cirencester–Northleach road (A429); approach from A429 via Yanworth or from A436 via Withington

**Opening**
Mar–mid-Nov Tue–Sun 11am–4pm; Bank Hol Mon 10am–5pm

**Admission**
Adult £5, Child £2.50

**Contact**
Yanworth, nr Cheltenham GL54 3LJ

t 01242 890256
w nationaltrust.org.uk
e chedworth@nationaltrust.org.uk

## 268 Cheltenham

# Cheltenham Art Gallery & Museum

1 hr   All year

This collection has been built up over the last 100 years by generous residents who have donated their collections and items. There is a nationally important Arts & Crafts collection and one room is dedicated to Edward Wilson who travelled with Scott to Antarctica.

* Started with donation of 43 important paintings in 1897
* Oriental gallery with Chinese pottery & costume

**Location**
Cheltenham town centre

**Opening**
Mon–Sat 10am–5.20pm; closed Bank Hols

**Admission**
Free, donations appreciated

**Contact**
Clarence Street, Cheltenham GL50 3JT

t 01242 237431
w cheltenham.artgallery.museum
e artgallery@cheltenham.gov.uk

269 Cheltenham

# Holst Birthplace Museum

1 hr    Feb–Dec

This Regency terrace house is where Gustav Holst, composer of *The Planets Suite,* was born in 1874. The story of the man and his music is told alongside a fascinating display of personal belongings, including his piano.The museum is also a fine period house.

* Working Victorian kitchen & laundry
* Regency drawing room & Edwardian nursery

**Location**
In Pitville area of Cheltenham, opposite Pitville Park

**Opening**
Tue–Sat 10am–4pm
(tours by appointment)

**Admission**
Adult £3.50, Child & Concs £3

**Contact**
4 Clarence Road, Cheltenham GL52 2AY

t  01242 524846
w  holstmuseum.org.uk
e  holstmuseum@btconnect.com

270 Chipping Campden

# Hidcote Manor Gardens

2 hrs+    Apr–Sep

One of England's great gardens created early in the C20 by the horticulturist Major Lawrence Johnston. A series of small gardens are separated by walls and hedges of different species. The varied style of the outdoor 'rooms' ensures an interesting visit at any time.

* Rare & unusual plants from around the world

**Location**
4 miles NE of Chipping Campden, off B4081

**Opening**
Please phone for details

**Admission**
Please phone for details

**Contact**
Hidcote Bartrim,
Chipping Campden GL55 6LR

t  01386 438333
w  nationaltrust.org.uk/hidcote
e  hidcote@nationaltrust.org.uk

271 Chipping Campden

# Kiftsgate Court Garden

1 hr    Apr–Sep

A series of interconnecting gardens each with a distinct character, including a sheltered Mediterranean garden. There are many unusual plants that have been collected by the garden's creators – three generations of women.

* Newly added water garden
* Views stretch to the Bredon & the Malvern Hills

**Location**
SE of Mickleton and 4 miles NE of Chipping Campden off B4081

**Opening**
Apr, Aug & Sep Sun, Mon & Wed
2pm–6pm; May–July Sat–Wed
12noon–6pm

**Admission**
Adult £5.50, Child £1.50

**Contact**
Chipping Campden GL55 6LN

t  01386 438777
w  kiftsgate.co.uk
e  info@kiftsgate.co.uk

272  Cinderford

# Dean Heritage Centre

2 hrs+     All year

This is the museum of the Forest of Dean, situated by a mill pond in a wooded valley, with woodland walks, adventure playground and picnic site. There are exhibits reflecting the area's social and industrial history, including a beam engine and a water-wheel.

* Traditional charcoal-burning demonstrations annually
* Various woodland craft workshops also at this site

    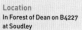

**Location**
In Forest of Dean on B4227
at Soudley

**Opening**
Daily: British Summer Time
10am–5.30pm;
British Winter Time 10am–4pm

**Admission**
Adult £4.50, Child £2.50, Concs £3.50

**Contact**
Camp Mill, Soudley,
Cinderford GL14 2UB

t  01594 822170
w  deanheritagemuseum.com
e  deanmuse@btinternet.com

273  Gloucester

# Clearwell Caves – Ancient Iron Mines

2 hrs     All year

Mining in the Forest of Dean is believed to have started more than 7,000 years ago as people migrated back into the area after the last Ice Age. Large-scale iron-ore mining continued until 1945. Visitors are allowed to walk into some of the oldest underground mines in Britain.

* Working mine-extracts coloured iron oxides for paint
* 9 caverns open, deep-level visits by appointment

**Location**
1½ miles S of Coleford

**Opening**
Mid-Feb–Oct 10am–5pm; Nov–Dec
Christmas Fantasy, phone for details;
Jan–Feb weekends only 10am–5pm

**Admission**
Adult £4.50, Child £2.80, Concs £4

**Contact**
Clearwell Caves & Ancient Iron Mines,
nr Coleford, Royal Forest of Dean,
Gloucester GL16 8JR

t  01594 832535
w  clearwellcaves.com
e  jw@clearwellcaves.com

274  Gloucester

# Gloucester City Museum & Art Gallery

1 hr     All year

This museum is nearly 150 years old and in that time it has acquired a fine collection of art, archaeological, geological and natural history items. Many local people have donated their collections and these include paintings by Rembrandt and Turner.

* Hands-on & interactive computer displays
*Special exhibition, activities & events

**Location**
Gloucester city centre at junction with
Parliament Street

**Opening**
Tue–Sat 10am–5pm;

**Admission**
Free

**Contact**
Brunswick Road GL1 1HP

t  01452 396131
w  livinggloucester.co.uk
e  culture@gloucester.gov.uk

# Gloucester Folk Museum

1 hr+    All year

Housed in splendid Tudor and Jacobean buildings which date from the C16 and C17. Displays include local history, such as the Siege of Gloucester (1643), Severn fishing and farming and an attractive garden. Craft industries including pin-making, shoemaking and toys and games.

\* Exhibition of domestic life - kitchen & laundry
\* Displays of a dairy, ironmongers & carpenters

| Location | Contact |
|---|---|
| Gloucester city centre, near the docks | 99–103 Westgate Street GL1 2PG |
| **Opening** | t 01452 396868/396869 |
| Tue–Sat 10am–5pm; | w livinggloucester.co.uk |
| Please phone for details | e folk.musuem@livinggloucester. |
| **Admission** | co .uk |
| Free | |

# National Waterways Museum

2 hrs    All year

Housed in the historic Gloucester docks, the museum charts the story of Britain's canals with a nationally important collection. You enter through a replica lock complete with running water and the exhibits show what it was like to live and work on the waterways.

\* Discover Gloucester's role as an important historical dock
\* For boat trips please phone to check availability

| Location | Contact |
|---|---|
| Follow signs for Historic Docks | Llanthony Warehouse, Gloucester Docks GL1 2EH |
| **Opening** | t 01452 318200 |
| Daily 10am–5pm; closed 25 Dec | w nwm.org.uk |
| **Admission** | e bookingsnwml@thewater |
| Adult £5, Child & Concs £4 | waystrust.org |
| Occasionally subject to change, please phone for details | |

# Soldiers of Gloucestershire Museum

1 hr+    All year

Housed in the Customs House in Gloucester's historic docks, the museum tells the story of how two regiments (one an infantry regiment of the regular Army, the other a territorial Yeomanry cavalry regiment) have brought honour to Gloucestershire.

\* The Gloucestershire Regiment (regular Army)
\* The Royal Gloucestershire Hussars (territorials)

| Location | Contact |
|---|---|
| Follow signs to Historic Docks | Gloucester Docks GL1 2HE |
| **Opening** | t 01452 522682 |
| Daily 10am–5pm; closed winter Mons & Christmas (last admission 4.30pm) | w glosters.org.uk |
| **Admission** | e regimental-secretary@rgbw.army. |
| Adult £4.25, Child £2.25, Concs £3.25 | mod.uk |

278 Lower Slaughter

# Old Mill Museum

½ hr+     All year

A C19 flour mill on the banks of the River Eye is home to a museum and an organic ice-cream parlour renowned for its handmade ice-cream. Owned by jazz singer Gerald Harris, the mill has been extensively restored and has become a popular Cotswold attraction.

* Free ice-cream tasting Apr–Oct
* Riverside tea room terrace

**Location**
Off A429 between Stow-on-the-Wold and Bourton-on-the-Water

**Opening**
Daily 10am–6pm, when clocks change 10–dusk; closed 18–25 Dec

**Admission**
Adult £1.25, Child 50p

**Contact**
Mill Lane, Lower Slaughter GL54 2HX
t  01451 820052
w  oldmill-lowerslaughter.com
e  info@oldmill-lowerslaughter.com

279 Moreton-in-Marsh

# Sezincote Gardens

1 hr+     Jan–Nov

Built in a Moghul architectural style, a mixture of Hindu and Muslim, Sezincote is a very unusual English house. The gardens are fascinating and include canals, Moghul paradise gardens and a small Indian-style pavilion. The water gardens contain many rare plants.

* Indian bridge decorated with Brahmin bulls
* Sezincote comes from Cheisnecote, 'the home of the oaks'

**Location**
1¼ miles W of Moreton-in-Marsh on A44

**Opening**
House May–Jul & Sep Thu & Fri 2.30pm–6pm
Gardens Jan–Nov Thu, Fri & Bank Hol Mon 2pm–6pm or dusk if earlier

**Admission**
House & Gardens £6 (no children)
Gardens Adult £4, Child £1.50

**Contact**
nr Moreton-in-Marsh GL56 9AW
t  01386 700444

280 Moreton-in-Marsh

# Wellington Aviation Museum

1 hr    All year

Near a training school for Bomber Command during WWII the museum now contains an extensive collection of artefacts from the war years including a Vickers-Armstrong Wellington bomber. A separate tail section shows the famous Barnes-Wallis structure.

* Thousands of documents to investigate
* Collection of aviation & military art

**Location**
On A44 NE of Cheltenham

**Opening**
Tue–Sun 10am–12.30pm & 2pm–5pm;
Jan–Feb weekends only

**Admission**
Adult £2, Child £1

**Contact**
British School House,
Moreton-in-Marsh GL56 0BG

t  01608 650323
w  wellingtonaviation.org

---

281 North Cerney

# Cerney House Gardens

1 hr    Apr–Jul

This beautiful 'secret' garden sits high above the Churn Valley in the heart of the Cotswolds. It has many features including a lovely Cotswold walled garden with lots of old-fashioned roses, a well-labelled herb garden and kitchen garden, as well as plenty of scenic views.

* Near to Chedworth Roman Villa
* Walks available in surrounding woodland

**Location**
On A435 Cheltenham road. Turn left
opposite Bathurst Arms

**Opening**
Apr–Jul Tue, Wed, Fri & Sun
10am–5pm

**Admission**
Adult £3, Child £1

**Contact**
North Cerney GL7 7BX

t  01285 831205
w  cerneygardens.com
e  enquiries@cerneygardens.com

---

282 Painswick

# Painswick Rococo Garden

2 hrs    Jan–Oct

The rococo style was a short but important design period more often associated with art or architecture. Few such gardens survive and its mixture of formal and informal creates a unique effect. Characterised by winding paths, the garden is full of fascinating features.

* Plunge pool, geometric kitchen garden & maze
* An interesting mixture of building styles

**Location**
Off A46, then B4073 ½ mile N
of Painswick

**Opening**
Daily: Jan–Oct 11am–5pm

**Admission**
Adult £5, Child £2.50, Concs £4

**Contact**
Painswick GL6 6TH

t  01452 813204
w  rococogarden.co.uk
e  info@rococogarden.co.uk

---

283 Tetbury

# Chavenage House

1 hr+    May–Sep

This wonderful Elizabethan manor house, with Cromwellian connections, has changed little in 400 years. The house is noted for Cromwell's room, the main hall with its magnificent stained-glass windows, the ballroom and the Oak Room.

* Set in beautiful gardens
* A favourite with filmmakers

**Location**
On B4014, 1½ miles NW of Tetbury

**Opening**
May–Sep Thu, Sun & Bank Hols
2pm–5pm

**Admission**
Please phone for details

**Contact**
nr Tetbury GL8 8XP

t  01666 502329
w  chavenage.com
e  info@chavenage.com

284 Tetbury

# Tetbury Police Museum

½ hr  All year

This museum is housed in the town's original police station and cells of a former magistrates' court. The building is Victorian with an interesting collection of artefacts from the Gloucestershire Constabulary. An under court room display demonstrates what a trial would have been like.

\* See early police batons, helmets & gas-masks
\* Extensive photographic collection

**Location**
5 min walk from town centre

**Opening**
Mon–Fri 9am–3pm; closed Bank Hols

**Admission**
Free, donations appreciated

**Contact**
The Old Court House, 63 Long Street, Tetbury GL8 8AA
t 01666 504670
w tetbury.org/policemuseum
e tetburycouncil@virgin.net

285 Tetbury

# Westonbirt Arboretum

3 hrs+  All year

Westonbirt has one of the finest collections of trees in the world today with 18,000 trees and shrubs in 600 acres of landscaped countryside. There is also an extensive array of wild flowers, fungi, birds and animals throughout the year.

\* Many events & concerts throughout the year
\* Maples restaurant & court-side café

**Location**
3 miles S of Tetbury on A433 to Bath

**Opening**
Daily: 10am–8pm or dusk if earlier

**Admission**
Prices change with the seasons
Adult £5–7.50, Child £1,
Concs available, phone for details

**Contact**
Westonbirt,
nr Tetbury GL8 8QS
t 01666 880220
w forestry.gov.uk/westonbirt
e westonbirt@forestry.gsi.gov.uk

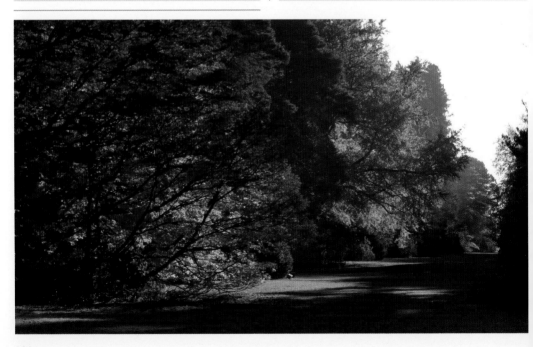

286 Uley

# Owlpen Manor House & Gardens

2 hrs+    Apr–Sep

This Tudor manor house (1450–1616) has a splendid great hall and stands at the centre of a clutch of medieval buildings. The terraced garden is a rare survival of an early formal garden with magnificent yew topiary, old roses and box parterres.

* Queen Margaret of Anjou is said to haunt the manor
* Contains a great collection of furniture, textiles & paintings

| Location | Contact |
|---|---|
| 1 mile E of Uley, off B4066 | nr Uley, Dursley GL11 5BZ |
| **Opening** | t  01453 860261 |
| Apr–Sep Tue, Thu & Sun 2pm–5pm | w  owlpen.com |
| **Admission** | e  sales@owlpen.com |
| Adult £4.80, Child £2 | |
| *Gardens only* £2.80, £1 | |

287 Westbury-on-Severn

# Westbury Court Garden

1 hr    Mar–Oct

Originally laid out at the turn of the C17, this is the only restored Dutch water-garden in the country. It was also the National Trust's first garden restoration, completed in 1971, and is planted with species pre dating 1700.

* Replica C17 panelling installed in pavilion
* Parterre & vegetable plots reinstated to C17 style

| Location | Admission |
|---|---|
| 9 miles SW of Gloucester on A48 | Adult £4, Child £2 |
| **Opening** | **Contact** |
| Mar–Jun Wed–Sun 10am–5pm; | Westbury-on-Severn GL14 1PD |
| Jul–Aug daily 10am–5pm; | t  01452 760461 |
| Sep–Oct Wed–Sun 10am–5pm | w  nationaltrust.org.uk |
| | e  westburycourt@nationaltrust.org.uk |

288 Winchcombe

# Sudeley Castle & Gardens

2 hrs+    Mar–Oct

Sudeley Castle is steeped in history. With royal connections spanning a thousand years, it has played an important role in the turbulent and changing times of England's past. It has played host to Henry VIII, Elizabeth I and Charles I – the latter during the Civil War.

* Home & tomb of Queen Katherine Parr.
* Spoiled in the Civil War, restoration began in 1837

| Location | Contact |
|---|---|
| 8 miles NE of Cheltenham on B4632 | Winchcombe GL54 5JD |
| **Opening** | t  01242 602308 |
| Mar–Oct 10.30am–5pm | w  sudeleycastle.co.uk |
| **Admission** | e  enquiries@sudeley.org.uk |
| Adult £7.20, Child £4.20, Concs £6.20 | |
| Peak pricing Jun–Aug | |

289   Barrington

# Barrington Court

2 hrs+    Mar–Oct

An enchanting formal garden laid out in a series of walled rooms, including the white garden, the rose and iris garden and the lily garden. The working kitchen garden has espaliered apple, pear and plum trees trained along high stone walls.

\* Tudor manor house restored in the 1920s

| Location | Contact |
|---|---|
| 5 miles NE of Ilminster on A358 | Barrington TA19 0NQ |
| **Opening** | t  01460 241938 |
| Mar & Oct Thu–Sun 11am–4.30pm; | w  nationaltrust.org.uk |
| Apr–Sep daily (closed Wed) | e  barringtoncourt@ |
| 11am–5.30pm | nationaltrust.org.uk |
| **Admission** | |
| Please phone for details | |

290   Bath

# The American Museum & Gardens

2 hrs    Mar–Oct

Learn how Americans lived from the time of the early European settlers to the American Civil War. Rooms include a replica C18 tavern where all visitors are given a piece of home-cooked gingerbread. A wonderful collection of quilts, native American objects and folk art.

\* Events occurring throughout the year
\* Beautiful skyline walls & stunning American arboretum

| Location | Contact |
|---|---|
| Off A36 S of Bath at Claverton | Claverton Manor, |
| (5 min drive from city) | Bath BA2 7BD |
| **Opening** | t  01225 460503 |
| 19 Mar–30 Oct, 12noon–5.30pm; | w  americanmuseum.org |
| closed Mon, open Bank Hols | e  info@americanmuseum.org |
| **Admission** | |
| Adult £6.50, Child £4, Concs £6 | |

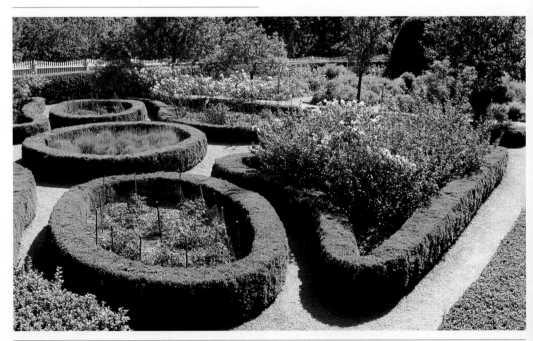

291 Bath

# Bath Abbey – Heritage Vaults Museum

1 hr    All year

Situated on the south side of Bath's C15 abbey (itself built on the site of a Saxon abbey), the vaults have been beautifully restored. They provide an atmospheric setting for objects that have survived from the abbey's fascinating past.

| Location | Contact |
|---|---|
| S side of abbey, in city centre | Bath BA1 1LT |
| **Opening** | t 01225 422462 |
| *summer* 9am–6pm | w bathabbey.org |
| *winter* 9am–4pm | e office@bathabbey.org |
| (Please phone in advance) | |
| **Admission** | |
| Adult £2.50 | |

292 Bath

# Bath Aqua Theatre of Glass

1 hr    All year

In this living/working museum, glass is produced for church windows, art projects and private commissions. You can see the beautiful aquamarine glass being blown in the theatre during regular public demonstrations.

* Signed & dated pieces available in shop
* Exhibition of old & new stained glass

| Location | Admission |
|---|---|
| 5 min walk W out of city centre | Adult £3.50 Child & Concs £2 |
| **Opening** | **Contact** |
| Daily 10am–1pm & 1.45pm–5pm | 105–107 Walcot Street, |
| Preferred viewing times 10.15am, | Bath BA1 5BW |
| 11.15am, 12.15pm, 2.15pm, 3.15pm, last | t 01225 428146 |
| demo at 4pm | w bathaquaglass.com |
| Oct–Apr closed Sun | |

293 Bath

# Bath Balloon Flights

3–4 hrs    Apr–Oct

Balloons launch from Royal Victoria Park, close to the city centre. Booking ahead is essential and all flights are subject to suitable weather conditions. Flight direction is wind-dependent, but the central start point ensures fantastic views of the city and its surroundings.

* Bookings available for singles, couples & groups
* Champagne served during flight

| Location | Contact |
|---|---|
| Royal Victoria Park is 5 min walk from | 8 Lambridge, London Road, |
| the city centre | Bath BA1 6BJ |
| **Opening** | t 01225 466888 |
| Apr–Oct (office open all year) | w balnet.co.uk |
| **Admission** | e bath@balnet.co.uk |
| Please phone for details | |

294 Bath

# Bath Postal Museum

3 hrs+    All year

The first letter sent with a stamp (the Penny Black) was sent from this building in 1840. The former post office now illustrates 4,000 years of communication, including Egyptian clay tablets, various writing implements and the story of the first air mail sent from Bath to London.

* Special exhibitions
* Pillar boxes through the ages

| Location | Contact |
|---|---|
| In Broad Street, in city centre | 8 Broad Street, Bath BA1 5LJ |
| **Opening** | t 01225 460333 |
| Mon–Sat 11am–5pm | w bathpostalmuseum.org |
| **Admission** | e info@bathpostalmuseum.org |
| Adult £2.90, Child £1.50, Concs £2.40 | |

## 295 Bath

# Holburne Museum of Art

1 hr+   All year

This jewel among Bath's splendid array of museums and galleries displays the treasures collected by Sir William Holburne: superb English and continental silver, porcelain, majolica, glass and Renaissance bronzes, and paintings include works by Gainsborough and Turner.

\* Regular specialist exhibitions & lectures
\* Book & gift shop

| Location | Contact |
|---|---|
| 5 min walk from Pulteney Bridge at end of Great Pulteney Street | Great Pulteney Street, Bath BA2 4DB |
| **Opening** | t 01225 466669 |
| Tue–Sat 10am–5pm, Sun 11pm–5pm; open Bank Hols | w bath.ac.uk/holburne |
| | e holburne@bath.ac.uk |
| **Admission** | |
| Adult £5.50, Concs £3 | |

## 296 Bath

# The Jane Austen Centre

1 hr   All year

Jane Austen is perhaps the best loved of Bath's many famous residents and visitors. She spent two long periods here at the end of the C18 and start of the C19 and the city featured in her work. There are period costumes and exhibits that explore Jane's life in Bath.

\* New Regency tea room

| Location | Contact |
|---|---|
| City centre N of Queen Square | 40 Gay Street, Bath BA1 2NT |
| **Opening** | t 01225 443000 |
| Daily: Mon–Sun 10am–5.30pm | w janeausten.co.uk |
| **Admission** | e info@janeausten.co.uk |
| Adult £5.95, Child £2.95, Concs £4.50 | |

## 297 Bath

# Museum of Costume & Assembly Rooms

2 hrs   All year

The story of fashion over the last 400 years is brought to life with one of the world's finest collections of fashionable dress. There are more than 150 dressed figures illustrating changing styles for both men and women. Each of the museum's 30,000 items is original.

\* Combined ticket savings with Roman Baths
\* Nureyev Style display until August 2006

| Location | Contact |
|---|---|
| City centre, just off The Circus | Bennett Street, Bath BA1 2QH |
| **Opening** | t 01225 477789 |
| Daily: Nov–Jan 11am–4pm; Mar–Oct 11am–5pm | w museumofcostume.co.uk |
| | e costume@enquiries.gov.uk |
| **Admission** | |
| Adult £6.25, Child £4.25, Concs £5.25 | |

## 298 Bath

# Roman Baths & Pump Rooms

2 hrs   All year

This is Bath's most famous attraction. Britain's only natural hot spring flourished between the C1 and the C5 and the remains are among the finest in Europe. Walk where Romans walked on ancient stone pavements around the steamy pool.

\* Taste the water in the C18 Pump Room above the Temple
\* Combined ticket savings with Museum of Costume

| Admission | |
|---|---|
| Adult £9.50, Child £5.30, Concs £8.50 | |

| Location | Contact |
|---|---|
| City centre near the abbey | Abbey Church Yard, Bath BA1 1LZ |
| **Opening** | t 01225 477785 |
| Jan–Feb & Nov–Dec 9.30am–4.30pm; Mar–June & Sep–Oct 9am–5pm; July–Aug 9am–9pm (last exit 1 hr after close) | w romanbaths.co.uk |
| | e romanbath_bookings@bathnes.gov.uk |

## 299  Bath

# Sally Lunn's Refreshment House & Museum

1 hr   All year

Sally Lunn's famous bun is still served from what is Bath's oldest building (c.1482). The museum shows remains of Roman, Saxon and medieval buildings on the site. The ancient kitchen used by Sally Lunn in the late C17 can also be seen.

* Three themed refreshment rooms
* Historic Trencher dinner is served from 6pm

| Location | Contact |
|---|---|
| Between Abbey Green & North Parade | 4 North Parade Passage, Bath BA1 1NX |
| **Opening** | |
| Daily: Mon–Sat 10am–10pm, Sun 11am–10pm | t 01225 461634 |
| | w sallylunns.co.uk |
| | e info@sallylunns.co.uk |
| **Admission** | |
| Adult 30p, Child & Concs free | |

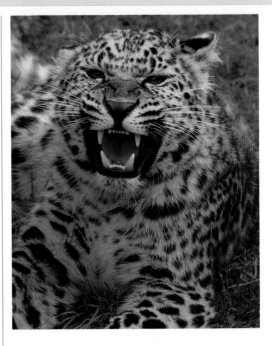

## 300  Bath

# William Herschel Museum

1 hr+   Feb–Dec

The home of C18 astronomer and musician William Herschel where he made important discoveries such as Uranus and infrared radiation. The museum is furnished in the style of the period and is representative of Bath's famous mid-Georgian town houses.

* Georgian garden & audio tours
* Education programmes available on request

| Location | Contact |
|---|---|
| 5 min walk W of city centre | 19 New King Street, Bath BA1 2BL |
| **Opening** | |
| Daily: 1 Feb–16 Dec 1pm–5pm (closed Wed); weekends 11am–5pm | t 01225 446865 |
| | w bath-preservation-trust.org.uk |
| | e debbie@herschelbpt.fsnet.co.uk |
| **Admission** | |
| Adult £3.50, Child £2, Concs £3 | |

## 301  Chard

# The Wildlife Park at Cricket St Thomas

3–5 hrs   All year

This park is home to more than 600 animals, including lemur, monkeys, leopards, oryx, zebra, camels, wallabies, cheetahs and birds. Through its captive breeding programmes the park plays an important part in the conservation of rare and endangered species.

* Licensed for civil marriages
* Safari train, crazy golf & mini car ride

| Location | Contact |
|---|---|
| 3 miles from Chard on A30. Signed from M5 junction 25 and A303 | Chard, Somerset TA20 4DB |
| **Opening** | t 01460 30111 |
| *summer* Mon–Sun 10am–6pm | w wild.org.uk |
| *winter* Mon–Sun 10am–4.30am | e wildlifepark.cst@bourne-leisure.co.uk |
| **Admission** | |
| Please phone for details | |

## 302 Cheddar

# Cheddar Gorge & Caves

3 hrs+     All year

The highest inland limestone cliffs in Britain and the famous cathedral-like caves form a 360-acre nature reserve owned by Lord Bath (of Longleat). The gorge walk is worth the effort for the fantastic views across Somerset from the top.

* New 'Cheddar Man & the Cannibals' attraction
* Open-top bus tour runs through gorge Apr–Sep

**Location**
Follow signs from junction 22 on M5 & A38 or take B3135 from A37 and E

**Opening**
Jul–Aug 10am–5pm
Sep–Jun 10.30am–4.30pm

**Admission**
Explorer ticket for all attractions
Adult £10.90, Child £7.90

**Contact**
Cheddar BS27 3QF

t 01934 742343
w cheddarcaves.co.uk
e info@cheddarcaves.co.uk

---

## 303 Dunster

# Dunster Castle

2 hrs     Mar–Nov

Dramatically sited on top of a wooded hill, there has been a castle here at least since Norman times. The present building was remodelled between 1868 and 1872. A sheltered terrace to the south is home to the National Collection of strawberry trees.

* C13 gatehouse survives
* Surrounded by beautiful parkland for walking

**Location**
Off A39, 3 miles SE Minehead

**Opening**
Castle Daily: 18 Mar–5 Nov 11am–5pm; (closed Thu & Fri)
Gardens & Park Daily: 10am–5pm

**Admission**
Castle Adult £7.20, Child £3.60
Gardens & Park £3.90, £1.70

**Contact**
Dunster, nr Minehead TA24 6SL

t 01643 821314
w nationaltrust.org.uk
e dunstercastle@nationaltrust.org.uk

---

## 304 Farleigh Hungerford

# Farleigh Hungerford Castle

2 hrs     All year

The ruins of this C14 castle lie in the beautiful valley of the River Frome. A free audio guide tells the story of the castle, its sinister past and the occupants during the Middle Ages. The impressive castle has a chapel that contains wall paintings and stained glass.

* Important collection of death masks in chapel crypt
* Programme of living history throughout the year

**Location**
8 miles SE of Bath off A36

**Opening**
Daily: Apr–Jun & Sep 10am–5pm;
Jul–Aug 10am–6pm;
Oct–Mar Sat & Sun 10am–4pm

**Admission**
Adult £3.30, Child £1.70, Concs £2.50

**Contact**
Farleigh Hungerford, nr Trowbridge BA2 7RS

t 01225 754026
w english-heritage.org.uk/farleigh hungerford
e customers@english-heritage.org.uk

## 305 Glastonbury

# Glastonbury Abbey

2 hrs    All year

The abbey is set in 36 acres of peaceful parkland in the centre of this ancient market town. One of the oldest religious sites in Great Britain visited, so legend has it, by Joseph of Arimathea and St David and St Patrick. It is believed by many to be the burial site of King Arthur.

\* Visitor centre with award-winning museum
\* Period-dressed guides in summer months

**Location**
Take A39 from junction 23 of M5, follow signs once in Glastonbury

**Opening**
Daily: Jun–Aug 9am–6pm (or dusk if earlier); Mar–May & Sep–Nov 9.30am–6pm; Dec–Feb 10am–dusk

**Admission**
Adult £4, Child £1.50, Concs £3.50

**Contact**
Abbey Gatehouse, Magdalene Street, Glastonbury BA6 9EL

t  01458 832267
w  glastonburyabbey.com
e  info@glastonburyabbey.com

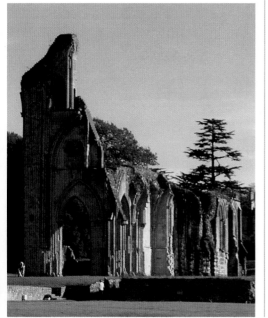

## 306 Highbridge

# Alstone Wildlife Park

1 hr+    Easter–Nov

A small, non commercial family-run park and licensed zoo with camels, pigs, deer, ponies, emu, owls and llama. Special features include Theodore the friendly camel, tame red deer, and a pets' corner.

\* Heaviest Steer in U.K.

**Location**
A38 Highbridge–Bridgwater road, signed turning on the right ½ mile from Highbridge

**Opening**
Daily: Easter–mid-Nov 10am–5.30pm

**Admission**
Adult £4, Child £3, Concs £3.50

**Contact**
Alstone Road, Highbridge
Somerset TA9 3DT

t  01278 782405

## 307 Sparkford

# Haynes Motor Museum

3 hrs    All year

The museum contains a unique collection of hundreds of classic, veteran and vintage cars and motorcycles, all in full working order. Features the famous red collection of 1950s and 1960s sports cars.

\* Fabulous collection of American sports cars
\* 70-seater video theatre

**Location**
½ mile N of Sparkford on A359

**Opening**
Daily: Mar–Oct 9.30am–5.30pm;
Nov–Feb 10am–4pm;

**Admission**
Adult £6.95, Child £3.75, Concs £5.50

**Contact**
Sparkford BA22 7LH

t  01963 440804
w  haynesmotormuseum.co.uk
e  info@haynesmotormuseum.co.uk

## 308 Taunton

# Hestercombe Gardens

2 hrs+   All year

Hestercombe is a unique combination of a Georgian landscape created by Bampfylde in the 1750s, Victorian terraces and Edwardian gardens by Lutyens and Jekyll. The landscaped park (40 acres) has walks, lakes, temples, woods and stunning views.

* Jekyll's original planting faithfully restored

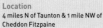

| Location | Contact |
|---|---|
| 4 miles N of Taunton & 1 mile NW of Cheddon Fitzpaine | Cheddon Fitzpaine, Taunton TA2 8LG |
| **Opening** | t 01823 413923 |
| Daily 10am–6pm (last admission 5pm) | w hestercombegardens.com |
| **Admission** | e info@hestercombegardens.com |
| Adult £5.75, Concs £5.25 | |

## 309 Weston-super-Mare

# The Helicopter Museum

2 hrs   All year

Marvel at more than 80 helicopters from Britain, Europe and the USA. A team of conservationists restore the aircraft and prepare them for show. The museum organises special events throughout the year, including open-cockpit days and Air Experience flights.

* World's largest helicopter museum
* Weston-super-Mare's largest all-weather attraction

| Location | Admission |
|---|---|
| On A371, off M5 (junction 21) | Adult £4.95, Child £2.95 |
| **Opening** | **Contact** |
| Apr–Oct Wed–Sun 10am–5.30pm; | The Heliport, Locking Moor Road, |
| Nov–Mar 10am–4.30pm; | Weston-super-Mare BS24 8PP |
| Easter & summer school hols daily | t 01934 635227 |
| 10am–5.30pm | w helicoptermuseum.co.uk |

## 310 Williton

# The Bakelite Museum

1 hr+   Mar–Sep

Set in peaceful Somerset countryside, and housed within a historic watermill, this is the largest collection of vintage plastics in Britain. See exhibits from the inter war period, stylish Art Deco and hundreds of interesting domestic items.

* Thousands of quirky & rare items on show
* Before Bakelite – a display of Victorian plastics

| Location | Contact |
|---|---|
| Williton is at junction of A39 & A358, NW of Taunton | Orchard Mill, Williton TA4 4NS |
| **Opening** | t 01984 632133 |
| Mar–Sept 10.30am–6pm; | w bakelitemuseum.co.uk |
| Only Thur–Sun in term time | e info@bakelitemuseum.co.uk |
| **Admission** | |
| Adult £3.50, Child £2, Concs £3 | |

## 311 Wookey Hole

# Wookey Hole Caves & Papermill

4 hrs   All year

One of Britain's most spectacular complexes of caves, cut into the Mendip Hills. The story of the famous Witch of Wookey is a highlight of the cave tour. The C19 papermill has demonstrations of papermaking with the opportunity for visitors to make their own.

* Magical mirror maze & penny arcade
* Virtual tour of caves & new Dinosaur Park

| Location | Contact |
|---|---|
| Junction 22 of M5 & then follow signs A39 from Bath to Wells | Wookey Hole, nr Wells BA5 1BB |
| **Opening** | t 01749 672243 |
| Daily: Apr–Oct 10am–5pm; | w wookey.co.uk |
| Nov–Mar 10am–4pm | e witch@wookey.co.uk |
| **Admission** | |
| Adult £9.90, Child & Concs £7.50 | |

312 Yeovil

# Fleet Air Arm Museum

3 hrs+    All year

The Fleet Air Arm Museum is one of the 'Must see' attractions when in the South West. Among Europe's largest collection of naval aircraft, see Concorde, harriers, helicopters and the award-winning Aircraft Carrier Experience. There is even a nuclear bomb.

* Ark Royal Aircraft Carrier Experience
*Concorde

**Location**
1 mile off A303/A37 roundabout

**Opening**
Daily: Apr–Oct 10am–5.30pm;
Nov–Mar Wed–Sun 10am–4.30pm;
open Bank Hols & school hols

**Admission**
Adult £9, Child £6, Concs £7

**Contact**
PO Box D6, RNAS, Yeovilton,
Illchester BA22 8HT

t  01935 840565
w  fleetairarm.com
e  info@fleetairarm.com

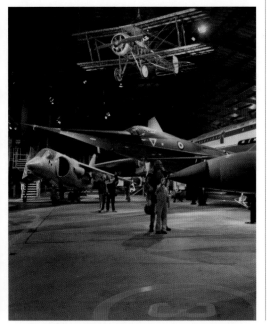

313 Yeovil

# Montacute House & Gardens

3 hrs+    Mar–Oct

A glittering Elizabethan house with splendid Renaissance features. The magnificent state rooms, including a long gallery (the largest of its type in England), are full of fine C17 and C18 furniture and period portraits from the National Portrait Gallery.

* Featured in the film *Sense and Sensibility*
* Parkland & gardens including historic rose garden

**Location**
On A30, 5 miles W of Yeovil

**Opening**
*House* 22 Mar–29 Oct Wed–Mon
11am–5pm
*Gardens* Mar–Oct Wed–Mon
11am–6pm; Nov–Mar Wed–Sun
11am–4pm

**Admission**
Please phone for details

**Contact**
Montacute,
Yeovil TA15 6XP

t  01935 823289
w  nationaltrust.org.uk
e  montacute@nationaltrust.org.uk

314 Yeovil

# Tintinhull House & Gardens

1 hr    Mar–Sep

This small manor house (mainly a C17 farmhouse with Queen Anne façade) stands in a beautiful formal garden created by Mrs Phyllis Reiss. The garden is divided into seven 'rooms' by clipped yew hedges and walls, and has a pool garden, fountain garden and kitchen garden.

* Striking mixed borders & colour schemes

**Location**
Tintinhull is just off A303 S of Yeovil,
follow signs from village

**Opening**
22 Mar–29 Oct Wed–Sun 11am–5pm;
open Bank Hols

**Admission**
Please phone for details

**Contact**
Montacute,
Yeovil TA15 6XP

t  01935 822545
w  nationaltrust.org.uk
e  montacute@nationaltrust.org.uk

## 315 Amesbury

# Stonehenge

1 hr    All year

Stonehenge is a ring of upright stones set in a circle – each stone towering about 19 feet (6metres). Its original purpose is unclear, but theories range from a temple made to worship ancient deities to an astronomical observatory. Others claim it was a sacred burial site.

* World Heritage site
* Audio tours in 9 languages

**Location**
2 miles W of Amesbury on junction of A303 & A360

**Opening**
Daily: Please phone for details

**Admission**
Adult £5.50, Child £2.80, Concs £4.10

**Contact**
Stonehenge Information Line

t 0870 333 1181
w english-heritage.org.uk/stonehenge
e customers@english-heritage.org.uk

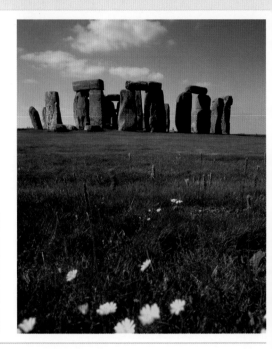

## 316 Avebury

# Avebury

2 hrs+    All year

One of the most important megalithic monuments in Europe dating back to *c.* 3000BC. The great stone circle, encompassing part of the village of Avebury, is roughly a quarter of a mile across. It encloses an area of about 28 acres and has two smaller circles within it.

* World Heritage site
* World's biggest megalithic monument

**Location**
6 miles W of Marlborough, 1 mile N of Bath road (A4) on A4361 and B4003

**Opening**
Daily: Apr–Oct 10am–6pm; Nov–Mar 10am–4pm

**Admission**
Adult £4.20, Child £2.1o

**Contact**
nr Marlborough SN8 1RF

t 01672 539250
w nationaltrust.org.uk
e avebury.estateoff@nationaltrust.org.uk

## 317 Corsham

# Corsham Court

1 hr+    All year

Corsham Court is based on an Elizabethan house dating from 1582. It was bought by Paul Methuen to house a collection of C16 and C17 paintings and, after alterations to the house in C19, more Italian Old Masters and works of art were added.

* Works by Van Dyck, Carlo Dolci & Reynolds
* Picture gallery boasts a rare ornate ceiling

**Location**
Signed 4 miles W of Chippenham from Bath road (A4)

**Opening**
20 Mar–30 Sep closed Mon & Fri (open Bank Hols) 2pm–5.30pm;
1 Oct–19 Mar Sat & Sun 2pm–4.30pm (last entry 30 mins before close)

**Admission**
*House & Gardens* Adult £6.50, Child £3, Concs £5 *Gardens* £2.50, £1.50, £2

**Contact**
Corsham SN13 0BZ

t 01249 701610
w corsham-court.co.uk
e staterooms@corsham-court.co.uk

318 Chippenham

# Lacock Abbey & Fox Talbot Museum

2 hrs+   Mar–Oct

Founded in 1232 and converted into a country house *c.* 1540, the medieval cloisters, sacristy, chapter house and monastic rooms of the abbey have survived largely intact. The museum commemorates the achievements of William Henry Fox Talbot, photographic pioneer.

* Harry Potter movies filmed here
* Beautiful Victorian woodland garden

| Location | Admission |
|---|---|
| 3 miles S of Chippenham, just E of A350 | Adult £7.40, Child £3.70 |
| **Opening** | **Contact** |
| *Abbey* Mar–Oct Wed–Mon 11am–5.30pm | Chippenham SN15 2LG |
| *Museum* Mar–Oct 11am–5.30pm; winter open weekends only | t 01249 730141<br>w nationaltrust.org.uk |

319 Devizes

# Broadleas Gardens

1 hr+   Apr–Oct

Lady Anne Cowdray's valley garden, bought in 1946, has been developed since the early 1960s. Treasures include a secret garden, winter garden, woodland, a sunken rose garden and a silver border packed with plants that are unusual or rarely seen.

* Afternoon teas on Sundays
* Rose pergola, herbaceous borders, rose garden & dell

| Location | Contact |
|---|---|
| A360 road to Salisbury, 1 mile S of Devizes | Broadleas Gardens Charitable Trust Limited, Broadleas, Devizes SN10 5JQ |
| **Opening** | |
| Apr–Oct Sun, Wed & Thu 2pm–6pm | t 01380 722035 |
| **Admission** | |
| Adult £5, Child £1.50 | |

320 Salisbury

# Larmer Tree Gardens

2 hrs   Apr–Oct

These gardens were created by General Pitt Rivers in 1880 and have been restored over the last 10 years. An open-air theatre, Roman temple, Nepalese carved buildings and water features cover the land. Ornamental pheasants and peacocks roam the gardens.

* Site available for events & weddings
* Victorian tea room open on Sundays only

| Location | Contact |
|---|---|
| On the B3081 off A354 Salisbury–Blandford road | Tollard Royal, Salisbury SP5 5PT |
| **Opening** | t 01725 516228 |
| Apr–Oct Sun–Thurs 11am–4.30pm | w larmertreegardens.co.uk<br>e larmer.tree@rushmore estate.co.uk |
| **Admission** | |
| Adult £3.75, Child £2.50, Concs £3 | |

321 Salisbury

# Old Sarum

1½ hrs   All year

This great earthwork, with more than 2,000 years of history; and its huge banks and ditches was created by Iron Age people around 500BC, and later occupied by Romans, Saxons and the Normans. See the remains of the prehistoric fortress, the palace, castle and cathedral.

* William the Conqueror paid off his army here in 1070
* Beautiful views to surrounding chalk downs

| Location | Contact |
|---|---|
| 2 miles N of Salisbury off A345 | English Heritage, Castle Road, Salisbury SP1 3SD |
| **Opening** | t 01722 335398 |
| Apr–Jun 10am–5pm; Jul–Aug 9am–6pm; Sep, Oct, Mar 10am–4pm; Nov–Mar 11am–3pm | w english-heritage.org.uk/oldsarum<br>e old_sarum.castle@english-heritage.org.uk |
| **Admission** | |
| Adult £2.90, Child £1.50, Concs £2.20 | |

322  Salisbury

# Salisbury Cathedral

1 hr    All year

Salisbury Cathedral is one of the finest medieval cathedrals in Britain. Started in 1220, it was completed by 1258, with the spire, the tallest in England (404ft/123m) added a generation later. It also boasts the largest and best-preserved cathedral close in Britain.

\* Voluntary guide tours of cathedral & chapter house
\* Chapter House contains rare original Magna Carta

| Location | Contact |
|---|---|
| Centre of city | Visitor Services, 33 The Close, Salisbury SP1 2EJ |
| **Opening** | |
| Daily: 7.15am–6.15pm, times vary depending on services; Please phone for details | t  01722 555120 |
| | w  salisburycathedral.org.uk |
| | e  visitors@salcath.co.uk |
| **Admission** | |
| Recommended voluntary donation Adult £4, Child £2, Concs £3.50 | |

323  Salisbury

# Salisbury & South Wiltshire Museum

1 hr+    All year

The museum holds material from major archaeological sites in Salisbury and south Wiltshire. Exhibitions cover the entire range of the museum's interests, which, in addition to archaeology, include fine and decorative arts, costume and social history.

\* Temporary exhibitions all year round & gift shop
\* A collection of Turner watercolours

| Location | Contact |
|---|---|
| In Cathedral Close, opposite the West Front | The King's House, 65 The Close, Salisbury SP1 2EN |
| **Opening** | |
| Mon–Sat 10am–5pm Jul & Aug open Sun 2pm–5pm | t  01722 332151 |
| | w  salisburymuseum.org.uk |
| | e  museum@salisburymuseum.org.uk |
| **Admission** | |
| Adult £4, Child £1, Concs £3 | |

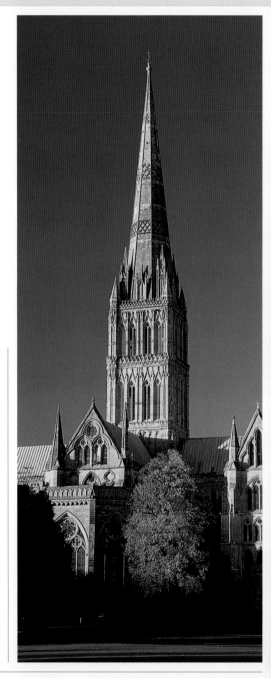

## 324 Stourhead

# Stourhead Gardens

3 hrs+    Mar–Oct

The gardens were designed by Henry Hoare II. Classical temples, including the Pantheon and the Temple of Apollo, are set around the central lake. Vistas change as the visitor walks around the paths and through the magnificent mature woodland.

\* Palladian mansion & gift shop
\* King Alfred's Tower, a 50m red brick folly

**Location**
Just off A303 at Mere

**Opening**
*House* Mar–Oct; closed Wed & Thur
*Gardens* Daily

**Admission**
*Gardens or House* Adult £5.80, Child £3.20 *Both* £9.90, £4.80

**Contact**
Stourhead Gardens,
nr Warminster BA12 6QD

t  01747 842020
w  nationaltrust.org.uk
e  stourhead@nationaltrust.org.uk

---

## 325 Swindon

# STEAM – Museum of the Great Western Railway

2 hrs    All year

This museum tells the story of the men and women who built, operated and travelled on the Great Western Railway. The museum celebrates Isambard Kingdom Brunel and the thousands of ordinary people who made the GWR one of the world's greatest railways.

\* Special events running throughout the year
\* World-famous GWR locomotives

**Location**
Follow signs from Swindon town centre

**Opening**
Daily: 10am–5pm

**Admission**
Adult £5.95, Child & Concs £3.95

**Contact**
Kemble Drive, Swindon SN2 2TA

t  01793 466646
w  swindon.gov.uk/steam
e  steammuseum@swindon.gov.uk

---

## 326 Warminster

# Longleat

4 hrs+    Feb–Nov

Longleat is set in more than 900 acres of Capability Brown landscaped parkland with further woodlands, lakes and farmland. Longleat House is one of the best examples of high Elizabethan architecture, and there are the safari park, mazes and murals to explore too.

\* Longleat hedge maze
\* Featured in the BBC programme *Animal Park*

**Location**
Off A36 between Bath & Salisbury
(A362 Warminster–Frome road)

**Opening**
Daily: Feb–Nov; Times vary
please phone for details

**Admission**
Please phone for details

**Contact**
The Estate Office, Longleat,
Warminster BA12 7NW

t  01985 844400
w  longleat.co.uk
e  enquiries@longleat.co.uk

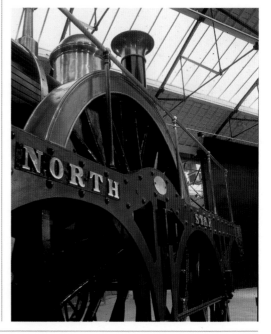

## 327 Warminster

# Shearwater Lake

2 hrs   All year

Surrounded by woodland, Shearwater Lake is one of the finest waterways in west Wiltshire. The 37-acre lake, which is part of the Longleat Estate, was designed in 1791 by Francis Drake of Bridgwater. It is known for its fishing and sailing.

* 20-mile cycleway to Salisbury begins here
* Regular fishing & sailing competitions

| Location | Contact |
|---|---|
| 1 mile off A350 at Crockerton | The Estate Office, Longleat Warminster BA12 7NW |
| Opening | |
| Daily: *summer* 7am–8pm | t 01985 844400 |
| *winter* 8am–5pm | w longleat.co.uk |
| | e enquiries@longleat.co.uk |
| Admission | |
| Car park £1 | |

## 328 Westbury

# Westbury White Horse & Bratton Camp

3 hrs+   All year

This famous landmark in west Wiltshire has fine views of the Wiltshire and Somerset countryside. Cut into a chalk hillside in 1778, the white horse is thought to rest on the site of an older horse that commemorated the defeat of the Danes by King Alfred at Ethandun in AD878.

*Neolithic barrow or burial mound

| Location | Contact |
|---|---|
| Between Westbury and B3098 | Westbury Tourist Information Centre |
| Opening | t 01373 827158 |
| Daily: Please phone for details | w english-heritage.org.uk |
| Admission | |
| Free | |

## 329 Wilton

# Wilton House

2 hrs   Easter–Oct

Wilton House contains many state rooms including the Double Cube Room, which houses a world-famous collection of Van Dyck paintings. Other attractions include the old riding school, a Tudor kitchen, a Victorian laundry and a new costume exhibition.

* Gardens & parkland bordered by the River Nadder
* A location for the feature film *Pride and Prejudice*

| Location | Contact |
|---|---|
| 3 miles W of Salisbury, situated on A30, off A36. 10 miles from A303 | The Estate Office, Wilton, Salisbury SP2 0BJ |
| Opening | t 01722 746720 |
| Phone or check the website for details | w wiltonhouse.com |
| | e tourism@wiltonhouse.com |
| Admission | |
| *House & Grounds* Adult £9.75, Child £5.50, Concs £8 | |
| *Grounds only* £4.50/£3.50 | |

# Eastern

Bedfordshire Cambridgeshire Essex
Hertfordshire Norfolk Suffolk

## 330 Bedford

# Cecil Higgins Art Gallery

2 hrs+     All year

The gallery is housed in a Victorian mansion, once home to the Higgins family who were wealthy brewers. Adjoining this is a modern gallery that houses an internationally renowned collection of watercolours, prints and drawings, ceramics, glass and lace.

* Rooms include items from the Handley-Read Collection
* Furniture by Victorian architect William Burges

**Location**
Just off the Embankment & high street

**Opening**
Tue–Sat 11am–4.45pm,
Sun & Bank Hols 2pm–4.45pm

**Admission**
Free, donations welcomed

**Contact**
Castle Lane, Bedford MK40 3RP
t  01234 211222
w  cecilhigginsartgallery.org
e  chag@bedford.gov.uk

## 331 Biggleswade

# The English School of Falconry

3 hrs+     Feb–Oct

This family-run centre is sited at Shuttleworth Old Warden Park to create a woodland setting as near as possible to the birds' natural surroundings. The centre is home to more than 300 birds of various species including falcons, hawks, eagles, vultures and owls.

* Three flying displays daily
* Hands-on experience

**Location**
Old Warden is 2 miles W of A1 where it bypasses Biggleswade

**Opening**
Daily: Feb–Oct 10am–5pm

**Admission**
Adult £6.50, Child £4, Concs £5.50

**Contact**
Old Warden Park, Biggleswade
SG18 9EA
t  01767 627527
w  shuttleworth.org
e  falconry.centre@virgin.net

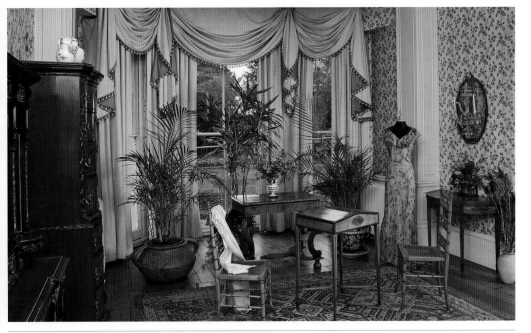

## 332 Biggleswade

# Shuttleworth Collection

2 hrs+    All year

This world-famous collection of aircraft, started by Richard Shuttleworth, depicts the history of flight from 1900 to the 1940s and ranges from a 1909 Bleriot to a WWII Spitfire. Cars, motorcycles and carriages are exhibited alongside the aircraft in eight hangars.

\* Regular flying displays in summer
\* Clayton & Shuttleworth steam-traction engine

**Location**
Shuttleworth Old Warden Aerodrome is 2 miles W of A1 where it bypasses Biggleswade

**Opening**
Daily: Apr–Oct 10am–5pm;
Nov–Mar 10am–4pm

**Admission**
Adult £7.50, Child free, Concs £6
Prices subject to change; please phone for details

**Contact**
Old Warden Pk, Biggleswade SG18 9EP
t 01767 627288
w shuttleworth.org
e collection@shuttleworth.org

## 333 Dunstable

# Leighton Buzzard Railway

2 hrs    Mar–Oct

One of the few narrow-gauge light railways to survive in England. Built more than 85 years ago to transport sand, the line has had a steam-hauled passenger train service since 1968, and passengers can now make a 70-minute round trip from Page's Park to Stonehenge Works.

\* Children's play area
\* Explore the Guntry terminus

**Location**
Off A4146 on edge of Leighton Buzzard, close to junction with A505 Dunstable-Aylesbury road

**Opening**
Early Mar–end Oct Sun & Bank Hols 10.40am–4.30pm; some Sats & Suns in Dec; please phone for details

**Admission**
Adult £6, Child (2–15) £3, Concs £5

**Contact**
Billington Road,
Leighton Buzzard LU7 4TN
t 01525 373888
w buzzrail.co.uk
e info@buzzrail.co.uk

## 334 Henlow

# Stondon Motor Museum

2 hrs    All year

This museum is one of the largest private collections in the country with more than 400 exhibits. It includes veteran cars from 1890 to 1993, housed in 5 different halls and some are for sale. An exclusive collection of Rolls-Royce and Bentley vehicles is a special feature.

\* Full-size replica of Captain Cook's *Endeavour*
\* Large free car park

**Location**
At Lower Stondon near Henlow off A600

**Opening**
Daily: 10am–5pm

**Admission**
Adult £6, Child £3, Concs £5

**Contact**
Station Road, Lower Stondon, Henlow SG16 6JN
t 01462 850339
w transportmuseum.co.uk
e info@transportmuseum.co.uk

## 335 Kensworth

# Dunstable Downs Countryside Centre & Whipsnade Estate

2 hrs+    All year

Dunstable Downs and Whipsnade comprise 510 acres of grassland and farmland, where the steep slopes are rich in flora and associated fauna. With outstanding views, it's a great place to walk, fly kites or watch paragliders. The centre has exhibits and kites for sale.

* Annual kite festival
* Designated Area of Outstanding Natural Beauty

| Location | Contact |
|---|---|
| 4 miles NE of Ashridge between B4540 & B4541 | Whipsnade Road, Kensworth, Dunstable LU6 2TA |
| **Opening** | t 01582 608489 |
| *Downs* All year | w nationaltrust.org.uk |
| *Centre* Daily: Apr–Oct 10am–5pm | e dunstabledowns@nationaltrust.org.uk |
| Nov–Apr, Sat–Sun 10am–4pm | |
| **Admission** | |
| Free | |

## 336 Leighton Buzzard

# Ascott House

2 hrs+    Mar–Aug

Ascott is a black and white C19 house set in 30 acres of grounds. It houses Anthony de Rothschild's collection of art, French and English furniture and Oriental porcelain. The garden has unusual trees, flower borders, topiary, a sundial, a Dutch garden and fountain statuary.

* Houses one of the foremost collections of Chinese three-colour ware ceramics in the world

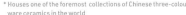

| Location | Admission |
|---|---|
| On A418 between Aylesbury & Leighton Buzzard, E of Wing | Adult £6.50, Child £3.25 |
| **Opening** | **Contact** |
| Daily: 15 Mar–30 Apr & 1–31 Aug except Mon 2pm–6pm; | Wing, Leighton Buzzard LU7 0PP |
| 2 May–29 Jul Tue–Thur 2pm–6pm | t 01296 688242 |
| | w ascottestate.co.uk |
| | e info@ascottestate.co.uk |

## 337 Luton

# Stockwood Craft Museum & Gardens

1 hr+    Apr–Oct

This award-winning museum covers nine centuries of garden history. There are displays on rural life and crafts, the Mossman Collection of horse-drawn vehicles, stunning period gardens and a programme of events that changes throughout the year.

* Conservatory tea room set in C18 walled garden
* Largest display of horse-drawn carriages in the UK

| Location | Contact |
|---|---|
| 2 miles S of Luton town centre, close to junction 10 of M1 | Farley Hill, Luton LU1 4BH |
| **Opening** | t 01582 738714 |
| Daily: Apr–Oct 10am–5pm | w lutonline.gov.uk |
| **Admission** | e museum.gallery@luton.gov.uk |
| Free, donations welcomed | |

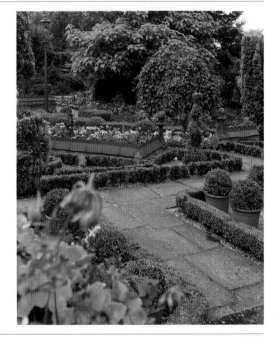

## 338 Milton Keynes

# Woburn Safari Park

6 hrs   All year

Situated in a 40-acre leisure park, the safari reserves allow you to experience wild animals roaming free at close quarters. During the hour-long drive you're likely to see rhino, eland, oryx, antelope, giraffe, zebra, elephants, tigers, wolves, bears, monkeys and hippos.

\* Visitor Attraction of the Year 2000

| Location | Admission |
|---|---|
| 5 minutes off M1 (junction 13). Follow signs | Please phone for details |
| Opening | Contact |
| Daily: Mar–Oct 10am–5pm; Nov–Feb open weekends 11am–3pm | Woburn MK17 9QN |
| | t 01525 290407 |
| | w discoverwoburn.co.uk |
| | e info@woburnsafari.co.uk |

## 339 Shefford

# Hoo Hill Maze

1 hr+   All year

Set within an orchard, this hedge maze measures 300 square feet by 7 feet high (30square metres x 2metres). Visitors are invited to picnic in the orchard, where there is also an open area. An adult garden maze is currently being constructed.

\* Three children's play houses
\* All three species of woodpecker present

| Location | Admission |
|---|---|
| Off A507 and A600 close to Shefford | Adult £3, Child £2, Concs £3 |
| Opening | Contact |
| Weekdays; Please phone for details; weekends, Bank Hol Mon & school hols 10am–6pm | Hoo Hill Maze, Hitchin Road, Shefford SG17 5JD |
| | t 01462 813475 |
| | e sheffordmaze@hotmail.com |

## 340 Silsoe

# Wrest Park Gardens

2 hrs+   Apr–Oct

Come and enjoy the magnificent gardens inspired by the great gardens of Versailles and the Loire Valley in France. Woodland walks and stunning formal gardens are complemented by the reflective expanses of water and wonderful stone and lead statuary.

\* Domed baroque pleasure pavilion
\* Chinese & Roman architecture

| Location | Admission |
|---|---|
| ¾ mile E of Silsoe off A6, 10 miles S of Bedford | Adult £4.30, Child £2.20, Concs £3.20 |
| Opening | Contact |
| Apr–Sep Sat, Sun & Bank Hols 10am–6pm; Oct Sat & Sun 10am–5pm | Silsoe MK45 4HS |
| | t 01525 860152 |
| | w english-heritage.org.uk |

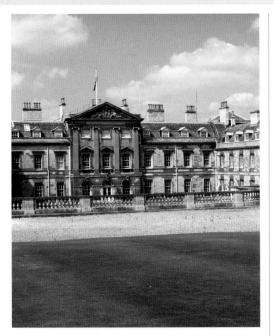

## 342 Cambridge

# Cambridge University Botanic Garden

3 hrs    All year

This tranquil 40-acre garden offers year-round interest to visitors. More than 10,000 labelled plant species grow in beautifully landscaped settings, including rock garden, lake, winter garden, woodland walk and glasshouses. There are and nine National Collections to admire.

\* Important collections of native English plants
\* Founded by mentor of Charles Darwin

| Location | Contact |
|---|---|
| 1 mile S of city centre | Cory Lodge, Bateman Street, Cambridge CB2 1JF |
| Opening | |
| Daily: Nov–Jan 10am–4pm; | t 01223 336265 |
| Feb & Oct 10am–5pm; | w botanic.cam.ac.uk |
| Mar–Sep 10am–6pm | e enquiries@botanic.cam.ac.uk |
| Admission | |
| Adult £3, Child £2, Concs £2.50 | |

## 341 Woburn

# Woburn Abbey

3 hrs+    Jan–Sep

A palatial C18 mansion founded in 1145 as a religious house for a group of Cistercian monks. In 1547 Edward VI gave Woburn Abbey to Sir John Russell who became the 1st Earl of Bedford. Tours include Queen Victoria's bedroom and the state dining room.

\* Woburn's treasures are acknowledged worldwide
\* Home to the Dukes of Bedfordshire for more than 400 years

| Location | Contact |
|---|---|
| Located on edge of village of Woburn | Woburn MK17 9WA |
| Opening | |
| Daily: Easter–Sept 11am–4pm; | t 01525 290666 |
| Sat–Sun only Jan–Mar | w woburnabbey.co.uk |
| Admission | e enquiries@woburnabbey.co.uk |
| Adult £9.50, Child £5, Concs £8.50 | |

343 Cambridge

# Fitzwilliam Museum

3 hrs+    All year

This is the art museum of the University of Cambridge with public access to its collection of international repute. See antiquities from ancient Egypt, rare printed books, Chinese jades and Japanese ceramics, plus paintings by Titian, Canaletto, Rubens, Monet and Picasso.

\* Fine collection of C20 art
\* Exhibition of medals from the Renaissance on

| Location | Contact |
|---|---|
| Approximately 500 yrds from city centre | Trumpington Street, Cambridge CB2 1RB |
| **Opening** | t 01223 332900 |
| Tue–Sat 10am–5pm; Sun 12noon–5pm | w fitzmuseum.cam.ac.uk |
| Closed Mon except summer Bank Hols | e fitzmuseum-enquiries@lists.cam.ac.uk |
| **Admission** | |
| Free, donations welcomed | |

344 Cambridge

# King's College

½ hr+    All year

King's is one of the oldest colleges in Cambridge, founded in 1441 by Henry VI. It is also the premier tourist attraction primarily thanks to the stunning architecture of its perpendicular chapel and its impressive interior that includes the painting Adoration of the Magi by Rubens.

\* Home to the world famous King's College choir

| Location | Admission |
|---|---|
| Take junction 11 or 12 from M11 follow signs for centre parking or park+ride | Adult £4.50, Child £3 |
| **Opening** | **Contact** |
| Daily: term time, Mon–Fri 9.30am–3.30pm, Sat 9.30am–3.15pm, Sun 1.15–2.15pm | King's College, Cambridge CB2 1ST |
| Out of term Mon–Sat 9.30am–4.30pm, Sun 10am–5pm | t 01223 331212 |
| | w kings.cam.ac.uk/visitors |
| | e visitor.manager@kings.cam.ac.uk |

# 345 Duxford

## Imperial War Museum Duxford

3 hrs+    All year

This former Battle of Britain airfield is now home to 200 historic aircaft including biplanes, Spitfires, Concorde and Gulf War jets – many of which still fly regularly. The 7 acres of indoor exhibition space also house one of the country's finest collections of military vehicles.

\* D-Day Experience complete with video story
\* Flying displays held throughout summer

| Location | Contact |
|---|---|
| Off junction 10 of M11 | Duxford CB2 4QR |
| **Opening** | t  01223 835000 |
| Daily: mid-Mar–mid Oct, 10am–6pm; | w  iwm.org.uk/duxford |
| winter 10am–4pm | e  duxford@iwm.org.uk |
| **Admission** | |
| Adult £12, Child free, Concs £9 | |

# 347 Ely

## Oliver Cromwell's House

1 hr+    All year

Home to Ely's most famous former resident, Cromwell's carefully restored house now contains Civil War exhibitions including weapons and armour. It also has illustrations of everyday C17 life and a history of the Fenlands and its transformation from marsh to farmland.

\* C15 inglenook fireplace restored to working order
\* Kitchen area has display of C17 recipes & ingredients

| Location | Contact |
|---|---|
| Ely town centre next to St Mary's Church | 29 St Mary's Street, Ely CB7 4HF |
| **Opening** | t  01353 662062 |
| Apr–Oct, daily 10am–5.30pm; | w  www.ely.org.uk/tic.htm |
| Nov–Mar Mon–Fri, 11am–4pm; | e  tic@ely.org.uk |
| Sat 10am–5pm, Sun 11.15–4pm | |
| **Admission** | |
| Adult £3.85, Child £2.60, Concs £3.35 | |

# 346 Ely

## Ely Cathedral

3 hrs+    All year

Begun by William the Conqueror, this magnificent cathedral stands on the site of a monastery founded in 673 by St Ethelreda. Essentially Romanesque, there is a blend of architectural styles complemented by many beautiful objects in stone, wood and glass.

\* Extensive renovation completed in 2000

| Location | Contact |
|---|---|
| Ely city centre | Chapter House, The College, Ely CB7 4DL |
| **Opening** | t  01353 667735 |
| Daily: summer 7am–7pm, | w  cathedral.ely.anglican.org |
| winter Mon–Sat 7.30am–6pm, | e  receptionist@cathedral.ely. |
| Sun 7.30am–5pm | anglican.org |
| **Admission** | |
| Adult £4.80, Concs £4.20, free on Sun | |

# 348 Ely

## Stained Glass Museum

1 hr    All year

The museum offers a unique insight into the story of stained glass, an artform practised in Britain for at least 1,300 years. This Trust, set up in the 1970s to rescue and preserve stained glass, now houses a National Collection of British stained glass.

\* Work by William Morris on display
\* One-day workshop of glass painting & fusing

| Location | Admission |
|---|---|
| Inside Ely Cathedral | Adult £3.50, Child & Concs £2.50 |
| **Opening** | **Contact** |
| Daily: Mon–Fri 10.30am–5pm, | Ely Cathedral, Ely CB7 4DL |
| Sat 10.30am–5.30pm (5pm in winter), | |
| Sun 12noon–6pm (4.30pm in winter) | t  01353 660347 |
| | w  stainedglassmuseum.com |
| | e  info@stainedglassmuseum.com |

## 349 Lode

# Anglesey Abbey

3 hrs   All year

This site of a former Augustinian priory (many C12 stonework features remain) was brought to its current splendour by Lord Fairhaven in the first half of the C20. He purchased the mill and the vast collection of paintings, and planned the elaborate gardens.

* Watermill can be seen working on 1st & 3rd Saturdays
* One of the country's finest collections of historic statuary

**Location**
6 miles NE of Cambridge on B1102

**Opening**
Daily: *summer House & Mill* 1pm–5pm
*Gardens* Apr–Nov 10.30am–5.30pm
*winter House & Mill* Sat–Sun
11am–3.30pm
*Gardens* 10.30am–4.30pm

**Admission**
*summer* House & Gardens **Adult £8,**
Child £4 *Gardens only* £4.50, £2.25
*winter* Adult £4, Child £2

**Contact**
Lode CB5 9EJ

t 01223 810080
w nationaltrust.org.uk/angleseyabbey
e angleseyabbey@nationaltrust.org.uk

## 350 Peterborough

# Flag Fen Bronze Age Centre

4 hrs   All year

Travel back in time to the Bronze Age and see how people lived more than 3,000 years ago. Discover tools, technology, clothes and food from 1000BC. The museum displays artefacts including swords, daggers and axes, and the earliest wheel ever discovered in England.

* Featured on the Channel 4 programme Time Team
* Set within a 20-acre park

**Location**
NE of Peterborough, off A1139 or A605

**Opening**
Daily: 10am–5pm (last admission 4pm)

**Admission**
Adult £4.25, Child £3, Concs £3.75

**Contact**
The Droveway, Northey Road,
Peterborough PE6 7QJ

t 01733 313414
w flagfen.com
e office@flagfen.freeserve.co.uk

## 351 Peterborough

# Nene Valley Railway

3 hrs+   All year

Embark on a 15-mile round trip through the beautiful Nene Park from Wansford to Peterborough. One of Britain's leading steam railways is home for a wide range of British and European engines and carriages, both steam and diesel.

* Train galas in March, June & September
* Talking Timetable 01780 784404

**Location**
Off southbound A1 at Stibbington
between A47 & A605 junctions

**Opening**
Daily: 9am–4.30pm

**Admission**
Adult £10, Child £5, Concs £7.50

**Contact**
Wansford Station, Stibbington,
Peterborough PE8 6LR

t 01780 784444
w nvr.org.uk
e nvrorg@aol.com

## 352 Peterborough

# Peterborough Cathedral

1 hr   All year

Today's cathedral is essentially the third abbey, founded in 1118 (the first dates from 655). It suffered badly at the hands of Oliver Cromwell, but many of its unique features remain to be admired today. The west front is a remarkable example of medieval architecture.

* Interior remains largely unchanged through 800 years
* Burial place for two queens

**Location**
Follow signs for city centre from
junction 16/17 of A1M

**Opening**
Daily: Mon–Fri 9am–6.30m, Sat
9am–5pm, Sun 7.30am–5pm

**Admission**
Free, donations encouraged

**Contact**
Little Prior's Gate, Minster Precincts,
Peterborough PE1 1XS

t 01733 355315
w peterborough-cathedral.org.uk
e a.watson@peterborough-cathedral.
org.uk

## 353 Royston

# Wimpole Estate

3 hrs+     Mar–Nov

First built in 1643 and much altered by subsequent owners, Wimpole has developed into the largest country house in Cambridgeshire. The 360 acres of beautiful parkland is the product of four celebrated designers including Capability Brown.

* Parkland includes restored lakes & Gothic tower
* Walks available through woodland & rolling hills

**Location**
8 miles SW of Cambridge
junction 12 off M11/junction 9 off A1(M)

**Opening**
Mar–Nov Sat–Wed (Fri during Aug &
Good Friday) 1pm–5pm (Bank Hol Mons
11am–5pm) *Farm & Gardens* Sat–Wed
10.30am–5pm

**Admission**
*Hall* Adult £6.90, Child £3.40
*Farm & Gardens* Adult £5.40, Child £3.40

**Contact**
Wimpole Hall, Arrington,
Royston SG8 0BW
t  01223 206000
w  wimpole.org
e  wimpolehall@nationaltrust.org.uk

## 354 Sawtry

# Hamerton Zoo Park

2 hrs+     All year

Opened as a conservation sanctuary in 1990, Hamerton's 15 acres of parkland provide a safe home for a fascinating array of beautiful creatures from around the world, including many endangered species and some that are extinct in the wild.

* Spacious indoor-outdoor enclosures for monkeys
* Opportunity to handle many different animals

**Location**
On A14, turn off to B660 at junction 15
on to A1M follow signs

**Opening**
Daily: 10.30am–6pm (4pm in winter)

**Admission**
Please phone for details

**Contact**
Hamerton, nr Sawtry PE28 5RE
t  01832 293362
w  hamertonzoopark.com
e  office@hamertonzoopark.com

## 355 Wisbech

# Fenland & West Norfolk Aviation Museum

1 hr+     Mar–Oct

Home to a range of aircraft and artefacts, including the cockpit from one of the MiG-29s that collided at RAF Fairford in 1995, a Boeing 747 simulator, uniforms and militaria, and weapons and armour. On a fine day, explore the cockpits of some of the aircraft on display.

* Aircraft park
* Café and souvenir shop

**Location**
Follow brown tourist signs from A47
Wisbech bypass; or take old B198 to
King's Lynn from Wisbech and
museum is ½ mile from bypass

**Opening**
Mar–Oct weekends & Bank Hols
9.30am–5pm (4pm in Mar & Oct)

**Admission**
Adult £1.50,  Child & Concs 75p

**Contact**
Old Lynn Road, West Walton,
Wisbech PE14 7DA
t  01945 461771
w  fawnaps.co.uk
e  bill@wwelbourne.freeserve.co.uk

## 356  Castle Hedingham

# Colne Valley Railway

2 hrs+   Mar–Oct

Take a ride on a period country railway with a pretty line, relocated station buildings, signal boxes and bridges all lovingly restored and rebuilt. A large collection of vintage steam and diesel engines, carriages and wagons are available to explore.

* Seven steam engines & 40 carriages & wagons
* Colne Valley Farm Park

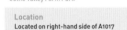

**Location**
Located on right-hand side of A1017
1 mile from Castle Hedingham

**Opening**
Please phone for details or check the website

**Admission**
Adult £6, Child £3, Concs £5

**Contact**
Yeldham Road, Castle Hedingham
CO9 3DZ

t  01787 461174
w  colnevalleyrailway.co.uk
e  info@colnevalleyrailway.co.uk

## 357  Chelmsford

# Chelmsford Museum & Essex Regiment Museum

1 hr+   All year

The museum is set in a Victorian mansion where visitors may follow the story of Chelmsford from the Ice Ages, via the Roman town, to the present day. See the superb Essex Regiment Museum housing many military artefacts as well.

* Bright & colourful Victorian pottery from Hedingham
* Period dress & room settings

**Location**
In Oaklands Park, off Moulsham Street

**Opening**
Daily: Mon–Sat 10am–5pm
Sun 2pm–5pm (winter 1pm–4pm)

**Admission**
Free, donations welcomed

**Contact**
Oaklands Park,
Chelmsford CM2 9AQ

t  01245 615100
w  chelmsfordmuseums.co.uk
e  oaklands@chelmsfordbc.gov.uk

## 358  Chelmsford

# RHS Garden Hyde Hall

3 hrs   All year

Some 40 years of work has transformed a windswept hill with just six mature trees, to the present-day garden of 24 acres. It contains the National Collection of viburnum and an attractive garden of 8 acres including woodland and a large collection of modern roses.

* Rope walk of climbing & pillar roses
* Ornamental ponds with lilies & fish

**Location**
From Rettendon follow flower signs

**Opening**
Daily: Oct–Mar 10am–dusk;
Apr–Sep 10am–6pm

**Admission**
Adult £5, Child £1

**Contact**
Rettendon,
Chelmsford CM3 8ET

t  01245 400256
w  rhs.org.uk/gardens/hydehall
e  hydehall@rhs.org.uk

## 359  Colchester

# Beth Chatto Gardens

      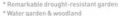

2 hrs+   All year

These gardens began in 1960 when the site was an overgrown wasteland between two farms. Faced with difficult conditions and with dry and damp soil in both sun and shade, the owners have put into practice what is now referred to as ecological gardening.

* Remarkable drought-resistant garden
* Water garden & woodland

**Location**
Located on A133. Approximately 4 miles E of Colchester and ¼ mile E of Elmstead Market

**Opening**
Mar–Oct Mon–Sat 9am–5pm;
Nov–Feb Mon–Fri 9am–4pm

**Admission**
Adult £4, Child free

**Contact**
Elmstead Market, Colchester CO7 7DB

t  01206 822007
w  bethchatto.co.uk
e  info@bethchatto.fsnet.co.uk

## 360 Colchester

# Colchester Castle Museum

2 hrs    All year

The museum covers 2,000 years of the most important events in British history. Once the capital of Roman Britain, Colchester has experienced devastation by Boudicca, invasion by the Normans and a siege during the English Civil War.

* Year-round events that bring history to life
* 2250BC Dagenham idol

**Location**
Situated in Castle Park at the E end of the high street

**Opening**
Daily: Mon–Sat 10am–5pm,
Sun 11am–5pm

**Admission**
Adult £4.50, Concs £2.90

**Contact**
High Street, Castle Park, Colchester
CO1 1TJ

t 01206 282939 Minicom 01206507806
w colchestermuseums.org.uk
e museum@colchester.gov.uk

## 361 Colchester

# Colchester Zoo

6 hrs    All year

Colchester Zoo has some of the best cat and primate collections in Europe. See a white tiger eye to eye in White Tiger Valley, or get closer to the zoo's chimpanzees at Chimp World. Other enclosures include Penguin Shores and Lions Rock for African lions.

* Playa Patagonia – sealion underwater experience
* Tiger campaign earned a Platinum Certificate

**Location**
Take A1124 exit from A12

**Opening**
Daily: summer 9.30am–5.30pm
winter 9.30am–1 hr before dusk

**Admission**
Please phone for details or visit the website

**Contact**
Maldon Road, Stanway, Colchester
CO3 0SL

t 01206 331292
w colchester-zoo.co.uk
e enquiries@colchester-zoo.co.uk

## 362 Colchester

# High Woods Country Park

2hrs+    All year

This country park boasts areas of woodland, wetland, grassland and farmland. Numerous footpaths provide an opportunity to see a wide range of wildlife. A visitor centre houses exhibits of local history and natural history.

* Quality Assured Visitor Attraction

**Location**
Accessible from Mile End Road &
Ipswich Road, travelling N from
Colchester

**Opening**
Daily: Visitor centre 1 Apr–30 Sep
Mon–Sat 10am–4.30pm, Sun & Bank
Hols 11am–5.30pm; 1 Oct–31 Mar
weekends only 10am–4pm

**Admission**
Free

**Contact**
Turner Road
Colchester CO4 5JR

t 01206 853588
w colchester.gov.uk
e yvonne.cook@colchester.gov.uk

## 363 East Mersea

# Cudmore Grove Country Park

1 hr    All year

Cudmore Grove is at the eastern end of Mersea Island, with fine views across the Colne and Blackwater estuaries. Walk the sea wall, explore the shore and watch for wildlife. Behind the sandy beach is a tranquil area of cliff top and grassland.

\* Wildside walk & bird hides
\* Ranger-led guided walks available by request

**Location**
Take B1025 S of Colchester & Mersea Island. Take left-hand fork to East Mersea – signed

**Opening**
Daily: 8am–dusk

**Admission**
£1 per hour per car, £2 per day per car

**Contact**
Bromans Lane, East Mersea CO5 8UE
t 01206 383868
w essexcc.gov.uk
e cudmoregrove@essexcc.gov.uk

## 364 Halstead

# Hedingham Castle

½ hr+    Apr–Sep

This is one of the best-preserved Norman keeps in England. Built in 1140, it possesses four floors including a magnificent banqueting hall with a minstrels' gallery and Norman arch. It is approached by a Tudor bridge, built in 1496 to replace the drawbridge.

\* Woodlands & lake with a pretty C18 dovecote
\* 1920s bog garden contains camellias & azaleas

**Location**
Situated in Castle Hedingham, ½ mile from A1017 between Cambridge & Colchester

**Opening**
Apr–Sep Sun 10am–5pm

**Admission**
Adult £4.50, Child £3.50, Concs £4

**Contact**
Halstead CO9 3DJ
t 01787 460261
w hedinghamcastle.co.uk
e hedinghamcastle@aspects.net.co.uk

## 365 Pitsea

# The Motorboat Museum

2 hrs+    All year

This museum is devoted to the history and evolution of sports and leisure motorboats, with more than 30 exhibits of motorboats from 1873 to today. From state-of-the-art offshore powerboats to the early days of steamers, trace the history of these wonderful craft.

* New 2005 model boat pond
* Carstais Collection

| Location | Contact |
|---|---|
| Well signed from Pitsea | Wat Tyler Country Park, Basildon SS16 4UH |
| Opening | t 01268 550077 |
| Thu-Mon 10am–4.30pm, daily during school hols | w motorboatmuseum.org.uk |
| Admission | |
| Free | |

## 366 Saffron Walden

# Audley End House & Gardens

3 hrs+    Mar–Oct

The house was built by the first Earl of Suffolk, Lord Treasurer to James I, on the scale of a great royal palace. Parts of the house were demolished in the early C18 and what remains is one of the most significant Jacobean houses in England.

* Historic kitchen & dry laundry
* Landscaped garden walks

| Location | Admission |
|---|---|
| 1 mile W of Saffron Walden on B1383 (M11 exits 8 and 9, northbound only, and 10) | Adult £8.50, Child £4.30, Concs £6.40 |
| | Contact |
| Opening | Saffron Walden CB11 4JT |
| Mar–Oct Wed–Sun 10am–6pm | t 01799 522399 |
| | w english-heritage.org.uk |

## 367 Saffron Walden

# Mole Hall Wildlife Park

2 hrs    Easter–Oct

This family-owned wildlife park was first opened to the public in 1963 and has continued to grow. The collection of animals and birds contains many exotic species including otters, primates including chimpanzees, owls, birds and many more.

* Tropical butterfly pavilion
* Animal adoption scheme

| Location | Contact |
|---|---|
| Signed from B1383 & junction 8 of M11 | Widdington, nr Saffron Walden CB11 3SS |
| Opening | t 01799 540400 |
| Daily: Easter–Oct 10.30am–6pm (dusk in winter months) | w molehall.co.uk |
| | e enquiries@molehall.co.uk |
| Admission | |
| Adult £5.80, Child £4, Concs £4.50 | |

## 368 Stansted

# Mountfitchet Castle & Norman Village

2 hrs    Mar–Nov

This is a Norman motte and bailey castle and village, reconstructed on its original ancient site. A vivid exhibition of village life at the time of the Norman Conquest includes houses, a seige tower and a church. Computerised figures give historical information.

* Iron Age fort, Roman, Saxon & Viking settlements

| Location | Contact |
|---|---|
| 2 miles from junction 8 of M11 | Stansted CM24 8SP |
| Opening | t 01279 813237 |
| Daily: Mar–Nov 10am–5pm | w mountfitchetcastle.com |
| | e info@mountfitchetcastle.com |
| Admission | |
| Adult £6, Child £5, Concs £5.50 | |

369  Tilbury

# Tilbury Fort

2 hrs     All year

The finest surviving example of C17 military engineering in England, Tilbury Fort remains largely unaltered. Today exhibitions, the powder magazine and bunker-like casemates, demonstrate how the fort protected the city. Visitors can even fire an anti-aircraft gun.

* Regular military collectors fairs
* Designed by Charles II's chief engineer

| Location | Admission |
|---|---|
| Located 5 miles E of Tilbury off A126 | Adult £3.30, Child £1.70, Concs £2.50 |
| **Opening** | **Contact** |
| Daily: Apr–Sep 10am–6pm; | Tilbury, RM18 7NR |
| Oct–Nov 10am–5pm; | t  01375 858489 |
| Dec–Apr Wed–Sun 10am–4pm | w  english-heritage.org.uk |

370  Waltham Abbey

# Royal Gunpowder Mills

3 hrs+    Apr–Sep

The world of explosives is uncovered with a range of interactive and static displays following the trail back to the C17. This unique museum traces the evolution of gunpowder technology and reveals the impact it had on the history of Great Britain.

* Muskets, rifles, pistols and machine guns
* Munitionettes – photo exhibits of women workers in WWII

| Location | Contact |
|---|---|
| 1 mile from junction 26 of M25, A121 | Beaulieu Drive, Waltham Abbey EN9 1JY |
| **Opening** | |
| Sat, Sun & Bank Hols only 11am–5pm | t  01992 707370 |
| (last admission 3.30pm) | w  royalgunpowdermills.com |
| **Admission** | e  info@royalgunpowdermills.com |
| Adult £5.90, Child £3, Concs £4.70 | |

371  Barnet

# Museum of Domestic Design & Architecture

1 hr      All year

The museum (MoDA) houses one of the most important and comprehensive collections of late C19 and C20 decorative design for the home. MoDA offers a wide-ranging programme alongside its permanent exhibition, Exploring Interiors: Decoration of the Home 1900–1960.

* Wallpapers & textiles from 1870s to 1960s
* Crown Wallpaper archive

| Location | Contact |
|---|---|
| *Underground* Oakwood, from where there is a university shuttle bus. Or M25 junction 24 on to A111 for 3 miles | Middlesex University, Cat Hill, Barnet EN4 8HT |
| **Opening** | t  020 8411 5244 |
| Tue–Sat 10am–5pm, Sun 2pm–5pm | w  moda.mdx.ac.uk |
| **Admission** | e  moda@mdx.ac.uk |
| Free, donations welcomed | |

## 372 Berkhamsted

# Ashridge Estate

1 hr+     All year

This estate, situated amidst 5,000 acres along the main ridge of the Chiltern Hills, offers a variety of picturesque walks, supporting a variety of wildlife in the commons, woodlands and chalk downland. The focal point is the Duke of Bridgewater Monument, erected in 1832.

\* Splendid views from Ivinghoe Beacon
\* Visitor centre with exhibition room

| Location | Admission |
|---|---|
| Between Northchurch & Ringshall just off B4506 | *Estate* Free *Monument* Adult £1.30, Child 60p |
| **Opening** | **Contact** |
| All year *Visitor centre* 1 Apr–mid-Dec 12noon–5pm | Ringshall, Berkhamsted HP4 1LT<br>t 01442 851227<br>w berkhamsted.info.co.uk<br>e ashridge@nationaltrust.org.uk |

## 373 Berkhamsted

# Berkhamsted Castle

2 hrs+     All year

Berkhamsted Castle is a good example of a motte and bailey castle where the original wooden defences were later rebuilt in stone. It consists of a large bailey and a motte to one side, on which there are traces of a stone tower. The only double-moated Norman castle in the UK.

\* Built in late C11 by Robert of Mortain
\* Further improvements were made by King John

| Location | Contact |
|---|---|
| Adjacent to Berkhamsted station | Berkhamsted HP4 1LJ |
| **Opening** | t 01442 871737 |
| Daily: Apr–Oct 10am–6pm; Nov–Mar 10am–4pm | w english-heritage.org.uk<br>e customers@english-heritage.org.uk |
| **Admission** | |
| Free | |

## 374 Broxbourne

# Paradise Wildlife Park

2 hrs+     All year

The park is a special place, with a relaxed and friendly atmosphere. It has a range of animals from monkeys to lions, zebra to tigers, cheetahs to camels. What makes it rare is the fact that you can get really close, meeting and feeding many of the animals.

\* Paradise lagoon, the brand-new paddling pool
\* Parrot Olympic training

| Location | Contact |
|---|---|
| Junction 25 of M25 on to A10, signed from Broxbourne | White Stubbs Lane, Broxbourne EN10 7QA |
| **Opening** | t 01992 470490 |
| Daily: Mar–Oct 9.30am–6pm; Nov–Feb 10am–5pm | w pwpark.com<br>e info@pwpark.com |
| **Admission** | |
| Adult £10, Child &Concs £7 | |

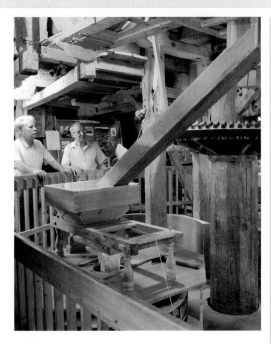

## 375 Hatfield

# Hatfield House

2 hrs+     Easter–Sep

This Jacobean house stands in its own great park and is the home of the Marquess of Salisbury. The state rooms are rich in paintings, furniture, fine tapestries and historic armour. Superb examples of Jacobean craftsmanship can be seen throughout the house.

\* Beautifully carved wooden grand staircase
\* Rare stained-glass window in private chapel

**Location**
Signed from junction 4 of A1(M).
Entrance opposite Hatfield station

**Opening**
Daily: Easter–Sep Wed–Sun & Bank
Hol Mon *House* 12noon–4pm *Gardens*
11am–5.30pm; Thu, tours of house and
garden available, phone for details

**Admission**
Adult £8, Child £4

**Contact**
Hatfield AL9 5NQ

t 01707 287010
w hatfield-house.co.uk
e s.jessup@hatfield-house.co.uk

## 376 Hatfield

# Mill Green Museum & Mill

1 hr+     All year

This museum is housed in what was for centuries the home of the millers who worked in the adjoining watermill. The watermill is fully restored and operational. It probably stands on the site of one of four Hatfield mills listed in the *Domesday Book*.

\* Waterwheel in action every day
\* Watch milling of organic flour on Tue, Wed & Sun

**Location**
Located in Mill Green, between
Hatfield and Welwyn Garden City

**Opening**
Tue–Fri 10am–5pm
Sat, Sun & Bank Hols 2pm–5pm

**Admission**
Free

**Contact**
Mill Green, Hatfield AL9 5PD

t 01707 271362
w hertsmuseums.org.uk/millgreen
e museum@welhat.gov.uk

## 377 Knebworth

# Knebworth House

3 hrs+    Apr–Sep

Knebworth House is a beautiful Gothic mansion set in 250 acres of parkland with formal gardens, a dinosaur trail, children's outdoor adventure playground, miniature railway, licensed tea room and gift shop.

* Constance Lytton fought for votes for women in 1900s
* The stately home of rock music

| Location | Admission |
|---|---|
| 29 miles N of London off junction 7 of the A1(M) at Stevenage | House Adult £9, Child & Concs £8.50 Gardens £7, £7, £7 |
| Opening | Contact |
| House & Exhibition 12noon–5pm Park & Gardens 11am–5.30pm Opening times vary, please phone for details | Knebworth SG3 6PY t 01438 812 661 w knebworthhouse.com e info@knebworthhouse.com |

## 378 Stevenage

# Fairlands Valley Park

4 hrs+    All year

This beautiful 120-acre park is home to an 11-acre lake used for a range of watersport courses; its waters are kept well stocked for anglers. There is a kids' area with paddling pool and play equipment. The park is also home to a wide selection of wildlife and wildfowl.

* Children's play area
* Paddling pools open during summer months

| Location | Contact |
|---|---|
| Situated on Six Hills Way, 1 mile E of Stevenage | Six Hills Way, Stevenage SG2 0BL |
| Opening | t 01438 353241 |
| Daily: 8am–dusk | w stevenage-leisure.co.uk/fairlands |
| Admission | e fairlands@stevenage-leisure.co.uk |
| Free | |

## 379 St Albans

# The Verulamium Museum

1 hr+    All year

Discover the life and times of a major Roman city at St Albans in the museum of everyday life in Roman Britain. Displays and activities include recreated Roman rooms, hands-on discovery areas and some of the best mosaics and wall plasters outside the Mediterranean.

* Excavation video & accessible collections
* Roman mosaic & hypocaust building new in 2005

| Location | Contact |
|---|---|
| Signed from St Albans | St Michaels, St Albans AL3 4SW |
| Opening | t 01727 751810 |
| Daily: Mon–Sat 10am–5.30pm, Sun 2pm–5.30pm | w stalbansmuseums.org.uk e museums@stalbans.gov.uk |
| Admission | |
| Adult £3.30, Child & Concs £2 | |

## 380 Tring

# Walter Rothschild Zoological Museum

1 hr+    All year

This collection, started in 1890 by Walter Rothschild, contains thousands of birds, mammals, reptiles, fish, insects and even dressed fleas. The Victorian setting gives it a unique atmosphere and it's a fascinating insight into the life of a classic English eccentric.

* Come face to face with a giant anaconda
* Part of the Natural History Museum since 1937

| Location | Admission |
|---|---|
| Tring is on A41, 12 miles W of Hemel Hempstead and 33 miles N of London. Museum is off Tring high street | Free |
| | Contact |
| Opening | Akeman Street, Tring HP23 6AP |
| Daily: Mon–Sat 10am–5pm, Sun 2pm–5pm | t 020 7942 6171 w nhm.ac.uk/museum/tring e tring-enquiries@nhm.ac.uk |

## 381 Welwyn
# Shaw's Corner

1 hr+        Mar–Oct

This Edwardian villa was the home of George Bernard Shaw from 1906 until his death in 1950. The rooms remain much as he left them, with many literary and personal effects and many touches evoking the individuality and genius of this great dramatist.

* Edwardian Arts & Crafts-influenced house
* Kitchen & outbuildings evocative of early C20 life

| Location | Admission |
|---|---|
| Junction 4 of A1(M) signed from B653 & B656 | Adult £3.80, Child £1.90 |
| | Contact |
| Opening | Ayot St Lawrence, |
| 18 Mar–29 Oct Wed–Sun & Bank Hols | Welwyn AL6 9BX |
| House 1pm–5pm | t 01438 820307 |
| Gardens 12noon–5.30pm | w nationaltrust.org.uk/shawscorner |
| | e shawscorner@nationaltrust.org.uk |

## 382 Aylsham
# Blickling Hall, Garden & Park

3 hrs+       Mar–Nov

One of England's great Jacobean houses, it is famed for its spectacular long gallery, superb library and fine collections of furniture, pictures and tapestries. The gardens are full of colour all year, and the extensive parkland features a lake and a series of beautiful walks.

* Superb Jacobean plaster ceiling in long gallery
* Formal woodland, parterre & wilderness garden

| Location | Admission |
|---|---|
| N of B1354, 1½ miles NW of Aylsham on A140 | Adult £7.30, Child £3.65 |
| | Gardens only £4.20, £2.10 |
| Opening | Contact |
| End Mar–Nov Wed–Sun | Blickling, Norwich NR11 6NF |
| Hall 1pm–4.30pm | t 01263 738030 |
| Gardens & Park 10.15am–5.15pm | w nationaltrust.org.uk |
| | e blickling@nationaltrust.org.uk |

## 383 Aylsham
# Bure Valley Railway

2 hrs+       All year

Bure Valley Railway is one of England's premier narrow-gauge railways serving enthusiasts, travellers and tourists. Its steam and diesel trains pass through scenery that is as varied, interesting and beautiful as any to be seen on a railway journey in England.

* Two main stations at Aylsham & Wroxham
* Easy to combine with cruise on Norfolk Broads

| Location | Admission |
|---|---|
| Aylsham station is situated mid-way between Norwich and Cromer on A140 | Please phone for details |
| | Contact |
| Opening | Norwich Road, Aylsham |
| Mar–Sep 10am–5.30pm | Norfolk NR11 6BW |
| plus school hols; | t 01263 733858 |
| please phone for details of other | w bvrw.co.uk |
| opening times | e info@bvrw.co.uk |

## 384 Blakeney

# Blakeney Point

3 hrs    All year

One of Britain's foremost bird sanctuaries, the point is a 3½-mile sand and shingle spit, noted for its colonies of breeding terns and for the rare migrants that pass through in spring and autumn. Both common and grey seals can also be seen.

* Information centre at Morston Quay provides further details
* Restricted access during main bird-breeding season

**Location**
Morston Quay, Blakeney and Cley are all off A149 Cromer–Hunstanton road

**Opening**
Daily: all reasonable times

**Admission**
Free

**Contact**
The Warden, 35 The Cornfield, Langham, Holt NR25 7DQ
t 01263 740480 (Apr–Sep)
  01263 740241 (Oct–Mar)
w nationaltrust.org.uk
e blakeneypoint@nationaltrust.org.uk

## 385 Dereham

# Roots of Norfolk

4 hrs+    Mar–Oct

Set in 50 acres of beautiful countryside, this exhibition of rural Norfolk life is housed in a Georgian workhouse dating from 1777. There is a traditional farm, worked by heavy horses. Explore village life, agriculture and the workhouse through hands-on displays.

* Recent £3.5 million refurbishment
* Family-friendly displays & adventure playground

**Location**
3 miles NW of Dereham. Follow signs

**Opening**
Daily: Mar–Oct 10am–5pm

**Admission**
Adult £6.60, Child £4.40, Concs £5.50

**Contact**
Gressenhall, Dereham NR20 4DR
t 01362 860563
w norfolk.gov.uk/museums
e gressenhall.museum@norfolk.gov.uk

## 386 Downham Market

# Denver Windmill

1–3 hrs    All year

Visit a working windmill set on the edge of the Fens. Recently restored, this unique set of buildings allows visitors to explore the story of windmilling in England and of the people who have lived and worked at the windmill since it was built in 1835.

* Tours to very top of windmill tower
* See mill working – wind & miller permitting

**Location**
Signed from A10

**Opening**
Daily: Apr–Oct Mon–Sat 10am–5pm,
Sun 12noon–5pm;
Nov–Mar Mon–Sat 10am–4pm,
Sun 12noon–4pm

**Admission**
Adult £3.50, Child £2, Concs £3

**Contact**
Denver, Downham Market PE38 0EG
t 01366 384009
w denvermill.co.uk
e enquiries@denverwindmill.fsnet.
  co.uk

387 Fakenham

# Thursford Collection

2 hrs    Easter–Sep

An Aladdin's cave of old road engines and mechanical organs of magical variety all gleaming with colour. Live musical shows feature nine mechanical pipe organs and Robert Wolfe stars in the Wurlitzer Show. Old farm buildings are transformed into a small village.

| Location | Contact |
| --- | --- |
| A148 between Fakenham & Holt | Thursford, Fakenham NR21 0AS |
| Opening | t 01328 878477 |
| 9 Apr–24 Sep Sun–Fri 12noon–5pm | w thursford.com |
| Admission | e admin@thursfordcollection.co.uk |
| Please phone for details | |

388 Great Yarmouth

# Tolhouse Museum

1 hr+    Apr–Oct

This C13 museum is one of the oldest civic buildings in the country. Once Great Yarmouth's courtroom and gaol, it illustrates aspects of local history, including the dungeons in which Victorian figures can be seen lurking in their cells. Brass rubbings can be made and costumes worn.

* Audio guide brings to life the stories & characters
* Museum of local history

| Location | Contact |
| --- | --- |
| Great Yarmouth, near Historic South Quay | Tolhouse Street, Great Yarmouth NR30 2SH |
| Opening | t 01493 858900 |
| Daily: 1 Apr–29 Oct Mon–Fri 10am–5pm, Sat & Sun 1.15pm–5pm | w museums.norfolk.gov.uk |
| | e yarmouth.museums@norfolk.gov.uk |
| Admission | |
| Adult £2.70, Child £1.50, Concs £2.30 | |

389 Holt

# Baconsthorpe Castle

1–2 hrs    All year

Reached via a maze of tiny lanes are the remains of this C15 castle, built by Sir John Heydon as a manor house and wool-processing factory during the Wars of the Roses. In the 1560s Sir John's grandson added the outer gate house, which was inhabited until the 1920s.

* English Heritage property

| Location | Contact |
| --- | --- |
| Off the A148 & B1149, ¾ mile N of village of Baconsthorpe, off an unclassified road. 3 miles E of Holt | Baconsthorpe, Holt |
| | t 01604 730325 |
| | w english-heritage.org.uk |
| Opening | |
| Daily: All reasonable times | |
| Admission | |
| Free | |

## 390 Hunstanton

# Hunstanton Sea Life Centre

1 hr+ All year

At this sanctuary you will see otters, penguins and more than 30 permanent displays all showcasing the diversity of life under the waves. The centre also provides a safe haven for sick, injured or orphaned seal pups that are cared for at the sanctuary.

* Penguin sanctuary, home to rare Humboldt penguins
* Marine Hospital new in 2005

**Location**
Take A140 from King's Lynn to Hunstanton. Follow signs

**Opening**
Daily: 10am–4pm
Times may vary during winter, please phone for details

**Admission**
Adult £7.75, Child £4.95, Concs £5.50

**Contact**
Southern Promenade, Hunstanton PE36 5BH

t 01485 533576
w sealsanctuary.co.uk
e hunstantonsealifecentre@
  merlinentertainments.biz

## 391 King's Lynn

# Sandringham

3 hrs Apr–Oct

The country retreat of Her Majesty The Queen and His Royal Highness The Duke of Edinburgh. Sandringham is a friendly and informal place and tours include ground-floor rooms within the house, a museum within the stable blocks and beautiful grounds.

* Nature trails & woodland walks in the Country Park
* Collection of vintage Royal motor vehicles

**Location**
Signed from King's Lynn

**Opening**
Daily: Apr–Sep
*House* 11am–4.45pm Oct 11am–3pm;
*Museum* 11am–5pm Oct 11am–4pm;
*Gardens* 10.30am–5pm Oct 11am–4pm

**Admission**
*House, Gardens & Museum* Adult £8, Child £5, Concs £6.50
*Gardens & Museum* £5.50, £3.50, £4.50

**Contact**
Estate Office, Sandringham PE35 6EN

t 01553 612908
w sandringhamestate.co.uk
e visits@sandringhamestate.co.uk

## 392 Little Walsingham

# Walsingham Shirehall Museum & Abbey Grounds

1 hr+ All year

Walsingham is one of the main centres for Christian pilgrimage in England. It has been an important site since 1061 and in 1153 an Augustinian priory was founded in the village. It was destroyed in 1538, but the remains and site of the original shrine can still be seen.

* Picturesque, tranquil grounds & snowdrop walks
* Shirehall Museum – unaltered hands-on courtroom

**Location**
4 miles NE of Fakenham off A149

**Opening**
Daily: 10am–4.30pm

**Admission**
Adult £3, Child & Concs £1.50

**Contact**
Common Place, Little Walsingham NR22 6BP

t 01328 820510/820259
e walsingham.museum@farmline.com

## 393 Norwich

# Felbrigg Hall, Garden & Park

2 hrs+    Mar–Oct

This handsome house owes much of its splendour to William Windham II. The interior was remodelled in the 1750s to provide a sumptuous setting for his art treasures. The state rooms contain superb C18 furniture and paintings, and there is an outstanding library.

* Orangery has a fine display of camellias in spring
* Walled garden, extensive parkland, lake & woods

| Location | Admission |
|---|---|
| In Felbrigg, 2 miles SW of Cromer, off B1346. Signed from A140 & A148 | Please phone for details |
| | Contact |
| Opening | Felbrigg, Norwich NR11 8PR |
| Mar–Oct Sat–Wed | t 01263 837444 |
| *Hall* 1pm–5pm | w nationaltrust.org.uk |
| *Gardens* 11am–5pm | e felbrigg@nationaltrust.org.uk |

## 394 Norwich

# Norwich Cathedral

1 hr+    All year

This is a magnificent Norman building. The nave roof bosses, illustrating the Bible from Creation to the Day of Judgement, and the Saxon bishop's throne, are unique features. The cloisters are the largest monastic cloisters in the country, and the spire the second highest.

* Nurse Edith Cavell buried here
* Famous collection of medieval carvings

| Location | Contact |
|---|---|
| Signed from city centre | 62 The Close, Norwich NR1 4EH |
| Opening | t 01603 218321/218300 |
| Daily: *summer* 7am–7pm | e vis-proffice@cathedral.org.uk |
| *winter* 7am–6pm | w cathedral.org.uk |
| Admission | |
| Free, donations welcomed | |

## 395 Norwich

# Sainsbury Centre for Visual Arts

1 hr    Spring–Dec

In an internationally renowned building designed by Norman Foster, discover the delights of the Sainsbury art collection. There are more than 1,200 items, spanning thousands of years and many cultures. Alongside African masks are works by Picasso and Bacon.

* Degas's *Little Dancer*
* Giacometti's *Standing Woman*

| Location | Contact |
|---|---|
| On university campus. Signed | University of East Anglia, Earlham Road, Norwich NR4 7TJ |
| Opening | t 01603 593199 |
| Tue–Sun 11am–5pm, Wed 11am–8pm | w scva.ac.uk |
| Please phone for details | e scva@uea.ac.uk |
| Admission | |
| Free | |

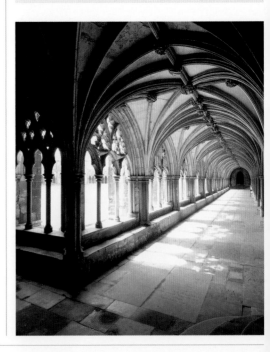

## 396 Sheringham

# The Muckleburgh Collection

2 hrs   Apr–Nov

This is a collection of military vehicles, many of which are in full working order. Further displays feature the Royal Flying Corps and the modern armed forces. Several aero engines and missiles are on show. Frequent tank demonstrations take place.

* The Meteor is on loan from the Imperial War Museum
* Gama Goat Rides – in a US Personnel Carrier

**Location**
Signed from A149 W of Cromer, 3 miles W of Sheringham

**Opening**
Daily: Apr–Nov 10am–5pm

**Admission**
Adult £5.50, Child £3, Concs £4.50

**Contact**
Weybourne Military Camp, Holt NR25 7EG

t 01263 588210
w muckleburgh.co.uk
e info@muckleburgh.co.uk

---

## 397 Swaffham

# Castle Acre Priory

1 hr   All year

The priory's ruins span seven centuries and include a C12 church with an elaborately decorated great west front that still rises to its full height, a C15 gatehouse and a porch and prior's lodging. Visit the recreated herb garden, growing both culinary and medicinal herbs.

* Regular events held throughout the year
* One of the first Cluniac priories in England

**Location**
¼ mile W of village of Castle Acre, 5 miles N of Swaffham

**Opening**
Daily: Apr–Sep 10am–6pm;
Oct–Mar Wed–Sun 10am–4pm

**Admission**
Adult £4.20, Child £2.10, Concs £3.20

**Contact**
Stocks Green PE32 2XD

t 01760 755394
w english–heritage.org.uk
e castleacre–priory@english–heritage.org.uk

---

## 398 West Runton

# Norfolk Shire Horse Centre

2 hrs+   Apr–Oct

See magnificent heavy shire horses working just as they did in days gone by. Take time to look around the rural museum and video show, see the small farm animals and the mares with their foals, and join in with feeding times.

* Displays twice daily
* Special events include blacksmith demonstrations

**Location**
Rail & bus services to West Runton

**Opening**
Apr–Oct Sun–Fri 10am–5pm;
closed Sat except Bank Hols

**Admission**
Adult £6, Child £4, Concs £5

**Contact**
West Runton, Nr Cromer NR27 9QH

t 01263 837339
w norfolk-shirehorse-centre.co.uk
e bakewell@norfolkshirehorse.fsnet.co.uk

## 399 Brandon

# High Lodge Forest Centre

8 hrs+    All year

This centre in the heart of Thetford Forest offers walks, cycle trails, cycle hire, an adventure playground, a ropes course, one of the largest mazes in Europe, and a giant sculpture trail. Special events include bird walks, a deer safari and family-fun walks.

| Location | Contact |
|---|---|
| Just off A11 on B1107 midway between Thetford & Brandon | Thetford Forest Park, Santon Downham, Brandon IP27 0TJ |
| Opening | |
| Daily: 9am–dusk | t 01842 815434 (High Lodge Centre) |
| Please phone for details | 01842 810271 (Forestry Commission) |
| Admission | w forestry.gov.uk |
| £4 per car | e e.anglia.fdo@forestry.gsi.gov.uk |

## 400 Bungay

# Norfolk & Suffolk Aviation Museum

2 hrs+    All year

The museum constitutes an impressive collection of aircraft and equipment. It also houses the Royal Observer Corps Museum, the 446th (H) Bomb Group Museum, the RAF Bomber Command Museum and the Air Sea Rescue and Coastal Command Museum.

* 40 aircraft within seven hangars
* Aircraft from before WWI to the present day

| Location | Contact |
|---|---|
| On B1062, off A143, 1 mile W of Bungay | The Street, Flixton NR35 1NZ |
| Opening | t 01986 896644 |
| Apr–Oct Sun–Thu 10am–5pm; | w aviationmuseum.net |
| Nov–Mar Tue Wed & Sun 10am–4pm; | e lcurtis@aviationmuseum.net |
| Closed 15 Dec–15 Jan | |
| Admission | |
| Free, donations welcomed | |

## 401 Bury St Edmunds

# Ickworth House

4 hrs+    Mar–Dec

Ickworth is an elegant Italianate house set amid spectacular English parkland. The central rotunda and curving wings were intended to house treasures collected from all over Europe. Today the state rooms display works by Titian, Velasquez and Gainsborough.

* Noted for its Georgian silver & Regency furniture
* Enchanting gardens & woodland walks

| Location | Admission |
|---|---|
| On A143, 2 miles S of Bury St Edmunds, signed from A14 | Please phone for details |
| | Contact |
| Opening | Bury St Edmunds IP29 5QE |
| House Mar–Sep 1pm–5pm; Oct–Nov 1pm–4.30pm closed Wed & Thu Nov–end Dec Sat & Sun 12noon–4pm | t 01284 735 270 |
| | w nationaltrust.org.uk |
| Gardens Daily: Opening times vary, please phone for details | e julia.vinson@nationaltrust.org.uk |

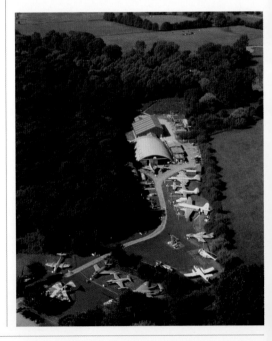

402 Bury St Edmunds

# Manor House Museum

1 hr+    All year

The museum, a Georgian town house in Bury St Edmunds's Great Churchyard, houses a superb series of collections. The displays feature some of the finest clocks and watches to be found anywhere in the world, and costumes and textiles from the C17 to the present day.

* Hear the polyphon longcase clock striking
* 1920s costume collection

| Location | Contact |
|---|---|
| Signed within Bury St Edmunds | 5 Honey Hill, Bury St Edmunds IP33 1RT |
| Opening | |
| Wed–Sun 11am–4pm | t 01284 757076/757074 |
| Admission | w stedmundsbury.gov.uk/manorhse |
| Adult £2.60, Child £2.10, Concs £2.10 | e manor.house@stedsbc.gov.uk |

---

403 Felixstowe

# Landguard Fort

1 hr    Apr–Oct

The remains of this fort, originally built during the C16, date back to the C18. Still standing are parts of the walls and casemate rooms within, dating from the fort of 1744 and later changes made during Queen Victoria's reign. It overlooks the Orwell Estuary.

* Some hoists for raising ammunition are still *in situ*
* Submarine minefield observation position

| Location | Admission |
|---|---|
| On Viewpoint Road, Landguard Point, off A14 | Adult £3, Child £1, Concs £2.50 |
| | Contact |
| Opening | 49 Looe Road, Felixstowe IP11 9QB |
| Apr daily 10am–5pm; | |
| May–Sep daily 10am–6pm; | t 01394 277767 |
| Oct daily 10am–5pm | w english-heritage.org.uk |

---

404 Framlingham

# Framlingham Castle

1 hr+    All year

This is a fine example of a late C12 castle. It has 13 hollow towers connected by a large curtain wall, 42 feet high and 8 feet thick (13 x 2.5metres), similar to those at Dover and Windsor castles. The castle has fulfilled a number of roles including fortress, prison, poorhouse and school.

* Walk along the impressive wall walk
* Explore the outer courts, moat & mere

| Location | Admission |
|---|---|
| In Framlingham on B1116 | Adult £4.20, Child £2.10, Concs £3.20 |
| | Contact |
| Opening | Framlingham, Woodbridge IP13 9BP |
| Daily: Apr–Sep 10am–6pm; | |
| Oct 10am–5pm; Nov–Mar 10am–4pm | t 01728 724189 |
| | w english-heritage.org.uk |

## 405 Ipswich

# Ipswich Transport Museum

1 hr   Mar–Nov

This museum has the largest collection of transport items in Britain devoted to just one town. Everything was either made or used in and around Ipswich. The collection, started in 1965, consists of around 100 major exhibits, and numerous smaller transport-related items.

\* Timetables, photographs, maps, tickets & uniforms
\* Varied programme of events as advertised

| Location | Contact |
|---|---|
| SE of Ipswich near junction 57 of A14 | Old Trolleybus Depot, Cobham Road, Ipswich IP3 9JD |
| Opening | t 01473 715666 |
| Mar–Nov Sun & Bank Hols 11am– 4pm; school hols Mon–Fri 1pm–4pm | w ipswichtransportmuseum.co.uk |
| Admission | e enquiries@ipswichtransportmuseum. co.uk |
| Adult £3, Child £2, Concs £2.50 | |

## 406 Leiston

# Long Shop Museum

1 hr+   Apr–Oct

The Long Shop was built in 1852 as Britain's first production line for steam engines. Traction engines, steamrollers, electric trolleybuses and even ammunition were also produced here. Learn how the Victorians worked and explore our industrial heritage.

\* Discover the amazing range of Garrett products
\* A collection of unique & fascinating exhibits

| Location | Contact |
|---|---|
| In town centre, off A12 at Saxmundham | Main Street, Leiston IP16 4ES |
| Opening | t 01728 832189 |
| Daily: Apr–Oct Mon–Sat 10am–5pm, Sun 11am–5pm | w longshop.care4free.net |
| Admission | e longshop@care4free.net |
| Adult £3.50, Child £1, Concs £3 | |

## 407 Long Melford

# Melford Hall

1 hr   Apr–Oct

One of East Anglia's most celebrated Elizabethan houses, little changed externally since 1578 and with a beautiful panelled banqueting hall. There is a Regency library, as well as Victorian bedrooms and good collections of furniture and porcelain.

\* Small collection of Beatrix Potter memorabilia
\* Garden contains a charming banqueting house

| Location | Admission |
|---|---|
| In Long Melford off A134, 14 miles S of Bury St Edmunds, 3 miles N of Sudbury | Adult £5, Child £2.50 |
| | Contact |
| Opening | Long Melford, Sudbury CO10 9AA |
| Apr Sat –Sun 2pm–5.30pm; May–Sep Wed–Sun 2pm–5.30pm; Oct Sat–Sun 2pm–5.30pm | t 01787 379228/376395 |
| | w nationaltrust.org.uk |
| | e melford@nationaltrust.org.uk |

## 408 Lowestoft

# Lowestoft Maritime Museum

1 hr+   Easter–Oct

The museum specialises in the history of the Lowestoft fishing fleet and early commercial activities, from the early days of sail, to steam and on to modern diesel vessels. Methods of fishing are also recorded, including the art of herring driftnet fishing.

\* Fine exhibition of evolution of lifeboats
\* Collection of shipwright's & cooper's tools

| Location | Contact |
|---|---|
| Under Lighthouse on Whaplode Road in Sparrow's Nest Park | Whapload Road, Lowestoft NR32 1XG |
| Opening | t 01502 561963 |
| Daily: May–10 Oct, 23–31 Oct & Easter hols 10am–5pm | |
| Admission | |
| Adult 75p, Child 25p, Concs 50p | |

## 409 Newmarket

# National Horseracing Museum

1 hr+    Apr–Oct

The story of the people and horses involved in racing from royal origins to Lester Piggott, Frankie Dettori and other modern-day heroes. Highlights include the head of Persimmon, a great Royal Derby winner in 1896, and the colourful jackets of 'Prince Monolulu'.

\* Gift shop well stocked with a range of unusual souvenirs
\* Minibus tours – behind the scenes at Newmarket

**Location**
In town centre, well signed

**Opening**
Daily: 11am–4.30pm (last admission 4pm), 10am–4.30pm on race days

**Admission**
Adult £4.50, Child £2.50, Concs £3.50

**Contact**
99 High Street, Newmarket CB8 8JH

t 01638 667333
w nhrm.co.uk
e museum@nhrm.freeserve.co.uk

## 410 Sudbury

# Gainsborough's House

1 hr    All year

This is the birthplace of Thomas Gainsborough RA (1727–88). The Georgian-fronted town house with attractive walled garden displays more of the artist's work than any other gallery. The collection is shown together with C18 furniture and memorabilia.

\* Varied exhibitions of contemporary art
\* Includes works by Hubert Gravelot & Francis Hayman

**Location**
In town centre

**Opening**
Mon–Sat 10am–5pm

**Admission**
Adult £3.50, Child £1.50, Concs £2.80

**Contact**
46 Gainsborough Street, Sudbury CO10 2EU

t 01787 372958
w gainsborough.org
e mail@gainsborough.org

## 411 Southwold

# Coastal Voyager

1 hr+ · All year

Hop aboard this 9-metre rigid inflatable for a short, high-speed, fun trip around Sole Bay or for a longer 3-hour trip, perhaps as far as Scroby Sands to see the seals. It is fully equipped with wrap-round seats, seatbelts and lifejackets.

\* Powered by a 400 horse-power engine
\* Suitable for individuals or groups

**Location**
Trips depart from Southwold Harbour

**Opening**
Please phone or visit the website for details

**Admission**
½-hr high-speed blast:
Adult £16, Child (under-13s) £9

**Contact**
6 Strickland Place,
Southwold IP18 6HN
t 01502 726050
w coastalvoyager.co.uk
e thrills@southwold.ws

## 412 Woodbridge

# Orford Castle

1 hr+ · All year

Originally a keep and bailey castle with a walled enclosure and a great tower, the building we see today was constructed by Henry II as a coastal defence during the C12. The unique polygon keep survives almost intact with three immense towers.

\* The building records are the earliest in the UK
\* 50 minute Audio tours

**Location**
In Orford on B1084, 20 miles NE of Ipswich

**Opening**
Daily: Apr–Sep 10am–6pm;
Oct 10am–5pm;
Nov–Mar 10am–5pm (closed Tue–Wed)

**Admission**
Adult £4, Child £2, Concs £3

**Contact**
Orford, Woodbridge IP12 2ND
t 01394 450472
w english-heritage.org.uk

## 413 Woodbridge

# Sutton Hoo

2–3 hrs · All year

Excavations here in 1939 revealed the burial chamber of a 90ft ship, filled with treasures including a warrior's helmet, weapons, armour, ornaments, tableware and a purse with 37 gold coins from c. AD620. The exhibition hall houses a full-size reconstruction of the chamber.

\* Most important archaeological find in the UK
\* Largest Anglo-Saxon ship ever discovered

**Location**
Off B1083 Woodbridge–Bawdsey road, signed from A12

**Opening**
Daily: 11am–5pm (school hols);
term-time please phone for details

**Admission**
Please phone for details

**Contact**
Woodbridge IP12 3DJ
t 01394 389700
w www.nationaltrust.org.uk
e suttonhoo@nationaltrust.org.uk

Peak District National Park, Derbyshire

# East Midlands

Derbyshire  Leicestershire  Lincolnshire
Northamptonshire  Nottinghamshire  Rutland

©English Heritage Photographic Library

414 Alfreton

# Wingfield Manor

1 hr+    All year

Mary Queen of Scots was imprisoned three times in this C15 manor house. Now an imposing ruin, the building was begun by Ralph, Lord Cromwell, Chancellor of England, around 1429. Over the entrance are carved twin money bags, symbolising Cromwell's status.

* Impressive undercroft of the hall, with vaulted roof
* The ITV series *Peak Practice* & Zeffirelli's *Jane Eyre* were filmed here

| Location | Admission |
|---|---|
| On B5035, 5 miles S of South Wingfield | Adult £3.30, Child £1.70, Concs £2.50 |
| **Opening** | **Contact** |
| Apr–Sep Thu–Mon 10am–5pm; Oct–Mar Sat–Sun 10am–4pm | Garner Lane, South Wingfield D55 7NH |
| | t 01773 832060 |
| | w english-heritage.org.uk |

415 Bakewell

# Haddon Hall

2 hrs+    Apr–Oct

Once home to William the Conqueror's illegitimate son, Peverel. Little now remains of the original building (1087) but major restoration work undertaken from 1370 onwards means visitors can now experience what this Tudor hall and beautiful gardens were like in their heyday.

* Annual children's weekend
* Film location for *Jane Eyre & Elizabeth*

| Location | Contact |
|---|---|
| 2 miles S of Bakewell on A6 | Bakewell, Derbyshire DE45 1LA |
| **Opening** | t 01629 812855 |
| Apr–Sep daily 10.30am–4.30pm; Oct Thu–Sun, 10.30am–4.30pm | w www.haddonhall.co.uk |
| | e info@haddonhall.co.uk |
| **Admission** | |
| Adult £7.25, Child £3.75, Concs £6.25 | |

416 Bolsover

# Bolsover Castle

1 hr+    All year

Bolsover Castle is a C17 house, built on the site of a Norman fortress, and is a wonderful place to meander and muse in. Sir Charles Cavendish, son of Bess of Hardwick, started the construction of the little castle in 1612.

* Symbolic & erotic wall-paintings restored in 1970s
* Venus fountain garden has been restored

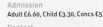

| Location | Admission |
|---|---|
| In Bolsover, on A632, 6 miles E of Chesterfield | Adult £6.60, Child £3.30, Concs £5 |
| **Opening** | **Contact** |
| Apr, Sep–Oct Thu–Mon 10am–5pm; May–Aug daily 10am–6pm; Nov–Mar Thu–Mon 10am–4pm | Castle Street, Bolsover S44 6PR |
| | t 01246 822844 |
| | w english-heritage.org.uk |
| | e bolsover.castle@english-heritage.org.uk |

417 Castle Donington

# Donington Grand Prix Collection

2–4 hrs    All year

Take a spin around the largest collection of Grand Prix cars and journey through motor sport history. Exhibits include a 1999 Ralf Schumacher Williams, a 1997 David Coulthard McLaren and the car in which Ayrton Senna won the 1993 European Grand Prix at Donington Park.

\* World's only complete collection of Vanwalls
\* Henry Seagrave's 1922 3-litre GP Sunbeam

| Location | Contact |
|---|---|
| M1 junction 23a/24, access from NW via A50 | Donington Park, Castle Donington DE74 2RP |
| **Opening** | t 01332 811027 |
| Daily: 10am–4pm | w doningtoncollection.com |
| **Admission** | e enquiries@doningtoncollection. co.uk |
| Adult £7, Child £2.50, Concs £5 | |

---

418 Castleton

# Blue John Cavern

1 hr    All year

An historic cavern containing the first known mined deposits of the Blue John mineral for which the area is famous. It was worked by the Romans more than 2,000 years ago. Tours take visitors through many colourful caves, including the crystallised and waterfall caverns.

\* Exhibition of C19 miners' working implements

| Location | Contact |
|---|---|
| 2 miles W of Castleton | Castleton S33 8WP |
| **Opening** | t 01433 620638/620642 |
| Daily: *summer* 9.30am–5.30pm | w bluejohn–cavern.co.uk |
| *winter* 9.30am–dusk | e lesley@bluejohn.gemsoft.co.uk |
| **Admission** | |
| Adult £7, Child £3.50, Concs £5 | |

419 Castleton

# Peak Cavern

1 hr    All year

Explore the mystery of the Great Cave and step into the unique world of Peak Cavern, with its unusual rock formations, eerie sounds of running water and echoes of a bygone age. The cavern's imposing entrance chamber is the largest natural cave entrance in the British Isles.

\* Riverside walk past historic miners' cottages
\* Guided tours & rope making demonstrations

| Location | Contact |
|---|---|
| On A6187, between Hathersage & Whaley Bridge | Peak Cavern Road, Castleton, Hope Valley S33 8WS |
| **Opening** | t 01433 620285 |
| Daily: 10am–5pm | w www.peakcavern.co.uk |
| **Admission** | e info@peakcavern.co.uk |
| Adult £6, Child £4, Concs £5 | |

## 420 Castleton

# Peveril Castle

1 hr    All year

Built shortly after the Norman Conquest of 1066 by one of King William's most trusted knights, the elegant tower of this stronghold still stands to its original height. The castle, perched high above the pretty village of Castleton, offers breathtaking views of the Peak District.

\* Some of the earliest herringbone masonry
\* Sir Walter Scott based one of his novels on the castle

| Location | Admission |
|---|---|
| On S side of Castleton, on A6187, 15 miles W of Sheffield | Adult £3, Child £1.50, Concs £2.30 |
| **Opening** | **Contact** |
| Apr, Sep–Oct daily 10am–5pm; May–Aug daily 10am–6pm; Nov–Mar Thur–Sun 10am–4pm | Market Place, Castleton S33 8WQ
t 01433 620613
w english-heritage.org.uk |

## 421 Crich

# The National Tramway Museum

3 hrs+    Mar–Dec

Visit the museum to see a variety of trams, including open, closed, double-deck, single-deck, horse-drawn, steam and vintage electric from all four corners of the globe. Electric trams also run through Period Street, and on to open countryside, giving panoramic views.

\* Exhibition hall houses impressive displays
\* Dramatic Tram at Night Experience

| Location | Admission |
|---|---|
| 8 miles from M1 junction 28 , via A38, A6, A61 & A52 | Adult £8.50, Child £4.50, Concs £7.50 |
| **Opening** | **Contact** |
| Daily: Mar–Nov 10am–5.30pm; Nov & Dec Sat–Sun 10.30am–4pm | Crich Tramway Village, Matlock DE4 5DP
t 01773 854321
w tramway.co.uk
e enquiry@tramway.co.uk |

## 422 Denby

# Denby Pottery Visitor Centre

1 hr+    All year

Admire and compare examples of Denby from early salt-glazed bottles and jars to the distinctive tableware of recent years. You can also see how Denby is made and have a go at painting a plate. There are extra activities for children during school holidays.

\* Watch free cookery demonstrations
\* Tours of the glass studio also available

| Location | Contact |
|---|---|
| Next to Denby Pottery on the B6179, off A38, 8 miles N of Derby | Derby Road, Denby nr Ripley DE5 8NX |
| **Opening** | t 01773 74099
w denbyvisitorcentre.co.uk
e visitor.centre@denby.co.uk |
| Daily: Mon–Sat 9.30am–5pm; Sun 10am–5pm | |
| **Admission** | |
| *Factory tour* Adult £4.95, Child& Concs £3.95 | |

# Derby Museum of Industry & History

1 hr     All year

Built on the site of one of the world's oldest factories, dating from 1702 and 1717, the museum tells the story of the industrial heritage and achievement of Derby and its people. There is a special emphasis on the development of Rolls-Royce aero engines and the railway industry.

\* On site of Derby's first silk mill
\* History of Midland Railway

**Location**
Off A6, near Derby Cathedral

**Opening**
Daily: Mon 11am–5pm,
Tue–Sat 10am–5pm,
Sun & Bank Hols 1pm–4pm
Please phone to confirm
holiday opening times

**Admission**
Free

**Contact**
Silk Mill Lane, off Full Street,
Derby DE1 3AF

t 01332 255308
w derby.gov.uk/museums

---

# Melbourne Hall & Gardens

2 hrs     Apr–Sep

An historic house and garden that was once the home of Prime Minister William Lamb, who as Lord Melbourne gave his name to the Australian city. It has interesting and extensive gardens that contain a wrought-iron arbour made around 1710 by Robert Bakewell of Derby.

\* Formal garden with yew tunnel
\* Best surviving example of work by London & Wise

**Location**
7 miles S of Derby

**Opening**
*House* Aug Daily: 2pm–4.15pm
except first two Mons
*Gardens* Apr–Sep Wed, Sat–Sun
& Bank Hols 1.30pm–5.30pm,

**Admission**
*House & Gardens* Adult £5.50,
Child £3.50, Concs £4.50
*Gardens* £3, £2, £3

**Contact**
Church Square, Melbourne DE73 1EN

t 01332 862502/864224
w melbournehall.com
e melbhall@globalnet.co.uk

---

# Royal Crown Derby Visitor Centre

2 hrs     All year

Tour the working factory and watch the production of tableware and giftware, from clay through to the finished hand-decorated product. The museum is full of treasures going back to 1750 and there are demonstrations of skills such as flower making, painting and gilding.

\* Working factory tour available on weekdays
\* Museum, demonstration studio & factory shop

**Location**
On A415, near Derby city centre

**Opening**
Daily: Mon–Sat 9.30am–4pm,
Sun 10.30am–4pm

**Admission**
Adult £2.95, Child & Concs £2.75
*Tour* Adult £4.95, Child & Concs £4.75

**Contact**
194 Osmaston Road, Derby DE23 8JZ

t 01332 712800
w royalcrownderby.co.uk
e enquiries@royalcrownderby.
co.uk

426  Matlock

# Chatsworth House

4–6 hrs    Mar–Dec

The 'Palace of the Peak' contains one of Europe's finest collections of treasures, displayed in more than 30 rooms, from the grandeur of the 1st Duke's hall and state apartments with their rich decoration and painted ceilings, to the C19 library and dining room.

* Kids' farmyard & woodland adventure playground
* Maze, rose, cottage & kitchen gardens

| Location | Admission |
|---|---|
| 8 miles N of Matlock, off B6012 | Please phone for details |
| Opening | Contact |
| Mid Mar–mid Dec: | Bakewell DE45 1PP |
| *House* 11am–4.30pm | t 01246 565300 |
| *Gardens* 11am–6pm | w chatsworth.org |
| | e visit@chatsworth.org |

427  Matlock Bath

# Masson Mills Working Textile Museum

1 hr+    All year

Sir Richard Arkwright built these mills as his showpiece on the banks of the River Derwent in 1783. Beautifully restored, Masson Mills house a working textile museum containing a unique and comprehensive collection of authentic historic working textile machinery.

* Internationally famous Grade II listed buildings
* Experience more than 200 years of industrial history

| Location | Contact |
|---|---|
| On A6, ½ mile S of Matlock Bath | 41 Derby Road, Matlock Bath DE4 3PY |
| Opening | t 01629 581001 |
| Daily: Mon–Fri 10am–4pm, Sat | w massonmills.co.uk |
| 11am–5pm, Sun 11am–4pm | |
| Admission | |
| Adult £2.50, Child £1.50, Concs £2 | |

428  Middleton by Wirksworth

# National Stone Centre

2 hrs+    All year

Deep in the heart of the Derbyshire Dales, this dramatic site is steeped in industrial history, but the centre tells the full story of stone. Through artefacts such as 330 million-year-old fossils and tropical reefs, it covers its history, the science and technology and its use in art.

* Gem panning
* Fossil rubbing

| Location | Contact |
|---|---|
| On B5035, S of Matlock, between | Porter Lane, Middleton by Wirksworth |
| Cromford & Carsington | DE4 4LS |
| Opening | t 01629 824833 |
| Daily: summer 10am–5pm | w nationalstonecentre.org.uk |
| winter 10am–4pm | e nsc@nationalstonecentre.org.uk |
| Admission | |
| *Site* **Free** *Discovery Centre* **Adult £1.80,** | |
| **Child 90p** | |

## 429  Swadlincote

# Beehive Farm Woodland Lakes

4–6 hrs    All year

Using specially laid-out trails, visitors can explore the beauty of this woodland landscape on foot or horseback. Alternatively, they can simply enjoy the atmosphere of the three tranquil fishing lakes – Horseshoe, Botany Bay and Jubilee.

* Woodland, meadow & wetland habitats
* Caravan & camping park

| Location | Contact |
|---|---|
| In Rosliston, near Burton upon Trent | Lullington Road, Rosliston, Swadlincote DE12 8HZ |
| Opening | t  01283 763981/763980 |
| Daily: 9.30am–5pm, Sun 9.30–4pm | w  beehivefarm-woodlandlakes.co.uk |
| Admission | e  info@beehivefarm-woodlandlakes.co.uk |
| Adult £2, Child £1 | |

## 430  Ashby-de-la-Zouch

# Ashby-de-la-Zouch Castle

1 hr+    All year

In the C15 Edward IV gave this property to Lord Hastings, who converted what was then a fortified manor house into a grand castle, adding a chapel and the Hastings Tower. Now partly ruined, the tower still soars to the great height of 80 feet.

* Wonderful views across Leicestershire
* The setting for jousting scenes in the film *Ivanhoe*

| Location | Contact |
|---|---|
| In Ashby-de-la-Zouch, 12 miles S of Derby, on A511 | South Street, Ashby-de-la-Zouch LE65 1BR |
| Opening | t  01530 413343 |
| Please phone for details | w  english-heritage.org.uk |
| Admission | e  customers@english-heritage.org.uk |
| Adult £3.20, Child £1.60, Concs £2.40 | |

431 Ashby-de-la-Zouch

# Conkers

4 hrs+     All year

Located at the heart of the national forest, Conkers offers a great mix of hands-on activities, from 4 indoor discovery zones for all ages to 23 outdoor activities, including lakeside walks, sculpture & nature trails, an assault course, train rides, playgrounds & water play.

* Visitor Attraction of the Year Finalist
* Adventure playground & assault course

| Location | Contact |
|---|---|
| 3 miles from Ashby-de-la-Zouch on B5003 | Rawden Road, Moira, nr Ashby-de-la-Zouch Leicestershire DE12 6GA |
| **Opening** | |
| Daily: *summer* 10am–6pm *winter* 10am–dusk | t  01283 216633 w  visitconkers.com e  info@visitconkers.com |
| **Admission** | |
| Adult £6.25, Child £4.25, Concs £5.25 | |

432 Coalville

# Manor House at Donington

1 hr+     Apr–Feb

Donington-le-Heath Manor House was built in the late C13 and renovated early in C17. Visitors can see restored rooms and displays on medieval life. The house is set in recently recreated C17-style gardens with herbaceous borders, herb gardens, an orchard and a maze.

* Re-enactments, hands-on displays & demonstrations
* Temporary exhibitions on a wide range of subjects

| Location | Admission |
|---|---|
| 1 mile S of Coleville, signed from M1 junction 22, on A50 | Free |
| **Opening** | **Contact** |
| Daily: Apr–Dec 11am–4pm; Jan–Feb Sat–Sun 11.30am–3pm | Donington-le-Heath, Coalville LE67 2FW |
| | t  01530 831259 w  leics.gov.uk/museums e  dlhmanorhouse@leics.gov.uk |

433 Coalville

# Snibston Discovery Park

6 hrs     All year

A popular museum, Snibston is situated on the site of a former colliery. It displays a rich collection of historic objects telling the story of transport, mining and quarrying, engineering and the fashion industry.
A visit includes a tour of the historic colliery buildings.

* Train ride along the newly restored colliery railway
* Sculpture trail

| Location | Contact |
|---|---|
| On A511, on edge of Coalville town centre | Ashby Road, Coalville LE67 3LN |
| **Opening** | t  01530 278444 |
| Daily: 10am–5pm; Closed in early Jan, please phone for details | w  leics.gov.uk/museums e  snibston@leics.gov.uk |
| **Admission** | |
| Adult £5.70, Child £3.60, Concs £3.90 | |

## 434 Desford

# Tropical Birdland

2 hrs+     All year

Created in 1982, this exotic bird lover's dream is set in beautiful surroundings and features more than 85 species of birds. You can walk through aviaries, visit the chick room, see spectacular free-flying birds, take a woodland stroll and visit the koi carp ponds.

\* Take tea with free-to-fly birds in the café
\* Boarding service for pet birds when you go on holiday

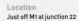

**Location**
Just off M1 at junction 22

**Opening**
Daily: 10am–5pm

**Admission**
Adult £5, Child &Concs £3.50

**Contact**
Lindridge Lane, Desford,
Leicester LE9 9N

t 01455 824603
w tropicalbirdland.co.uk
e info@tropicalbirdland.co.uk

## 435 Leicester

# Jewry Wall

1 hr     All year

One of Leicester's most famous landmarks, this rare example of Roman walling has survived for nearly 2,000 years. Originally part of the Roman public baths, it separated the exercise hall, which stood on the site of St Nicholas Church, from the rest of the baths.

\* Archaeologists discovered remains of Roman baths
\* Museum tells the story of Leicester from the Iron Age

**Location**
In St Nicholas Street, W of
St Nicholas Church

**Opening**
Sat 11am–4.30pm, Sun 1pm–4.30pm;
school hols Mon–Fri 11am–4.30pm

**Admission**
Free

**Contact**
St Nicholas Circle, Leicester LE1 4LB

t 0116 2254971
w english-heritage.org.uk

436 Leicester

# The National Gas Museum, Leicester

1 hr    All year

Established in 1977 to preserve the knowledge and skills of the gas industry during a period of rapid technological and economic change, the museum contains many artefacts collected during the conversion to natural gas and tells the story of gas from 1667 to the present day.

| Location | Admission |
|---|---|
| Off the A426, S of Leicester city centre | Free |
| **Opening** | **Contact** |
| Tue–Thu 12noon–4.30pm; closed Bank Hols | 195 Aylestone Road, Leicester LE2 7QH |
| Opening at other times by special arrangement | t  0116 2503190 |
| | w  gasmuseum.co.uk |
| | e  information@gasmuseum.co.uk |

437 Leicester

# National Space Centre

4–6 hrs    All year

This centre is dedicated to space science and astronomy. From its futuristic Rocket Tower discover the stories, personalities and technology of the past and present, and explore our current understanding of space and how it affects our future.

* Six themed galleries with hands-on activities
* Space theatre show

| Location | Contact |
|---|---|
| Just off A6, 2 miles N of city centre | Exploration Drive, Leicester LE4 5NS |
| **Opening** | t  0870 607 7223 |
| Tue–Sun 10am–5pm; school hols daily 10am–5pm | w  spacecentre.co.uk |
| | e  info@spacecentre.co.uk |
| **Admission** | |
| Adult £9.95, Child & Concs £7.95 | |

438 Leicester

# New Walk Museum

1 hr+    All year

The museum's permanent collections include the Ancient Egypt Gallery and the Natural History Room, with dinosaur skeletons and interesting fossils. It is also a major art gallery with a collection of German Expressionist and European art dating from the C15.

* Decorative arts gallery
* Wild space exhibition

| Location | Admission |
|---|---|
| Short walk from city centre | Free |
| **Opening** | **Contact** |
| Daily: Mon–Sat 10am–5pm | 53 New Walk, Leicester LE1 7EA |
| Sun 11am–5pm | t  0116 225 4900 |
| | w  leicester.gov.uk/museums |
| | e  museums@leicester.gov.uk |

439 Loughborough

# Great Central Railway

2 hrs+    All year

Mainline steam trains run every weekend throughout the year. Experience the famous expresses of the steam age. See freight and parcel train demonstrations or relax in the comfort of classic corridor trains, which are steam-heated in winter.

* Steam through the glorious Leicester countryside
* Driver's view of bridges, trains & hidden sidings

| Location | Admission |
|---|---|
| SE of Loughborough town centre | Adult £12, Child & Concs £8 |
| **Opening** | **Contact** |
| Trains run at weekends all year & midweek Jun–Aug, Please phone for details | Great Central Road, Loughborough LE11 1RW |
| | t  01509 230 726 |
| | w  gcrailway.co.uk |
| | e  booking_office@gcrailway.co.uk |

440 Lutterworth

# Stanford Hall

1 hr    Easter–Sep

Stanford, on the River Avon, has been the home of the Cave family since 1430. In the 1690s Sir Roger Cave commissioned Smiths of Warwick to pull down the old manor house and build the present hall, which is a superb example of their work.

\* Collection of Stuart royal portraits

| Location | Admission |
|---|---|
| Just off M1/M6 interchange, near A14 | House & Grounds Adult £5, Child £2<br>Grounds £3, £1 |
| Opening | Contact |
| Easter–Sep Sun & Bank Hols only<br>House 1.30pm–5.30pm<br>Grounds 12noon–5.30pm | Lutterworth LE17 6DH<br>t 01788 860250<br>w stanfordhall.co.uk<br>e enquiries@stanfordhall.co.uk |

441 Market Harborough

# Rockingham Castle

3 hrs    May–Sep

Built by William the Conqueror more than 900 years ago, the castle stands in beautiful grounds, with superb views across the Welland Valley. As well as a stronghold, it was an important seat of government. It is now home to the Saunders Watson family.

\* Winner of numerous education awards
\* Regular events including kite & Viking days

| Location | Contact |
|---|---|
| Off A6003, 1 mile N of Corby | Rockingham, Market Harborough,<br>Leicestershire LE16 8TH |
| Opening | t 01536 770240 |
| Easter Sun & Mon;<br>May–Sep Sun, Tue & Bank Hols<br>12pm–5pm | w rockinghamcastle.com<br>e estateoffice@rockinghamcastle.com |
| Admission | |
| Adult £7.50, Child £4.50, Concs £6.50 | |

442 Newtown Linford

# Bradgate Country Park

3 hrs+    All year

With 850 acres of heathland, small woods, herds of deer and the River Lin, this is Leicestershire's largest country park. It also includes the ruins of Bradgate House, the birthplace of Lady Jane Grey, who was famously Queen of England for just nine days.

\* Old John Tower folly

| Location | Admission |
|---|---|
| 3 miles from M1 junction 22,<br>signed on A50 | Park Free, charges for car park<br>Visitor centre Adult £1.20, Child 60p |
| Opening | Contact |
| dawn–dusk | Deerbarn Buildings, Newtown<br>Linford LE6 OHE<br>t 0116 2362713 |

## 443 Alford

# Claythorpe Watermill & Wildfowl Gardens

1 hr+  Easter–Oct

At the tip of the Lincolnshire wolds, Claythorpe is home to more than 500 animals and birds and visitors are able to experience their environment and habitat first hand. Visit the bygone exhibit area, which depicts the history of the site's milling and baking industry.

* Enchanted woods in which fairy tales come to life
* Otters, red squirrels & wallabies

**Location**
Signed off A16

**Opening**
Daily: Easter–Oct 10am–5pm
early & late season 10am–4pm

**Admission**
Adult £4.25, Child £3.25, Concs £3.75

**Contact**
Aby, nr Alford LN13 0DU

t 01507 450687
w claythorpewatermill.
  fsbusiness.co.uk
e info@claythorpewatermill.co.uk

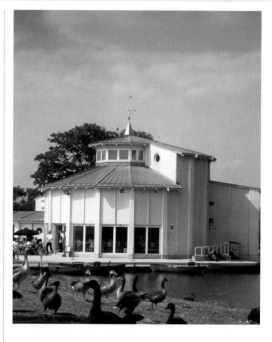

## 444 Boston

# Sibsey Trader Windmill

1 hr  All year

Built in 1877 in typical Lincolnshire style, to replace a small post mill, this is one of the few six-sailed mills remaining in England. It's not exceptionally tall, but the slender tower and surrounding flat landscape create the impression that it's bigger than it really is.

* Grade I listed working windmill
* Range of fresh, organic, stoneground flour available

**Location**
Off A16, 5 miles N of Boston, ½ mile W
of Sibsey

**Opening**
Apr–Sep Tue 10am–6pm,
& Sat–Sun 11am–6pm;
Oct–Mar Sat 11am–5pm;
Bank Hols 10am–6pm

**Admission**
Adult £2, Child £1, Concs £1.50

**Contact**
Frith Ville Road, Sibsey PE22 0SY

t 01205 750036/460647
w sibsey.fsnet.co.uk
e traderwindmill@sibsey.fsnet.co.uk

## 445 Cleethorpes

# Cleethorpes Humber Estuary Discovery Centre

1 hr  All year

Located on the boating lake, surrounded by fantastic views and friendly wildlife. The hands-on exhibition explores Cleethorpes's Victorian seaside history, the seaside and nature. The second-floor observatory has outstanding views over the Humber Estuary.

* On the edge of an important habitat

**Location**
From A180 & A16 follow signs for the
lakeside

**Opening**
Daily: Jan–Jun, Sep–Oct 10am–5pm;
Jul–Aug 10am–6pm;
Nov–Dec 10am–4pm

**Admission**
Adult £1.95, Child £1.30

**Contact**
Lakeside, Kings Road, Cleethorpes
DN35 0AG

t 01472 323232
w cleethorpesdiscoverycentre.co.uk
e lynne.emeny@nelincs.gov.uk

446  Colsterworth

# Woolsthorpe Manor

2 hrs    Mar–Oct

This C17 manor house was the birthplace and home of the scientist Sir Isaac Newton. Visitors can see his childhood scribblings on the walls. A gnarled old apple tree in the garden may be a descendant of the famous specimen that inspired Newton in his work.

* An interactive science discovery centre
* Replica of principle of differential calculus

**Location**
From A1 take B676 at Colsterworth roundabout, turn right at second crossroads & follow signs

**Opening**
5 Mar–27 Mar Sat–Sun 1pm–5pm;
1 Apr–30 Sep Wed–Sun 1pm–5pm;
1 Oct–30 Oct Sat–Sun 1pm–5pm

**Admission**
Adult £4.20, Child £2.10

**Contact**
23 Newton Way, Woolsthorpe-by-Colsterworth, nr Grantham NG33 5NR

t 01476 860338
w nationaltrust.org.uk
e woolsthorpemanor@national
  trust.org.uk

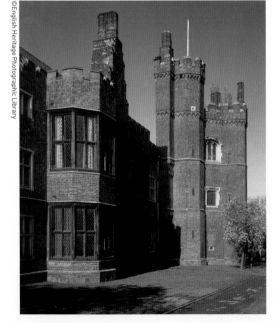

447  Gainsborough

# Gainsborough Old Hall

2 hrs    All year

This is a large C15 timber-framed medieval house, with a magnificent great hall and brick tower built on the site of an earlier C13 manor house. In 1483 Richard III stayed at the Old Hall and in 1541 Henry VIII was a guest.

* Special events throughout the year
* Lectures on first Tuesday of each month

**Location**
Town centre, off Parnell Street

**Opening**
Daily: Easter–Oct Mon–Sat 10am–5pm
Sun 1pm–4.30pm
Nov–Easter Mon–Sat 10am–5pm

**Admission**
Adult £3.25, Child /Concs £2.50

**Contact**
Parnell Street, Gainsborough
DN21 2NB

t 01427 612669
w lincolnshire.gov.uk/
  gainsborougholdhall
e gainsborougholdhall@
  lincolnshire.gov.uk

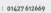

## 448  Grantham

# Belton House

6 hrs   Mar–Dec

A stunning example of Restoration country house architecture, Belton was built in 1685–88 and later altered by James Wyatt. The interiors contain fine plasterwork and wood carving, as well as collections of paintings, furniture, tapestries and silverware.

\* Formal gardens, orangery & landscape park
\* Edward VIII often came to stay before his abdication

**Location**
On A607 3 miles NE of Grantham, signed from A1

**Opening**
*House* Mar–Oct Wed–Sun 12.30pm–5pm
*Gardens* Mar–Oct Wed–Sun 11am–5.30pm;
Nov–Dec Fri–Sun 12noon–4pm

**Admission**
Adult £8, Child £4.50

**Contact**
Grantham NG32 2LS
t 01476 566116
w nationaltrust.org.uk
e belton@nationaltrust.org.uk

## 449  Grantham

# Grantham Museum

½ hr   All year

The museum interprets the archaeology and social history of Grantham and includes exhibits on famous residents such as Sir Isaac Newton and Margaret Thatcher, who has given many personal items to the museum. There is also a section on the Dambusters.

\* Dambusters mission planned here
\* 1851 Great Exhibition gold medal-winning doll

**Location**
Central Grantham

**Opening**
Mon–Sat 10am–5pm

**Admission**
Free

**Contact**
St Peter's Hill, Grantham NG31 6PY
t 01476 568783
w lincolnshire.gov.uk/ granthammuseum
e grantham.museum@ lincolnshire.gov.uk

## 450  Grimsby

# National Fishing Heritage Centre

2 hrs   All year

The centre tells the story of the area's fishermen, their boats and the waters they fished in. The dangers and hardships of life at sea are explained and there is a reconstruction of a 1950s sea voyage, complete with authentic aromas and a moving deck.

\* Collection of historic vessels in adjacent dock
\* Reconstruction of streets & alleys of 1950s Grimsby

**Location**
Next to Alexandra Dock, 2 min walk from town centre

**Opening**
Daily: Mon–Fri 10am–4pm,
Sat–Sun & Bank Hols 11am–3pm

**Admission**
Adult £6, Child £2, Concs £4

**Contact**
Alexandra Dock, Grimsby DN31 1UZ
t 01472 323345
w nelincs.gov.uk
e ann.hackett@nelincs.gov.uk

## 451  Lincoln

# Lincoln Medieval Bishop's Palace

1 hr   All year

Standing in the shadow of Lincoln Cathedral, the palace acted as the administrative centre of the largest diocese in medieval England and now forms an impressive bishop's house. Don't miss the East Hall, with its stunning vaulted undercroft, or the chapel.

\* Heritage garden
\* Panorama of the Roman, medieval & modern city

**Location**
S side of Lincoln Cathedral

**Opening**
Apr–Jun & Sep–Oct 10am–5pm;
Jul–Aug 10am–6pm;
Nov–Mar Thu–Mon 10am–4pm

**Admission**
Adult £3.60, Child £1.80, Concs £2.70

**Contact**
Minster Yard, Lincoln LN2 1PU
t 01522 527468
w english-heritage.org.uk

## 452 Lincoln

# Usher Gallery

1 hr+    All year

Set in the beautiful grounds of the Temple Gardens, the gallery houses a collection of fine and decorative arts. The original Usher bequest of clocks and watches, porcelain, silver, enamels, miniatures and coins remains the core of the gallery's permanent collection.

* From neo-classical sculpture to contemporary portraiture
* C17-C20 glass, including English drinking glasses

| Location | Contact |
|---|---|
| Lincoln city centre | Lindum Road, Lincoln LN2 1NN |
| **Opening** | t 01522 527980 |
| Daily: 10am–5pm | w thecollection@lincoln.museum |
| **Admission** | e thecollection@lincolnshire.gov.uk |
| Free, charges for special exhibitions | |

## 453 Scunthorpe

# Normanby Hall Country Park

4 hrs    All year

Set in the heart of tranquil North Lincolnshire, the 300 acres of country park provide the perfect day out for all the family. Learn about Lincolnshire's rich rural heritage in the fascinating Farm Museum or step back in time in the award-winning Victorian walled garden.

* Extensive woodland with a wealth of wildlife
* Adventure playground for younger children

| Location | Contact |
|---|---|
| 4 miles N of Scunthorpe on B1430 | Normanby, Scunthorpe DN15 9HU |
| **Opening** | t 01724 720588 |
| *Hall & Museum* Easter–Sep 1pm–5pm | w northlincs.gov.uk/normanby |
| *Gardens* All year 10.30am–5pm | e normanby.hall@northlincs.gov.uk |
| *Park* All year 9am–dusk | |
| **Admission** | |
| Adult £4.20, Child £2.10, Concs £3.80 | |

## 454 Skegness

# Gibraltar Point National Nature Reserve & Visitor Centre

2 hrs+    All year

This area of unspoilt coastline comprises sand dunes, saltmarshes and freshwater habitats for rare plants and animals, including seals, water voles and pygmy shrews. There are five bird-watching hides, a nature trail, an interpretation centre, and various activities and events.

* Area of international scientific interest
* Home to many rare plants, insects & animals

| Location | Admission |
|---|---|
| 1½ miles S of Skegness, signed from town centre | Free |
| **Opening** | **Contact** |
| *Reserve* daily 10.30am–dusk | Gilbraltar Road, Skegness PE24 4SU |
| *Visitor centre* May–Oct daily 10.30am–4pm; | t 01507 526667 |
| Nov–Apr Sat–Sun & Bank Hols 10.30am–4pm | w lincstrust.org.uk |
| | e info@lincstrust.co.uk |

## 455 Skegness

# Skegness Natureland Seal Sanctuary

2 hrs    All year

The sanctuary houses seals, penguins and tropical birds. There are reptiles in a tropical house and a display of free-flying tropical butterflies. Natureland is well known for rescuing abandoned seal pups and visitors can view the hospital unit and large seascape pool.

\* Family Attraction of the Year 2004
\* Underwater viewing pool

| Location | Contact |
|---|---|
| Signed from town centre | North Parade, Skegness PE25 1DB |
| **Opening** | t 01754 764345 |
| Daily: Jun–Sep 10am–5pm; | w skegnessnatureland.co.uk |
| Oct–May 10am–4pm | e natureland@fsbdial.co.uk |
| **Admission** | |
| Adult £5.20, Child £3.40, Concs £4.15 | |

## 456 Spalding

# Baytree Garden Centre & Owl Centre

2 hrs+    All year

Set in 16 acres, this garden centre and nursery has something for all gardeners, including bulbs, plants, pets and aquatics. The centre is also home to more than 100 owls and birds of prey, including very rare Mexican striped owls. There are regular flying displays.

\* Absorbing interactive experience
\* Visit tropical owls in the Hot House

| Location | Contact |
|---|---|
| On main A151 at Weston between | High Road Weston, Spalding, |
| Spalding & Holbeach | Lincolnshire PE12 6JU |
| **Opening** | t Garden Centre 01406 370242 |
| Please phone for details | Owl Centre 01406 372840 |
| **Admission** | w baytree-gardencentre.com |
| Please phone for details | e info@baytree-gardencentre.com |

## 457 Spalding

# The Butterfly & Wildlife Park

4hrs    Mar–Oct

Set in the heart of the Fens, the park has a tropical house, a reptile area with crocodiles and snakes, a creepy-crawlie house and an ant room. Outdoor attractions include a birds of prey centre that runs twice-daily flying displays, an animal centre and an adventure playground.

\* Quality Assured Visitor Attraction
\* Lincolnshire Family Attraction of the Year 2003

| Location | Contact |
|---|---|
| Signed off A17 at Long Sutton | Long Sutton, Spalding |
| **Opening** | PE12 9LE |
| Daily: end Mar–end Oct from 10am | t 01406 363833 |
| Please phone for details | w butterflyandwildlifepark.co.uk |
| **Admission** | e butterflypark@hotmail.com |
| Please phone for details | |

## 458 Stamford

# Burghley House

3 hrs    Mar–Oct

Built between 1555 and 1587 by William Cecil, Lord Treasurer to Elizabeth I, Burghley was based on designs of other great houses of the period, but has European influences. Externally, it is largely as it was when completed by Cecil's masons.

\* Paintings include work by John Frederick Herring
\* Sculpture park

| Location | Contact |
|---|---|
| 1½ miles from Stamford, well signed | Stamford PE9 3JY |
| **Opening** | |
| *House* Mar–Oct Sun–Thur 11am–5pm; | t 01780 752451 |
| *Sculpture Park* Sun–Thur; 10am–5pm | w burghley.co.uk |
| | e burghley@burghley.co.uk |
| **Admission** | |
| Adult £8.20, Child £3.70, Concs £7.20 | |

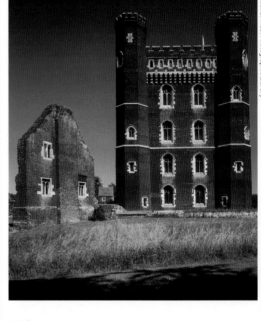

## 459 Spilsby

# Lincoln Aviation Heritage Centre

4 hrs    All year

This aircraft museum is based on a 1940s bomber airfield and has a number of exhibits, ranging from the original control tower and war time blast shelter to Barnes Wallis's bouncing bomb and squadron and airfield photographs.

\* Avro Lancaster bomber NX611 Just Jane
\* RAF Escaping Society

| Location | Contact |
|---|---|
| On A155, between Revesey & | East Kirkby Airfield, nr Spilsby |
| East Kirkby | PE23 4DE |
| **Opening** | |
| Easter–Oct Mon–Sat 9.30am–5pm; | t 01790 763207 |
| Nov–Easter Mon–Sat 10am–4pm | w lincsaviation.co.uk |
| | e enquiries@lincsaviation.co.uk |
| **Admission** | |
| Adult £6.50, Child £2, Concs £5.50 | |

## 460 Tattershall

# Tattershall Castle

1 hr    Mar–Dec

A large medieval fortified and moated redbrick tower, built for Ralph Cromwell, Lord Treasurer of England. The building was restored by Lord Curzon in 1911–14 and contains four great chambers with enormous Gothic fireplaces, tapestries and brick vaulting.

\* Spectacular views from the battlements

| Location | Admission |
|---|---|
| On S side of A153, 15 miles NE of | Adult £4, Child £2 |
| Sleaford, 10 miles SW of Horncastle | **Contact** |
| **Opening** | Tattershall, Lincoln LN4 4LR |
| Apr–Oct Mon–Wed & Sat–Sun | t 01526 342543 |
| 11am–5pm; | w nationaltrust.org.uk |
| Mar, Nov–Dec Sat–Sun 12noon–4pm | e tattershallcastle@nationaltrust. |
| | org.uk |

461 Althorp

# Althorp House

4 hrs    Jul–Sep

The home of the Spencer family since 1508. The park came to world attention on 6 September 1997, when Diana, Princess of Wales was laid to rest there. See her final resting place on the island in the Round Oval, surrounded by her family's ancestral heritage.

* Magnificent Palladian stable block for 100 horses
* One of the world's finest collections of portraiture

**Location**
7 miles W of Northampton off A428.
Clearly signed from Junction 16 of M1

**Opening**
Jul–Sep 11am–5pm;
Aug 31 closed

**Admission**
Adult £12, Child £6, Concs £10

**Contact**
The Stables, Althorp
Northampton NN7 4HQ
t 01604 770107
w althorp.com
e mail@althorp.com

462 Brixworth

# Brixworth Country Park

2 hrs+    All year

The park has many facilities including a café, cycle hire, play area, sensory garden and waymarked trails. It is now the main gateway to Pitsford Water and the 10km safe walking/cycling route called the Pitsford Water Trail. The park is also linked with the Brampton Valley Way.

* Take a walk along our sculpture trail
* Watch birds from our bird hide

   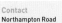

**Location**
Close to Brixworth Village & 7 miles N of Northampton on A508 Northampton –Market Harborough road

**Opening**
Daily: dawn–dusk

**Admission**
Free *Car Park* £1.20 per hour, £2 all day

**Contact**
Northampton Road
Brixworth NN6 9DG
t 01604 883920
w explorenorthamptonshire.co.uk
e brixworth@northamptonshire.gov.uk

463 Corby

# Deene Park

2 hrs    Jun–Aug

Deene Park is a largely C16 house incorporating a medieval manor. It's built around a courtyard and had important rooms added during the reign of George III. It was the seat of the 7th Earl of Cardigan, who led the charge of the Light Brigade at Balaklava in 1854.

* Crimean War exhibition of uniforms & memorabilia
* Beautiful gardens & parkland

**Location**
6 miles NE of Corby, off A43

**Opening**
Jun–Aug Sun & Bank Hols 2pm–5pm

**Admission**
Adult £6.50, Child £3, Concs £6

**Contact**
Corby NN17 3EW
t 01780 450278
w deenepark.com
e admin@deenepark.com

464 Corby

# Kirby Hall

1–2 hrs    All year

Featuring decorative carving and ornate gardens fit for a queen, Kirby Hall is one of the great Elizabethan houses, built in the hope of a royal visit. The Great Hall and state rooms have recently been refitted and redecorated to authentic C17 and C18 designs.

* Elizabethan festivals

**Location**
On an unclassified road off A43,
4 miles NE of Corby

**Opening**
24 Mar–30 Jun Thurs–Mon 10am–5pm;
1 Jul–31 Aug daily 10am–6pm;
1 Sep–31 Oct Thurs–Mon 10am–5pm;
1 Nov–31 Mar Thurs–Mon 10am–4pm

**Admission**
Adult £4.30, Child £2.20, Concs £3.20

**Contact**
Kirby Hall Deene, nr Corby
NN17 5EN
t 01536 203230
w english-heritage.org.uk

465 Cottesbrooke

# Cottesbrooke Hall & Gardens

2 hrs+    May–Sep

An architecturally magnificent Queen Anne house with a renowned picture collection, featuring sporting and equestrian subjects. Other collections include fine furniture and porcelain. Cottesbrooke is reputed to be the model for Jane Austen's Mansfield Park.

* HHA/Christie's Garden of the Year 2000
* Guided tours of the house available

**Location**
At A14 junction 1 head S on A5199, signed for Cottesbrooke

**Opening**
May–Jun, Wed–Thu & Bank Hols, 2pm–5.30pm;
Jul–Sep, Thu & Bank Hols 2pm–5.30pm

**Admission**
*Hall & Gardens* Adult £7.50, Child £3.50, Concs £6
*Gardens* £5, £2.50, £4

**Contact**
Cottesbrooke, Northampton NN6 8PF
t 01604 505808
w cottesbrookehall.co.uk
e enquiries@cottesbrooke.co.uk

466 Daventry

# Canons Ashby House

1 hr+    Apr–Oct

Constructed in the mid-C16, this charming house has survived substantially unaltered since 1710. The interior contains wall paintings and Jacobean plasterwork, with rich panelling in the Winter Parlour. Edward Dryden's formal gardens have been restored.

* Remains of an Augustinian priory
* Orchard containing varieties of typical C16 apple trees

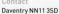

**Location**
Between Northampton & Banbury

**Opening**
Apr–Sep Sat–Wed 1pm–5pm;
Oct Sat–Wed 12noon–4pm

**Admission**
*House* Adult £5.80, Child £2.90
*Gardens* £2

**Contact**
Daventry NN11 3SD
t 01327 860044
w nationaltrust.org.uk
e canonsashby@nationaltrust.org.uk

467 Kettering

# Rushton Triangular Lodge

1 hr    Apr–Oct

This triangular building was designed and built by Sir Thomas Tresham in 1593 as a testament to his Catholicism, for which he had been imprisoned. Consequently, the lodge is emblazoned with references to the number three and the Holy Trinity.

* Colourful house adorned with dates & emblems
* Three windows, three floors, three roof gables

**Location**
1 mile W of Rushton, on A6, on unclassified road 3 miles from Desborough

**Opening**
Apr–Oct Thur–Mon 10am–5pm

**Admission**
Adult £2.30, Child £1.20, Concs £1.70

**Contact**
Rushton, Kettering NN14 1RP
t 01536 710761
w english-heritage.org.uk

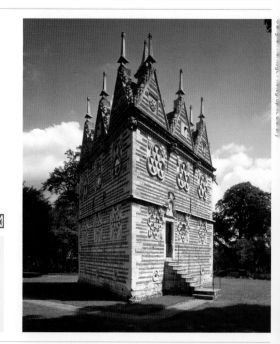

## 468 Market Harborough

# Kelmarsh Hall & Gardens

2 hrs+  Easter–Sep

This early C18 Palladian-style house was designed by James Gibbs. It includes a Chinese room with handpainted wallpaper, interesting gardens, a lake and woodland walks. A herd of British white cattle roam the parkland.

* Managed by the Kelmarsh Trust
* Regular events throughout the season

**Location**
On A508 at Kelmarsh village

**Opening**
House **Easter–4 Sep Sun & Bank Hols**
2pm–5pm
Gardens Tues–Thur 2pm–5pm

**Admission**
House & Gardens Adult £4.50,
Child £2.50, Concs £4
Gardens £3.50, £2, £3

**Contact**
Kelmarsh, Northampton NN6 9LU

t 01604 686543
w kelmarsh.com
e enquiries@kelmarsh.com

## 469 Northampton

# Holdenby House, Gardens & Falconry Centre

2 hrs  Apr–Sep

Across the fields from Althorp lies Holdenby, a house whose royal connections go back more than 400 years. Its history is complemented by a regal collection of birds of prey, including the only naturally reared male black eagle in captivity anywhere.

* Based on the remaining kitchen wing of the old palace
* Built in 1583 by Sir Christopher Hatton

**Location**
6 miles NW of Northampton, off A5199
or A428

**Opening**
Gardens & Falconry Centre
Easter–Sep Sun & Bank Hols
1pm–5pm
House Pre-booked tours only

**Admission**
Gardens & Falconry Centre
Adult £4.50, Child £3, Concs £4

**Contact**
Holdenby, Northampton NN6 8DJ

t 01604 770074
w holdenby.com
e enquiries@holdenby.com

## 470 Northampton

# Northampton Museum & Art Gallery

1 hr  All year

Reflecting the town's proud standing as Britain's boot and shoe capital, the Northampton Museum & Art Gallery features the world's largest collection of footwear. Other displays include British and Oriental pottery and porcelain and a display of fine glassware.

* Programme of temporary exhibitions and events
* The town's history from the Stone Age to the present day

**Location**
Northampton town centre

**Opening**
Daily: Mon–Sat 10am–5pm,
Sun 2–5pm

**Admission**
Free

**Contact**
4–6 Guildhall Road,
Northampton NN1 1DP

t 01604 838111
w northampton.gov.uk/museums
e museums@northampton.gov.uk

## 471 Northampton South

# Abington Museum

3 hrs+  All year

Housed in a C15 manor house that was once the home of Shakespeare's granddaughter, Elizabeth Bernard, the museum is now home to displays of Victorian curiosities, Northamptonshire military history, a costume gallery, local history and a leathercraft gallery.

* C17 oak-panelled room
* C19 fashion gallery

**Location**
Approximately 1½ miles E of town centre

**Opening**
March–Oct Sun–Tues 1pm–5pm;
Nov–Feb Sun–Tues 1pm–4pm;
Bank Hol Mon 1pm–5pm

**Admission**
Free

**Contact**
Abington Park, Park Avenue,
South Northampton NN1 5LW

t 01604 838110
w northampton.gov.uk/museums

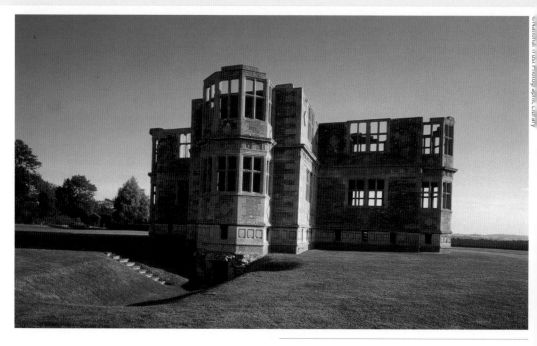

©National Trust Photographic Library

472 Oundle

# Lyveden New Bield

1 hr+    Feb–Nov

This incomplete Elizabethan garden lodge remains unaltered since building work stopped 400 years ago. Designed in the shape of a cross, with fascinating architectural stonework, the lodge is set in beautiful countryside adjoining the remains of a moated garden.

* Designed by Sir Thomas Tresham
* Elizabethan water-gardens

**Location**
4 miles SW of Oundle on A427, 3 miles E of Brigstock, leading off A6116

**Opening**
Apr–Jul & Sep–Oct Wed–Sun 10.30am–5pm;
Aug daily 10.30am–5pm
Nov, Feb & March Sat–Sun 10.30am–4pm

**Admission**
Adult £3.50, Child Free

**Contact**
nr Oundle, Peterborough PE8 5AT

t  01832 205358
w  nationaltrust.org.uk/lyveden
e  lyvedennewbield@nationaltrust.org.uk

473 Towcester

# Canal Museum

2–4 hrs    All year

Housed in an old corn mill on the Grand Union Canal are exhibits from two centuries of canal history, including a reconstructed narrowboat, with all its traditional furniture and equipment. Trips can be taken through the mile-long Blisworth Tunnel.

* Cruise along the Grand Union Canal

**Location**
S of Northampton, 10 mins from M1 junction 15 of M1 & A5, on Grand Union Canal S of Blisworth Tunnel

**Opening**
Oct–Mar Tue–Sun 10am–4pm;
Apr–Sep Tue–Sun 10am–5pm

**Admission**
Adult £3.75, Child £2.50, Concs £3.25

**Contact**
Stoke Bruerne, Towcester NN12 7SE

t  01604 862 229
w  waterwaystrust.org
e  canal.museum@waterwaystrust.org

## 474 Wansford

# Prebendal Manor House

2 hrs+     Easter–Sep

This C13 Grade I listed manor house is the oldest surviving dwelling in Northamptonshire and is steeped in history. The recreated medieval gardens are unique to the area and are the largest in Europe. Visit the C16 dovecote and the large C18 tithe barn museum.

\* Rare breeds of sheep & pigs & medieval farming
\* Explore the history of the Prebends

**Location**
A few miles from A1 & A605, signed from nearby villages

**Opening**
Easter–Sep 1pm–5.30pm

**Admission**
Adult £5.50, Child £2.50, Concs £5

**Contact**
Nassington, Peterborough PE8 6QG
t 01780 782575
w prebendal-manor.co.uk
e info@prebendal-manor.co.uk

## 475 Eastwood

# D H Lawrence Birthplace Museum

2 hrs+     All year

The recreation of the birthplace and early home of D H Lawrence gives a fascinating glimpse into the cramped realities of a Victorian mining family. The museum also uses an interactive wash house, exhibition room and video to interpret the writer's roots and his community.

\* Combine with a visit to Durban House Heritage Centre
\* See the style in which the local mine owner lived

**Location**
From M1 Junction 26 or 27 follow signs towards Eastwood, then signed

**Opening**
Apr–Oct 10am–5pm;
Nov–Mar 10am–4pm

**Admission**
Weekdays free; Sat, Sun & Bank Hols Adult £2, Child £1.20, Concs £1.20

**Contact**
Mansfield Road, Eastwood, Nottingham NG16 3DZ
t 01773 717353
w broxtowe.gov.uk
e culture@broxtowe.gov.uk

## 476 Wellingborough

# Irchester Country Park

4–6 hrs     All year

Explore a network of trails running across 83 hectares of mixed woodland and observe the wealth of wildlife, including woodpeckers and sparrowhawks. A Forestry Centre of Excellence, the park balances conservation with timber production and recreation.

\* Ironstone railway museum
\* Accessible trails & orienteering trail

**Location**
2 miles S of Wellingborough, on B570, off A509, in the Nene Valley

**Opening**
Park Daily: 24 hrs
Car park 24hrs
Lower car park 9am–6pm

**Admission**
Free. Car park £2

**Contact**
Gypsy Lane, Little Irchester, Wellingborough NN29 7DL
t 01933 276866
w northamptonshire.gov.uk
e irchester@northamptonshire.gov.uk

## 477 Edwinstowe

# Sherwood Forest Country Park & Visitor Centre

2 hrs     All year

A good place to begin any exploration of Sherwood Forest is the visitor centre. Find out what life would have been like for outlaws, kings and commoners in Sherwood Forest during the Middle Ages. Enjoy the trails and discover the forest yourself.

\* See the Major Oak, Robin Hood's hiding place
\* National Nature Reserve

**Location**
In Edwinstowe village, off B6034

**Opening**
Visitor centre Daily: summer 10am–5pm, winter 10am–4.30pm
Park dawn–dusk

**Admission**
Free. Car park £1.50–£3

**Contact**
Edwinstowe, nr Mansfield NG21 9HN
t 01623 823202
w nottinghamshire.gov.uk/country parks
e sherwood.forest@nottscc.gov.uk

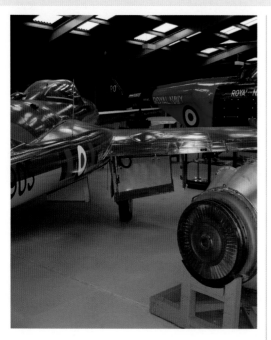

# Mansfield Museum & Art Gallery

1 hr    All year

Explore the history of Mansfield and the surrounding area. Permanent displays illustrate the social, industrial and natural history of the area. Enjoy the 'Xplorative' hands-on environmental exhibition.

\* Pottery pieces from Derby, Pinxton & Mansfield
\* Varied programme of temporary exhibitions

| Location | Contact |
|---|---|
| 5 min walk from market place | Leeming Street, Mansfield NG18 1NG |
| **Opening** | t  01623 463088 |
| Mon–Sat 10am–5pm; | w  mansfield.gov.uk |
| closed Bank Hols | e  lweston@mansfield.gov.uk |
| **Admission** | |
| Free | |

# Newark Air Museum

2 hrs    All year

The museum's impressive collection currently stands at more than 70 aircraft and cockpit sections, including transport, training and reconnaissance aircraft and helicopters and a diverse selection of jet fighters and bombers.

\* Post war air-to-air missile display
\* History of RAF Winthorpe, wartime bomber training

| Location | Contact |
|---|---|
| Easily accessible from A1, A46, A17, | Winthorpe Showground, Newark |
| A1133 & Newark bypass | NG24 2NY |
| **Opening** | t  01636 707170 |
| Daily: Mar–Oct 10am–5pm; | w  newarkairmuseum.co.uk |
| Nov–Feb 10am–4pm | e  newarkair@onetel.com |
| **Admission** | |
| Please phone for details | |

# Angel Row Gallery

1–2 hrs    All year

This is one of the region's leading contemporary art galleries, with a programme of exhibitions that covers a whole range of art, including painting, photography, video and installations. The gallery also runs workshops and hosts talks by leading artists.

\* Temporary exhibitions change throughout the year

| Location | Contact |
|---|---|
| Central Nottingham | Central Library Building, 3 Angel Row, |
| | Nottingham NG1 6HP |
| **Opening** | t  0115 915 2869 |
| Mon, Tue & Thu–Sat 10am–5pm, | w  angelrowgallery.com |
| Wed 10am–7pm | e  angelrow.info@ |
| **Admission** | nottinghamcity.gov.uk |
| Free | |

481 Nottingham

# City of Caves

1 hr+    All year

Descend under the city to manmade Anglo-Saxon tunnels to discover an enchanted well, a medieval tannery that includes a pillar cave (AD 1250), original Victorian slums and the Anderson shelter, used during the Blitz. Learn more about ongoing archaeological digs.

\* Have a go at real archaeology
\* Special events throughout the year

**Location**
Nottingham city centre. Inside Broadmarsh shopping centre on upper level

**Opening**
Daily: 10.30am–4.30pm

**Admission**
Adult £4.95, Child & Concs £3.95

**Contact**
Drury Walk,
Broadmarsh Centre,
Nottingham NG1 7LS

t  0115 988 1955
w  cityofcaves.org.uk
e  info@cityofcaves.com

---

482 Nottingham

# Galleries of Justice

2–3 hrs    All year

A tour through three centuries of crime, punishment and law. Located in the Shire Hall, it includes a Victorian street, courtrooms, an C18 prison, an exercise yard, cave cells, a women's prison with bath house and laundry, medieval cave system and an Edwardian police station.

\* Costumed interpreters bring the experience to life
\* Series of temporary exhibitions

**Location**
In central Nottingham, near Broadmarsh shopping centre

**Opening**
Tue–Sun & Bank Hols 10am–5pm

**Admission**
Adult £7.95, Child & Concs £5.95

**Contact**
Shire Hall, High Pavement,
Lace Market, Nottingham NG1 1HN

t  0115 952 0555
w  galleriesofjustice.org.uk
e  nnco@galleriesofjustice.org.uk

---

483 Nottingham

# Nottingham Castle

1–2 hrs    All year

Looming high above the city and set in scenic Victorian gardens, Nottingham Castle has a turbulent history with a new ducal mansion built over the original medieval site. The castle has displays about its history, and a fine collection of paintings, sculptures and china.

\* Network of caves & passageways beneath the castle
\* Robin Hood statue

**Location**
In central Nottingham

**Opening**
Daily: 10am–5pm

**Admission**
Mon–Fri Adult £3, Child & Concs £1.50;
Sat–Sun & Bank Hols £2, Child & Concs £1

**Contact**
Lenton Road, Nottingham NG1 6EL

t  0115 915 3700
w  nottinghamcity.gov.uk/museums
e  helens@ncmg.demon.co.uk

## 484 Nottingham

# Tales of Robin Hood

1–2 hrs    All year

The swashbuckling adventures of Robin Hood have inspired storytellers for more than 700 years. Explore the world of this infamous and endearing outlaw and experience medieval life, legend and adventure by fleeing through the forest to escape the evil Sheriff.

* Regular Robin Hood events
* Medieval banquets are held on Fridays & Saturdays

| Location | Contact |
|---|---|
| In city centre, next to castle, signed from M1 | 30–38 Maid Marian Way, Nottingham NG1 6GF |
| Opening | t 0115 948 3284 |
| Daily: 10am–5.30pm | w robinhood.uk.com |
| | e robinhoodcentre@mail.com |
| Admission | |
| Adult £7.95, Child £5.95, Concs £6.95 | |

## 485 Nottingham

# Wollaton Hall Museum

3 hrs+    All year

Set in more than 500 acres of historic deer park, Wollaton Hall is a spectacular Tudor building, designed by Robert Smythson and completed in 1588. It is now home to the city's natural history museum, an industrial museum, a visitor centre, and a gallery.

* steam-engine house

| Location | Admission |
|---|---|
| 3 miles from city centre | Mon–Fri Free, Sat–Sun Each museum Adult £2.50, Child & Concs £1.50 |
| Opening | Contact |
| *Natural History Museum, Industrial Museum & Yard Gallery* | Wollaton Park, Nottingham NG8 2AE |
| Daily: Oct–Mar 11am–4pm; Apr–Sep 11am–5pm | t 0115 915 3900 |
| | w nottinghamcity.gov.uk |
| | e carolbf@ncmg.demon.co.uk |

## 486 Ollerton

# Holocaust Centre, Beth Shalom

2–3 hrs    All year

Beth Shalom is set in 2 acres of beautiful gardens and provides a range of facilities for visitors to explore the history and implications of the Holocaust. The main features are its redbrick memorial building, permanent exhibition on the Nazi period and memorial gardens.

* New exhibition The Journey - Children of the Holocaust
* Survivors regularly speak at the centre

| Location | Contact |
|---|---|
| Large buildings on right between Laxton & Ollerton | Laxton, nr Ollerton NG22 0PA |
| Opening | t 01623 836627 |
| Please phone for details | w holocaustcentre.net |
| | e office@bethshalom.com |
| Admission | |
| Adult £6, Child & Concs £4 | |

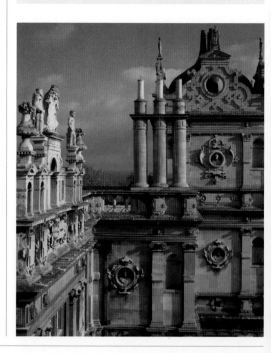

## 487 Ollerton

# Rufford Abbey & Country Park

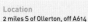

4 hrs   All year

This ruined, former Cistercian monastery was founded in the C12, but after its dissolution in 1536 its lands were granted to George Talbot, 4th Earl of Shrewsbury. The Talbot family then went on to transform the buildings into a country house.

* Stable block houses a contemporary craft exhibition
* The gardens were re established in the late 1970s

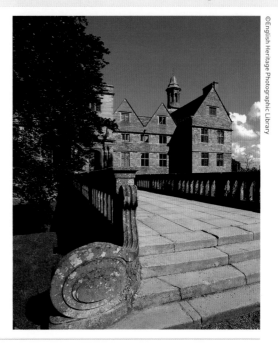

| Location | Contact |
|---|---|
| 2 miles S of Ollerton, off A614 | Ollerton, nr Newark NG22 9DF |
| **Opening** | t 01623 822944 |
| Daily: Apr–Oct 10am–5pm | w nottinghamshire.gov.uk/country- |
| Nov–Mar 10am–4pm | parks |
| **Admission** | e rufford.park@nottscc.gov.uk |
| Free, Charges for car park Sat–Sun & Bank Hols | |

---

## 488 Southwell

# Southwell Minster

2 hrs   All year

Southwell Minster, with its majestic Norman nave and glorious C13 chapter house, is one of the least-known jewels in the crown of Nottinghamshire. Nearby is the Minster Centre with an audio-visual theatre showing a film on the life of the Minster, a library, gallery and bookshop.

* Dedicated education officer who organises events talks for children

| Location | Admission |
|---|---|
| Southwell town centre | Free but donations welcome |
| **Opening** | **Contact** |
| *Minster* Daily | Southwell, Nottinghamshire |
| *Minster Centre* Mon–Fri 9am–5pm, | t 01636 812649 |
| Sat 10am–4pm, Sun 1pm–4pm | w southwellminster.org.uk |
| | e nikki-di@southwellminster.org.uk |

---

## 489 Southwell

# Southwell Workhouse

1 hr+   Mar–Nov

The lives of the poor and destitute in the C19 and C20 are revealed at Southwell Workhouse. Explore the building and its history, including the segregated staircases and rooms, and unlock the stories of the people who lived and worked there.

* Play the Master's Punishment game
* Meet some of the 'characters' who lived here

| Location | Contact |
|---|---|
| 13 miles from Nottingham on A612, | Upton Road, Southwell NG25 0PT |
| 8 miles from Newark on A617 & A612 | t 01636 817250 |
| **Opening** | w nationaltrust.org.uk |
| Mar–Jul & Sep–Nov Thu–Mon | e theworkhouse@ |
| 12noon–5pm; Aug 11am–5pm | nationaltrust.org.uk |
| **Admission** | |
| Adult £4.40, Child £2.20 | |

## 490 Worksop

# Clumber Park

2–3 hrs  All year

Part of Nottinghamshire's famed 'Dukeries', at Clumber Park there are more than 3,800 acres of parkland, woods, open heath and rolling farmland with a superb serpentine lake at their heart. Although the house was demolished in 1938, many features of the estate remain.

* Walled kitchen garden
* Bicycle hire available

| Location | Contact |
|---|---|
| 4 miles SE of Worksop | The Estate Office, Clumber Park, Worksop S80 3AZ |
| **Opening** | |
| *Park* Daily: dawn–dusk | t 01909 476592 |
| *Gardens* Daily: Mar–Oct 10am–5.30pm, | w nationaltrust.org.uk/clumberpark |
| Sat–Sun 10am–6pm | e clumberpark@nationaltrust.org.uk |
| **Admission** | |
| £4 per car | |

## 491 Worksop

# Harley Gallery

1 hr  All year

The Harley Foundation, set up as a charitable trust in 1977 by the late Ivy, Duchess of Portland, is based in the Ducal Estate of Welbeck. As well as offering studio space to artists and craftspeople, it funds an art gallery and programme of exhibitions.

* Historical gallery exhibiting decorative & fine art
* Full programme of events

| Location | Contact |
|---|---|
| 5 miles S of Worksop on A60 | Welbeck, Mansfield Road, Worksop S80 3LW |
| **Opening** | |
| 15 Jan–Dec Tue–Sun & Bank Hols | t 01909 501700 |
| 10am–5pm | w harleygallery.co.uk |
| **Admission** | e info@harley-welbeck.co.uk |
| Free | |

## 492 Worksop

# Mr Straw's House

1 hr+  Apr–Nov

This modest semi-detached Edwardian house provides an intriguing insight into early C20 everyday life. The interior has remained unaltered since the 1930s and features contemporary wallpaper, Victorian furniture and household objects.

* Displays of family clothes
* A typical suburban garden

WC

| Location | Contact |
|---|---|
| Follow signs to Bassetlaw General Hospital, signed from Blyth Road | 5 Blyth Grove, Worksop S81 0JG |
| **Opening** | t 01909 482380 |
| Apr–Nov Tue–Sat 11am–4.30pm | w nationaltrust.org.uk |
| **Admission** | e mrstrawshouse@ nationaltrust.org.uk |
| Pre-booked timed ticket only Adult £4.60, Child £2.30 | |

## 493 Barnsdale

# Drought Garden & Arboretum

½ hr    All year

Designed by the late Geoff Hamilton with refurbishment by Nick Hamilton, this garden – on a south-facing clay slope at Barnsdale – has survived dry summers and penetrating frost. The arboretum shows the species of trees planted around the reservoir.

\* Accolade Winner 2002
\* The Best of its Kind 2003

| Location | Contact |
|---|---|
| Accessed from A606 Oakham–Stamford road. | Barnsdale, Rutland Water |
| | t 01572 653026 |
| Opening | w anglianwaterleisure.co.uk |
| Daily: all reasonable times | e tic@anglianwater.co.uk |
| Admission | |
| Free | |

## 494 Clipsham

# Clipsham Yew Tree Avenue

1½ hrs    All year

The Yew Tree Avenue is a unique collection of 150 clipped yew trees, most more than 200 years old, once the drive to Clipsham Hall. The topiary was begun in 1870 by Amos Alexander, the estate's head forester, who lived in the gate lodge at the foot of the avenue.

\* Clipping each autumn by Forestry Commission
\* Muntjac may be seen crossing the avenue

| Location | Contact |
|---|---|
| Less than 1 mile E of Clipsham on Castle Bytham road | Forest Enterprise, North Hants Top Lodge, Fineshade NN17 3BB |
| | t 01780 444394 |
| Opening | w forestry.gov.uk |
| Daily: all reasonable times | e northants@forestry.gsi.gov.uk |
| Admission | |
| Free | |

## 495 Lyddington

# Lyddington Bede House

1 hr    Apr–Oct

Lyddington Bede House was originally a wing of a medieval rural palace belonging to the bishops of Lincoln. In 1600 the building was converted into an alms house and it remained a home for pensioners until the 1930s.

\* Great Chamber features a beautiful ceiling cornice
\* Bedesmen's rooms with tiny windows & fireplaces

| Location | Contact |
|---|---|
| In Lyddington, 6 miles N of Corby, 1 mile E of A6003, next to church | Bluecoat Lane, Lyddington LE15 9LZ |
| | t 01572 822438 |
| Opening | w english-heritage.org.uk |
| Please phone for details | |
| Admission | |
| Adult £3.30, Child £1.70, Concs £2.50 Prices for events vary | |

## 496 Oakham

# Oakham Castle

½ hr    All year

The Great Hall, built in about 1180–90, is a fine example of late C12 domestic architecture. The remains of other parts of the house lie beneath the grass of the inner bailey. The hall possesses a range of C12 figure sculpture.

\* Stonework by masons from Canterbury Cathedral
\* More than 200 horseshoes hang on the castle walls

| Location | Admission |
|---|---|
| In Oakham town centre, just off market place | Free |
| **Opening** | **Contact** |
| Mon–Sat 10.30am–5pm, weekdays closed 1pm-1.30pm, Sun 2pm–4pm | c/o Rutland County Museum, Catmose Street, Oakham LE15 6HW |
| | t 01572 758440 |
| | e museum@rutland.gov.uk |

## 497 Oakham

# Rutland County Museum

1 hr+    All year

Rutland Museum is a perfect introduction to England's smallest county. The new Welcome to Rutland Gallery is a guide to the house of Rutland and leads into displays of local archaeology and history, and an extensive rural life collection.

\* Rare Saunderson tractor
\* Tools & equipment of village tradesmen

| Location | Admission |
|---|---|
| Off A603, near town centre | Free |
| **Opening** | **Contact** |
| Daily: Mon–Sat 10.30am–5pm, Sun 2pm–4pm | Catmose Street, Oakham LE15 6HW |
| | t 01572 758440 |
| | e museum@rutland.gov.uk |

## 498 Oakham

# Rutland Water

2 hrs+    All year

The largest manmade lake in western Europe, this attractive 3,100-acre reservoir has an international reputation for balancing leisure activities with wildlife conservation. Visitors may windsurf, rock-climb or canoe; hire a dinghy, bike or fishing boat; or just relax.

\* Butterfly & Aquatic Centre & bird-watching
\* Range of craft available for hire or launch your own

| Location | Contact |
|---|---|
| Just off A606, signed from A1 | Tourist Information Centre, Sykes Lane, Empingham, Rutland LE 15 8PX |
| **Opening** | t 01572 653026 |
| Daily: 10am-5pm | w anglianwaterleisure.co.uk |
| **Admission** | e tic@anglianwaterleisure.co.uk |
| Free. Car park charge | |

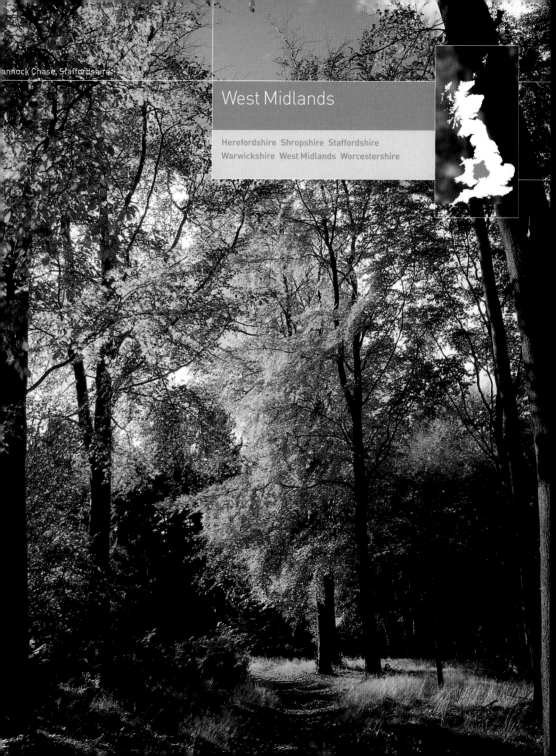

Cannock Chase, Staffordshire

# West Midlands

Herefordshire  Shropshire  Staffordshire
Warwickshire  West Midlands  Worcestershire

499 Abbeydore

# Dore Abbey

1 hr    All year

Founded by French monks in 1147, Dore Abbey is remarkable for the wealth of features dating back to the C12. Today only the chancel area and transepts remain but the foundations of the nave, cloisters, chapter house and domestic buildings are all still in evidence.

* The only Cistercian monastery in Britain founded from Morimond, France

| Location | Contact |
|---|---|
| In Abbeydore village on B4347 | Abbeydore, Hereford, Herefordshire HR2 0AD |
| **Opening** Daily | w doreabbey.org.uk |
| **Admission** Free | t 01981 570251 |

500 Bringsty

# The Garden at The Bannut

2 hrs    Easter–Sep

Set in the Herefordshire countryside with beautiful views of the Malvern Hills, the magnificent garden has been developed over the past 20 years by one couple. Manicured hedges divide the garden into formal and informal rooms, each with its own specific interest.

* Laburnum Walk and intriguing Secret Garden
* Plants for sale

| Location | Contact |
|---|---|
| On A44 2½ miles E of Bromyard, near entrance to Brockhampton | Bringsty, WR6 5TA |
| **Opening** Easter–Sep 12.30–5pm | t 01885 482206 |
| **Admission** Adult £3, Child £1.50 | w bannut.co.uk |
| | e everettbannut@zetnet.co.uk |

501 Bromyard

# Brockhampton Estate

1 hr    All year

This 1,700-acre estate still maintains farms and has extensive areas of woodland, including ancient oak and beech. Visitors can enjoy a variety of walks through both park and woodland. At the heart of the estate lies Lower Brockhampton House, a late C14 moated manor house.

* Timber-framed gatehouse and ruined chapel
* Woodland is home to interesting range of wildlife

| Location | Admission |
|---|---|
| 2 miles E of Bromyard on A44 | Adult £3.60, Child £1.80 |
| **Opening** | **Contact** |
| *House* Mar Sat–Sun 12noon–4pm; Apr–Sep Wed–Sun 12noon–5pm; Oct Wed–Sun 12noon–4pm | Greenfields, Bringsty WR6 5TB |
| *Estate* All year dawn–dusk | t 01885 488099/482077 |
| | w nationaltrust.org.uk |
| | e brockhampton@nationaltrust.org.uk |

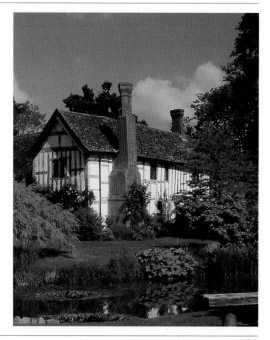

## 502 Bromyard

# Bromyard Heritage Centre

½ hr    Apr–Oct

Based in an C18 stable block, Bromyard Heritage Centre displays aspects of Bromyard's past, together with an extensive exhibition of hops and hop growing. This traces the growing and picking cycle and changing methods of cultivation since the C15.

\* Host to highly successful Year of the Hop exhibition
\* Exhibition of rural & urban developments in the town

| Location | Contact |
|---|---|
| Signposted from A44 | Rowberry Street, Bromyard HR7 4DU |
| **Opening** | t 01432 260692 |
| Apr–Oct Mon–Sat 10am–4pm | w visitorlinks.com |
| **Admission** | |
| Free | |

## 503 Bromyard

# Shortwood Family Farm

4 hrs+    Easter–Oct

Ideal for all the family, this organic farm offers visitors the opportunity to collect eggs, feed animals, see at first hand the benefits of organic farming, buy fresh produce, visit Mini-Farm World and pets' corner, follow the farm trail, and take a trailer ride.

\* Milk a cow by hand

| Location | Admission |
|---|---|
| Signed from A417 between Burley Gate, Bodenham & from Pencombe village | Adult £5, Child £3.20 |
| | **Contact** |
| **Opening** | Pencombe, |
| Daily: Easter–Oct from 10am | Bromyard HR7 4RP |
| | t 01885 400205 |
| | w shortwoodfarm.co.uk |

## 504 Hereford

# The Cider Museum

1 hr    All year

Learn the story of traditional cidermaking: how apples were harvested, milled and pressed, and how the resulting juice was fermented to produce cider. You can also walk through a reconstructed farm cider house and see the 300-year-old travelling cidermaker's 'tack'.

\* Visit the original champagne cider cellars
\* See the distillation process being used for cider brandy

| Location | Admission |
|---|---|
| In W Hereford, off A438 | Adult £3, Child £2, Concs £2.50 |
| **Opening** | **Contact** |
| Daily: 12noon–4pm | 21 Ryelands Street, Hereford HR4 0LW |
| | t 01432 354 207 |
| | w cidermuseum.co.uk |
| | e e-mail@cidermuseum.co.uk |

## 505 Hereford

# Hereford Cathedral, Mappa Mundi & Chained Library

2 hrs    All year

Housed within the cathedral's C15 south-west cloister and the new library building is an exhibition that uses models and original artefacts to reveal the secrets of Mappa Mundi, the largest and most elaborate complete pre-C15 world map in existence.

\* The world's largest chained library – 1,500 rare books
\* Working stonemason's yard & cathedral shop

| Location | Admission |
|---|---|
| Hereford town centre | Adult £4.50, Child & Concs £3.50 |
| **Opening** | **Contact** |
| Daily: *summer* Mon–Sat 10am–4.15pm, Sun 11am–3.15pm | 5 College Cloisters, Cathedral Close, Hereford HR1 2NG |
| *winter* Mon–Sat 11am–3.15pm | t 01432 374200 |
| | w herefordcathedral.org |
| | e visits@herefordcathedral.org |

## 506 Hereford

# The Weir

1 hr+    Jan–Oct

A delightful riverside garden, particularly spectacular in early spring and with fine views over the River Wye and the Black Mountains. The late C18 house (not open to the public) sits on top of steep slopes that fall away to the river.

* Walks through beech woodland high above the river
* Created by the Parr family in the 1920s

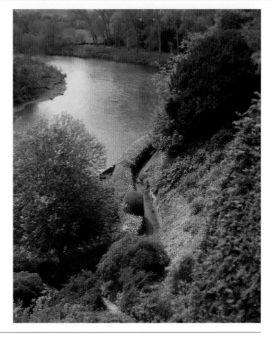

**Location**
5 miles W of Hereford, signed from A438

**Opening**
21 Jan–22 Jan 11am–4pm;
28 Jun–29 Jun 11am–4pm;
1 Feb–26 Feb Wed–Sun 11am–4pm;
27 Feb–2 Apr daily 11am–4pm;
Apr–Oct daily 11am–5pm

**Admission**
Adult £3.60, Child £1.80

**Contact**
Swainshill, nr Hereford HR4 7QF

t 01981 590509
w nationaltrust.org.uk
e theweir@ntrust.org.uk

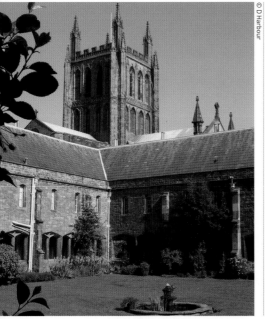

© D Harbour

## 507 Kington

# Hergest Croft Gardens

2 hrs+    May–Oct

In the heart of the Welsh Marches, with stunning views towards the Black Mountains, Hergest Croft was created over 100 years by three generations of the Banks family. There are hidden valleys, woodland glades, open parkland and flower borders for year-round beauty.

* National Collection of birch & maples
* Rhododendrons and azaleas

**Location**
Signed on A44 from Kington

**Opening**
May–June 12noon–6pm;
Mar Sat–Sun 12.30pm–5pm;
3 Apr–31 Oct 12.30pm–5.30pm

**Admission**
Adult £5, Child free

**Contact**
Kington HR5 3EG

t 01544 230160
w hergest.co.uk
e gardens@hergest.co.uk

## 508 Leominster

# Berrington Hall

2 hrs   Mar–Oct

With sweeping views to the Brecon Beacons, this elegant Henry Holland house was built in the late C18 and is set in parkland designed by Capability Brown. A rather austere external appearance belies a surprisingly delicate interior.

* Beautiful ceilings & a spectacular staircase hall
* Good collection of furniture & paintings

| Location | Contact |
|---|---|
| 3 miles N of Leominster | Leominster HR6 0DW |
| **Opening** | t 01568 615721 |
| Times vary, please phone for details | w nationaltrust.org.uk |
| **Admission** | e berrington@nationaltrust.org.uk |
| Adult £5, Child £2.50 | |

## 509 Leominster

# Croft Castle

2 hrs   Mar–Oct

Croft Castle has an extensive range of showrooms to complement the fine Georgian interior and period furnishings. The gardens and park offer pleasant walks and magnificent views.

* Joint tickets with Berrington Hall available
* Beautiful period walled garden

| Location | Admission |
|---|---|
| 5 miles NW of Leominster | *House & Gardens* Adult £4.80, Child £2.40 |
| **Opening** | *Gardens* £3.40, Free |
| 6 Mar–28 Mar Sat–Sun 1pm–5pm; | |
| 1 Apr–30 Sep Wed–Sun 1pm–5pm; | **Contact** |
| 1 Oct–31 Oct Sat–Sun 1pm–5pm | nr Leominster HR6 9PW |
| | t 01568 780246 |
| | w nationaltrust.org.uk |
| | e croftcastle@nationaltrust.org.uk |

## 510 Ludlow

# Wigmore Castle

2 hrs   All year

One of the most remarkable ruins in England, Wigmore Castle was abandoned before the C17 and left to deteriorate naturally. Today it has been buried up to first-floor level by fallen upper floors, but its towers and curtain walls survive to their full height.

* WARNING: The castle has steep steps to the summit that are hazardous in icy conditions

| Location | Contact |
|---|---|
| 8 miles W of Ludlow on A4110 | English Heritage West Midlands, 112 Colmore Row, |
| **Opening** | Birmingham B3 3AG |
| Daily: All reasonable times | |
| **Admission** | t 0121 625 6820 |
| Free | w english-heritage.org.uk |
| | e customers@englishheritage.org.uk |

## 511  Ross-on-Wye

# Goodrich Castle

1 hr    All year

This fortified baronial palace stands majestically on a red sandstone crag, commanding the passage of the River Wye into the picturesque wooded valley of Symonds Yat. Much of the stone used was quarried from the rock around the base of the castle, creating a deep moat.

* Cannon that destroyed the castle in 1645 is now on display
* Views over River Wye & Symonds Yat

| Location | Admission |
|---|---|
| 5 miles S of Ross-on-Wye off A40 | Please phone for details |
| **Opening** | **Contact** |
| Daily: Mar–May & Sep–Oct 10am–5pm; | Ross-on-Wye HR9 6HY |
| Daily: Jun–Aug 10am–6pm; | t 01600 890538 |
| Nov– Feb Thurs–Mon 10am–4pm | w english-heritage.org.uk |

## 512  Symonds Yat

# Amazing Hedge Puzzle

1 hr    All year

Planted more than 20 years ago by brothers Lindsay and Edward Heyes, the Amazing Hedge Puzzle is one of Herefordshire's most popular and fun private tourist attractions. Learn about mazes through history and the myths surrounding them in the maze museum.

* Hands-on displays allow you to build your own maze
* Set in the beautiful countryside of the Wye Valley

| Location | Admission |
|---|---|
| Follow signs on B4164, off A40 | Please phone for details |
| between Ross-on-Wye & Monmouth | **Contact** |
| **Opening** | Jubilee Park, Symonds Yat West, |
| Daily: Jan–Feb & Nov–Dec 11am–3pm; | Ross-on-Wye HR9 6DA |
| Apr–Sep and half-terms 11am–5pm; | t 01600 890360 |
| Mar & Oct 11am–4pm | w mazes.co.uk |
| | e info@mazes.co.uk |

## 513  Bishop's Wood

# Boscobel House & The Royal Oak

2 hrs+    Apr–Oct

A refuge for Charles II before he fled to France, this timber-framed farmhouse was later converted into a hunting lodge. It was called Boscobel after the Italian *'bosco bello'*, meaning 'in the midst of fair woods' and reflecting the woodland that once surrounded it.

* Its true use is thought to have been to hide Catholics
* Escape from Worcester and farm exhibition

| Location | Contact |
|---|---|
| 8 miles NW of Wolverhampton, on | Brewood, Bishop's Wood ST19 9AR |
| minor road between A41 & A5 | t 01902 850244 |
| **Opening** | w english-heritage.org.uk |
| Daily: Apr–Sep 10am–6pm; | e boscobelhouse@english-heritage. |
| Oct 10am–5pm | org.uk |
| **Admission** | |
| Adult £4.60, Child £2.30, Concs £3.50 | |

## 514 Bridgnorth

# Dudmaston

2 hrs+    Mar–Sep

A late C17 house with intimate family rooms containing fine furniture and Dutch flower paintings, as well as a fabulous collection of important contemporary paintings and sculpture. The gardens are a mass of colour in spring and include a wooded valley or dingle.

\* C20 art includes Nicholson, Moore & Hepworth

**Location**
4 miles SE of Bridgnorth, on A442

**Opening**
*House* Mar–Sep Tue–Wed & Sun
2pm–5.30pm
*Gardens* Mon–Wed & Sun 12noon–6pm

**Admission**
*House & Gardens* Adult £4.75, Child
£2.40 *Gardens only* £3.50, £1.50

**Contact**
Quatt, nr Bridgnorth WV15 6QN
t  01746 780866
w  nationaltrust.org.uk
e  dudmaston@nationaltrust.org.uk

## 515 Bridgnorth

# Rays Farm Country Matters

2 hrs    Mar–Oct

Animals both large and small and woodland walks with mystical moments are the main attractions at Rays Farm. There are also more than 40 owls on display, many of whom have been rescued from the wild, and llamas, reindeers, red deer, axis deer and many more.

\* Pull 'Excalibur' from its stone
\* Many varieties of deer and goats

**Location**
Signed off B4363 near Billingsley
between Bridgnorth and Cleobury
Mortimer

**Opening**
Daily: Mar–Oct 10am–5.30pm

**Admission**
Adult £5.50, Child £4, Concs £5

**Contact**
Billingsley, Bridgnorth
Shropshire WV16 6PF
t  01299 841255
w  raysfarm.com

## 516 Bridgnorth

# Severn Valley Railway

3 hrs+    All year

A full-size standard-gauge line running regular steam-hauled passenger trains between Kidderminster and Bridgnorth, a distance of 16 miles. For most of the way, the route follows the meandering course of the River Severn closely.

\* Crosses impressive Victoria Bridge
\* Passengers may break the journey at any station

**Location**
Stations in Kidderminster, Bridgnorth
& Bewdley

**Opening**
Daily: May–Sep & Oct–Apr Sat–Sun
Full timetable on the website

**Admission**
Please visit the website for full details

**Contact**
The Railway Station,
Bewdley DY12 1BG
t  01299 403816
w  svr.co.uk

## 517 Broseley

# Benthall Hall

1 hr+    Apr–Sep

Situated on a plateau above the gorge of the Severn, this C16 stone house has mullioned and transomed windows and a stunning interior with carved oak staircase, decorated plaster ceilings and oak panelling. There is also an interesting Restoration church.

* Carefully restored plantsman's garden
* Old kitchen garden

**Location**
On B4375, 1 mile NW of Broseley, 1 mile SW of Ironbridge

**Opening**
Apr–Jun Tue–Wed, Bank Hols & Sun of Bank Hols;
Jul–Sep Tue, Wed, Sun & Bank Hols
*House* 2pm–5.30pm
*Gardens* 1.30pm–5.30pm

**Admission**
Please phone for details

**Contact**
Broseley TF12 5RX

t 01952 882159
w nationaltrust.org.uk

## 518 Church Stretton

# Acton Scott

3 hrs    Apr–Oct

Experience daily life on an upland farm at the turn of the C20. The waggoner and his team of heavy horses work the land with vintage farm machines. Every day you can see milking by hand and buttermaking in the dairy. You will also see the farrier and the blacksmith.

* Lambing, shearing, cidermaking etc. in season
* Children's holiday activities

**Location**
Off A49, 17 miles S of Shrewsbury, 14 miles N of Ludlow

**Opening**
Apr–Oct Tue–Sun & Bank Hols
10am–5pm

**Admission**
Adult £4.50, Child £2.25, Concs £4

**Contact**
nr Church Stretton SY6 6QN

t 01694 781306
w actonscottmuseum.co.uk
e acton.scott.museum@shropshire-cc.gov.uk

## 519 Craven Arms

# Secret Hills – Shropshire Hills Discovery Centre

2 hrs+    All year

A stylish and imaginative new building with a grass roof set within 25 acres of the Onny Meadows. Designed to improve understanding of the landscape, culture and heritage of the area, the centre provides a base for year-round entertainment and hands-on activities.

* Craft gallery & activities area
* Find out about earthquakes

**Location**
Off A49, 7 miles N of Ludlow

**Opening**
Daily: Apr–Oct 10am–4.30pm;
Nov–Mar 10am–3.30pm

**Admission**
Adult £4.25, Child £2.75

**Contact**
School Road, Craven Arms SY7 9RS

t 01588 676000/676040
w shropshire-cc.gov.uk/discover.nsf
e secrethills@shropshire-cc.gov.uk

## 520 Ludlow

# Angel Gardens

1 hr+    May–Sep

Angel Gardens has spectacular landscaped ornamental gardens at 1,000 feet with magnificent views over Stretton and the Welsh hills. Take lunch or afternoon tea in the lakeside pavilion tea rooms and admire other harmonious design structures.

* Exotic planting and fernery
* Chinese seat swing

**Location**
Between Kidderminster & Ludlow on A4117

**Opening**
May–Sep Sun–Tue 12noon–5pm

**Admission**
Adult £4, Child free

**Contact**
Springfield, Angel Lane
Bitterley, Ludlow SY8 3HZ

t 01584 890381
w stmem.com/angelgardens
e angelgardens@sy83hz.fsnet.co.uk

## 521 Ludlow

# Stokesay Castle

1 hr    All year

Strength and elegance are united in this fortified medieval manor house, built by renowned wool merchant Lawrence of Ludlow. In 1291 a 'licence to crenellate' was obtained from Edward I at Hereford for the three-storey south tower.

* Magnificent Great Hall largely untouched
* Timber-framed Jacobean gatehouse

**Location**
Off A49, 7 miles NW of Ludlow

**Opening**
Mar–May Thu–Mon 10am–5pm;
Jun–Aug daily 10am–6pm;
Sep–Oct Thu–Mon 10am–5pm;
Nov–Feb Fri–Sun 10am–4pm

**Admission**
Adult £4.60, Child £2.30, Concs £3.50

**Contact**
Craven Arms SY7 9AH

t 01588 672544
w english-heritage.org.uk

## 522 Market Drayton

# Wollerton Old Hall Garden

2 hrs    Easter–Sep

Wollerton Old Hall Garden is a 4-acre plantsman's garden developed around a C16 house (not open) in rural Shropshire. The strong formal design has created many separate gardens, each with its own character, and there are many rare and unusual plants.

* Present garden developed from 1984
* Difficult-to-obtain perennials available in nursery

**Location**
Off A53, between Market Drayton &
Shrewsbury

**Opening**
Good Fri–Sep Fri, Sun & Bank Hols
12noon–5pm

**Admission**
Adult £4, Child £1

**Contact**
Wollerton, Market Drayton TF9 3NA

t 01630 685760
w wollertonoldhallgarden.com
e info@wollertonoldhallgarden.com

## 523 Shifnal

# The RAF Museum – Cosford

3 hrs+    All year

Follow the story of man's flight – the successes and failures – through one of the largest aviation collections in the UK. More than 70 historic aircraft are displayed in three wartime hangars on an active airfield. The collection spans nearly 80 years of aviation history.

* Visitor Attraction of the Year 2003
* State-of-the-art flight simulator

**Location**
On A41, less than 1 mile from M54 junction 3

**Opening**
Daily: 10am–6pm (last admission 4pm)

**Admission**
Free, charges for special events
Under-16s must be accompanied by an adult

**Contact**
Cosford, Shifnal TF11 8UP

t  01902 376200
w  rafmuseum.org
e  cosford@rafmuseum.com

## 524 Shifnal

# Weston Park

2 hrs+    Mar–Sep

The house was first mentioned in the *Domesday Book* in the C11, but Weston owes its unique character to the developments of the C17, directed by Lady Wilbraham. The beautiful landscaped gardens are the work of Capability Brown, though they were restored in 1991.

* Mary, daughter of George V, honeymooned here
* G8 Summit held here in 1998

**Location**
On A5, 3 miles off M54 junction 3

**Opening**
Dates vary, please phone for details
*House* 1pm–5pm
*Park & Gardens* 11am–6.30pm

**Admission**
*House, Park & Gardens* Adult £6.50,
Child £4.50, Concs £5.50;

*Park & Gardens* £3.50, £2.50, £3

**Contact**
Weston-under-Lizard,
Shifnal TF11 8LE

t  01952 852100
w  weston-park.com
e  enquiries@weston-park.com

## 525 Shrewsbury

# Attingham Park

2 hrs+    All year

One of the great houses of the Midlands, this elegant mansion was built in 1785 for the first Lord Berwick, to the design of George Steuart, and has a picture gallery by John Nash. The Regency interiors contain collections of silver, Italian furniture and Grand Tour paintings.

* Park with walk by River Tern landscaped by Repton
* Environmental activity room opened in 2003

   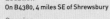

**Location**
On B4380, 4 miles SE of Shrewsbury

**Opening**
Please phone for details

**Admission**
Please phone for details

**Contact**
Shrewsbury SY4 4TP

t  01743 708123
w  nationaltrust.org.uk
e  attingham@nationaltrust.org.uk

## 526 Shrewsbury

# Hawkstone Park

4 hrs    Jan–Oct

Created in the C18, Hawkstone became one of the greatest historic parklands in Europe. The park is centred around the Red Castle and the awe-inspiring Grotto Hill, and features intricate pathways, ravines, arches and bridges, towering cliffs and follies.

* Woodland full of ancient oaks
* The attraction has won numerous awards

**Location**
Off A49, between Shrewsbury & Whitchurch

**Opening**
Jan–Feb Sat–Sun 10am–3pm;
21 Mar–30 Oct daily 10am–4pm

**Admission**
Adult £5.75, Child £3.75, Concs £4.75

**Contact**
Weston-under-Redcastle,
Shrewsbury SY4 5UY

t  01939 200611
w  hawkstone.co.uk
e  info@hawkstone.co.uk

## 527 Shrewsbury

# Wroxeter Roman City

1 hr    All year

The largest excavated Roman British city to have escaped development, Wroxeter was originally home to 6,000 people. The most impressive ruins are the C2 municipal baths and the remains of a huge dividing wall. Local finds are on display in the visitor centre.

* Fourth-largest Roman settlement in Britain

**Location**
On B4380, 5 miles E of Shrewsbury

**Opening**
Daily: Apr–Sep 10am–6pm;
Oct 10am–5pm;
Nov–Mar 10am–1pm & 2pm–4pm

**Admission**
Adult £4, Child £2, Concs £3

**Contact**
Wroxeter, Shrewsbury SY5 6PH

t  01743 761330
w  english-heritage.org.uk

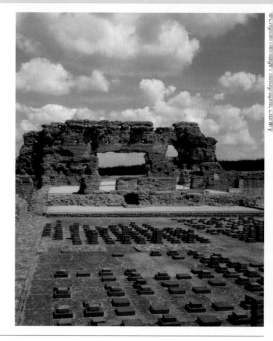

## 528 Telford

# Ironbridge Gorge Museums

1–6 hrs    All year

There are ten award-winning museums spread along what is often called 'the valley that changed the world'. That valley, beside the River Severn, is still spanned by the world's first iron bridge. See the products that set industry on its way and the machines that made them.

* Various workshops, including ceramic and iron working
* Enginuity – hands-on design & tech experiences

**Location**
5 miles S of Telford, signed from M54 junction 4

**Opening**
Daily: 10am–5pm; some areas close in winter

**Admission**
*Passport ticket to all 10 attractions*
Adult £13.25, Child £8.75, Concs £11.50

**Contact**
Ironbridge, Telford TF8 7DQ

t  01952 884 391
w  ironbridge.org.uk
e  tic@ironbridge.org.uk

## 529 Telford

# Enginuity

2 hrs   All year

Based in the Ironbridge World Heritage Site, this museum explains the science and design behind the gadgets we see and use every day. The interactive displays provide fascinating insights into energy generation, robotics and other engineering feats.

\* World Heritage Site
\* Be an apprentice engineer for the day

| Location | Contact |
|---|---|
| Follow brown tourist signs from M54 junction 4 | Ironbridge Gorge Museum Trust, Coach Road, Coalbrookdale, Telford TE8 7DQ |
| **Opening** | |
| Daily: 10am–5pm | t 01952 884391 |
| | w ironbridge.org.uk |
| **Admission** | e tic@ironbridge.org.uk |
| Adult £5.45, Child & Concs £3.80 | |

## 530 Ashbourne

# Sudbury Hall & Museum of Childhood

3 hrs   Mar–Oct

This spectacular late C17 house has sumptuous interiors and a fine collection of portraits. The great staircase is one of the most elaborate of its kind in an English house. The C19 service wing is home to the Museum of Childhood with displays about children from the C18 onwards.

\* Featured in the BBC production of *Pride and Prejudice*
\* 'Behind the Scenes' tours

| Location | Admission |
|---|---|
| 6 miles E of Uttoxeter at junction of A50 Derby–Stoke and A515 Ashbourne | *Hall* Adult £5.50, Child £2.50 |
| | *Museum* £5.50, £3.50 |
| **Opening** | *Hall & Museum* £11, £6 |
| *Hall & Museum* 11 Mar–29 Oct Wed–Sun 1pm–5pm | **Contact** |
| *Grounds* 11 Mar–29 Oct Wed–Sun 11am–6pm; Open Bank Hols | Sudbury, Ashbourne DE6 5HT |
| | t 01283 585337 |
| | w nationaltrust.org.uk |
| | e sudburyhall@nationaltrust.org.uk |

## 531 Burslem

# Ceramica

1½ hrs+   All year

Ceramica is an interactive experience in the heart of the English Potteries, at the centre of the ceramic industry. Learn how clay is transformed into china and the important part ceramics play in everyday life. Discover the past, present and future of ceramics in the displays.

\* See a reconstruction of the inside of a bottle oven
\* Josiah Wedgwood's kiln, discovered by Channel 4's *Time Team*

| Location | Contact |
|---|---|
| In town centre, beside A50 | Market Place, Burslem, Stoke-on-Trent ST6 3DS |
| **Opening** | |
| Daily: Mon–Sat 9.30am–5pm, Sun 10.30am–4.30pm | t 01782 832001 |
| | w ceramicauk.com |
| **Admission** | e info@ceramicauk.com |
| Adult £3.95, Child & Concs £2.75 | |

## 532   Burton upon Trent

# Coors Visitor Centre

2 hrs+   All year

Beer has been brewed in Burton upon Trent for centuries and the Museum of Brewing charts its heritage. It provides a blend of living heritage, historic galleries and family entertainment. The centre is home to two teams of shire horses and a vintage vehicle collection.

* See a working stationary steam engine
* Visit the micro brewery

| Location | Contact |
|---|---|
| A511 in centre of Burton upon Trent (follow signs for Burton North and Stretton) | Horninglow Street Burton upon Trent DE14 1YQ |
| | t  0845 600 0598 |
| Opening | w  coorsvisitorcentre.com |
| Daily: 10am–5pm (last admission 4pm) | e  enquiries@coorsbrewers.com |
| Admission | |
| Adult £6, Child £3, Concs £4 | |

## 533   Halfpenny Green

# Halfpenny Green Vineyards

1 hr   All year

Information boards describe many of the French, German and hybrid varieties of vine planted here and visitors to Halfpenny Green can follow the self-guided vineyard trail. After touring the vineyard, inspect the winery and taste the wines.

* Award-winning wines
* Vineyard trail & craft centre

| Location | Contact |
|---|---|
| Off B4176, near Halfpenny Green Airfield | Tom Lane, Halfpenny Green DY7 5EP |
| | t  01384 221122 |
| Opening | w  halfpenny-green-vineyards.co.uk |
| Daily: 10.30am–5pm | e  sales@halfpenny-green-vineyards. co.uk |
| Admission | |
| Free | |
| *Basic tour* £2 | |
| *Guided tour*  £9.95 (pre-booked) | |

## 534   Hanley

# The Potteries Museum & Art Gallery

2 hrs   All year

At the home of the greatest collection of Staffordshire ceramics you can see Reginald Mitchell's WWII Spitfire and all sorts of art and craft. The award-winning museum also hosts a lively programme of changing exhibitions with national touring shows and events.

* World's finest collection of Staffordshire ceramics
* A collection of more than 650,000 objects

| Location | Admission |
|---|---|
| A500 junction 15 , signed from town centre | Free |
| | Contact |
| Opening | Bethesda Street, Hanley ST1 3DW |
| Daily: Mar–Oct Mon–Sat 10am–5pm, Sun 2pm–5pm; Nov–Feb Mon–Sat 10am–4pm, Sun 1pm–4pm | t  01782 232323 |
| | w  stoke.gov.uk/museums |
| | e  museums@stoke.gov.uk |

## 535   Lichfield

# Erasmus Darwin's House

1 hr   All year

An elegant C18 house near Lichfield Cathedral, this was home to Charles Darwin's grandfather, Erasmus, a renowned doctor, philosopher, inventor, scientist and poet. Period furnishings and audio-visual and interactive displays tell the story of this remarkable man.

* Conference facilities
* Licensed weddings

| Location | Contact |
|---|---|
| In town centre, near cathedral | Beacon Street, Lichfield WS13 7AD |
| | t  01543 306 260 |
| Opening | w  erasmusdarwin.org |
| Please phone for details | e  enquiries@erasmusdarwin.org |
| Admission | |
| Adult £2.50, Child £2 | |

## 536 Lichfield

# Lichfield Heritage Centre

1 hr+    All year

The centre gives an account of Lichfield's varied history. It is home to the Staffordshire Millennium Embroideries, which are displayed in their own gallery, as well as fine examples of city, diocesan and regimental silver, ancient charters and archives.

\* Audio-visual presentations
\* Collection of photographs of Lichfield, old & new

| Location | Admission |
|---|---|
| In town centre | Please phone for details |
| **Opening** | **Contact** |
| Mon–Sat 10am–5pm, | Market Square, Lichfield WS13 6LG |
| Sun 10.30am–5pm | t 01543 256611 |
| | w lichfieldheritage.org.uk |
| | e info@lichfieldheritage.org.uk |

## 537 Lichfield

# Wall Roman Site (Letocetum)

1 hr    Apr–Oct

Wall was an important staging post on the Roman military road to North Wales. It provided overnight accommodation and a change of horse for travelling Roman officials and imperial messengers. The foundations of a hotel and bath house can be seen.

\* Many excavated finds displayed in the museum
\* Audio tour with Gallas the Roman soldier

| Location | Contact |
|---|---|
| Off A5, near Lichfield | Watling Street, nr Lichfield WS14 0AW |
| **Opening** | t 01543 480768 |
| Daily: May–Sep 10am–6pm; | w english-heritage.org.uk |
| Oct 10am–5pm | |
| **Admission** | |
| Adult £2.90, Child £1.50, Concs £2.20 | |

## 538 Longton

# Gladstone Working Pottery Museum

2 hrs+    All year

Gladstone is the only surviving complete Victorian pottery factory from the days when coal-burning ovens made the world's finest bone china. Traditional skills, original workshops and huge bottle kilns make for a convincing and atmospheric time-warp.

\* Try your hand at pottery crafts
\* Cobbled yard & huge bottle kilns

| Location | Contact |
|---|---|
| From M6 follow A500, then take A50 | Uttoxeter Road, Longton, |
| to Longton | Stoke-on-Trent ST3 1PQ |
| **Opening** | t 01782 319232 |
| Daily: 10am–5pm | w stoke.gov.uk/gladstone |
| **Admission** | e gladstone@stoke.gov.uk |
| Adult £4.95, Child £3.50, Concs £3.95 | |

## 539 Market Drayton

# Dorothy Clive Garden

1 hr+   Mar–Oct

A wide range of unusual plants can be seen in this lovely garden. Features include a quarry garden with a waterfall, a woodland garden and a scree and water-garden. The summer borders are spectacular and the autumn crocus and dwarf cyclamen are mindblowing.

\* Lovely views of three counties
\* Japanese maples add to autumn colours

**Location**
On A51, between Nantwich & Stone

**Opening**
Daily: 12 Mar–30 Oct 10.30am–5.30pm

**Admission**
Adult £4, Child £1, Concs £3.40

**Contact**
Willoughbridge,
Market Drayton TF9 4EU

t  01630 647237
w  dorothyclivegarden.co.uk
e.  info@dorothyclivegarden.co.uk

## 540 Milford

# Shugborough

3 hrs+   Mar–Oct

In 1693 the original manor house was demolished and a three-storey house was built. This survives and forms the centre of the house today, but between 1745 and 1748 the architect Thomas Wright transformed the property into a magnificent Georgian mansion.

\* Living history museum with costumed servants
\* Fully working Georgian farm complete with animals

**Location**
6 miles from M6 junction 13

**Opening**
Daily: Mar–28 Oct 11am–5pm

**Admission**
Adult £8, Concs £5

**Contact**
Shugborough, Milford ST17 0XB

t  01889 881388
w  shugborough.org.uk
e  shugborough.promotions
@staffordshire.gov.uk

## 541 Stafford

# Stafford Castle

3 hrs+   All year

Built by William the Conqueror to subdue rebellious local people, Stafford Castle has dominated the landscape throughout 900 years of turbulent history. Visitors today will find a more peaceful setting – follow the castle trail, explore the castle ruins and take in the panoramic view.

\* Try on armour & chainmail
\* Host of archaeological finds

**Location**
Off A518, 1 mile SW of Stafford

**Opening**
Apr–Oct Tue–Sun & Bank Hols
10am–5pm;
Nov–Mar Sat–Sun 10am–4pm

**Admission**
Free

**Contact**
Castle Bank, Newport Road, Stafford
ST16 1DJ

t  01785 257698
w  stafforddc.gov.uk

## 542 Stoke-on-Trent

# Biddulph Grange Garden

1 hr+    Easter–Dec

A rare survival of a high Victorian garden, restored by the National Trust. The garden is divided into a series of themed spaces, including a Chinese temple, Egyptian court, pinetum, dahlia walk, glen, avenues and many other settings.

* Inspiration of the C19 horticulturist James Bateman
* Egyptian garden contains topiary obelisks of yew

**Location**
Off A527, on N side of Biddulph

**Opening**
25 Mar–29 Oct Wed–Sun & Bank Hol
Mon 11.30am–5.30pm; 4 Nov–17 Dec
Sat–Sun only 11am–3pm

**Admission**
*summer* Adult £5.30, Child £2.60
*winter* Adult £2, Child £1

**Contact**
Grange Road, Biddulph,
Stoke-on-Trent ST8 7SD

t 01782 517999
w nationaltrust.org.uk
e biddulphgrange@ationaltrust.org.uk

## 543 Stoke-on-Trent

# Spode Museum & Visitor Centre

1 hr+    All year

Visitors will see a collection of Spode ceramics, including teaware, dessertware and dinnerware, as well as beautiful ornamental pieces. The display includes items from the 1790s to 1833, illustrating the genius of two Josiah Spodes, I and II.

* Display includes designs for the royal family
* Fully guided factory tours available

**Location**
From M6 junction 15 take A500, go left
at 2nd roundabout, then follow signs

**Opening**
Daily: Mon–Sat 9am–5pm, Sun
10am–4pm, Bank Hols 9am–5pm

**Admission**
Free

**Contact**
Church Street, Stoke-on-Trent
ST4 1BX

t 01782 744011
w spode.co.uk
e spodemuseum@spode.co.uk
e visitorcentre@spode.co.uk

## 544 Tamworth

# Middleton Hall

2–3 hrs    Apr–Sep

The hall has an interesting architectural history, with its oldest buildings dating from 1300 and others dating from the C16 to the early C19. Attractions include the 11-bay Georgian west wing and the impressive C16 Great Hall, the restoration of which was completed in 1994.

* 24 embroideries on history of Sutton Coldfield
* Links to Lady Jane Grey, Elizabeth I & Jane Austen

**Location**
On A4091, 4 miles S of Tamworth,
between Belfry & Drayton Manor Park

**Opening**
Apr–Sep Sun 2pm–5pm;
Bank Hols 11am–5pm

**Admission**
Adult £5, Child £1, Concs £3

**Contact**
Middleton, Tamworth B78 2AE

t 01827 283095
w middletonhalltrust.co.uk
e middletonhall@btconnect.com

## 545 Tamworth

# Tamworth Castle

1 hr    All year

This is a Norman shell-keep castle with intact apartments from the C12 to the C19. Fifteen period rooms are open to visitors, including the Great Hall, dungeon and haunted bedroom. There is also a permanent exhibition on Norman castles.

* The Tamworth Story is an interactive local history exhibit
* Living images also known as 'talking heads'

**Location**
Take A51 & A453 through town centre,
signed from A51

**Opening**
Tue–Sun 12noon–5.15pm;
Aug daily 12noon–5.15pm;
Autumn/winter times differ,
please phone for details

**Admission**
Adult £4.75, Child £2.75, Concs £3.75

**Contact**
The Holloway, Ladybank
Tamworth B79 7NA

t 01827 709629/709626
w tamworth.gov.uk
e heritage@tamworth.gov.uk

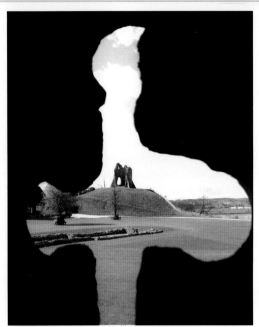

546   Tutbury

# Tutbury Castle

2 hr   Easter–Sep

Built in the 1070s for one of William the Conqueror's barons, Tutbury Castle has been involved in some of the most dramatic events in English history. A bloody place of siege and battle, on four occasions it acted as a prison for Mary Queen of Scots.

* Authentic Tudor privy garden & medieval herbery
* Secret staircase to the Great Hall recently uncovered

**Location**
Exit M1 junction 24a or M6 junction 15, near A50

**Opening**
Easter–17 Sep Wed–Sun 11am–5pm

**Admission**
Adult £4.50, Child & Concs £4

**Contact**
Tutbury, Burton-on-Trent DE13 9JF
t  01283 812129
w  tutburycastle.com
e  info@tutburycastle.com

---

547   Winkhill

# Blackbrook Zoological Park

2–4 hrs   All year

Set amid the Staffordshire Moorlands, this zoo contains a large and varied collection of some of the most rare and endangered species to be found in the world, from swans and geese to vultures and flamingos from meerkats and marmots to piranhas and pythons.

* Largest collection of wildfowl in Britain
* Largest collection of cranes & storks in Britain

**Location**
From Leek, take A523 & 1st right, signed to the park, then 1st right again

**Opening**
Daily: 10.30am–5.30pm (earlier closing in winter)
*Café* Open in summer only

**Admission**
Please phone for details

**Contact**
Winkhill ST13 7QR
t  01538 308293
w  blackbrookzoologicalpark.co.uk
e  enquiries@blackbrookzoologicalpark.co.uk

---

548   Wolverhampton

# Moseley Old Hall

2 hrs+   Mar–Dec

An Elizabethan house, famous for its associations with the fugitive King Charles II who hid here in 1651. Faced with brick in the 1870s, inside it remains as Charles would have known it, with timber framing, oak panelling, period furniture and ingenious hiding places.

* Knot garden recreated in C17 style
* Exhibition of Charles II's escape after Battle of Worcester

**Location**
4 miles N of Wolverhampton, S of M54 between A449 & A460

**Opening**
18 Mar–29 Oct Wed, Sat–Sun 1pm–5pm;
5 Nov–19 Nov Sun only 1pm–4pm;
26 Nov–17 Dec Sun 1pm–4pm (also special Christmas events)
All Bank Hol Mons & following Tues

**Admission**
Adult £5, Child £2.50

**Contact**
Moseley Old Hall Lane, Fordhouses, Wolverhampton WV10 7HY
t  01902 782808
w  nationaltrust.org.uk
e  moseleyoldhall@nationaltrust.org.uk

## 549 Alcester

# Coughton Court

3 hrs   Mar–Oct

This beautiful Tudor house has been a family home since 1409. There is a fine collection of family portraits, furniture and a fascinating exhibition about the Gunpowder Plot. The gatehouse and courtyard are complemented by an Elizabethan knot garden.

* Stunning displays of roses & herbaceous plants
* There are two churches to visit

**Location**
On A435, 2 miles N of Alcester

**Opening**
Mar & Oct Sat–Sun 11–5pm;
Apr–Jun & Sep Wed–Sun 11am–5pm;
Jul–Aug Tue–Sun 11am–5pm

**Admission**
Adult £8.60, Child £4.30

**Contact**
nr Alcester B49 5JA

t 01789 400777
w coughtoncourt.co.uk
e sales@throckmortons.co.uk

## 550 Alcester

# Kinwarton Dovecote

1 hr   Apr–Oct

Beside Kinwarton Church is a field full of archaeological interest, in particular an impressive circular C14 dovecote, which still houses doves. Visitors will see an unusual pivoted ladder from which access to the nesting boxes is possible.

**Location**
S of B4089, 1 mile NE of Alcester

**Opening**
Apr–Oct daily 9am–6pm

**Admission**
£1

**Contact**
Kinwarton, nr Alcester B49 5DN

t 01743 708100
w nationaltrust.org.uk
e kinwartondovecote@ntrust.org.uk

## 551 Alcester

# Ragley Hall

5 hrs    Apr–Sep

Ragley Hall is set in 27 acres of beautiful formal gardens. The home contains baroque plasterwork, the stunning C20 mural *The Temptation*, and a collection of paintings, china and furniture. In addition to the beautiful house, there are the formal gardens and parkland.

\* Ever-changing gardens
\* Game fair & other events throughout the year

**Location**
Off Alcester bypass, signed at A46 junction

**Opening**
*House* Apr–Sep Thu–Sun & Bank Hols 12noon–5.30pm
*Park & Gardens* Apr–Sep Thu–Sun & Bank Hols 10am–6pm

**Admission**
Adult £7.50, Child £4.50, Concs £6.50

**Contact**
Alcester B49 5NJ
t 01789 762090
w ragleyhall.com
e info@ragleyhall.com

## 552 Banbury

# Farnborough Hall

2 hrs+    Apr–Sep

A beautiful honey-coloured stone house, richly decorated in the mid-C18 and the home of the Holbech family for more than 300 years. The interior plasterwork is breathtaking and the charming grounds contain C18 temples, a terrace walk and an obelisk.

\* Terrace walk open by prior appointment only

**Location**
6 miles N of Banbury, W of A423

**Opening**
2 Apr–28 Sep Wed & Sat 2pm–5.30pm

**Admission**
Adult £4, Child £2

**Contact**
Banbury OX17 1DU
t 01295 690002
w nationaltrust.org.uk
e farnboroughhall@nationaltrust.org.uk

## 553 Banbury

# Upton House

1 hr+    Apr–Oct

Once owned by Walter Samuel, 2nd Viscount Bearsted and chairman of Shell 1921–46, Upton contains an outstanding collection of English and continental Old Master paintings, including works by Hogarth, Stubbs, Guardi, Canaletto, Brueghel and El Greco.

\* Exhibition of Shell paintings & publicity posters
\* Tapestries, French porcelain & Chelsea figures

   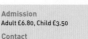

**Location**
On A422, 7 miles NW of Banbury, 12 miles SE of Stratford-upon-Avon

**Opening**
*House* 3 Apr–31 Oct Mon–Wed & Sat–Sun 1pm–5pm
*Gardens* 3 Apr–Oct Sat–Sun 12noon–4pm

**Admission**
Adult £6.80, Child £3.50

**Contact**
nr Banbury OX15 6HT
t 01295 670266
w nationaltrust.org.uk
e uptonhouse@nationaltrust.org.uk

## 554 Coventry

# Brandon Marsh Nature Centre

1 hr+    All year

A visit to Brandon Marsh Nature Centre starts at the visitor centre, opened by Sir David Attenborough in 1998. This contains displays, hands-on activities and information about the nature reserve, which covers 220 acres and features many lakes and bird hides.

\* Warwickshire Wildlife Trust Centre

**Location**
Off A45

**Opening**
Daily: Mon–Sat 9am–4.30pm, Sun 10am–4pm

**Admission**
Adult £2.50, Child £1, Concs £1.50

**Contact**
Brandon Lane, Coventry CV3 3GW
t 02476 308999
w wildlifetrust.org.uk
e enquiries@wkwt.org.uk

## 555  Henley-in-Arden

# Henley-in-Arden Heritage & Visitor Centre

1 hr          Easter–Oct

Henley-in-Arden's history is recorded in the town's oldest house, part of which is C14. Exhibits include a model of the Norman castle that once stood on the mount and information on the ancient Market Cross and the tradition of town criers.

* Audio diaries of early memories
* Tales of industrial, social & sporting life in the town

| Location | Contact |
|---|---|
| In town centre | Joseph Hardy House,150 High Street, Henley-in-Arden B95 5BS |
| **Opening** | t  01564 795919 |
| Easter–Oct Tue–Fri 10.30am–4.30pm, | w  heritagehenley.org.uk |
| Sat–Sun & Bank Hols 2.30pm–4.30pm | e  info@heritagehenley.org.uk |
| **Admission** | |
| Free | |

## 556  Gaydon

# Heritage Motor Centre

3 hrs         All year

The Heritage Motor Centre is home to the largest collection of classic, vintage and veteran British cars in the world. There are 200 vehicles on display, charting the history of the British car industry from the turn of the century to the present day.

* 1963 Morris Mini Cooper
* Regular programme of events

| Location | Contact |
|---|---|
| 2 mins from M40 junction 12 | Banbury Road, Gaydon CV35 0BJ |
| **Opening** | t  01926 641188 |
| Daily: 10am–5pm | w  heritage-motor-centre.co.uk |
| **Admission** | e  enquiries@heritage-motor-centre. co.uk |
| Adult £8, Child £6, Concs £7 | |

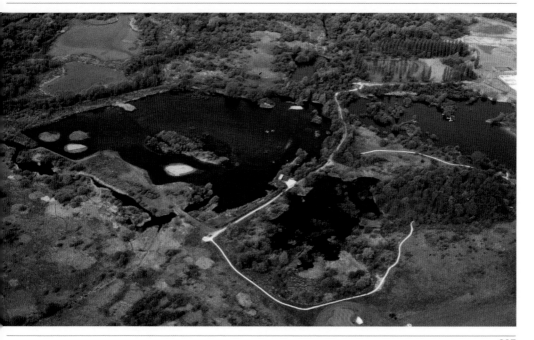

## 557 Kineton

# Compton Verney Art Gallery

2hrs+    Mar–Oct

An innovative art gallery, in an C18 mansion, designed by Robert Adam and set in 120 acres of Capability Brown landscape. The Peter Moores collections include artefacts from Naples 1450–1800, China 3000BC–AD1500 and a collection of British folk art.

* Major temporary exhibitions
* Projects for schools & groups

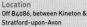

**Location**
Off B4086, between Kineton & Stratford-upon-Avon

**Opening**
Mar–Oct Tue–Sun 11am–5pm

**Admission**
Adult £6, Child £2, Concs £4

**Contact**
Compton Verney CV35 9HZ

t  01926 645500
w  comptonverney.org.uk
e  info@comptonverney.org.uk

## 558 Kenilworth

# Kenilworth Castle

2 hrs+    All year

The largest castle ruin in England and the scene of many sieges and murders, Kenilworth Castle has been linked with some of the most important names in English history. Explore its impressive Norman keep, Tudor gardens and John of Gaunt's Great Hall.

* Walks to Old Kenilworth & ruined abbey
* Elizabethan festival & Shakespeare performances

**Location**
In town centre

**Opening**
Mar–May 10am–5pm;
Jun–Aug 10am–6pm;
Sep–Oct 10am–5pm;
Nov–Feb 10am–4pm

**Admission**
Adult £4.95, Child £2.50, Concs £3.70

**Contact**
Castle Mews, Kenilworth CU8 1NE

t  01926 852078
w  english-heritage.org.uk/
   kenilworthcastle

## 559 Knowle

# Baddesley Clinton

3 hrs+    Mar–Nov

This moated manor house dates from the C15 and little has changed since 1634. During the Elizabethan era it was a haven for persecuted Catholics and there are three priest-holes. The garden includes stewponds, a lake and a nature walk.

* 70-seater restaurant
* Replica priest's hole, part of children's trail

**Location**
W of A4141, between Warwick & Birmingham, 7 miles NW of Warwick

**Opening**
1 Mar–5 Nov Wed–Sun 1.30pm–5pm

**Admission**
*House & Gardens* Adult £6.80, Child £3.40
*Gardens* £3.40, £1.70

**Contact**
Rising Lane, Baddesley Clinton, Knowle, Solihull B93 0DQ

t  01564 783294
w  nationaltrust.org.uk
e  baddesleyclinton@nationaltrust.org.uk

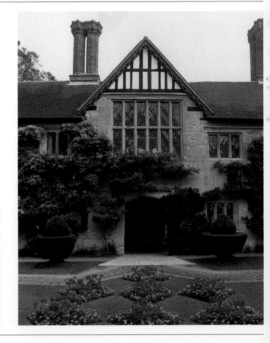

## 560 Nuneaton

# Arbury Hall

½ hr+    Bank Hols

This Elizabethan house was built on the site of a C12 Augustinian priory. Transformed in the C18 to become a fine example of Gothic Revival architecture, the house contains collections of antique furniture, pictures, glass and china. Many rooms are open to the public.

* Delightful landscaped gardens, wooded walks & lake
* Chimneypiece based on tomb of Aymer de Valence

| Location | Contact |
|---|---|
| Signed from Nuneaton | Nuneaton CV10 7PT |
| | t 02476 382804 |
| **Opening** | e brenda.newell@arburyhall.net |
| Sun & Mon of Bank Hols only | |
| 2pm–6pm; | |
| **Admission** | |
| *House & Gardens* Adult £6.50, Child £4 | |
| *Gardens* Adult £5, Child £3.50 | |

## 561 Nuneaton

# Bosworth Battlefield Visitor Centre & Country Park

2 hrs+    Jan–Oct

This is the site of one of the most famous battles in English history, between Richard III and Henry Tudor. The result gave England a new king and marked the beginning of the Tudor dynasty. Discover what it was like to be a soldier and follow the battle trail.

* Walk down a medieval street
* Annual re enactment of the battle

| Location | Admission |
|---|---|
| 2 miles S of Market Bosworth near the village of Sutton Cheney | Adult £3.25, Concs £2.25 |
| **Opening** | **Contact** |
| *Visitor centre* Mar Sat–Sun 11am–5pm; Apr–Oct daily 11am–5pm | Sutton Cheney, Nuneaton, Warwickshire CV13 0AD |
| *Country Park* Jan–Oct daily 7am onwards. Closing times vary | t 01455 290429 |
| | w leics.gov.uk |
| | e bosworth@leics.gov.uk |

## 562 Royal Leamington Spa

# Royal Pump Rooms

1 hr    All year

The historic Royal Pump Rooms have been redeveloped and now include an art gallery and museum. Visitors can explore life in a Victorian spa town, relax in the magnificent Turkish Room and discover the water treatments used at the Royal Pump Rooms.

* Historic hammam room
* Temporary exhibition space & interactive gallery

| Location | Contact |
|---|---|
| Town centre | The Parade, Royal Leamington Spa CV32 4AA |
| **Opening** | |
| Tue, Wed, Fri–Sat 10.30am–5pm, | t 01926 742700 |
| Thu 1.30–8pm, Sun 11am–4pm | w royal-pump-rooms.co.uk |
| **Admission** | e prooms@warwickdc.gov.uk |
| Free | |

## 563 Rugby

# Rugby Art Gallery

1 hr+    All year

This gallery contains a collection of paintings, prints and drawings by well-known British artists such as Sir Stanley Spencer, L S Lowry, Percy Wyndham Lewis, Paula Rego, Barbara Hepworth, Bridget Riley and Lucian Freud.

* Rugby's collection of modern art
* Roman artefacts & local social history objects

| Location | Contact |
|---|---|
| Signed from town centre | Little Elbarow Street, Rugby CV21 3BZ |
| **Opening** | t 01788 533201 |
| Tue & Thu 10am–8pm, Wed & Fri 10am–5pm, Sat 10am–4pm, Sun & Bank Hols 1pm–5pm | w rugbygalleryandmuseum.org.uk |
| | e rugbyartgallery&museum@rugby.gov.uk |
| **Admission** | |
| Free | |

## 564 Stratford-upon-Avon

# Anne Hathaway's Cottage

1 hr    All year

Anne Hathaway's cottage was home to Shakespeare's wife before they married in 1582. Besides being the place where the teenage Shakespeare courted his future bride, the Hathaway home is regarded as the quintessential English country cottage.

\* Inhabited by Hathaway family until the C19
\* Shakespeare tree garden, maze, orchard & brook

| Location | Admission |
|----------|-----------|
| 1 mile from town centre | Adult £5.20, Child £2, Concs £4 |
| **Opening** | **Contact** |
| Daily: Nov–Mar 10am–4pm; | Cottage Lane, Shottery CV37 9HH |
| Apr–May & Sep–Oct Mon–Sat | |
| 9.30am–5pm, Sun 10am–5pm; | t 01789 292100 |
| Jun–Aug Mon–Sat 9am–5pm, | w shakespeare.org.uk |
| Sun 9.30am–5pm | e info@shakespeare.org.uk |

## 565 Stratford-upon-Avon

# Hall's Croft

1 hr    All year

One of the finest half-timbered, gabled houses in Stratford-upon-Avon, named after Dr John Hall, who married Shakespeare's daughter, Susanna. Dr Hall was a pioneering medical practitioner and displays in the house reflect his wealth and status in the community.

\* Outstanding paintings & furniture
\* Exhibition of medical artefacts from the C16 & C17

| Location | Admission |
|----------|-----------|
| Near town centre | Adult £3.50, Child £1.70, Concs £3 |
| **Opening** | **Contact** |
| Daily: Nov–Mar 11am–4pm; | Old Town, Stratford-upon-Avon CV37 |
| Apr–May & Sep–Oct 11am–5pm; | |
| Jun–Aug Mon–Sat 9.30am–5pm, | t 01789 292107 |
| Sun 10am–5pm | w shakespeare.org.uk |
| | e info@shakespeare.org.uk |

566 Stratford-upon-Avon

# Harvard House

1 hr    May–Sep

Harvard House was home to Katherine Rogers, mother of John Harvard, whose bequest founded Harvard University. Built in 1596, the property is a fine example of an Elizabethan town house. It boasts the most ornately timber-framed frontage in Stratford.

* Home to the first museum of British pewter
* Many architectural features of interest

 WC

**Location**
In town centre

**Opening**
May–Sep Fri–Sun & Bank Hols
11am–4pm

**Admission**
Adult £2, Child free

**Contact**
High Street, Stratford-upon-Avon

t  01789 204507
w  shakespeare.org.uk
e  info@shakespeare.org.uk

567 Stratford-upon-Avon

# Holy Trinity Church

½ hr+    All year

Visit Shakespeare's grave and the graves of Anne Hathaway, Dr John Hall and his wife Susanna Shakespeare, and Thomas Nash in the chancel of Holy Trinity Church. Also in the chancel are 26 fine C15 carved misericords.

* Beautiful church situated on banks of River Avon
* Church is approached along an avenue of lime trees

**Location**
Signed from town centre

**Opening**
Mar & Oct Mon–Sat 9am–5pm,
Sun 12pm–5pm; Apr–Sep Mon–Sat
8.30am–6pm, Sun 12noon–5pm;
Nov–Feb Mon–Sat
9am–4pm, Sun 12noon–5pm

**Admission**
*Shakespeare's Grave* Adult £1,
Child & Concs 50p *Church* free

**Contact**
Old Town, Stratford-upon-Avon
CV37 6BG

t  01789 266316
w  stratford-upon-avon.org.uk
e  office@stratford-upon-avon.org.uk

568 Stratford-upon-Avon

# Nash's House & New Place

1 hr    All year

This building belonged to Thomas Nash, a rich property owner married to Shakespeare's granddaughter. The House contains exceptional C17 tapestries and oak furniture, exhibits on the history of Stratford-upon-Avon and interesting Roman, Saxon and Bronze Age artefacts.

* Stratford's first Shakespeare festival staged here
* Elizabethan-style knot garden

 WC

**Location**
Signed from town centre

**Opening**
Daily: Nov–Mar 11am–4pm; Apr–May
& Sep–Oct 11am–5pm; Jun–Aug
Mon–Sat 9.30am–5pm, Sun 10am–5pm

**Admission**
Adult £3.50, Child £1.70, Concs £3

**Contact**
Chapel Street, Stratford-upon-Avon
CV37 6EP

t  01789 292325
w  shakespeare.org.uk
e  info@shakespeare.org.uk

## 569 Stratford-upon-Avon

# Packwood House

2 hrs    Mar–Nov

The original C16 house was restored between the world wars by Graham Baron Ash. The interior contains a fine collection of C16 textiles and furniture. The gardens have renowned herbaceous borders and a famous collection of yews.

\* A curious feature is the large number of sundials
\* Glorious gardens

| Location | Admission |
|---|---|
| On A3400, 2 miles E of Hockley Heath | House & Gardens Adult £6.20, Child £3.10 Gardens £3.10, £1.55 |
| Opening | |
| House 1 Mar–5 Nov Wed–Sun 12noon–4.30pm | Contact |
| Gardens 1 Mar–5 Nov Wed–Sun 11am–4.30pm | Lapworth, Solihull B94 6AT |
| | t 01564 783294 |
| | w nationaltrust.org.uk |
| | e packwood@nationaltrust.org.uk |

## 570 Stratford-upon-Avon

# Shakespeare's Birthplace

1 hr    All year

Experience the Tudor world of William Shakespeare by visiting the house where, in 1564, he was born. Shakespeare's Birthplace provides an insight into his childhood. Family rooms have been recreated with furniture, utensils and wall-hangings from the period.

\* Exhibitions tell the story of the house
\* Exhibits of rare period items including First Folio (1623)

| Location | Admission |
|---|---|
| Signed from town centre | Adult £6.70, Child £2.60, Concs £5.50 |
| Opening | |
| Nov–Mar Mon–Sat 10am–4pm | Contact |
| Sun 9.30–5pm; | Henley Street, Stratford-upon-Avon |
| Apr–May & Sep–Oct Mon–Sat 10am–5pm, Sun 10.30am–5pm; | CV37 6QW |
| Jun–Aug Mon–Sat 9am–5pm, Sun 10.30am–4pm | t 01789 201823 |
| | w shakespeare.org.uk |
| | e info@shakespeare.org.uk |

## 571 Stratford-upon-Avon

# The Shakespeare Countryside Museum & Mary Arden's House

1 hr+    All year

Mary Arden was the mother of William Shakespeare and this site contains her family home. Comprising two C16 farmhouses – Mary Arden's house itself and Palmer's farm – these houses, outbuildings and the adjoining land demonstrate life on a Tudor working farm.

\* Falconry displays
\* Rare breeds farm

| Location | Admission |
|---|---|
| 3 miles outside Stratford-upon-Avon | Adult £5.70, Child £2.50, Concs £5 |
| Opening | |
| Daily: Jun–Aug Mon–Sat 9.30am–5pm, Sun 10am–5pm; | Contact |
| | Station Road, Wilmcote CV37 9UN |
| Apr–May & Sep–Oct daily 10am–5pm; | t 01789 293455 |
| Nov–Mar daily 10am–4pm | w shakespeare.org.uk |
| | e info@shakespeare.org.uk |

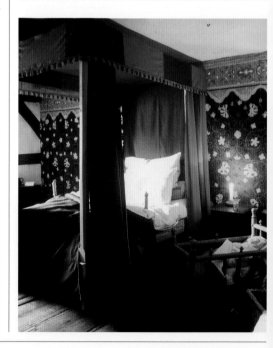

## 572 Sutton Coldfield

# Kingsbury Water Park

2 hrs+    All year

Warwickshire's premier waterside attraction. Kingsbury Water Park has 15 lakes in more than 600 acres of country park. Stroll along the surfaced paths, explore hidden corners, spot birds and wildlife, hire a bike, join an organised event. There is also an adventure playground and a farm.

\* Day-ticket fishing
\* Miniature railway new for 2006

| Location | Contact |
|---|---|
| Exit at Junction 9 of the M42 & follow A4097 towards Kingsbury | Bodymoor Heath Sutton Coldfield B76 0DY |
| **Opening** | t  01827 872660 |
| Please phone for details | w  warwickshire.gov.uk/countryside |
| **Admission** | e  parks@warwickshire.gov.uk |
| Car park £2.50 | |

## 573 Warwick

# Lord Leycester Hospital

1 hr    All year

A historic group of timber-framed buildings from the late C14 clustered round the Norman gateway into Warwick. For 150 years it was the home of Warwick's medieval guilds. Under Elizabeth I it became a retirement home for old warriors and their wives.

\* Museum of Queen's Own Hussars in Chaplain's Hall
\* Master's garden

| Location | Admission |
|---|---|
| Near Tourist Information Centre | Adult £4.90, Child £3.90, Concs £4.40 |
| **Opening** | Gardens £2 |
| Tue–Sun & Bank Hols 10am–5pm | **Contact** |
| Closed 25 Dec & Good Fri | High Street, Warwick CV34 4BH |
| | t  01926 491422 |
| | w  lordleycester.com |
| | e  lordleycester@btinternet.com |

## 574 Warwick

# St John's House

1 hr+    May–Sep

A charming Jacobean house dating from about 1620, St John's became a branch of the Warwickshire Museum in 1961 and houses the social history collection. The galleries have themes such as costume, domestic life and school life, and are changed frequently.

\* Museum of Royal Warwickshire Regiment
\* Ever-changing display of costume

| Location | Contact |
|---|---|
| Signed from town centre | Warwick CV34 4NF |
| **Opening** | t  01926 412500 |
| May–Sep Tue–Sat & Bank Hols | w  warwickshire.gov.uk/museum |
| 10am–5pm, Sun 2.30pm–5pm | e  museum@warwickshire.gov.uk |
| **Admission** | |
| Free | |

## 575 Warwick

# Warwick Castle

2–3 hrs    All year

Built by William the Conqueror in 1068, this is a fine example of a medieval castle. Today visitors can see the mill and engine house where the power of the River Avon ground grain for 600 years, the conservatory, peacock garden, and exquisite Victorian rose garden.

\* Quality Assured Visitor Attraction

| Location | Admission |
|---|---|
| 2 miles from junction 15 of M40. Warwick Castle is easily accessible by road or rail | Please phone for details |
| | **Contact** |
| **Opening** | Warwick CV34 4QU |
| Daily: Apr–Sep 10am–6pm; Oct–Mar 10am–5pm | t  0870 442 2000 |
| | w  warwick-castle.co.uk |
| | e  customer.information@warwick-castle. co.uk |

## 576  Warwick

# Warwickshire Museums

1 hr+    All year

The Warwickshire Museum Service is housed in the C17 market hall. This is one of the few buildings in central Warwick that survived a huge fire in the town in 1694. Displays of geology, biology and archaeology illustrate the natural and historical heritage of the county.

* Famous Sheldon tapestry map of Warwickshire
* 180 million-year-old plesiosaur from Jurassic Period

| Location | Contact |
|---|---|
| In town centre | Market Place, Warwick CV34 4SA |
| **Opening** | t  01926 412500 |
| May–Sep Tue–Sat 10am–5pm, | w  warwickshire.gov.uk |
| Sun & Bank Hols 11.30am–5pm; | e  museums@warwickshire.gov.uk |
| Oct–Apr Tue–Sat 10am–5pm | |
| **Admission** | |
| Free | |

## 577  Wellesbourne

# Charlecote Park

2 hrs+    Mar–Dec

The mellow brickwork and great chimneys of Charlecote sum up the essence of Tudor England. There are associations with both Elizabeth I and Shakespeare – he knew the house well and is alleged to have been caught poaching the estate deer.

* Contains objects from Beckford's Fonthill Abbey
* Formal garden & Capability Brown deer park

| Location | Contact |
|---|---|
| 1 mile W of Wellesbourne, 5 miles | Warwick CV35 9ER |
| E of Stratford, on N side of B4086 | t  01789 470277 |
| **Opening** | w  nationaltrust.org.uk |
| Please phone for details | e  charlecote.park@nationaltrust.org.uk |
| **Admission** | |
| Adult £6.40, Child £3.20 | |

## 578  Wellesbourne

# Wellesbourne Watermill

2 hrs    Easter–Sep

Visitors to this historic watermill can see the mill's machinery being driven by one of the country's largest wooden waterwheels. There are regular demonstrations of how stoneground flour is milled. Coracles are used on the millpond, which is a tranquil haven for wildlife.

* Children's play area
* Animal farm park & maize maze

| Location | Admission |
|---|---|
| On B4086, between Kineton & | Adult £4.50, Child £3, Concs £3.50 |
| Stratford-upon-Avon | **Contact** |
| **Opening** | Kineton Road, Wellesbourne |
| 18 Mar–Sep Wed–Sun & Bank Hols | CV35 9HG |
| 10am–5pm; 22 Jul–1 Sep Tue–Sun | t  01789 470237 |
| 10am–5pm | w  wellesbournemill.co.uk |
| | e  charhutsby@talk21.com |

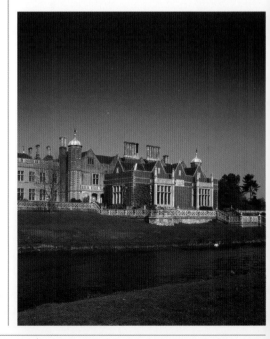

## 579 Aston

# Aston Hall

1 hr    Easter–Oct

A fine Jacobean house, built between 1618 and 1635 by Sir Thomas Holte, featuring elaborate plasterwork ceilings and friezes, a magnificent carved oak staircase and a spectacular 136ft (40m) Long Gallery. Period rooms contain fine furniture, paintings, textiles and metalwork.

\* Biannual candlelight event
\* Regular programme of events

| Location | Contact |
|---|---|
| Off M6 junction 6, 3 miles N of city centre | Trinity Road, Aston, Birmingham B6 6JD |
| **Opening** | t  0121 327 0062 |
| Easter–Oct Tue–Sun & Bank Hols 11.30am–4pm | w  bmg.org.uk |
| **Admission** | |
| Free | |

## 580 Baginton

# Lunt Roman Fort

2 hrs    Apr–Oct

This is a partial reconstruction of the fort established here in AD60. Visitors enter the fort by the reconstructed eastern gateway, which is built entirely of timber and based on depictions from Trajan's Column. There is also a museum of Roman military life with archaeological finds.

\* Events & re enactments with the XIII Legion
\* Museum of army life

| Location | Admission |
|---|---|
| In Baginton, near Coventry. Can be approached from A45 & A46 | Adult £2,  Child & Concs £1 |
| **Opening** | **Contact** |
| Apr–Mid Jul, Mid Sep–Oct Sat–Sun 10.30am–4.30pm; 16 Jul–18 Sep Wed–Sun 10.30am–4.30pm Prebooked parties at other times please phone for details | Coventry Road, Baginton CV8 3AJ |
| | t  02476 832565/303567 |

## 581 Baginton

# Midland Air Museum

2 hrs    All year

Exhibits range from the Avro Vulcan bomber through more than 30 other historic aircraft, both civil and military, aero-engines and other artefacts, to a wide range of memorabilia. The Heritage Centre houses a collection of material relating to Sir Frank Whittle.

\* Giant 1959 Armstrong Whitworth Argosy freighter
\* Meteor, Vulcan, Hunter, Starfighter & Phantom

| Location | Admission |
|---|---|
| Off A45, between roundabout & Baginton | Adult £4.25, Child £2.50, Concs £3.75 |
| **Opening** | **Contact** |
| Daily: Apr–Oct Mon–Sat 10am–5pm, Sun & Bank Hols 10am–6pm; Nov–Mar 10.30am–4.30pm | Coventry Airport, Baginton, Coventry CV8 3AZ |
| | t  02476 301033 |
| | w  midlandairmuseum.org.uk |
| | e  midlandairmuseum@aol.com |

## 582 Birmingham

# Birmingham Museum & Art Gallery

2 hrs    All year

This magnificent building houses one of the world's finest collections of Pre-Raphaelite art, as well as displays of silver, sculpture, ceramics, archaeology and social history. British watercolours and Arts & Crafts Movement work is also on show.

\* Permanent collection of famous Pre-Raphaelite work
\* Gas hall exhibition space

| Location | Contact |
|---|---|
| Adjacent to Council House, signed from end of New Street | Chamberlain Square, Birmingham B3 3DH |
| **Opening** | t  0121 303 2834 |
| Daily: Mon–Thu & Sat 10am–5pm, Fri 10.30am–5pm, Sun 12.30pm–5pm | w  bmag.org.uk |
| **Admission** | e  bmag_enquiries@birmingham. gov.uk |
| Free | |

## 583 Birmingham

# Ikon Gallery

1 hr        All year

One of Europe's leading contemporary art galleries, Ikon exhibits the best in international and British art in a changing programme of exhibitions and events. A variety of media are represented, including sound, video, mixed media, photography, painting, sculpture and installation.

\* Exhibitions in Ikon's events room & tower room
\* Situated in a converted neo-Gothic school building

| Location | Contact |
|---|---|
| 15 mins from city centre, signed from Victoria Square | 1 Oozells Square, Brindleyplace, Birmingham B1 2HS |
| **Opening** | t  0121 248 0708 |
| Tue–Sun & Bank Hols 11am–6pm | w  ikon-gallery.co.uk |
| **Admission** | e  marketing@ikon-gallery.co.uk |
| Free | |

## 584 Birmingham

# Museum of the Jewellery Quarter

1 hr+       All year

Visit a real jewellery factory that has changed little since the early part of the last century. The museum tells the story of jewellery making in Birmingham from its origins in the Middle Ages to the present day, and includes an explanation of jewellery-making techniques.

\* Free entry includes a guided tour of factory

| Location | Contact |
|---|---|
| Adjacent to Jewellery Quarter Clock & Jewellery Quarter Station | 75–79 Vyse Street, Birmingham B18 6HA |
| **Opening** | t  0121 554 3598 |
| Nov–Easter Tue–Sat 11.30am–4pm; Easter–Oct Tue–Sun 11.30am–4pm | w  bmag.org.uk |
| **Admission** | e  bmag.enquiries@ birmingham. gov.uk |
| Free | |

## 585 Birmingham

# National Sea Life Centre

3 hrs       All year

A unique insight into the lives of a myriad creatures – from shrimps to sharks. The unique, one-million-litre tropical ocean display has a Hawaiian volcanic theme, and the completely transparent 360° submarine tunnel provides a home for two giant green turtles.

\* Programme of talks & feeding demonstrations
\* Totally tropical centre

| Location | Admission |
|---|---|
| Between National Indoor Arena & International Convention Centre | Adult £11, Child £8.25, Concs £9 |
| **Opening** | **Contact** |
| *summer* daily 10am–5pm; | The Waters Edge, Brindleyplace, Birmingham B1 2HL |
| *winter* Mon–Fri 10am–4pm, Sat–Sun 10am–5pm | t  0121 643 6777 / 633 4700 |
| | w  sealifeeurope.com |
| | e  slcbirmingham@ merlinentertainments.biz |

# 586 Birmingham

## Royal Birmingham Society of Artists Gallery

2 hrs    All year

One of the oldest art societies in the UK, the Royal Birmingham Society of Artists was given royal status in 1868 by Queen Victoria and played an important part in the Pre-Raphaelite movement. The gallery exhibits the work of members and local designers.

* Regularly changing programme of exhibitions
* Craft gallery, including ceramics, jewellery & more

| Location | Contact |
|---|---|
| Follow New Hall Street to Brook Street | 4 Brook Street, St Paul's Square, Birmingham B3 1SA |
| Opening | t 0121 236 4353 |
| Mon–Wed & Fri 10.30am–5.30pm, | w rbsa.org.uk |
| Thu 10.30am–7pm, Sat 10.30am–5pm | e secretary@rbsa.org.uk |
| Admission | |
| Free | |

# 587 Birmingham

## ThinkTank

4 hrs    All year

Thinktank is Birmingham's science museum, a wonderfully modern attraction offering ten galleries of historical artefacts, modern interactives and futuristic facts. Visitors can explore everything from aircraft and steam engines to intestines and tastebuds!

* Planetarium new in Dec 2005
* Also 3 brand new exhibits exploring the theme of space

| Location | Contact |
|---|---|
| Follow blue banners, 15 min walk from New Street | Curzon Street, Birmingham B4 7XG |
| | t 0121 202 2222 |
| Opening | w thinktank.ac |
| Daily: 10am–5pm | e findout@thinktank.ac |
| Admission | |
| Adult £6.95, Child £4.95, Concs £5.50 | |

# 588 Birmingham

## Tolkien's Birmingham

2 hrs    Apr–Sep

J R R Tolkien garnered inspiration from childhood haunts in Birmingham. The imagery he skilfully created can be attributed to various places and buildings in the city. See where Tolkien dreamed up *The Hobbit* and *Lord of the Rings* for yourself or choose a guided tour.

* In depth knowledge from specialist tour guide for groups only
* Please wear appropriate footwear

| Location | Contact |
|---|---|
| Various areas of Birmingham | 50 Springfield Road, Kings Heath, |
| Opening | Birmingham B14 7DU |
| Apr–Sep by appointment | |
| Please phone for details of guided tours | t 0121 444 4046 |
| | w birminghamheritage.org.uk |
| Admission | e balti1@compuserve.com |
| Adult £5, Child £2.50 | |

# 589 Bournville

## Cadbury World

 ... 

3 hrs    Feb–Dec

Chocolate through the centuries – from Aztec rainforests to Victorian England. Learn about the Cadbury family and their early triumphs and struggles to develop the business. Follow the journey of chocolate from its origins as cocoa to liquid chocolate in the factory.

* Learn how chocolate is used to make famous brands
* Chocolate Coronation Street!

| Location | Contact |
|---|---|
| Signed from M42 | Linden Road, Bournville, Birmingham B30 2LU |
| Opening | |
| Feb–Dec; times vary, please phone for details | t 0121 451 4159 |
| | w cadburyworld.co.uk |
| Admission | e cadbury.world@csplc.com |
| Adult £10.50, Child £7.90, Concs £8.30 | |
| Prebooking recommended | |

## 590  Bournville

# Selly Manor

2 hrs    All year

Dating back to at least 1327, Selly Manor is a medieval timber-framed manor house with Tudor extensions. By the late C19 it was due for demolition but it was saved by George Cadbury, who had it moved piece by piece and rebuilt in the village of Bournville.

* In the unique village of Bournville near Cadbury World

**Location**
3 miles S of Birmingham city centre on Maple Road next to Bournville village green

**Opening**
Tue–Fri 10am–5pm;
Apr–Sep, Sat–Sun & Bank Hols only, 2pm–5pm

**Admission**
Adult £3, Child £1, Concs £2

**Contact**
Bournville, Birmingham B30 1UB
t  0121 472 0199
w  bvt.org.uk/sellymanor
e  sellymanor@bvt.org.uk

## 591  Castle Bromwich

# Castle Bromwich Hall Gardens

2 hrs+    Apr–Sep

This unique example of an English baroque garden is being restored to the period 1680–1740. The 10-acre walled garden contains rare and interesting period plants, vegetables and herbs. Classical patterned parterres can be seen at the end of the Holly Walk.

* C19 holly maze, plant & gift shop
* Restored summer house & greenhouse

**Location**
Signed from M6 junction 5

**Opening**
Apr–Sep Wed–Fri 12noon–4pm,
Sat, Sun & Bank Hols 1pm–5pm

**Admission**
Adult £3.50, Child £1.50, Concs £2.50

**Contact**
Chester Road, Castle Bromwich, Birmingham B36 9BT
t  0121 749 4100
w  cbhgt.colebridge.net
e  admin@cbhgt.colebridge.net

## 592  Coventry

# Coventry Cathedral

1 hr+    All year

Coventry Cathedral was bombed and destroyed in 1940, during WWII. The striking new cathedral, designed by Basil Spence, was consecrated in 1962 and is filled with work from leading artists of the time.

* Stunning tower views & Blitz exhibition
* Bookshop & gift shops open daily

**Location**
Central Coventry

**Opening**
Daily: 9am–5pm (services permitting)

**Admission**
Free

**Contact**
1 Hilltop, Coventry CV1 5AB
t  02476 521200
w  coventrycathedral.org.uk
e  information@coventrycathedral.org.uk

## 593  Coventry

# Herbert Art Gallery & Museum

1 hr    All year

The Herbert is currently undergoing a major redevelopment. Although most of the galleries are closed until late 2007, a programme of exhibitions and events will be taking place throughout the year, including activities for families with children.

* Archaeological finds from Saxon & medieval times
* Objects from Coventry's Asian communities

**Location**
Central Coventry, near Cathedral, next to Tourist Information Centre

**Opening**
Daily: Mon–Sat 10am–5.30pm,
Sun 12noon–5pm

**Admission**
Free

**Contact**
Jordan Well, Coventry CV1 5QP
t  0247 6832386
w  theherbert.org
e  info@theherbert.org

594 Dudley

# Black Country Living Museum

3 hrs+   All year

Set amid 26 acres, the museum occupies an urban heritage park. Historic buildings from around the Black Country have been moved and rebuilt to create a tribute to the traditional skills and enterprise of the people who lived in the heart of industrial Britain.

* Tramcars & trolleybuses transport visitors
* Costumed demonstrators & working craftsmen

**Location**
On A4037, 3 miles from M5 junction 2

**Opening**
Daily: Mar–Oct 10am–5pm;
Nov–Feb Wed–Sun 10am–4pm

**Admission**
Adult £9.95, Child £5.75, Concs £8.75

**Contact**
Tipton Road, Dudley DY1 4SQ

t 0121 557 9643
w bclm.co.uk
e info@bclm.co.uk

595 Dudley

# Dudley Canal Trust

1 hr   Feb–Nov

Explore Dudley's subterranean world of limestone mines and canal systems. Visitors can see the mining and engineering feats of the men from the C18 and modern tunnelling techniques of today. Computer displays show scenes from the past 200 years of mining.

* See the geological history of the area
* Special events throughout the year

**Location**
Follow signs to Dudley past Black Country Living Museum to traffic lights, turn left & the attraction is on the left

**Opening**
Mar–Oct 10am–5pm;
Feb & Nov 10am–4pm

**Admission**
Adult £4.15, Child £3.50, Concs £3.80

**Contact**
The Ticket Office, Todds End Towpath,
Tipton Road, Dudley

t 01384 236275
w dudleytunneltrips.org
e dcttrips@btclick.com

## 596 Dudley

# Dudley Museum & Art Gallery

½ hr+    All year

This museum contains a collection of C17, C18 and C19 British and European paintings, furniture and ceramics, together with Oriental ceramics, Japanese netsuke and inro, Bilston enamels, commemorative medals, and Greek, Roman and Egyptian pottery.

* Geological collection of fossils, rock & minerals
* Regular & varied art exhibitions

**Location**
Off Priory Street, near bus station

**Opening**
Mon–Sat 10am–4pm

**Admission**
Free

**Contact**
St James' Road, Dudley DY1 1HU

t 01384 815575
w dudley.gov.uk
e dudley.museums@dudley.gov.uk

## 597 Edgbaston

# Birmingham Botanical Gardens & Glasshouses

2 hrs+    All year

The gardens originally opened in 1832 and today tropical, sub tropical, Mediterranean and desert glasshouses stand in 15 acres of beautiful gardens. This fine collection of plants includes more than 200 trees and the National Bonsai Collection.

* Designed by J C Loudon, a leading garden planner
* Sculpture trail, waterfowl & exotic birds

**Location**
Signed from Edgbaston

**Opening**
Daily: Mon–Sat 9am–5pm,
Sun 10am–5pm

**Admission**
Adult £5.90, Child & Concs £3.50

**Contact**
Westbourne Road, Edgbaston,
Birmingham B15 3TR

t 0121 454 1860
w birminghambotanicalgardens.
   org.uk
e admin@birminghambotanicalgardens.
   org.uk

## 598  Kingswinford

# Broadfield House Glass Museum

2 hrs      All year

The museum has a collection of British glass, much of which was made locally, from C18 tableware to Victorian cameo vases to modern sculptural pieces. Permanent displays and temporary exhibitions celebrate the art of glassmaking. There is also a glassmaking studio.

* Watch & wonder at the glassblowers' skills
* The Glass Dance windows made by David Prytherch

**Location**
Off A491, between Stourbridge & Wolverhampton

**Opening**
Tue–Sun & Bank Hols 12noon–4pm

**Admission**
Free

**Contact**
Compton Drive, Kingswinford DY6 9NS

t  01384 812745
w  glassmuseum.org.uk
e  glass.museum@dudley.gov.uk

## 599  Walsall

# New Art Gallery

2 hrs      All year

This Arts Lottery-funded gallery opened in 2000 and is said to be one of the most exciting art galleries to be built in the UK in the past 20 years. Traditional art is showcased in the Garman Ryan Collection, donated by Lady Kathleen, widow of sculptor Sir Jacob Epstein.

* Building designed by Caruso St John Architects
* Exhibitions dedicated to best of contemporary art

**Location**
A454 on Wolverhampton Street

**Opening**
Tue–Sat & Bank Hols 10am–5pm, Sun 12noon–5pm

**Admission**
Free

**Contact**
Gallery Square, Walsall WS2 8LG

t  01922 654400
w  artatwalsall.org.uk
e  info@artatwalsall.org.uk

## 600  Walsall

# Walsall Leather Museum

2 hrs      All year

Located at the heart of Britain's saddlery and leather goods trade, this fascinating museum tells the story of Walsall's leather workers, past and present. Regular demonstrations of traditional leather crafts take place in historic workshops.

* Collection of contemporary designer leatherwork
* Regular exhibitions & special events

**Location**
On A4148

**Opening**
Mar–Oct Tue–Sat 10am–5pm, Sun 12noon–5pm;
Nov–Apr Tue–Sat 10am–4pm, Sun 12noon–4pm

**Admission**
Free

**Contact**
Littleton Street West, Walsall WS2 8EQ

t  01922 721153
w  walsall.gov.uk/leathermuseum
e  leathermuseum@walsall.gov.uk

## 601  Wolverhampton

# Bantock House & Park

1 hr+      All year

This Grade II listed family home was built in 1788. The ground floor has recently been restored to its Edwardian splendour, while the upstairs features superb displays of enamels, Japanned ware and steel jewellery, with lots of hands-on activities for all ages.

**Location**
Signed from Wolverhampton ring road

**Opening**
Apr–Oct Tue–Sun 11am–5pm;
Nov–Mar Tue–Sun 12noon–4pm

**Admission**
Free

**Contact**
Finchfield Road, Wolverhampton WV3 9LQ

t  01902 552195
w  wolverhampton.gov.uk

## 602 Wolverhampton

# Wightwick Manor

2 hrs   Mar–Dec

This is a fine example of a house built and furnished in the Arts & Crafts Movement style. It features many original William Morris wallpapers and fabrics, Pre-Raphaelite paintings, Kempe glass and tiles by William de Morgan.

\* Beautiful garden designed by Thomas Mawson
\* Talks & tours bring the house to life

| Location | Contact |
|---|---|
| Off A454, beside Mermaid Inn, 3 miles W of Wolverhampton | Wightwick Bank, Wolverhampton WV6 8EE |
| **Opening** | t  01902 761400 |
| Mar–24 Dec Thu & Sat 12.30pm–5pm | w  nationaltrust.org.uk |
| **Admission** | e  wightwickmanor@nationaltrust.org.uk |
| Adult £6.50, Child £3.30 | |
| Timed ticket & guided tour only | |

## 603 Wolverhampton

# Wolverhampton Art Gallery

1 hr+   All year

The gallery has an innovative programme of temporary exhibitions, alongside a series of workshops and special events. The collection includes British and American Pop Art as well as traditional C18 and C19 paintings by Gainsborough, Turner and Landseer.

\* Contemporary art collection is the finest in the region
\* Sensing Sculpture, a tactile sculpture court

| Location | Contact |
|---|---|
| Opposite Tourist Information Centre | Lichfield Street, Wolverhampton WV1 1DU |
| **Opening** | |
| Mon–Sat 10am–5pm ; | t  01902 552055 |
| closed Bank Hols | w  wolverhamptonart.org.uk |
| **Admission** | e  info@wolverhamptonart.org.uk |
| Free | |

## 604 Bewdley

# West Midland Safari & Leisure Park

3 hrs+   Apr–Oct

A 4-mile drive-through safari covers an area of more than 150 acres and is home to a variety of exotic and unusual animals including rare and beautiful white tigers, elephants, rhino, giraffes, lions, wallabies, emus, camels, zebra, bison, wolves and llamas.

\* Safari bus tours
\* Discovery trail

| Location | Contact |
|---|---|
| On A456 between Kidderminster & Bewdley | Spring Grove, Bewdley DY12 1LF |
| **Opening** | t  01299 402114 |
| Daily: Mon–Fri 10am–5pm, | w  wmsp.co.uk |
| Sat–Sun 10am–5.30pm | e  info@wmsp.co.uk |
| **Admission** | |
| Please phone for details | |

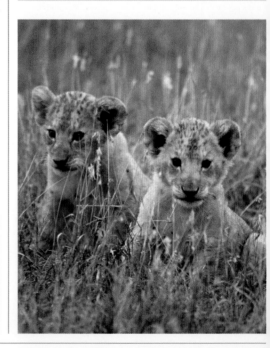

## 605 Broadway

# Broadway Tower & Country Park

½ hr+    All year

Built on an ancient beacon site, the tower has a colourful history as – among others – home to the renowned printing press of Sir Thomas Phillips and country retreat for Pre-Raphaelite artists, notably the artist, designer, writer, craftsman and socialist William Morris.

\* Today houses exhibition connected with its past
\* Said to be one of England's outstanding viewpoints

**Location**
Off A44 1 mile SE of Broadway

**Opening**
Daily: Apr–Oct 10.30am–5pm;
Nov–Mar Sat Sun 11am–3pm

**Admission**
Adult £3.50, Child £2, Concs £3

**Contact**
Middle Hill, Broadway WR12 7LB
t 01386 852390
w broadway-cotswolds.co.uk
e broadwaytower1@aol.com

## 606 Bromsgrove

# Avoncroft Museum of Historic Buildings

3 hrs    Mar–Nov

Avoncroft is a fascinating world of historic buildings spanning seven centuries, rescued and rebuilt on a beautiful open-air site. You can see craftsmen working in a C19 nailshop, furnished historic houses and a variety of craft demonstrations.

\* Visit rural Victorian England at the Toll Cottage
\* See a church, gaol & working windmill

**Location**
2 miles S of Bromsgrove off A38

**Opening**
Mar Tues–Thurs, Sat–Sun
10.30am–4pm; Apr–Jun, Sep & Oct
Tues–Fri 10.30am–4.30pm, Sat–Sun
10.30am–5pm; Jul–Aug daily
10.30am–5pm; Nov Sat–Sun
10.30am–4.30pm

**Admission**
Adult £6, Child £3, Concs £5

**Contact**
Stoke Heath,
Bromsgrove B60 4JR
t 01527 831363
w avoncroft.org.uk
e avoncroft1@compuserve.com

## 607 Droitwich

# Hanbury Hall

2 hrs+    Mar–Oct

Completed in 1701, this homely William and Mary-style house is famed for its beautiful painted ceilings and staircase, and has other fascinating features including an orangery, ice house, pavilions and working mushroom house, as well as beautiful parkland walks.

\* Tercentenary exhibition opened in 2001
\* Garden surrounded by 160 acres of parkland

**Location**
Near junction 5 of M5, 5 miles
W of Droitwich

**Opening**
4 Mar & 11 Mar Sat–Sun 1pm–5pm;
18 Mar–31 Oct Sat–Wed 1pm–5pm

**Admission**
Please phone for details

**Contact**
School Road, Droitwich WR9 7EA
t 01527 821214
w nationaltrust.org.uk
e hanburyhall@nationaltrust.org.uk

## 608 Kidderminster

# Bodenham Arboretum

2 hrs+    All year

Bodenham Arboretum is a collection of more than 2,700 trees set in 156 acres, with 11 pools, 5 miles of footpaths and a working farm with a herd of pedigree Herefords. In addition there is an award-winning visitor centre set in the hillside overlooking the Big Pool.

\* Christmas Nativity trail
\* Laburnum Tunnel is a highlight in late May/June

**Location**
Signed from Wolverley

**Opening**
Jan–Feb Sat–Sun 11am–5pm;
Mar–Dec Wed–Sun 11am–5pm

**Admission**
Adult £5, Child £2

**Contact**
Wolverley, Kidderminster DY11 5SY
t 01562 852444
w bodenham-arboretum.co.uk

## 609 Kidderminster

# Harvington Hall

2 hrs  Mar–Oct

A moated medieval and Elizabethan manor house.
Many of the rooms still have their original Elizabethan
wall-paintings that were discovered under whitewash
in 1936. The hall also contains the finest series of
priest-holes anywhere in the country.

* Elizabethan malt house & Georgian chapel in garden
* Moat broadens into a small lake, home to waterfowl

**Location**
3 miles SE of Kidderminster just off
A450 Birmingham to Worcester road

**Opening**
Mar & Oct Sat–Sun 11.30am–4.30pm;
Apr–Sep Wed–Sun 11.30am–4.30pm

**Admission**
Adult £4.50, Child £3, Concs £3.80

**Contact**
Harvington, Kidderminster DY10 4LR
t 01562 777846
w harvingtonhall.com
e thehall@harvington.fsbusiness.
co.uk

## 610 Malvern

# Great Malvern Priory

½ hr  All year

Malvern Priory is one of the greater parish churches in
the country. It was founded in 1085 and contains the
finest collection of stained glass after York Minster,
together with carved misericords from the C15 and C16
and the largest collection of medieval floor and wall tiles.

* Venue for many concerts
* Newly restored organ in 2004

**Location**
Just off A449 in Malvern

**Opening**
Daily: Apr–Sep 9am–6.30pm;
Oct–Mar 9am–4.30pm

**Admission**
Free, donations welcomed

**Contact**
Church Street, Malvern WR14 2AY
t 01684 561020
w greatmalvernpriory.org.uk
e office@greatmalvernpriory.org.uk

## 611 Pershore

# Croome Park

2 hrs    Mar–Dec

Capability Brown's first complete landscape design, Croome is being restored to its C18 splendour with generous support from the Heritage Lottery Fund. Admire the beauty, enjoy relaxing walks or take part in one of our many activities.

\* 1st phase of National Trust's ten-year restoration project
\* Restoration of park buildings also in progress

**Location**
8 miles S of Worcester & E of A38

**Opening**
Mar–May, Sep–Oct Wed–Sun 10am–5.30pm;
Jun–Aug daily 10am–5.30pm;
Nov–Dec Wed–Sun 10am–4pm;
Open all Bank Hols 10am–4pm

**Admission**
Adult £3.70, Child £1.80

**Contact**
NT Estate Office, The Builders' Yard, High Green, Severn Stoke WR8 9JS

t 01905 371006
w nationaltrust.org.uk
e croomepark@nationaltrust.org.uk

## 612 Stourbridge

# Hagley Hall

1 hr    Jan–Feb

Commissioned in 1756 and designed by Sanderson Miller, this was the last of the great Palladian houses to be built. Van Dyck paintings, Chippendale furniture and exquisite rococo plasterwork are displayed throughout the house.

\* Surrounded by 350 acres of landscaped deer park
\* See where two of the Gunpowder Plot conspirators hid

**Location**
E of Kidderminster, junction 4 of M5, signed from junction of A456 and A491

**Opening**
Jan–Feb Sun–Fri 2pm–5pm;
all Bank Hols and their weekends
Times limited, please phone or visit the website for details

**Admission**
Adult £5, Child & Concs £2.50

**Contact**
Hagley DY9 9LG

t 01562 882408
w hagleyhallcom
e hagleyhall@aol.com

## 613 Worcester

# The Commandery

1½ hrs    All year

The building was originally founded as a hospital in 1085 by the then Bishop of Worcester, St Wulfstan. Over the centuries it has been adapted for different uses while retaining the fabric of its history. It currently houses a variety of historical exhibitions.

* Try on original armour & weapons
* Relive the Battle of Worcester

| Location | Contact |
|----------|---------|
| Just outside city walls at Sidbury Gate | Sidbury, Worcester WR1 2HU |
| **Opening** | t 01905 361821 |
| Daily: Mon–Sat 10am–5pm, | w worcestercitymuseums.org.uk |
| Sun 1.30pm–5pm | e thecommandery@cityofworcester. |
| | gov.uk |
| **Admission** | |
| Adult £4.10, Child £3.10 | |

## 614 Worcester

# Leigh Court Barn

½ hr+    Apr–Sep

This is a striking example of medieval architecture. At 130 feet long and 36 feet wide (40 x 11m), the barn is the largest cruck structure in the UK. Once part of Leigh Court Manor, the barn has ten bays and two porches.

* Originally built for the monks of Pershore Abbey

| Location | Contact |
|----------|---------|
| 5 miles W of Worcester on unclassified road off A4103 | Leigh, Worcester WR6 5LB |
| **Opening** | t 0121 625 6820 |
| Apr–Sep Thur–Sun & Bank Hols 10am–6pm | w english–heritage.org.uk |
| **Admission** | |
| Free | |

## 615 Worcester

# Royal Worcester Porcelain Works

4 hrs+  All year

The works were established in 1751 along the banks of the River Severn. Our Royal Worcester Shops offer an extensive range of quality bone china, porcelain & giftware with great savings and special offers all year. You can also paint your own design on a plate.

* One of the world's leading ceramics museums
* Huge variety of porcelain, bone china & earthenware

**Location**
3 miles from junction 7 of M5, follow signs to city centre – near cathedral

**Opening**
Daily: Mon–Sat 9am–5.30pm Sun 11am–5pm

**Admission**
Prices vary, please see the website or phone for details

**Contact**
Severn Street, Worcester WR1 2NE

t  01905 746000
w  worcesterporcelainmuseum.org
e  museum@royal-worcester.co.uk

## 616 Worcester

# Sir Edward Elgar Birthplace Museum

1 hr  Feb–Dec

The cottage and the Elgar Centre together tell the story of Sir Edward Elgar, composer of much of England's best-known classical music. Visit his study with his gramophone. See family photographs and countless mementos including his books and his golf clubs.

* In the Elgar Centre see manuscripts & music scores
* Watch historic film of his final years

**Location**
3 miles from Worcester on A44 towards Leominster

**Opening**
Daily: 11am–5pm*
closed 23 Dec–1 Feb

**Admission**
Adult £5, Child £2, Concs £4.50

**Contact**
Crown East Lane, Lower Broadheath WR2 6RH

t  01905 333224
w  elgarmuseum.org
e  birthplace@elgarmuseum.org

## 617 Worcester

# Spetchley Park Garden

2 hrs  Apr–Sep

Virtually hidden from the road and largely unaltered in the past century, this lovely 30-acre Victorian paradise boasts an enviable collection of plant treasures from every corner of the globe. Clipped hedges and tumbling borders mix with olives and pineapple scented flowers.

* Year-round colour
* Unexpected vistas provide views of the Malvern Hills

**Location**
2 miles E of Worcester on A44, leave M5 at junction 6

**Opening**
Apr–Sep Tue–Fri 11am–5pm, Sun 2pm–5pm; Bank Hols 11am–5pm Deer park closed in Jun

**Admission**
Adult £5, Child £2

**Contact**
Spetchley, Worcester WR5 1RS

t  01453 810303
w  spetchleygardens.co.uk
e  hb@spetchleygardens.co.uk

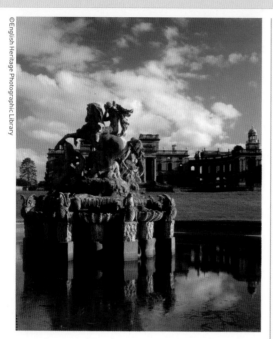

©English Heritage Photographic Library

# Upton Heritage Centre

1 hr+    All year

Located in the oldest surviving building in Upton, the Pepperpot, are displays illustrating the growth and development of the town and its involvement in the Civil War of 1651.

\* Battle of Upton display
\* Sited in old bell tower

| Location | Admission |
|---|---|
| On the B4211 from Great Malvern & A38 & A4104 from Worcester | Free |
| | Contact |
| Opening | Church Street, Upton-upon-Severn, |
| Daily: Apr–Sep 1.30pm–4.30pm; open some mornings please phone for details | Worcester WR8 0HT |
| | t 01684 592679 |

# Witley Court

2 hrs    All year

An early Jacobean manor house, Witley Court was converted in the C19 into a vast Italianate mansion with porticos by John Nash. The spectacular ruins of this once-great house are surrounded by magnificent landscaped gardens.

\* Huge stone fountains that once shot 120 feet upwards
\* £1m garden renovation in past two years

| Location | Contact |
|---|---|
| 10 miles NW of Worcester on A443 | Great Witley WR6 6JT |
| Opening | t 01299 896636 |
| Daily: Apr–Oct 10am–6pm (5pm in Oct); Nov–Mar Thur–Sun 10am–4pm | w english-heritage.org.uk |
| | e mark.badger@english-heritage. org.uk |
| Admission | |
| Adult £4.95, Child £2.50, Concs £3.70 | |

# Worcester Cathedral

1 hr    All year

Worcester Cathedral has been a place of prayer and worship since AD680. The present building was begun in 1084. Its many attractions include King John's tomb, Prince Arthur's Chantry, the early C12 Chapter House and St Wulstan's crypt.

\* Tower open 10.30am–4.30pm, Sat & summer holidays
\* Magnificent Victorian stained-glass windows

| Location | Contact |
|---|---|
| City centre, off College Street | 10a College Green, Worcester WR1 2LH |
| Opening | |
| Daily: 7.30am–6pm, services three times daily | t 01905 28854 |
| | w cofe-worcester.org.uk |
| Admission | e info@worcestercathedral.org.uk |
| Free, donations welcomed | |

Llynnau Mymbyr, Gwyneed

# Wales

Mid Wales  North Wales  South Wales

## 621 Aberystwyth

# Animalarium

3 hrs    All year

Meet a wide collection of exotic and domestic animals, birds and reptiles, including monkeys, marmosets, lemurs and wallabies. Pony rides run twice daily from Easter to September. There is an animal-petting area, a fruit bat cave and a daily snake-handling demonstration.

* Wales Tourist Board seal of approval

**Location**
At Borth, between Aberystwyth & Machynlleth

**Opening**
Daily: *summer* 10am–6pm
*winter* 11am–4pm

**Admission**
Adult £6.50, Child £4.50, Concs £5.50

**Contact**
Borth, Ceredigion SY25 6RA

t 01970 871224

## 622 Aberystwyth

# Vale of Rheidol Railway

1 hr+    Apr–Oct

Take a ride on a steam train for 11 miles from Aberystwyth to Devil's Bridge. During the hour-long journey you'll have spectacular views of the wooded Rheidol Valley. From Devil's Bridge there are walks to Mynach Falls, Devil's Punchbowl and Jacob's Ladder.

* One of the Great Little Trains of Wales
* Last steam railway owned by British Rail

**Location**
Trains depart from Aberystwyth centre, beside main railway station

**Opening**
Please phone for details

**Admission**
*Return* Adult £12, Child from £3, Concs £10.50

**Contact**
Park Avenue, Aberystwyth, Cardiganshire SY23 1PG

t 01970 625819
w rheidolrailway.co.uk
e vor@rheidolrailway.co.uk

## 623 Brecon

# Brecon Beacons National Park Visitor Centre

1 hr+    All year

The attractions of the Brecon Beacons National Park range from lush, green, open countryside to historical and cultural heritage. There are attractions to suit all the family including museums, theatres and family activity centres, plus beautiful walks and rides.

* Centre of internationally renowned festivals
* Selection of guided walks available

**Location**
National Park Mountain Centre is 5½ miles SW of Brecon

**Opening**
Daily; Mar–Jun & Sep–Oct 9.30am–5pm; Jul–Aug 9.30am–6pm; Nov–Feb 9.30am–4.30pm

**Admission**
Free. Car park charges vary

**Contact**
NPVC, Libanus, Brecon, Powys LD3 8ER

t 01874 623366
w breconbeacons.org
e mountain.centre@breconbeacons .org

## 624 Cardigan

# Felinwynt Rainforest & Butterfly Centre

1 hr+   Easter–Oct

This tropical rainforest in the heart of Wales is home to exotic and unusual plants, birds, insects and butterflies from all over the world. You'll see the American glass-wing butterfly, the Asian scarlet swallowtail and the giant atlas moth.

* Welsh Tourist Board Star Attraction
* Video room

**Location**
Off A487, 6 miles N of Cardigan. Follow brown tourist signs

**Opening**
Daily: Easter–Oct 10.30am–5pm

**Admission**
Adult £3.90, Child £1.75, Concs £3.70

**Contact**
Felinwynt, Cardigan
Ceredigion SA43 1RT
t 01239 810882/810250
w butterflycentre.co.uk

## 625 Dolgellau

# Quaker Heritage Centre

½ hr   All year

Find out all about the Quaker community that was once established here and the persecution that forced its members to emigrate. They settled in America in 1681 after buying 40,000 acres of land in what became known as Pennsylvania.

* Pennsylvania still has numerous Welsh names

**Location**
Town centre, off Sgwar Eldon Square

**Opening**
*summer* Daily: 10am–6pm
*winter* Thu–Mon: 10am–5pm

**Admission**
Free

**Contact**
Tŷ Meirion, Sgwar Eldon Square, Dolgellau
t 01341 424442
w gwynedd.gov.uk
e amgueddfeydd–museums@gwynedd.gov.uk

## 626 Llandrindod Wells

# The National Cycle Collection

1 hrs+   All year

How big is a penny-farthing's wheel? And just how uncomfortable were those early bikes compared with today's high-tech versions? See more than 250 bicycles from 1819, such as the hobby horse, boneshakers and penny-farthings up to the most modern cycles of today.

* The Dunlop story
* Displays about past racing stars

**Location**
Just off Temple Street in town centre. Llandrindod Wells is on A483

**Opening**
Mar–Oct daily 10am–4pm;
Nov–Feb Tue, Thu & Sun 10am–4pm

**Admission**
Adult £2.50, Child £1, Concs £2

**Contact**
The Automobile Palace, Temple Street Llandrindod Wells, Powys LD1 5DL
t 01597 825531
w cyclemuseum.org.uk
e cycle.museum@care4free.net

## 627 Llangorse

# Llangorse Rope & Riding Centre

4 hrs+   All year

The centre offers a range of indoor and outdoor climbing and riding activities, from rock surfaces and rope bridges to trekking and hacking. There are qualified instructors and onsite accommodation is available.

* Largest indoor climbing & riding centre in Wales
* WTB's Best New Business in Wales Award

**Location**
On B4560, off A40
Brecon–Abergavenny road

**Opening**
*Climb* Mon–Sat 9am–10pm;
Sun 9am–6pm
*Ride* Daily: 9.30am–4.30pm

**Admission**
*Climb* From £11.50 per person
*Ride* From £12.50 per person

**Contact**
Gilfach Farm, Llangorse, Brecon Beacons, Powys LD3 7UH
t 01874 658272
w activityuk.com
e info@activity.uk.com

## 628 Llannwrda

# Dolaucothi Gold Mines

2 hrs    Easter–Oct

These unique gold mines are set amid wooded hillsides overlooking the beautiful Cothi Valley. The Romans, who exploited the site almost 2,000 years ago, left behind a complex of pits, channels, adits and tanks. Mining resumed in the C19 and peaked in 1938.

\* Historical tours
\* Opportunity to pan for gold

**Location**
Between Lampeter & Llanwrda on A482

**Opening**
Daily: Easter–Oct 10am–5pm

**Admission**
Adult £3.20, Child £1.60

**Contact**
Pumsaint, Llanwrda SA19 8US

t 01558 650177
w nationaltrust.org.uk
e dolaucothi@nationaltrust.org.uk

## 629 Llanwyddyn

# Lake Vyrnwy Nature Reserve

2 hrs+    All year

This manmade lake was completed in 1888. In dry weather, if the water level drops far enough, the ruins of the submerged village of Llanwyddyn reappear. With various hides, vantage points and nature trails, it is a spectacular place for bird-watching.

\* Moorland, woodland & water habitats
\* Good bird-watching all year round

**Location**
10 miles W of Llanfyllin

**Opening**
Apr–Dec daily 10.30am–5.30pm;
Jan–Mar Sat–Sun only 10.30am–5.30pm

**Admission**
Free

**Contact**
Brynawel, Llanwyddyn,
Powys SY10 0LZ

t 01691 870278
w rspb.org.uk
e vyrnwy@rspb.org.uk

## 630 Machynlleth

# Celtica

1 hr+    All year

A unique and stimulating experience of Celtic heritage and culture. Your journey takes you through eight galleries – the foundry, the origins gallery, the village, the round house, the forest, the otherworld, the vortex and Yma o Hyd. A headset provides commentary.

\* Award-winning attraction
\* Member of Dyfi Valley Attractions

**Location**
In Machynlleth village

**Opening**
Daily: 10am–6pm; closed Christmas

**Admission**
Adult £5, Child £4, Concs £4.40

**Contact**
Y Plas, Machynlleth,
Powys SY20 8ER

t 01654 702702
w celticawales.com
e celtica@celticawales.com

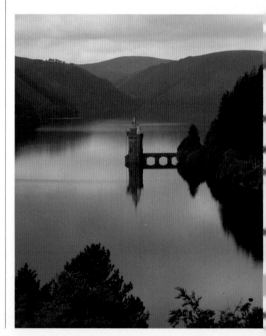

## 631 Machnylleth

# Centre for Alternative Technology

3 hrs+    All year

This is a 40-acre haven of biodiversity. It has examples of wind, water and solar power; energy conservation; environmentally-sound buildings; self-builds; organic agriculture and alternative sewage systems. In summer entry is via a unique water-balanced cliff railway.

\* Largest public display centre of its kind in Europe
\* Multi-award winner

**Location**
3 miles N of Machynlleth on A487 to Dolgellau. Clearly signed

**Opening**
Daily: mid-Jul–Aug 9.30am–6pm;
Sep–Oct 10am–5.30pm;
Nov–Mar 10am–5pm;
Apr–mid-Jul 10am–5.30pm

**Admission**
Adult £8, Child £5.50, Concs £7.20

**Contact**
Machynlleth, Powys SY20 9AZ
t 01654 705950
w cat.org.uk
e information@cat.org.uk

## 632 Machynlleth

# Corris Craft Centre

2 hrs+    Apr–Oct

Corris Craft Centre is home to ten craft workshops in which visitors are invited to see the skills of the craftworkers and to buy from the displays of wooden toymaking, pottery, jewellery, leatherwork, handcarved candles, glassware, wood turning and card designing.

\* Also buy patchwork quilting & rustic furniture

**Location**
On A487 between Machynlleth & Dolgellau

**Opening**
Daily: Apr–Oct 10am–5.30pm
Please phone for details of winter opening times

**Admission**
Free

**Contact**
Corris, Machynlleth,
Powys SY20 9RF
t 01654 761584
w kingarthurslabyrinth.com
e king.arthurs.labyrinth@corris-wales.co.uk

## 633 Machynlleth

# King Arthur's Labyrinth

2 hrs+    Apr–Nov

Take a boat underground through a waterfall and deep into the spectacular caverns under the mountains where tales of King Arthur are told with stunning sound and light effects. Back above ground, join the Bard's Quest to search for legends lost in the Maze of Time.

\* Large fully operational craft centre
\* Shop sells items on the Arthurian theme

**Location**
On A487 between Machynlleth & Dolgellau

**Opening**
Daily: Apr–5 Nov 10am–5pm
(last tour 5pm)

**Admission**
Adult £5.50, Child £3.90, Concs £4.95

**Contact**
Corris, Machynlleth,
Powys SY20 9RF
t 01654 761584
w kingarthurslabyrinth.com
e king.arthurs.labyrinth@corris-wales.co.uk

## 634 Rhayader

# Gigrin Farm

1 hr+    All year

A family-run upland sheep farm with wonderful views of the Wye and Elan valleys. It has breeding ewes along with ponies, assorted ducks and a number of pea fowl. In 1994 it became the Official Kite Country, Red Kite feeding station – a big draw for bird-watchers.

\* Farm & nature trail
\* New wetland project

**Location**
On A470, ½ mile S of Rhayader

**Opening**
Daily: 1pm–5pm

**Admission**
Adult £3, Child £1, Concs £2.50

**Contact**
South Street, Rhayader,
Powys LD6 5BL
t 01597 810243
w redkitecentre.co.uk
e kites@gigrin.co.uk

Mid Wales | North Wales

## 635 Presteigne

# The Judge's Lodging

1 hr+ Mar–Dec

Explore the gas-lit world of the Victorian judges, their servants and felonious guests, at this national award-winning, historic house. It is totally hands-on, with an eavesdropping audio tour. Grim cells and a vast courtroom echo to the trial of a local duck thief.

\* Family friendly with kids' activity boxes
\* Local history exhibition

**Location**
From A49, take B4362. The museum is in town centre.

**Opening**
Mar–Oct 10am–6pm;
Nov–Dec Wed–Sun 10am–4pm;
Closed 22Dec–Feb

**Admission**
Adult £4.95, Child £3.95, Concs £4.50

**Contact**
Broad Street, Presteigne
Powys, Mid Wales LD8 2AD
t 01544 260650
w judgeslodging.org.uk
e info@judgeslodging.org.uk

## 636 Welshpool

# Powis Castle & Garden

3 hrs Mar–Oct

This world-famous garden, overhung with enormous clipped yews, shelters rare and tender plants, statues, an orangery and an aviary on the terraces. The medieval castle contains one of the finest collections of paintings and furniture in Wales.

\* Collection of Indian treasures at the Clive Museum
\* Beautiful interiors dating from 1600 to 1904

**Location**
1 mile S of Welshpool; signed from A483

**Opening**
Please phone for details

**Admission**
Adult £8.80, Child £4.40

**Contact**
Welshpool SY21 8RF
t 01938 551944
w nationaltrust.org.uk
e powiscastle@nationaltrust.org.uk

## 637 Anglesey

# Anglesey Sea Zoo

2 hrs+ Feb–Oct

This is Wales's largest marine aquarium, nestling on the shores of the Menai Strait. With more than 50 displays, the Sea Zoo has recreated the habitats of the fauna and flora found around Anglesey and the North Wales coastline.

\* Major seahorse conservation project
\* Lobster hatchery gift & pearl shop

**Location**
On A55 cross the Britannia Bridge on to Anglesey & follow brown lobster signs to Brynsiencyn. Nearest train station Bangor, then no.42 bus

**Opening**
Daily; Feb–Mar 11am–3pm;
Easter–Oct 10am–6pm

**Admission**
*Low season* Adult £5.95, Child £4.95,
Concs £5.50

**Contact**
Brynsiencyn, Isle of Anglesey LL61 6TQ
t 01248 430411
w angleseyseazoo.co.uk
e info@angleseyzoo.co.uk

## 638 Anglesey

# Plas Newydd

3 hrs Apr–Oct

This C18 house built by Wyatt is an interesting mixture of classical and Gothic. Restyled in the 1930s, the house is famous for its association with Whistler, whose work is exhibited.There is also a museum for the 1st Marquess of Anglesey who led the cavalry at the Battle of Waterloo.

\* Marine walk on the Menai Strait
\* Fine spring garden with Australasian arboretum

**Location**
Junction 7 & 8 off A55

**Opening**
Apr–Oct Sat–Wed
*House* 12pm–5pm
*Gardens* 11am–5.30pm

**Admission**
Adult £6, Child £3

**Contact**
Llanfairpwll, Anglesey LL61 6DQ
t 01248 715272/714795
w nationaltrust.org.uk
e plasnewydd@nationaltrust.org.uk

639 Blaenau Ffestiniog

# Llechwedd Slate Caverns

2 hrs    All year

Take two underground train rides: The Miner's Tramway takes passengers into the mountain, past early Victorian mining remains and spectacular caverns. The Deep Mine descends on Britain's steepest passenger railway, with a gradient of 1:1.8.

* Explore 10 chambers on foot
* Experience life in the Victorian village

**Location**
On A470 between Blaenau Ffestiniog & Dolwyddelan

**Opening**
Daily: from 10am

**Admission**
Adult £8.25, Child £6.25, Concs £7

**Contact**
Blaenau Ffestiniog LL41 3NB

t 01766 830306
w llechwedd-slate-caverns.co.uk
e info@llechwedd-slatecaverns.co.uk

640 Caernarfon

# Caernarfon Castle

1 hr+    All year

Designed to replicate the walls of Constantinople, with its unique polygonal towers, intimidating battlements and colour-banded masonry, the castle dominates the town. In 1969 it was the setting for the investiture of Prince Charles as Prince of Wales.

* World Heritage site
* Houses Museum of the Royal Welsh Fusiliers

**Location**
In town centre on A55. Nearest railway station is Bangor

**Opening**
Daily: Apr–May 9.30am–5pm;
Jun–Aug 9.30am–6pm;
Sep–Oct 9.30am–5pm;
Nov–Mar Mon–Sat 9.30am–4pm;
Sun 11am–4pm

**Admission**
Adult £4.75, Child & Concs £3.75

**Contact**
Castle Ditch, Caernarfon,
Gwynedd LL55 2AY

t 01286 677617
w cadw.wales.gov.uk

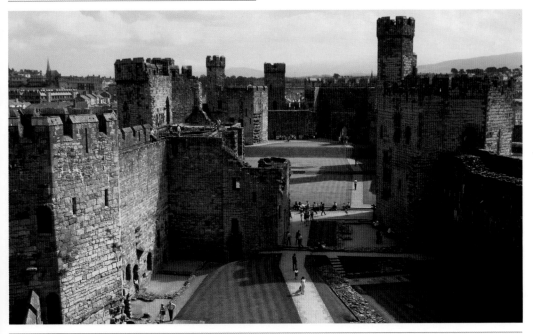

## 641 Caernarfon

# Welsh Highland Railway

3 hrs — All year

Take a 12-mile ride, from the coast to the slopes of Snowdon, on North Wales's newest railway. Enjoy the spectacular scenery of lakes, mountains and forest en route to the heart of Snowdonia itself.

**Location**
Main station on St Helens Road in Caernarfon, signed from A487

**Opening**
Daily: Mar–Oct; limited winter service, please phone for details

**Admission**
Adult £16, Child £8, Concs £12.80
(Adult price includes 1 child)

**Contact**
Harbour Station, Porthmadog, Gwynedd LL49 9NF
t 01766 516024
w festrail.co.uk
e enquiries@festrail.co.uk

## 642 Chirk

# Chirk Castle

2 hrs — Easter–Oct

A magnificent Marcher fortress, completed in 1310. The austere exterior belies the comfortable and elegant state rooms inside, with elaborate plasterwork, superb Adam-style furniture, tapestries and portraits. There is also a formal garden of clipped yew, roses and climbers.

* Renovated laundry room
* Terrace with stunning views & a classical pavilion

**Location**
1 mile off A5, 2 miles W of Chirk

**Opening**
Easter–Oct Wed–Sun 12noon–5pm

**Admission**
Adult £6.40, Child £3.20

**Contact**
Chirk, Wrexham LL14 5AF
t 01691 777701
w nationaltrust.org.uk
e chirkcastle@nationaltrust.org.uk

## 643 Colwyn Bay

# The Welsh Mountain Zoo

4 hrs+ — All year

The animals, from tigers and bears to penguins and parrots are housed in natural settings. There are falconry displays during the summer and the Chimpanzee World complex featuring the unique Chimp Encounter and a South American small monkey-breeding centre.

* New! Sealions' Rock
* Children's farm & Jungle Adventureland

**Location**
3 mins from the A55 (Rhos-on-Sea exit). Follow signs

**Opening**
Daily: summer 9.30am–6pm,
winter 9.30am–5pm

**Admission**
Adult £7.50, Child £5.35, Concs £6.40

**Contact**
Old Highway, Colwyn Bay,
North Wales LL28 5UY
t 01492 532938
w welshmountainzoo.org

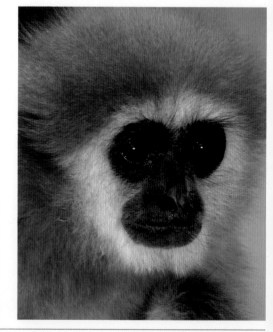

# 644 Conwy

## Conwy Castle

1 hr+    All year

This gritty, dark-stoned fortress has the rare ability to evoke an authentic medieval atmosphere. Commanding a rock above the Conwy Estuary, the castle demands as much attention as the dramatic Snowdonia skyline behind it.

* One of the great fortresses of medieval Europe
* Marvellous floodlit nighttime views

**Location**
On B5106 off the A55. Railway station is next to castle

**Opening**
Daily: 1 Apr–1 Jun 9.30am–5pm;
2 Jun–28 Sep 9.30am–6pm;
29 Sep–26 Oct 9.30am–5pm
27 Oct–31 Mar Mon–Sat 9.30am–4pm,
Sun 11am–4pm

**Admission**
Adult £4, Child & Concs £3.50

**Contact**
Cadw, Conwy LL32 8LD

t 01492 592358
w cadw.wales.gov.uk

# 645 Conwy

## The Royal Cambrian Academy

½ hr+    All year

The most prestigious art institution in Wales has been in Conwy for more than 122 years. Members come from all parts of the UK, but the majority come from Wales. The work shown here is a true reflection of contemporary Welsh art.

* Exhibited paintings are for sale
* Exhibitions change regularly

**Location**
In town centre, just off high street behind Plas Mawr

**Opening**
Tue–Sat 11am–5pm, Sun 1pm–4.30pm

**Admission**
Free

**Contact**
Crown Lane, Conwy LL32 8AN

t 01492 593413
w rcaconwy.org
e rca@rcaconwy.org

# 646 Ffestiniog

## Hydro Centre – Ffestiniog Power Station

1 hr    Easter–Oct

After a talk about generating electricity, visitors are taken on a tour of Britain's first hydro-electricity station. See the machine hall, generators, turbines, interactive models and displays. Drive to the top of the dam for magnificent views.

* Visitors must be able to climb 160 steep steps
* No children under 4

**Location**
On A487 N of Ffestiniog

**Opening**
Daily: Jul–Aug 10am–5pm;
Easter, May Bank Hols, Oct half-term,
Sep & June Tue–Sun 10am–4.30pm

**Admission**
Adult £4, Child £2, Concs £2.50
Visit to Stwlan Dam £3.50 per car

**Contact**
Tan–y–Grisiau,
Blaenau Ffestiniog LL41 3TP

t 01766 830465
w fhc.co.uk
e hydrocentre@edisonmission.com

# 647 Gwynedd

## Greenwood Forest Park

4 hrs+    Mar–Oct

Enjoy family adventure and fun at Greenwood Forest Park with its exciting Green Dragon family rollercoaster. Ride the Great Green Run, the longest sledge slide in Wales. Have a Jungle Boat Adventure, shoot traditional longbows, build dens or enjoy a Forest Theatre show.

* Adventure playgrounds & toddlers' village
* Mini-tractors, puzzle barn & big indoor exhibition

**Location**
Take A4144, leading to B4366

**Opening**
Daily: mid-Mar–Aug 10am–5.30pm;
School summer hols 10am–6pm;
Sep–Oct 10am–5pm

**Admission**
Please phone for details

**Contact**
Y Felinheli, Gwynedd
North Wales LL56 4QN

t 01248 670076
w greenwoodforestpark.co.uk
e info@greenwoodforestpark.co.uk

## 648 Llanberis

# Snowdon Mountain Railway

2½ hrs   Mar–Nov

This tremendously ambitious feat of engineering, is unique in Britain. The rack and pinion railway, which rises to within 66 feet of the summit of the highest mountain in England and Wales (3,560 feet), was built and opened in 1896.

\* 30-minute stay at the top & free audio-visual guide
\* Breathtaking views from the train & the summit

**Location**
Llanberis station on the A4086, 7½ miles from Caernarfon. 15 mins drive from A55/A5 junction at Bangor. Nearest railway station is Bangor

**Opening**
Daily: mid-March–Nov
Please phone for details

**Admission**
Adult £20, Child £14, Concs £17

**Contact**
Llanberis, Gwynedd LL55 4TY

t 0870 4580033
w snowdonrailway.co.uk
e info@snowdonrailway.co.uk

## 649 Llangollen

# Llangollen Wharf

1 hr+   Easter–Oct

Take a horse-drawn boat trip or a motorised aqueduct cruise along the beautiful Llangollen Canal. Longer horse-drawn trips can be arranged for large groups, and a self-steer day-hire boat for groups of up to 10 people is also available.

**Location**
Off A5 Shrewsbury road & near A483 to Chester

**Opening**
Daily: Easter–Oct 10am–5pm

**Admission**
*Horse-drawn boats* Adult £4.50, Child £2.50
*Aqueduct cruise* £8.50, £6.50

**Contact**
Welsh Canal Holiday Craft Ltd
The Wharf, Llangollen LL20 8TA

t 01978 860702

650  Minffordd

# Portmeirion

4 hrs+    All year

This unique village is set on a private peninsula on the southern shores of Snowdonia. It was created by the Welsh architect Clough Williams-Ellis (1883–1978) to demonstrate how a naturally beautiful place could be developed without spoiling it.

\* Used as the location for cult TV series *The Prisoner*
\* Cottages in the village let by Portmeirion Hotel

**Location**
Signed off A487 at Minffordd between Penrhyndeudraeth & Porthmadog

**Opening**
Daily: 9.30am–5.30pm

**Admission**
Adult £6, Child £3, Concs £5

**Contact**
Gwynedd LL48 6ET

t  01766 770000
w  portmeirion-village.com
e  info@portmeirion-village.com

651  Porthmadog

# The Ffestiniog Railway

4 hrs+    All year

Take a 13-mile ride on this historical railway. For 140 years steam-hauled trains have run from the harbour at Porthmadog to the mountains at Blaenau Ffestiniog, passing farmland and forest, mountains and moors, lakes and waterfalls.

\* Regular special events
\* Refurbished café/bar at Harbour station

**Location**
Next to harbour in Porthmadog on A487

**Opening**
Daily: Mar–Nov; limited winter service
Please phone for details

**Admission**
Adult £16, Child £8, Concs £12.80
(Adult price includes 1 child)

**Contact**
Harbour Station, Porthmadog, Gwynedd LL49 9NF

t  01766 516000
w  festrail.co.uk
e  info@festrail.co.uk

## 652 Blaenafon

# Big Pit National Mining Museum

3 hrs+    Feb-Nov

This is a real colliery. Kitted out in helmet, cap-lamp and battery pack, you descend 300 feet (90 metres) to another world – of shafts, coalfaces and levels, of underground roadways, air doors and stables. It includes new interactive exhibitions.

\* Enjoy simulated mining
\* Winding engine house & blacksmith's workshop

**Location**
Leave M4 at junction 25a/26, follow signs from A465

**Opening**
Daily; Feb-Nov 9.30am–5pm
Underground tours run 10am–3.30pm

**Admission**
Free

**Contact**
Blaenafon, Torfaen NP4 9XP
t 01495 790311
w nmgw.ac.uk
e bigpit@nmgw.ac.uk

## 653 Caerleon

# Roman Legionary Museum

1 hr+    All year

Some 2,000 years ago, Wales was the furthest outpost of the Roman Empire. A fortress was founded at Caerleon that would guard the region for 200 years. Today you can learn what made the Romans such a formidable force and how life would not be the same without them.

\* See how the Romans lived & fought
\* Most complete amphitheatre in Britain

**Location**
Caerleon lies N of Newport, just off junction 25 of M4

**Opening**
Mon-Sat 10am–5pm,
Sun 2pm–5pm

**Admission**
Free

**Contact**
High Street, Caerleon,
Gwent NP18 1AE
t 01633 423134
w nmgw.ac.uk
e rlm@nmgw.ac.uk

## 654 Caerphilly

# Caerphilly Castle

1 hr+    All year

Caerphilly Castle is one of the most impressive examples of medieval castle building in Britain. Spread over some 30 acres of land, it is the second largest castle in Britain after Windsor. In the words of the poet Tennyson, 'It isn't a castle – it's a town in ruins'.

\* 45-minute audio tours
\* Many summer demonstrations & events

**Location**
Exit M4 at junction 32, then take A470 or A469 for Caerphilly

**Opening**
Daily: 1 Apr–1 June 9.30am–5pm;
2 Jun–28 Sep 9.30am–6pm;
29 Sep–26 Oct 9.30am–5pm;
27 Oct–31 Mar Mon–Sat 9.30am–4.30pm,
Sun 11am–4pm

**Admission**
Adult £3, Child £2.50 & £2.50

**Contact**
Bridge Street, Caerphilly,
Wales CF83 1JD
t 02920 883143
w cadw.wales.gov.uk
e caerphilly.castle@cadw.co.uk

## 655 Cardiff

# Cardiff Castle

2 hrs+    All year

Cardiff Castle is one of Wales's leading tourist attractions. Situated in the very heart of the capital, alongside city-centre shopping and the magnificent Bute Park, the Castle's enchanting fairytale towers conceal an elaborate and splendid interior.

\* Guided tours of lavish & opulent interiors
\* Set in beautiful grounds

**Location**
Cardiff city centre

**Opening**
Daily: Mar–Oct 9.30am–6pm;
Nov–Feb 9.30am–5pm

**Admission**
Adult £6.50, Child £4, Concs £5

**Contact**
Castle Street, Cardiff CF10 3RB
t 02920 878100
w cardiffcastle.com
e cardiffcastle@cardiff.gov.uk

## 656 Cardiff

# Millennium Stadium Tours

1 hr    All year

Experience the moments before a match when Wales charge down the players' tunnel cheered on by tens of thousands of rugby and football fans. Feel the prematch tension and the joy of victory in the changing rooms before celebrating in the Cardiff Arms Suite.

\* Sit in the Royal Box & lift a trophy
\* One of the proposed venues for the 2012 Olympics

| Location | Contact |
|---|---|
| Cardiff city centre | Millennium Stadium Shop, Gate 3, Westgate Street, Cardiff CF10 1JE |
| Opening | |
| Daily: 9.30am–5.30pm | t 02920 822040 |
| Admission | w millenniumstadium.co.uk |
| Adult £5.50, Child £3, Concs £3.50 | |

## 657 Cardiff

# Museum of Welsh Life

3 hrs+    All year

Standing in the grounds of the magnificent St Fagan's Castle, this museum shows how the people of Wales have lived, worked and spent their leisure time over the past 500 years. More than 30 buildings have been moved from various parts of Wales and reassembled here.

\* Exhibitions of costume, daily life & farming tools

| Location | Contact |
|---|---|
| 4 miles W of Cardiff city centre | St Fagan's, Cardiff CF5 6XB |
| Exit M4 at junction 33 | t 02920 573500 |
| Opening | w nmgw.ac.uk |
| Daily: 10am–5pm | e post@nmgw.ac.uk |
| Admission | |
| Free. Car Park £2 | |

## 658 Cardiff

# Techniquest

2 hrs+    All year

This Science Discovery Centre in Cardiff Bay has more than 150 hands-on exhibits that bring science and technology to life. Among the amazing activities, visitors can fire a rocket, launch a hot-air balloon, play a giant keyboard and much more. Musiquest was new in autumn 2005.

\* Explore the universe in the planetarium
\* Enjoy a fascinating interactive Science Theatre Show

| Location | Admission |
|---|---|
| Exit M4 at junction 33 & then follow signs on A4232 | Adult £6.90, Child & Concs £4.80 |
| | Contact |
| Opening | Stuart Street, Cardiff CF10 5BW |
| Daily: Mon–Fri 9.30am–4.30pm | |
| Sat, Sun & Bank Hols 10.30am–5pm | t 02920 475475 |
| | w techniquest.org |
| | e info@techniquest.org |

## 659 Cardigan

# Cardigan Heritage Centre

1 hr    Mar–Oct

Set in a converted C18 warehouse on Teifi Wharf, the centre has permanent exhibits tracing the history of Cardigan from the days before the coming of the Normans. There are also static and interactive computer displays and regularly changing exhibitions.

\* Guided tours by appointment
\* Arts activities & quizzes for children

**Location**
Take A487 to Cardigan. Centre is on bank of River Teifi, next to Cardigan Bridge

**Opening**
Daily: mid-Mar–Oct from 10am–5pm

**Admission**
Adult £2, Child £1, Concs £1.50

**Contact**
Teifi Wharf, Cardigan, Wales
t 01239 614404

## 660 Carmarthen

# National Botanic Garden of Wales

2 hrs+    All year

The first national botanic garden in the UK for more than 200 years, it is dedicated to conservation, science, education, leisure and the arts. Set in the former C18 park of Middleton Hall, this 568-acre estate enjoys a pollution-free environment, spectacular views and a rich heritage.

\* Apiary gardens
\* Regular calendar of special events

**Location**
On A48 near Carmarthen, signed from the M4 & A40

**Opening**
Daily: Easter–Oct 10am–6pm; Oct–Mar 10am–4.30pm

**Admission**
Adult £7, Child £2, Concs £5

**Contact**
Garden of Wales, Llanarthne, Carmarthenshire SA32 8HG
t 01558 668768
w gardenofwales.org.uk
e reception@gardenofwales.org.uk

## 661 Chepstow

# Tintern Abbey

1 hr   All year

This Cistercian abbey is one of the greatest monastic ruins of Wales. Since the early C20 every effort has been made to maintain one of the finest and most complete abbey churches in the country. A favourite of many artists and the poet Wordsworth.

* Site exhibition
* Audio tour & Braille plan

**Location**
Off the A466 4 miles N of Chepstow

**Opening**
Daily: 1 Apr–1 Jun 9.30am–5pm;
2 Jun–28 Sep 9.30am–6pm;
29 Sep–26 Oct 9.30am–5pm;
27 Oct–31 Mar Mon–Sat 9.30am–4pm,
Sun 11am–4pm

**Admission**
Adult £3.25, Child £2.75 & £2.75

**Contact**
Plas Carew, Units 5–7 Cefn Coed,
Nantgarw, Cardiff CF15 7QQ

t 01291 689251
w cadw.wales.gov.uk
e brite.winterborn.cadw@wales.gsi.gov.uk

## 662 Dan-yr-Ogof

# National Showcaves Centre for Wales

2 hrs+   Apr–Oct

Descend below ground to explore a wonderland of stalactites, waterfalls and natural cave formations extending over 10 kilometres. The tour of the showcaves is self-guided but commentaries play at selected points so you can enjoy a visit at your own speed.

* Top Wales attraction
* Several other attractions

**Location**
On A4067 between Swansea & Brecon. Signed from junction 45 of M4

**Opening**
Daily: Apr–Oct 10am–3pm (last admission to caves 3pm)

**Admission**
Adult £9.50, Child £6

**Contact**
Dan-yr-Ogof, nr Abercraf,
Upper Swansea Valley, Powys SA9 1GJ

t 01639 730801
w showcaves.co.uk
e james@showcaves.co.uk

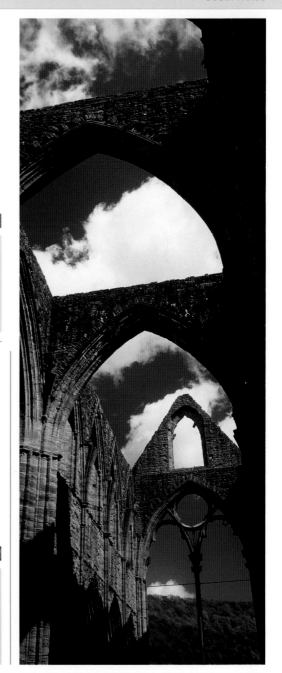

## 663 Monmouth

# Caldicot Castle & Country Park

2 hrs+     Mar–Oct

Founded by the Normans, developed in royal hands as a stronghold in the Middle Ages and restored as a Victorian family home, the castle is set in 55 acres of beautiful parkland. Explore the medieval towers and enjoy breathtaking views from the battlements.

* Audio tours for adults & children

**Location**
From M4 take junction 23 & B4245.
From M48 take junction 2,
A48 & B4245. Signed from B4245

**Opening**
Daily: Mar–Oct 11am–5pm

**Admission**
Please phone for details

**Contact**
Church Road,
Monmouthshire NP26 4HU

t 01291 420241
w caldicotcastle.co.uk

## 664 Narberth

# Colby Woodland Garden

3 hrs     Apr–Oct

This attractive woodland garden has a fine collection of rhododendrons and azaleas. There are beautiful walks through secluded valleys along open and wooded pathways. The house is not open to the public but there is access to the walled garden.

* Regular guided walks with garden staff

**Location**
1 mile inland from Amroth, follow
signs from A477 (Tenby/Carmarthen)

**Opening**
Daily; Apr–Oct 10am–5pm

**Admission**
Adult £3.60, Child £1.80

**Contact**
Amroth, Narberth SA67 8PP

t 01834 811885
w nationaltrust.org.uk

## 665 Neath

# Aberdulais Falls

½ hr+     Mar–Dec

For more than 400 years this famous waterfall provided the energy to drive the wheels of industry, from copper to tinplate. A unique hydro-electricity scheme makes Aberdulais Falls energy self-sufficient, producing power using a giant waterwheel.

\* Waterwheel is the largest used in Europe
\* Visited by famous artists, such as Turner in 1796

**Location**
On A4109, 3 miles NE of Neath,
4 miles from junction 43 of M4

**Opening**
Please phone for details

**Admission**
Adult £3.20, Child £1.60

**Contact**
Aberdulais, nr Neath SA10 8EU

t  01639 636674
w  nationaltrust.org.uk

---

## 666 Swansea

# Craig-y-nos Country Park

2 hrs     All year

An ideal place for a stroll through trees, alongside water and in grassy meadows. There are no rides, amusements, playgrounds or machines, just 40 acres of historic gardens to enjoy. The centre has a 'go-wild' zone for kids where they can listen to bats and climb inside a rotten tree.

**Location**
Midway between Brecon & Swansea
on A4067

**Opening**
Please phone for details

**Admission**
Free. Car park charge

**Contact**
Brecon Road, Pen-y-cae,
Swansea Valley SA9 1GL

t  01639 730395
w  breconbeacons.org
e  cyncp@breconbeacons.org

## 667 Tenby

# Heatherton Country Sports Park

4 hrs     All year

This leisure park has a wide range of activities including clay-pigeon shooting, coarse fishing, archery, pitch and putt, indoor bowls, baseball, go-karting, paintball, adventure golf, horse-riding, bumper boats, a driving range and a maze.

\* Play Robot Wars
\* Suitable for groups and birthday parties.

**Location**
2 miles outside Tenby on B4318
Tenby–Pembroke road

**Opening**
Daily; Jun–Sep 10am–10pm;
Oct–May 10am–6pm;
closed 25, 26 Dec & 1 Jan

**Admission**
Free. Pay-as-you-go activities

**Contact**
St Florence, Tenby,
Pembrokeshire SA69 9EE

t  01646 651025
w  heatherton.co.uk

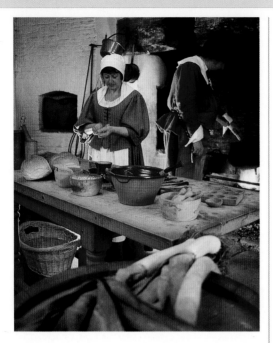

## 668 Tenby

# Manor House Wild Animal Park

4 hrs    Easter–Sep

Set in landscaped wooded grounds and floral gardens beside an C18 manor house, the zoo has a close-encounters unit where visitors can feed and pet animals, including snakes. There are daily falconry displays and informative talks.

* Visitors may be allowed to hold certain birds of prey

**Location**
3 miles outside Tenby on B4318

**Opening**
Daily: Easter–Sep 10am–6pm

**Admission**
Adult £6, Child & Concs £5

**Contact**
St Florence, Tenby,
Pembrokeshire SA70 8RJ

t 01646 651201
w manorhousewildanimalpark.co.uk
e mail@manorhousewildanimalpark.
co.uk

## 669 Treharris

# Llancaiach Fawr Manor

1 hr+    All year

This splendid semi-fortified, Tudor manor house has been refurbished to its C17 state. Step back in time to the year 1645 where the servants of the household will tell you tales of their lives during the Civil War years.

* Listen to the gossip of the day – 300 years ago
* Stroll in the formal gardens

**Location**
On B4254 between Nelson &
Gelligaer, 2½ miles from the A470

**Opening**
Daily: Mon–Fri 10am–5pm;
Sat–Sun 10am–6pm;
Nov–Feb closed Mon

**Admission**
Adult £4.95, Child £3.50, Concs £3.75

**Contact**
Nelson, Treharris CF46 6ER

t 01443 412248
w caerphilly.gov.uk/visiting

## 670 Trelewis

# Welsh International Climbing & Activity Centre

4 hrs+    All year

In addition to climbing, the centre offers a wealth of indoor and outdoor activities for all abilities, including abseiling, caving, potholing, gorge walking, kayaking, mountain walking and expeditions. It also has a fitness suite and family and bunk-house accommodation.

* One of the biggest indoor climbing walls in Europe
* High-ropes assault course

**Location**
From B4255 follow signs to Bedlinog,
then ½ mile from Trelewis

**Opening**
Daily: Mon–Fri 9am–10pm,
Sat–Sun 9am–7pm

**Admission**
Prices vary according to activity

**Contact**
Taff Bargoed Centre, Trelewis,
Merthyr Tydfil CF46 6RD

t 01443 710749
w indoorclimbingwalls.co.uk
e enquiries@indoorclimbingwalls.
co.uk

# Yorkshire

East Riding  North Yorkshire
South Yorkshire  West Yorkshire

Alston
Consett
Stanley
Washington
SUNDERLAND
Houghton le Spring
Chester-le-Street
873
DURHAM
Durham
864–869
Peterlee
Brandon
Spennymoor
A1(M)
Hartlepool
870
Appleby-in-Westmorland
Bishop Auckland
860–861
Newton Aycliffe
857–858
Stockton-on-Tees
871
Redcar
Brough
Darlington
872
Middlesbrough
862–863
691
Guisborough
Scotch Corner
TEESSIDE
Whitby
Richmond
Stokesley
Catterick
NORTH YORK MOORS
Scalby
Scarborough
Hawes
688
Leyburn
682
Northallerton
697–698
690
Thirsk
Pickering
Filey
NORTH YORKSHIRE
685
686
689
ENGLAND
Ripon
Easingwold
Malton
Flar
694–696
Bridlington
693
A1(M)
671–674
Settle
Knaresborough
Driffield
683–684
687
York
675
Harrogate
Wetherby
701–712
692
Pocklington
699–700
Skipton
Ilkley
Market Weighton
EAST RIDING OF YORKSHIRE
SHIRE
Clitheroe
807
Keighley
Yeadon
Tadcaster
Beverley
Colne
Bingley
LEEDS & BRADFORD
676
Nelson
Shipley
LEEDS
Selby
HULL
802–803
Burnley
BRADFORD
720–721
Garforth
677–681
M65
Accrington
Halifax
723–728
Hessle
Rawtenstall
722
Batley
Castleford
Barton-upon-Humber
Todmorden
Brighouse
M62
Pontefract
Goole
820
Brighouse
729–731
Wakefield
Immingha
Rochdale
Huddersfield
Hemsworth
Thorne
M18
Gr
Bury
M66
M62
Scunthorpe
450
Bolton
Middleton
Barnsley
453
M60
Oldham
Penistone
M1
Doncaster
M180
M181
M180
Brigg
4
822–834
Salford
SOUTH YORKSHIRE
713
Caistor
M62
MANCHESTER
Stocksbridge
A1(M)
749
751–752
Glossop
Rotherham
Bawtry
Gainsborough
Sale
Stockport
SHEFFIELD
715
714
447
Cheadle
716–719
Market Rasen
732
MANCHESTER
418–420
SHEFFIELD CITY
Worksop
Retford
451–452
Lincoln
The Wo
Wilmslow
Peak
Dronfield
490–492
Knutsford
Whaley Bridge
740–743
Buxton
District
Staveley
M1
Washingborough
Northwich
Macclesfield
415
Chesterfield
Worksop
Horncastle
M6
Bakewell
426
416
477
486–487
Congleton
Clay Cross
Mansfield
Otterton
Coning
750
Matlock
Sutton in Ashfield
478
460
736
Biddulph
427–428
Alfreton
Kirkby in Ashfield
488–489
Newark-on-Trent
479
Leek
547
Wirksworth
421
Ripley
Kidsgrove
Belper
DERBYSHIRE
NOTTINGHAM-LINCOLNSHI
531
534
Ashbourne
422
475
Sleaford
SHIRE
Boston
Newcastle-under-Lyme
STOKE-ON-TRENT
Ilkeston
NOTTINGHAM

**SOUTH YORKSHIRE**

**WEST YORKSHIRE**

**EAST RIDING**

**NORTH YORKSHIRE**

## 671 Bridlington

# Bempton Cliffs Nature Reserve

2 hrs   All year

One of the best places in Britain to see seabirds. More than 200,000 birds nest on the cliffs, including gannets, puffins, guillemots, razorbills and kittiwakes. Five safe viewing areas are situated along 3 miles of chalk cliffs. The first mile is suitable for wheelchairs.

* Gannets first colonised the cliffs in the 1920s
* Puffins can be seen in spring & summer

| Location | Admission |
|---|---|
| On cliff road from Bempton, on B1229 from Flamborough to Filey | £3.50 car park charge for non members |
| **Opening** | **Contact** |
| *Visitor centre* | 11 Cliff Lane, Bempton, |
| Daily: Mar–Nov 10am–5pm; | Bridlington YO15 1JD |
| Dec–Feb 9.30am–4pm | t 01262 851179 |
| | w rspb.org.uk |

## 672 Bridlington

# Bridlington Leisure World

4 hrs+   All year

The complex includes three swimming pools, one with waves, slides, storm effects and water features; a 25m training pool and a learner pool. There is also a multi-purpose hall for indoor bowling, family activities and a fitness studio.

* Small theatre and bar
* One of East Riding's premier leisure attractions

| Location | Contact |
|---|---|
| Off A165 (off the M62). Nearest town, is Scarborough | The Promenade, Bridlington, Yorkshire YO15 2QQ |
| **Opening** | t 01262 606715 |
| Please phone for details | w bridlington.net/leisureworld |
| **Admission** | |
| Activities individually priced | |

## 673 Bridlington

# Park Rose Owl & Bird of Prey Centre

3 hrs   Mar–Oct

Set in 3½ acres of natural woodland, the centre has 40 aviaries displaying hundreds of owls and birds of prey. There are daily guided information tours, and koi carp and aquatic plants to admire.

* Flying displays throughout summer season
* School visits & educational talks

| Location | Admission |
|---|---|
| On A165/A166, 2 miles S of Bridlington | Adult £2.50, Child £1.50 |
| **Opening** | **Contact** |
| Daily: Mar–Oct 10am–5pm | Carnaby Covert Lane, Bridlington YO15 3QF |
| | t 01262 606800 |

## 674 Bridlington

# Sewerby Hall & Gardens

3 hrs   Apr–Sep

Set in 50 acres of early C19 parkland in a dramatic cliff-top position, overlooking Bridlington Bay, the Hall contains a magnificent orangery, period rooms and art and photographic galleries. Attractions include a beautiful walled garden and a pitch and putt golf course.

* Display of Amy Johnson's awards & trophies
* Children's zoo includes monkeys & penguins

| Location | Contact |
|---|---|
| From Bridlington follow signs for Flamborough & then Sewerby | Church Lane, Sewerby, Bridlington YO15 1EA |
| **Opening** | t 01262 673769 |
| Daily: Apr–Sep 10am–5.30pm | w sewerby-hall.co.uk |
| **Admission** | e sewerby.hall@eastriding.gov.uk |
| Adult £3.30, Child £1.30, Concs £2.60 | |

# 675 Foston-on-the-Wold

## Cruckley Farm

2 hrs+    Easter–Sep

Watch the daily routines of feeding animals and milking cows on a working farm as well as a huge variety of rare breeds. You can also see the collection of vintage farm equipment that is regularly used by film companies. The farm keeps more than 50 varieties of animal.

\* Feed hand reared animals in the paddock
\* All seven rare breeds of pig

| Location | Contact |
|---|---|
| Just off B1249 between Driffield & Beeford | Foston-on-the-Wold, Driffield East YO25 8BS |
| **Opening** | t 01262 488337 |
| Good Fri–Sep 10.30am–5.30pm | w cruckley.co.uk |
| **Admission** | e cruckley@aol.com |
| Adult £3.50, Child £2.75, Concs £3.25 | |

# 676 Hornsea

## Hornsea Museum

1 hr+    Easter–Sep

This award-winning museum shows how village life has changed in North Holderness from the pre-industrial age of the early C17 through to post WWII. Sited in an C18 farmhouse, the museum has a Victorian kitchen and other domestic rooms plus rural craft workshops.

\* Local industrial display & photographic exhibition
\* Hornsea pottery collection

| Location | Contact |
|---|---|
| In Hornsea town centre, off B1242 | Burns Farm, 11 Newbegin, Hornsea HU18 1AB |
| **Opening** | t 01964 533443 |
| Easter–Sep Tue–Sat, Bank Hol Mons & autumn half-term 11am–5pm, Sun 2pm–5pm | w hornseamuseum.com |
| | e contact@hornseamuseum.com |
| **Admission** | |
| Adult £2.50, Child & Concs £2 | |

# 677 Hull

## The Deep

2–3 hrs    All year

Experience marine life and sea life close-up in this museum shaped like a ship. Take an underwater lift, walk through sub aqua tunnels and watch sharks galore swim overhead. Explore exhibitions about corals, Arctic sea life and the Big Bang.

\* 10m -deep tank containing 2.5 million litres of water
\* Lots of hands-on and interactive activities

| Location | Contact |
|---|---|
| Within walking distance of town centre on banks of Humber | Hull HU1 4DP |
| | t 01482 381000 |
| **Opening** | w thedeep.co.uk |
| Daily: 10am–6pm | e info@thedeep.co.uk |
| **Admission** | |
| Adult £7.50, Child £5.50, Concs £6 | |

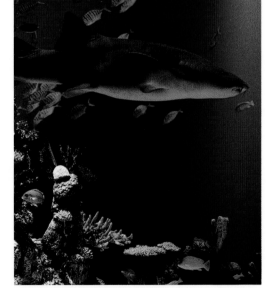

## 678 Hull

# Ferens Art Gallery

1 hr+    All year

Opened in 1927, the award-winning Ferens Art Gallery combines internationally renowned permanent collections with exhibitions and live art. The first-class permanent collection of paintings and sculpture spans centuries from the medieval period to the present day.

\* Innovative children's gallery new from Autumn 2005
\* Masterpieces by Canaletto, Spencer & Hockney

| Location | Contact |
|---|---|
| In city centre | Queen Victoria Square, Kingston upon Hull HU1 3RA |
| **Opening** | t 01482 613902 |
| Daily: Mon–Sat 10am–5pm, Sun 1.30pm–4.30pm | w hullcc.gov.uk/museums/ferens |
| | e museums@hull.gov.uk |
| **Admission** | |
| Free | |

## 679 Hull

# Fort Paull

2 hrs+    All year

Fort Paull has more than 1,000 years of history dating back to Viking landings. It has played a part in Britain's sea defences for almost 500 years – from its time as a fortress built by Henry VIII to the anti-aircraft defence visited by Sir Winston Churchill.

\* Only remaining Napoleonic fort in Yorkshire
\* Explore the underground labyrinths

| Location | Contact |
|---|---|
| Village of Paull is S of Hull in the direction of Hedon | Battery Road, Paull, Hull HU12 8FP |
| **Opening** | t 01482 882655 |
| Apr–Oct 10am–6pm; Nov–Mar 11am–4pm | w fortpaull.com |
| | e fortpaull@aol.com |
| **Admission** | |
| Adults £4.50, Child &Concs £3 | |

## 680 Hull

# Hull Arena

2 hrs+    All year

An Olympic-size ice rink that is home to the Hull Stingrays, who play in the British National Ice Hockey league. The rink is open to the public every day, with a variety of family sessions and discos. Times for these vary so it is best to phone in advance.

\* One of the North's leading music venues
\* See ice hockey played at the highest level

| Location | Admission |
|---|---|
| Just off A63 in centre of Kingston upon Hull | All skating £3 + £1 skate hire *Evening disco* £3.50 |
| **Opening** | **Contact** |
| *Public skating* Mon–Fri 12.15pm–3.30pm; Sat–Sun 10am–12noon & 2.15pm–4.15pm Please phone to confirm disco sessions | Kingston Street, Kingston upon Hull HU1 2DZ |
| | t 01482 325252 |
| | w hullcc.gov.uk/leisure |
| | e hullarena@hullcc.gov.uk |

## 681 Hull

# Streetlife Museum of Transport

2 hrs+    All year

Exciting developments opened recently, include a motor car gallery, a major extension of the popular carriage gallery, a larger street scene with several new shops and a hands-on interactive exhibition area.

\* Supported by Heritage Lottery Funding
\* Animated horses and simulated carriage rides

| Location | Contact |
|---|---|
| In high street near Wilberforce House | High Street, Hull HU1 1PS |
| **Opening** | t 01482 613902 |
| Daily: Mon–Sat 10am–5pm, Sun 1.30pm–4.30pm | w hullcc.gov.uk/museums/streetlife |
| | e museums@hull.gov.uk |
| **Admission** | |
| Free | |

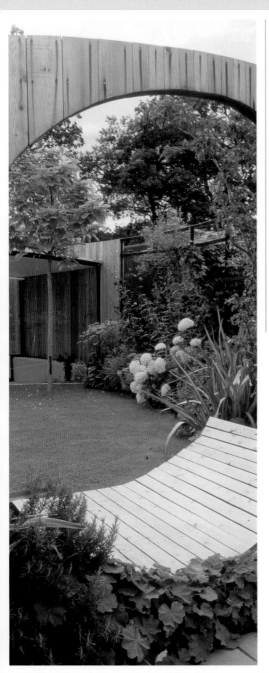

682 Bedale

# Big Sheep & Little Cow Farm

2 hrs | All year

This small family-run, family-friendly attraction is home to many farm animals. Bottle feed, bathe and pet lambs, piglets and calves under the supervision of a guide. Talk to the donkey and afterwards enjoy a homemade ice-cream.

* Sand play area & new play barn
* Quad bikes and pony rides

| Location | Admission |
|---|---|
| 11 miles S of Scotch Corner & 1 mile from A1 on A684 towards Bedale. Follow brown Farm Visitor Centre signs | Adult £4.50, Child £3.50, Concs £4 |
| | Contact |
| | nr Bedale |
| Opening | |
| Daily: Mar–Sep 10.30am–5pm; Oct–Feb Wed–Sun 10.30am–5pm | t 01677 422125 |
| | w farmattraction.co.uk |
| | e enquiries@farmattraction.co.uk |

683 Harrogate

# RHS Garden Harlow Carr

3 hrs | All year

One of Yorkshire's most relaxing yet inspiring locations. Highlights include the spectacular Gardens through Time, a streamside garden and contemporary herbaceous borders; alpines, scented and kitchen gardens; and woodland and wildflower meadows.

* Extensive plant centre
* All year colour & interest

| Location | Contact |
|---|---|
| Off B6162, 1½ miles from Harrogate town centre | Crag Lane, Harrogate HG3 1QB |
| | t 01423 565418 |
| Opening | w rhs.org.uk/harlowcarr |
| Daily: Mar–Oct 9.30am–6pm; Nov–Feb 9.30am–4pm | e admin-harlowcarr@rhs.org.uk |
| Admission | |
| Adult £6, Child £1.60, Concs £4 RHS members free | |

## 684 Harrogate

# Royal Pump Room Museum

1 hr+ · All year

Visit the strongest sulphur wells in Europe once popular with more than 15,000 people every summer. You can find out what Harrogate's link is with Russian royalty and also see a display of old-fashioned shops. Don't forget to taste the water – it is something you will not forget.

* See historical spa treatments
* Combine visit with Knaresborough Castle

**Location**
Easy walking distance from any town centre car park – follow signs

**Opening**
Apr–Oct Mon–Sat 10am–5pm
(4pm Nov–Mar)
Sun 2pm–5pm (4pm Nov–Mar)

**Admission**
Adult £2.80, Child £1.50, Concs £1.70

**Contact**
Crown Place, Harrogate HG1 2RY
t 01423 556188
w harrogate.gov.uk/museum
e museum@harrogate.gov.uk

## 685 Helmsley

# Duncombe Park

3 hrs · All year

Used as a girls' school for 60 years, Duncombe Park has been restored as a grand family home (200 rooms), housing a fine collection of English and continental furniture. Its naturally landscaped gardens have fine views over valley and moors.

* 450 acres of parkland is National Nature Reserve
* Way-marked walks through woods & river valley

**Location**
1 mile from Helmsley town centre

**Opening**
Sun–Thu 11am–5.30pm
*House tours* 12.30pm–3.30pm every 60 mins

**Admission**
Adult £6.50, Child £3, Concs £5

**Contact**
Helmsley YO62 5EB
t 01439 770213
w duncombepark.com
e info@duncombepark.com

## 686 Kirby Misperton

# Flamingo Land Theme Park & Zoo

6 hrs+ · Apr–Nov

The zoo is home to more than 1,000 animals, including tigers, zebra, monkeys, sea lions and meerkats, and the largest flock of pink flamingos in the country. The bird walk has birds of all sizes from finches to ostriches and the park has eight rollercoaster rides.

* Lost Kingdom display
* Children's farm

**Location**
Off A64 Scarborough–York road on A169 Malton–Pickering road

**Opening**
Daily: Apr–Nov 10am–5pm or 6pm please phone for details

**Admission**
Please phone for details

**Contact**
Kirby Misperton,
Malton YO17 6UX
t 01653 668287
w flamingoland.co.uk
e info@flamingoland.co.uk

## 687 Knaresborough

# Mother Shipton's Cave & Petrifying Well

1 hr+    Mar–Oct

Mother Shipton is perhaps England's most famous prophetess, foretelling the Spanish Armada and the Great Fire of London. She lived 500 years ago during the reigns of Henry VIII and Elizabeth I. Visit the cave, petrifying well, museum and 12 acres of historic woodland park.

\* Oldest tourist attractions in Britain
\* Free all-day parking

**Location**
Signed from A1 on A59

**Opening**
Mar Sat–Sun 10am–5.30pm;
Apr–Oct daily 10am–5.30pm

**Admission**
Adult £5.50, Child £3.75, Concs £4.50

**Contact**
Prophecy House,
Knaresborough HG5 8DD

t  01423 864600
w  mothershipton.co.uk
e  adrian@mothershipton.co.uk

## 688 Leyburn

# Bolton Castle

1 hr+    All year

This spectacular medieval fortress in the heart of the Yorkshire Dales was completed in 1399. Today visitors can explore five floors of displays depicting castle life in the C15 and see where Mary Queen of Scots was once imprisoned.

\* Film location for *Ivanhoe, Elizabeth & Heartbeat*

**Location**
6 miles W of Leyburn, just off A684.
Signed from Wensley

**Opening**
Daily: Mar–Nov 10am–5pm;
Dec–Feb 10am–4pm
Please phone for details

**Admission**
Adults £5, Child & Concs £3.50

**Contact**
Leyburn North Yorkshire DL8 4ET

t  01969 623981
w  boltoncastle.co.uk

## 689 Malton

# Eden Camp Modern History Museum

4 hrs    All year

In this unique military museum, historical scenes are reconstructed using movement, lighting, sound, smells and smoke machines. Attractions include an original prisoner of war camp built in 1942. It is the only museum of its kind in the world.

\* Covers complete C20 British military history
\* Multiple award–winning attraction

**Location**
Just 100 yards from A64
(York–Scarborough) & A169
(Malton–Pickering) interchange

**Opening**
Daily: 10am–5pm

**Admission**
Adult £4.50, Child & Concs £3.50

**Contact**
Malton YO17 6RT

t  01653 697777
w  edencamp.co.uk
e  admin@edencamp.co.uk

## 690 Middleham

# Middleham Castle

fine    1 hr    All year

The commanding views from this impressive fortress cover an area that has been inhabited by prehistoric, Roman, Viking and Norman settlers. The formidable stone keep was one of the largest in England. Many modifications have been made over the centuries.

\* Childhood home of Richard III
\* *James Herriott's Yorkshire* was filmed in the area

**Location**
2 miles S of Leyburn on A6108

**Opening**
Daily: Apr–Sep 10am–6pm;
Oct–Mar Thu–Mon 10am–4pm

**Admission**
Adult £3.30, Child £1.70, Concs £2.50

**Contact**
Castle Hill, Middleham,
Leyburn DL8 4QR

t  01969 623899
w  english-heritage.org.uk/yorkshire

691 Ormesby

# Ormesby Hall

2 hrs+    Apr–Oct

Set in 270 acres of parkland, this C18 Palladian mansion, now owned by the National Trust, is notable for its fine plasterwork and carved wood decoration. Visit the Victorian laundry, kitchen, game larder and stable block. There is also an attractive garden and holly walk.

* National Trust property
* large model railway

**Location**
3 miles SE of Middlesborough.
Take A174, A172 & follow signs

**Opening**
Apr–Oct Sat–Sun & Bank Hols
1.30pm–4.30pm

**Admission**
Adult £4.10, Child £2

**Contact**
Ormesby Hall,
Ormesby TS7 9AS

t 01642 324188
e yorkor@smtp.ntrust.org.uk

692 Pocklington

# Burnby Hall Gardens

4 hrs    Easter–Oct

Burnby Hall Gardens is world-famous for its National Collection of water lilies, which contains more varieties than anywhere else in Europe. There is also an extensive range of ornamental trees, plants, shrubs and numerous fish and birds.

* Winner of Yorkshire in Bloom 2004
* Two large lakes in 10 acres of beautiful gardens

**Location**
20 mins E of York off A1079

**Opening**
Daily: Easter–Oct 10am–6pm

**Admission**
Adult £3.25, Child £1.50, Concs £2.60
Gardens free in winter

**Contact**
The Ball, Pocklington YO42 2QF

t 01759 307125
w burnbyhallgardens.com
e brian@brianpetrie.plus.com

693 Ripley

# Ripley Castle & Gardens

2 hrs+    All year

Home to the Ingilby family for over 700 years, the castle is famous as the place where Jane Ingilby held Oliver Cromwell at gunpoint. Impressive collection of arms and armour from the English Civil War. Extensive hot houses, gardens and grounds.

* Guided tours leave front door every hour
* Home to the National Hyacinth Collection

**Location**
3 miles N of Harrogate on A61

**Opening**
Daily: Jul–Aug 10.30am–3.30pm;
Sep–Jun Tue, Thu, Sat–Sun & Bank
Hols, please phone for details as they
may vary

**Admission**
Adult £6.50, Child £4, Concs £5.50

**Contact**
The Ripley Castle Estate,
Harrogate HG3 3AY

t 01423 770152
w ripleycastle.co.uk
e enquiries@ripleycastle.co.uk

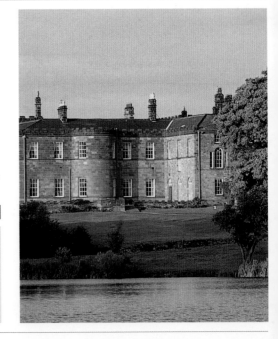

## 694 Ripon

# Fountains Abbey & Studley Royal Estate

4 hrs   All year

The spectacular ruins of this C12 Cistercian abbey stand alongside a deer park, a Victorian church and an elegant C18 landscape garden with water features and follies. On some evenings the abbey is floodlit.

\* Best surviving example of a monastic mill
\* Declared a World Heritage Site in 1987

| Location | Contact |
|---|---|
| 4 miles W of Ripon on B6265 | Ripon HG4 3DY |
| | t 01765 608 888 |
| Opening | w nationaltrust.org.uk |
| Daily: Nov–Feb 10am–4pm; | e webinfo@fmtp.ntrust.org.uk |
| Mar–Oct 10am–5pm; | |
| Nov–Jan closed Fri | |
| Admission | |
| Adult £5.50, Child £3 | |

## 696 Ripon

# Theakston Brewery & Visitor Centre

2 hrs+   All year

A visit to the Theakston Brewery in Masham will allow you to witness the creation of the famous ales first hand. Smell the aromas of the raw materials and then follow the entire brewing process from blending the ingredients through to filling the casks.

\* See coopers create beautiful wooden barrels
\* Home of world-famous Old Peculiar ale

| Location | Contact |
|---|---|
| Masham is on A6108 N of Ripon | Masham, Ripon HG4 4YD |
| | t 01765 684383 |
| Opening | w theakstons.co.uk |
| Daily: 10.30am–4pm | e info@theakstons.co.uk |
| Tours 11am–3.30pm | |
| Admission | |
| Adult £4.50, Child £2, Concs £3.50 | |

## 695 Ripon

# Newby Hall & Gardens

4 hrs   May–Sep

One of England's renowned Adam houses, this is an exceptional example of C18 interior decoration, recently restored to its original beauty. Contents include the Gobelins Tapestry Room, a famous gallery of classical statues and some of Chippendale's finest furniture.

\* 25 acres of award-winning gardens
\* Miniature railway, woodland walk & special events

| Location | Admission |
|---|---|
| Off B6265 between Boroughbridge | Adult £8.50, Child £5.70, Concs £7.20 |
| & Ripon | Contact |
| Opening | Ripon HG4 5AE |
| Jul–Aug daily 11am–5.30pm; | t 01423 322 583 |
| May–Jun, Sep & Bank Hols Tue–Sun | w newbyhall.com |
| 11am–5.30pm | e info@newbyhall.com |

## 697 Scarborough

# Scarborough Castle

1 hr   All year

Dominating the headland, this impressive castle was built in the early C13 and later enhanced by King John and Henry III. It suffered naval bombardment in 1914 and during WWII it was home to a secret listening post. There are wonderful views of the Yorkshire coastline.

\* Vast C13 fortress
\* Site of an Iron Age settlement

| Location | Contact |
|---|---|
| Castle Road, E of town centre | Castle Road, Scarborough |
| | t 01723 372451 |
| Opening | w english-heritage.org.uk/yorkshire |
| Apr–Sep daily 10am–6pm; | |
| Oct–Mar Thu–Mon 10am–4pm | |
| Admission | |
| Adult £3.30, Child £1.70, Concs £2.50 | |

## 698 Scarborough

# Wykeham Lakes

1 hr+    All year

The ideal place to enjoy a range of watersports, including sailing, windsurfing, boating, scuba-diving and canoeing.Tuition is available. If you prefer fishing, choose from two trout, three coarse-fishing lakes and pike fishing all year round.

* Fishing lakes under new management from 2005

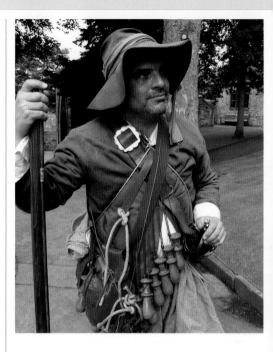

**Location**
6 miles W of Scarborough
off the A170 between West Ayton &
Wykeham

**Opening**
*Boating & watersports lake* **Daily:**
7am–dusk *Fishing* All year
*Bird watching* By arrangement with
Wykeham Estate

**Admission**
Prices vary according to activity/
duration please phone for details

**Contact**
Charm Park, Wykeham,
Scarborough

t *fishing* 07946 534001
  *sailing* 0845 4560164
w wykeham.co.uk

## 699 Skipton

# Bolton Abbey

2 hrs+    All year

This estate covers 30,000 acres of beautiful countryside in the Yorkshire Dales. There are medieval buildings, C12 priory ruins to explore, and 80 miles of moorland, woodland and riverside footpaths. A guide book and walks leaflets are available,there is also a gift shop.

* Landscape was inspiration for Wordsworth & Turner
* Grounds include a 6-mile stretch of River Wharfe

**Location**
Between Harrogate & Skipton, off A59
on B6160

**Opening**
Daily: 9am–dusk

**Admission**
Vehicle pass £5 (occupants free),
£3.50 for disabled badge holders

**Contact**
Skipton BD23 6EX

t 01756 718009
w boltonabbey.com
e tourism@boltonabbey.com

## 700 Skipton

# Skipton Castle

1 hr+    All year

More than 900 years old, the castle is one of England's most complete and best-preserved medieval castles; surviving a three-year siege during the Civil War. Climb from the depths of the dungeons to the very top of the watch tower, and visit the fantastic book shop.

* View the banqueting hall, kitchen & bedchambers
* Comprehensive tour sheets in nine languages

**Location**
In town centre

**Opening**
Mar–Sep Mon–Sat 10am–6pm,
Sun 12noon–6pm;
Oct–Feb 10am–4pm

**Admission**
Adult £5.20, Child £2.70, Concs £4.60

**Contact**
Skipton BD23 1AQ

t 01756 792442
w skiptoncastle.co.uk
e info@skiptoncastle.co.uk

## 701 York

# The Bar Convent

1 hr+    All year

The oldest working convent in England established in 1686. The foundress of the order, Mary Ward, was a pioneer of education for women and its members ran a school for 299 years. The Bar Convent Museum tells the early history of Christianity in the North of England.

* C18 neo classical chapel still used for weekly service
* Conference facilities & B&B available

| Location | Contact |
|---|---|
| 2 min walk from train station | 17 Blossom Street, York YO24 1AQ |
| Opening | t 01904 643 238 |
| *Museum tours* Mon–Fri 10am–4pm | w bar-convent.org.uk |
| Admission | e info@bar-convent.org.uk |
| Free | |

## 702 York

# Castle Howard

2 hrs+    Mar–Oct

One of Britain's finest stately homes, located in the beautiful Howardian hills. The magnificent house is distinguished by its famous dome and inside there are enormous collections of important art treasures. Spectacular gardens form part of a 10,000 acre estate.

* Adventure playground, boat trips & farm shop
* Outdoor guided tours & historical characters

| Location | Contact |
|---|---|
| 15 miles NE of York | North York YO60 7DA |
| Opening | t 01653 648 333 |
| Daily: Mar–Oct 10am–4pm | w castlehoward.co.uk |
| Admission | e house@castlehoward.co.uk |
| Adult £9.50, Child £6.50, Concs £8.50 | |

## 703 York

# Clifford's Tower

½ hr    All year

Clifford's Tower is all that remains of York Castle. The original wooden tower was burned down during anti-Jewish riots. The height of the motte was increased and the tower was rebuilt in stone. Today the tower is just a shell, but you can climb to the top for a good view of York.

* Used as a prison after the Civil War
* Castle continued to be used for executions until 1896

| Location | Contact |
|---|---|
| Opposite York Castle Museum | Tower Street, York YO1 9SA |
| Opening | t 01904 646940 |
| Daily: Apr–Sep 10am–6pm (5pm in Oct) | w english-heritage.org.uk/yorkshire |
| Nov–Mar 10am–4pm | e cliffords.tower@english-heritage.org.uk |
| Admission | |
| Adult £2.80, Child £1.40, Concs £2.10 | |

## 704 York

# Jorvik

1 hr    All year

Discover what life was like more than 1,000 years ago, see more than 800 Viking items uncovered here, and journey through a reconstruction of actual Viking streets complete with sounds and smells. Witness the skills of Viking craftsmen in a new interactive exhibition.

* Jorvik is the name given to York by Vikings in AD975
* Wheelchair users please phone 01904 543402

| Location | Contact |
|---|---|
| Take A64 to York | Jorvik, Coppergate, York YO1 9WT |
| Opening | t 01904 543403/643211 |
| Daily: Apr–Oct 10am–5pm; | w vikingjorvik.com |
| Nov–Mar 10am–4pm | e jorvik@yorkarchaeology.co.uk |
| Admission | |
| Adult £7.45, Child £5.25, Concs £6.30 | |
| Prebooking recommended for individual tours | |

## 705 York

# National Railway Museum

3 hrs+    All year

The collection includes 103 locomotives and 177 items of rolling stock from the *Rocket* to the *Eurostar*. Permanent displays include Palaces on Wheels with pre-Victorian Royal saloons, and a Japanese bullet train.

* Home of The *Flying Scotsman*
* Literally millions of photographs & artefacts

**Location**
200 yrds from train station, signed from town centre

**Opening**
Daily: 10am–6pm

**Admission**
Free, except for special events

**Contact**
Leeman Road, York YO26 4XJ
t  01904 621261
w  nrm.org.uk
e  nrm@nmsi.ac.uk

## 706 York

# Rievaulx Abbey

4 hrs+    All year

Founded by St Bernard of Clairvaux in the C13, this Cistercian abbey was once home to some 150 monks and 500 lay brethren. Although much of what was built by the monks is in ruins, recent digs reveal the monks ate strawberries and ran a flourishing iron industry.

* Towering medieval architecture
* Exhibition of the works of God

**Location**
In Rievaulx, 2¼ miles W of Helmsley on a minor road off B1257

**Opening**
Daily: Apr–Sep 10am–6pm; 14–22 Feb & Oct 10am–5pm; Nov–13 Feb & 23 Feb–Mar 10am–4pm

**Admission**
Adult £4, Child £2, Concs £3

**Contact**
Rievaulx, York YO62 5LB
t  01439 798228
w  english-heritage.co.uk/yorkshire

707 York

# York Art Gallery

1 hr+    All year

See some of Europe's finest art with examples of oil and canvas, watercolours and ceramics. The gallery traces 600 years of British and European art, from the time of the Wars of the Roses right up to the present day.

* Outstanding collection of Pioneer Studio pottery
* Full programme of temporary exhibitions

| Location | Contact |
|---|---|
| Opposite Tourist Information Centre, 3 mins walk from York Minster | Exhibition Square, York YO1 7EW |
| | t 01904 697979 |
| Opening | w york.art.museum |
| Daily: 10am–5pm | e art.gallery@ymt.org.uk |
| Admission | |
| Free | |

708 York

# York Castle Museum

1 hr+    All year

Experience life as a Victorian. Walk down cobbled streets and peer through windows of shops long gone. Take a journey through 400 years of life in Britain, from parlours to prisons, marriages to the mill house, and see the toys that children used to treasure.

* Stumble into the underworld of the highwayman
* City at War exhibition

| Location | Contact |
|---|---|
| In city centre | Eye of York, York YO1 9RY |
| | t 01904 650333 |
| Opening | w york.castle.museum |
| Daily: 9.30am–5pm | e castle.museum@ymt.org.uk |
| Admission | |
| Adult £6.50, Child £3.50, Concs £5 | |

709 York

# York Dungeons

1 hr    All year

Deep in the heart of historic York, buried beneath its paving stones, lies the North's most chilling horror attraction. The York Dungeons bring more than 2,000 years of gruesomely authentic history vividly back to life ... and death.

* See how torture was part of everyday life until the C19
* Judgement of Sinners new in 2005

| Location | Contact |
|---|---|
| In city centre | The York Dungeons, 12 Clifford Street, York YO1 9RD |
| Opening | t 01904 632599 |
| Daily: Apr–Sep 10am–5pm; Oct–Mar 10.30am–4.30pm | w thedungeons.com |
| | e yorkdungeons@merlinentertainments.biz |
| Admission | |
| Adult £9.95, Child (5–14) £7.95, Child (under 5) £7.95 free, Concs £8.95 | |

710 York

# York Minster

1½ hrs    All year

Savour the peaceful atmosphere of the largest Gothic cathedral in Northern Europe, a place of worship for more than 1,000 years, and a treasure house of stained glass. Take an audio tour of the undercroft, or a guided tour of the Minster.

* Climb the tower for an amazing view
* Visited by 2 million people every year

**Location**
In York city centre

**Opening**
Daily: Apr–Oct Mon–Sat 9am–4.45pm, Sun 12noon–3.45pm;
Nov–Mar Mon–Sat 9.30am–4.45pm, Sun 12noon–3.45pm
Tower: see website for details

**Admission**
Donations appreciated

**Contact**
Deangate, York YO1 7HH
t 01904 557216
w yorkminster.org
e visitors@yorkminster.org

---

711 York

# Yorkshire Air Museum

3 hrs    All year

Admire displays such as the restored control tower, air gunners museum, airborne forces display and Squadron Memorial Rooms. See Yorkshire's pioneering Cayley glider and with the Wright llyer, Halifax bomber, and modern jets like the Harrier GR3 and Tornado GR4.

* See the only restored Halifax bomber
* Historical aircraft from the earliest days of flight

**Location**
Take B1228 off A63/A1079 roundabout

**Opening**
Daily: *summer* (Apr–Sep) 10am–5pm
*winter* (Oct–Mar)10am–3.30pm

**Admission**
Adult £5, Child £3, Concs £4

**Contact**
Halifax Way, Elvington York YO41 4AU
t 01904 608595
w yorkshireairmuseum.co.uk
e museum@yorkshireairmuseum.co.uk

---

712 York

# Yorkshire Museum & Gardens

2 hrs    All year

Walk in the footsteps of Romans and Vikings. See beasts turned to stone from a time when dinosaurs ruled the planet and a host of outstanding archaeological finds. The museum is set in 10 acres of botanical gardens in the historic centre of York.

* Ruins of St Mary's Abbey in grounds
* 2006 exhibition of Constantine the Great, York's famous emperor

**Location**
5–10 min walk from train station

**Opening**
Daily: 10am–5pm

**Admission**
Adult £4, Child £2.50, Concs £3

**Contact**
Museum Gardens, York YO1 7FR
t 01904 687687
w york.yorkshire.museum
e yorkshire.museum@ymt.org.uk

South Yorkshire

## 713 Conisbrough

# Conisbrough Castle

2 hrs+    All year

The white circular keep of this C12 castle is a spectacular structure made of magnesian limestone and is the oldest of its kind in England. Recently restored, with two new floors and a roof, it is an outstanding example of medieval architecture.

* Inspiration for Sir Walter Scott's classic novel Ivanhoe
* Closed for private functions some Saturdays during Summer

**Location**
NE of town centre on A630

**Opening**
Daily: Apr–Sep 10am–5pm;
Oct–Mar 10am–4pm

**Admission**
Adult £4, Child £2.15, Concs £2.75

**Contact**
Castle Hill, Conisbrough DN12 3BU

t 01709 863329
w conisbroughcastle.org.uk
e info@conisbroughcastle.org.uk

## 714 Maltby

# Roche Abbey

1 hr    Apr–Sep

Founded in 1147, the fine early Gothic transepts of this Cistercian monastery still survive to their original height. In the C18 Capability Brown transformed an already beautiful valley, incorporating the ruins. Excavation has revealed the complete layout of the abbey.

* Visit the website for full programme of special events

**Location**
1½ miles S of Maltby off A634

**Opening**
Apr–Sep Thu–Mon 10am–5pm;
Jul–Aug daily 10am–5pm

**Admission**
Adult £2.90, Child £1.50, Concs £2.20

**Contact**
The Abbey Lodge, Maltby,
nr Rotherham S66 8NW

t 01709 812739
w english-heritage.org.uk/yorkshire

## 715 Rotherham

# Magna Science Adventure Centre

3 hrs+    All year

Set within a vast former steelworks, Magna is a hands-on visitor attraction that explores the powerful themes of earth, air, fire and water. Operate a real JCB, fire a water cannon or explode a rock face. Visit Europe's biggest high-tech, sci-tech playground.

* Feel the force of a tornado in the Air Pavilion
* Test your bravery as a virtual fireball races towards you

**Location**
Just off M1, 1 mile along A6178 from Meadowhall shopping centre

**Opening**
Daily: 10am–5pm

**Admission**
Adult £9, Child & Concs £7

**Contact**
Sheffield Road, Templeborough,
Rotherham S60 1DX

t 01709 720002
w visitmagna.co.uk
e info@magnatrust.co.uk

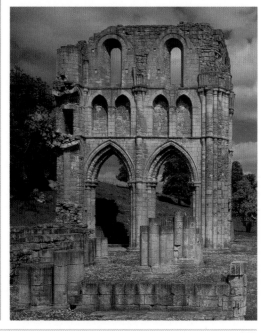

## 716 Sheffield

# The Graves Art Gallery

  1 hr  All year

Admire the city's collections of C19 and C20 British and European art. The paintings encapsulate the story of the development of modern art, the main trends traced through works by many well-known artists including Picasso, Bonnard and Spencer.

* Exciting programme of temporary exhibitions
* Sheffield's latest contemporary acquisition 'Kiss' by Marc Quinn

| Location | Contact |
| --- | --- |
| In city centre above Central Library | Surrey Street, Sheffield S1 1XZ |
| **Opening**<br>Mon–Sat 10am–5pm | t 0114 278 2600<br>w sheffieldgalleries.org.uk<br>e infosheffieldgalleries.org.uk |
| **Admission**<br>Free | |

## 717 Sheffield

# Millennium Galleries

  2 hrs+  All year

With four individual galleries under one roof, there is something for everybody to enjoy here. Admire treasures from the past and masterpieces from Britain's national collections and discover new creations by contemporary artists and makers.

* Material regularly borrowed from the Tate & the V&A museum
* Metalwork gallery

| Location | Contact |
| --- | --- |
| In city centre near Winter Garden | Arundel Gate, Sheffield S1 2PP |
| **Opening**<br>Mon–Sat 10am–5pm,<br>Sun 11am–5pm | t 0114 278 2600<br>w sheffieldgalleries.org.uk<br>e info@sheffieldgalleries.org.uk |
| **Admission**<br>Free, exhibitions may charge | |

## 718 Sheffield

# Renishaw Hall Gardens

  4 hrs+  Easter–Sep

The hall was home to the Sitwell family for more than 350 years, the beautiful Italianate garden, park and lake were created by the eccentric Sir George Sitwell. Today visitors can enjoy lakeside walks, various galleries and a sculpture trail.

* Hall open by special arrangement only
* Regular calendar of events

| Location | Admission |
| --- | --- |
| Just 2 miles from junction 30 off M1, between Ecrington & Renishaw on A6135 | Please phone for details |
| | **Contact**<br>Renishaw Hall, Sheffield |
| **Opening**<br>Easter–Sep Thu–Sun & Bank Hol Mon 10.30am–4.30pm. Please phone for details of special events | t 01246 432310<br>w sitwell.co.uk<br>e info@renishawhall.free-online.co.uk |

## 719 Sheffield

# Sheffield Ski Village

   3½ hrs      All year

This all-season dry-slope ski resort offers skiing, snowboarding and toboggan rides for all ages and abilities, with lessons available at all levels and equipment for hire. Afterwards relax in the authentic village inn pub. It is ideal for groups and parties.

* More than 1 mile of piste
* Thunder Valley Toboggan Run

  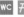

| Location | Admission |
| --- | --- |
| 5 mins from city centre, off A61 Penistone Road | Please phone for details |
| | **Contact**<br>Vale Road, Sheffield S3 9SJ |
| **Opening**<br>Daily: *summer* Mon–Fri 4pm–10pm,<br>Sat–Sun 10am–8pm, Bank Hols 10am–10pm; *winter* Mon–Fri 10am–10pm, Sat–Sun, Bank Hols & 26 Dec–2 Jan 9am–10pm | t 0114 276 9459<br>w sheffieldskivillage.co.uk<br>e info@sheffieldskivillage.co.uk |

## 720  Bradford

# Colour Museum

1 hr    All year

Europe's only museum of colour. This is the place to come to find out all about the weird and wonderful world of colour. Along with its interactive galleries and special exhibitions, the museum holds workshops on all aspects of colour.

* Situated in a former wool warehouse
* Workshops and educational programme (visit the website)

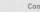

| Location | Contact |
|---|---|
| In city centre, near Metro Interchange | PO Box 244, Perkin House, 1 Providence Street, Bradford BD1 2PW |
| Opening | |
| Tue–Sat 10am–4pm | t  01274 390955 |
| | w  colour-experience.org.uk |
| Admission | e  museum@sdc.org.uk |
| Adults £2, Child & Concs £1.50 | |

## 721  Bradford

# National Museum of Photography, Film & Television

2 hrs+    All year

This is one of the most visited national museums outside London, located in Bradford in recognition of the city's historic contribution to the development of cinema and film making in the UK. The museum's archive includes the first negative and the earliest television footage.

* First moving pictures – 1888 film of Leeds Bridge
* More than 3 million historical items

| Location | Contact |
|---|---|
| City centre off Little Horton Lane | Bradford BD1 1NQ |
| Opening | t  0870 701 0200 |
| Tue–Sun & Bank & Public Hols 10am–6pm | w  nmpft.org.uk |
| | e  talk.nmpft@nmsi.ac.uk |
| Admission | |
| Free, except for cinemas | |

## 722  Halifax

# Shibden Hall

1 hrs+    All year

Built in 1420, the hall was home to the Lister family for more than 300 years and it contains furnishings from several different centuries. The barn houses a collection of horse-drawn vehicles and the folk museum is a reconstruction of an early C19 village.

* See coopers, wheelwrights, pharmacies, a Crispin Inn & an old ale brewery

| Location | Admission |
|---|---|
| Signed from Halifax & M62 | Adult £3.50, Child & Concs £2.50 |
| Opening | Contact |
| Daily: Mar–Nov Mon–Sat 10am–5pm, Sun 12noon–5pm; | Lister's Road, Halifax HX3 6XG |
| Dec–Feb Mon–Sat 10am–4pm, Sun 12noon–4pm | t  01422 352246 |
| (doors close 30 mins before closing time) | w  calderdale.gov.uk/tourism |
| | e  shibden.hall@calderdale.gov.uk |

## 723 Leeds

# Harewood House & Bird Gardens

3–4 hrs    Feb–Nov

This is one of the country's premier avian collections. More than 100 species of threatened and exotic birds are housed in sympathetic environments with the aim of promoting conservation and education. The Capability Brown gardens also provide many attractions.

* Boat trips across the lake & adventure playground
* Extensive collections of art & furniture in the house

| Location | Grounds Mon–Fri Adult £8.25, |
| On A61, 7 miles from Leeds | Child £5.50, Concs £7.50 |
| & Harrogate | Sat–Sun £10.25, £7, £9.50 |
| Opening | Contact |
| Daily: 4 Feb–Nov 10am–5pm | Harewood Estate, Harewood, |
| | Leeds LS17 9LQ |
| Admission | t  0113 218 1010 |
| All attractions Mon–Fri Adult £11, | w  harewood.org |
| Child £6.50, Concs £9.50 | e  info@harewood.org |
| Sat–Sun £13, £8, £11.50 | |

## 724 Leeds

# Leeds City Art Gallery

2 hr    All year

There is something for everyone at Leeds City Art Gallery, from traditional prints, watercolours, paintings and sculptures to contemporary works. The exhibitions are ever-changing, displaying some of the most outstanding works of British art outside London.

* Designated as a collection of national importance
* Features work by Turner, Rembrandt & Henry Moore

| Location | Contact |
| In city centre, next to Central Library | The Headrow, Leeds LS1 3AA |
| Opening | t  0113 247 8248 |
| Daily: Mon–Sat 10am–5pm, | w  leeds.gov.uk/gallery |
| Wed 10am–8pm, Sun 1pm–5pm, | |
| closed on Bank Hols | |
| Admission | |
| Free | |

## 725 Leeds

# Royal Armouries Museum

4 hrs    All year

The Royal Armouries Museum in Leeds was opened in 1996 as the new home for the National Collection of arms and armour. Five themed galleries cover war, tournament, self–defence, hunting and the arms and armour of the Orient.

* See Henry VIII's tournament armour
* Live action events & interactive technology

| Location | Contact |
| S of city centre, near junction 4 of M621 | Armouries Drive, Leeds LS10 1LT |
| Opening | t  08700 344344 |
| Daily: 10am–5pm | w  royalarmouries.org.uk |
| Admission | e  enquiries@armouries.org.uk |
| Free, charge payable for parking | |

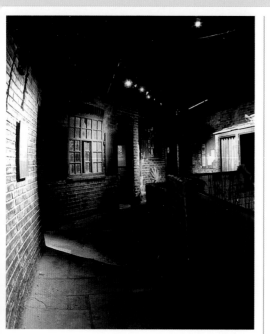

# Temple Newsam House & Farm

2 hrs    All year

This magnificent country house contains one of the most important collections of decorative arts in Britain, including splendid Chippendale furniture and silver. The 1,500 acres of parkland, woodland, farmland and gardens include a rare breeds centre with more than 400 animals.

* Largest rare breeds centre in the world
* Grounds ideal for picnics

**Location**
Temple Newsam Road, off Selby Road,
4 miles from city centre, off A63

**Opening**
Nov–Mar Tue–Sun 10.30am–4pm;
Apr–Oct Tue–Sun 10am–5pm
(last admission 30 mins before
closing)

**Admission**
*House* Adult £3.50, Child £2.50
*Farm* £3.50, £2.50
*House & Farm* £5.50, £3.50

**Contact**
Temple Newsam Road, Leeds LS15 0AE
t 0113 264 7321
w leeds.gov.uk/templenewsam
e tnewsamho.leeds@virgin.net

---

# Thackray Museum

3 hrs    All year

Established in a former workhouse building adjacent to St James's Hospital, the museum houses displays that show how people's lives have changed over the past 150 years as a result of improvements in public health, medicine and healthcare.

* Vast range of surgical instruments from the C19 to today
* Unique collection of pharmacy ceramics

**Location**
Follow signs for St James's Hospital,
museum is 100m past main entrance

**Opening**
Daily: 10am–5pm (last admission 3pm)

**Admission**
Adult £5.50, Child £4, Concs £4.50
Car park £1

**Contact**
Beckett Street, Leeds LS9 7LN
t 0113 244 4343
w thackraymuseum.org
e info@thackraymuseum.org

---

# Tropical World

2 hrs    All year

Explore the tropics in the butterfly house, home to 30–40 species, and the Coronation house, filled with unusual plants. The Amazon is recreated in the South American house and is home to whistling ducks and macaws. The nocturnal zone has bush babies and fruit bats.

* Largest collection of tropical plants outside Kew
* Insect zone and desert house

**Location**
Off A58 at Oakwood, 3 miles
N of city centre

**Opening**
Daily: 10am–6pm
(last admission 5.30pm)

**Admission**
Adult £3, Child (8–15) £2

**Contact**
Canal Gardens, Roundhay Park,
Leeds LS8 2ER
t 0113 266 1850

## 729 Wakefield

# National Coalmining Museum

3 hrs+    All year

Tours take visitors 140 metres underground and trace mining techniques and conditions through the ages from the C19, when women and children worked underground, to how pit ponies were used before mechanical systems were implemented.

\* Exhibition of modern mining methods
\* Each guide is a former local miner

| Location | Contact |
|---|---|
| On A642 between Wakefield & Huddersfield | Caphouse Colliery, New Road, Overton, Wakefield WF4 4RH |
| Opening | t 01924 848806 |
| Daily: 10am–5pm | w ncm.org.uk |
| | e info@ncm.org.uk |
| Admission | |
| Free | |

## 730 Wakefield

# Sandal Castle

1 hr+    All year

Originally a motte and bailey castle dating from the C12, the stone castle overlooking the River Calder was demolished on the orders of Parliament after being besieged during the Civil War in 1645. It was restored to its present state in the 1970s and 1980s.

\* Overlooks site of 1460 Battle of Wakefield
\* Spectacular views

| Location | Admission |
|---|---|
| On A61, 2 miles from city centre in the direction of Barnsley | Free |
| | Contact |
| Opening | Manygates Lane, Sandal, Wakefield WF2 7DG |
| Castle Daily: dawn–dusk | |
| Visitor centre Daily: Easter–Oct half-term 11am–4.30pm, otherwise weekends only Please phone for details | t 01924 249779 |

## 731 Wakefield

# Yorkshire Sculpture Park

2 hrs+    All year

One of Europe's leading open-air galleries showing modern and contemporary work by leading UK and international artists. A changing programme of exhibitions, displays and projects is held throughout 500 acres of the C18 landscaped grounds.

\* Four indoor galleries including underground gallery

| Location | Contact |
|---|---|
| 1 mile from M1 junction 38 on A637 | West Bretton, Wakefield WF4 4LG |
| Opening | t 01924 832631 |
| Daily: summer 10am–6pm | w ysp.co.uk |
| winter 10am–5pm | e info@ysp.co.uk |
| Admission | |
| Free. Car park £3 | |

# North West

Cheshire Cumbria Lancashire
Manchester Merseyside

Castle Douglas
Dalbeattie
Kirkcudbright

Brampton
**762**

Hexham
Gateshead — Jarr
**881–882**
**891** **892** **893**
**897** **859** Stan **904–905** Wash
Consett
Chester-le-Street
Durham **864–869**
Brandon
Spennymoor
Bishop Auckland
**860–861**
Newton Aycliffe
Stockton-on-Te
**862–863**
Darlington
TEESSI

Carlisle
**763–765**
Wigton
Alston
**873**

**M6**

CUMBRIA
Maryport
Cockermouth
**766–767**
**775**
Keswick
Workington
Whitehaven
Egremont

Penrith
**778–780**
Appleby-in-Westmorland
Brough
**857–858**
Scotch Corner
Richmond
Catterick

DURHAM

Lake District
**770**
Ambleside
Coniston
**771**
**768**
Windermere
**786–787**
Kendal
**776–777**
**772–774**
Sedbergh
Hawes
**688**
Leyburn
**682**
**690**
Thir

Millom
**769**
Ulverston
**781–785**
**760–761**
Grange-over-Sands
**804**
Kirkby Lonsdale
NORTH YORKSHIRE
Ripon
**694–696**
**693**

Barrow-in-Furness
Isle of Walney
Morecambe
Heysham
**813**
**810–812**
Carnforth
Lancaster
Settle
ENGLAND

Knare
**683–684**
**687**
Harrogate

Fleetwood
**808**
Garstang
Skipton
Ilkley
**699–700**
Keighley
Yeadon
LEEDS & BRADFORD
Bingley
Shipley
LEEDS
**720–721**
**723–728**

Blackpool
**791–794**
Lytham St Anne's
Kirkham
Warton
Preston
**815–818**
Blackburn
**789–790**
LANCASHIRE
Clitheroe
**807**
**806**
**802–803**
**788**
Accrington
Rawtenstall
Colne
Nelson
Burnley
Todmorden
BRADFORD
Halifax
**722**
Brighouse
**729–731** Wak

Southport
Formby
**814**
Leyland
**805**
**809**
Chorley
**819**
**820**
**795–801**
**821**
Standish
Wigan
Bury
Rochdale
Middleton
**M62**
Huddersfield

Crosby
Bootle
Wallasey
**856**
Ormskirk
Kirkby
Skelmersdale
**M58**
St Helens
Salford
**822–834**
MANCHESTER
**749**
**751–752**
Oldham
Penistone
SHEFFIELD

LIVERPOOL
**840–854**
**835–838**
Birkenhead
**855**
**839**
**759**
Warrington
**756**
**748**
**758**
Runcorn
Altrincham
**732**
Sale
Cheadle
Stockport
Glossop
Stocksbridge
**716–719**
**418–420**
Peak District
Dronfie

Great Ormes Head
Colwyn Bay
Prestatyn
Rhyl
**643**
Conwy
**644–645**
Llan
Abergele
St Asaph
Holywell
Flint
**744**
Ellesmere Port
**737–738**
Frodsham
**753**
Northwich
Knutsford
Whaley Bridge
**740–743**
Buxton
Macclesfield
**415**
**426**
Bakewell
Matlock
**427–428**
Clay Cross
Alfreto

Queensferry
**745–747**
Middlewich
CHESTER
**733–735**
**754–755**
Winsford
Crewe
Congleton
**750**
Biddulph
Leek
Kidsgrove
**534**
**547**
Wirksworth
**421**
Belper
DERBY

Blaenau Ffestiniog
Ffestiniog
Betws-y-coed
Llanrwst
CONWY
Ruthin
Mold
Denbigh
DENBIGHSHIRE
FLINTSHIRE
Wrexham
Nantwich
Whitchurch
**757**
Newcastle-under-Lyme
**531**
**542–543**
STOKE-ON-TRENT
**736**
Ashbourne
DERBY

Llandudno
Ruabon
Llangollen
**649**
WREXHAM

## 732 Altrincham

# Dunham Massey

2 hrs     Mar–Nov

This early Georgian house was extensively renovated in the early C20. The result is one of Britain's most sumptuous Edwardian interiors housing collections of C18 walnut furniture, paintings and Huguenot silver. You can also visit the extensive servants' quarters.

* Beautiful gardens with richly planted borders
* Orangery, Victorian bark house & well house

**Location**
3 miles SW of Altrincham, M6 junction 19, M56 junction 7

**Opening**
Mar–Sep Sat–Wed 12noon–5pm;
Oct–Nov Sat–Wed 12noon–4pm

**Admission**
Adult £6.50, Child £3.25

**Contact**
Altrincham WA14 4SJ

t  0161 941 1025
w  national-trust.org.uk
e  dunhammassey@ntrust.org.uk

## 733 Chester

# Chester Cathedral

1 hr     All year

This is the most complete medieval monastic complex standing in the UK. Records show a church has existed on this site since the early C10, and the foundation of a Benedictine monastery in 1092. In 1541 it became the Cathedral Church of Christ and the Blessed Virgin Mary.

* Restoration in latter part of C19 by Sir Gilbert Scott
* Stunning stained glass, fabrics & sculptures

**Location**
In city centre

**Opening**
Daily: Mon–Sat 9am–5pm
Sun 1pm–5pm

**Admission**
Adult £4, Child £1.50, Concs £3

**Contact**
12 Abbey Square, Chester CH1 2HU

t  01244 324756
w  chestercathedral.com
e  fry@chestercathedral.com

## 734 Chester

# Chester Zoo

5 hrs+     All year

Founded in 1934 and covering more than 100 acres, Chester Zoo is one of the largest zoos in the UK and has more than 1 million visitors each year. It is home to more than 7,000 animals, representing around 500 different species, and a spectacular plant collection.

* New elephant centre to open in Spring 2006
* Internationally renowned for innovative enclosures

**Location**
Easily accessible from M53 & M56, follow brown tourist signs

**Opening**
Daily: from 10am; closing times vary, please phone for details

**Admission**
*Peak season* Apr–Sep Adult £13.50, Child £10.50, Concs £12

*Off-peak* Oct–Mar £9.50, £7.50, £8.50

**Contact**
Upton-by-Chester, Chester CH2 1LH

t  01244 380280
w  chesterzoo.org
e  reception@chesterzoo.co.uk

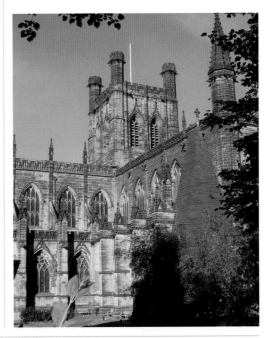

## 735 Chester

# Grosvenor Museum

1 hr+    All year

Hear the story of Chester from the Roman fortress of Deva to the present day. Learn about its Roman people, army and buildings, visit a Roman graveyard with tombstones of the Legion's soldiers and enjoy artists' views of the city's past.

* Discover the natural history of Cheshire
* Georgian house with re created period rooms

| Location | Contact |
|---|---|
| Chester city centre | 27 Grosvenor Street, Chester CH1 2DD |
| Opening | t  01244 402008 |
| Daily: Mon–Sat 10.30am–5pm, | w  grosvenormuseum.co.uk |
| Sun 1pm–4pm | e  srogers@chestercc.gov.uk |
| Admission | |
| Free | |

## 736 Congleton

# Little Moreton Hall

2 hrs    Mar–Dec

This moated house, with its irregular half-timbered façades opening on to a cobbled courtyard, was built in the mid-C15. The house was extended between 1570 and 1580 when the Long Gallery was added, giving the hall its curious top-heavy look.

* A warren of rooms, some no larger than cupboards
* *Moll Flanders* & *Lady Jane* were filmed here

| Location | Admission |
|---|---|
| 4 miles S of Congleton on A34, 10 mins from junctions 16 & 17 of M6 | Adult £5.25, Child £2.50 |
| Opening | Contact |
| Mar–Oct Wed–Sun 11.30am–5pm; | Congleton CW12 4SD |
| Nov–Dec Sat–Sun 11.30am–4pm | t  01260 272018 |
| | w  nationaltrust.org.uk |
| | e  littlemoretonhall@ntrust.org.uk |

## 737 Ellesmere Port

# Blue Planet Aquarium

2 hrs    All year

The aquarium features one of the world's largest underwater viewing tunnels. Visitors can get up close to huge sharks, graceful rays and hundreds of other fish. Exhibits span the Scottish Highlands, the mighty Amazon, the depths of Lake Malawi and mangroves.

* Shark-inhabited Caribbean reef
* Touchpools with anemones, rays and octopus play park

| Location | Contact |
|---|---|
| Nr junction 10 of M53, adjacent to Cheshire Oaks designer outlet village | Cheshire Oaks, Ellesmere Port CH65 9LF |
| Opening | t  0151 357 8800 |
| Daily: from 10am. Closing times vary, please phone for details | w  blueplanetaquarium.com |
| | e  info@blueplanetaquarium.com |
| Admission | |
| Adult £9.95, Child &Concs £7.50 | |

©National Trust Photographic Library

# The Boat Museum

4 hrs+   All year

Board some of the boats from the world's largest floating collection of traditional canal craft. Discover how people lived in homes no larger than the hallway of a modern house. Tour the Georgian and Victorian buildings full of fascinating exhibitions.

* Visit the Pump House & Power Hall
* Experience domestic life in dock workers' cottages

**Location**
Junction 9 off M53. Follow signs

**Opening**
Apr–Oct daily 10am–5pm;
Nov–Mar Sat–Wed 11am–4pm

**Admission**
Adult £6.45, Child £4.75, Concs £5.25

**Contact**
South Pier Road,
Ellesmere Port CH65 4FW

t  0151 355 5017
w  boatmuseum.org.uk
e  bookings@thewaterwaystrust.org

# Tatton Park

4 hrs+   Mar–Oct

An impressive estate with more than 1,000 acres of stunning parkland that is home to herds of red and fallow deer. Its major attractions include a Tudor hall, neo-classical mansion, working farm and award-winning gardens.

* Classic car show, fine food fairs & classical concerts
* Victorian kitchens & servants' quarters

**Location**
Signed from junction 19 of M6,
& junction 57 of M56

**Opening**
Mar–Oct Tue–Sun 12noon–5pm
Times for individual attractions vary,
please phone for details
*Gardens* From 10am

**Admission**
Adult £3, Child £2

**Contact**
Knutsford WA16 6QN

t  01625 534400
w  tattonpark.org.uk
e  tatton@cheshire.gov.uk

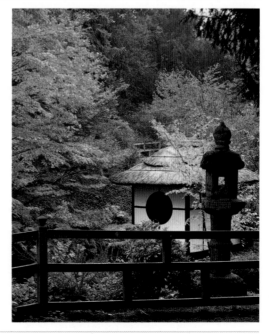

740 Macclesfield

# Capesthorne Hall

2–4 hrs   Apr–Oct

A turreted, redbrick C18 Jacobean-style building, Capesthorne Hall has collections including fine art, marble sculptures and tapestries, plus Regency, Jacobean and rococo antiques. Enjoy the treasured collections of Americana and children's toys.

* Guided tours by arrangement
* Grounds include a chapel, gardens & lakes

**Location**
Off A34 between Manchester & Stoke-on-Trent, 3 miles S of Alderly Edge, junction 6 of M56

**Opening**
Apr–Oct Sun, Wed & Bank Hols
12noon–5pm

**Admission**
Adult £6, Child £3, Concs £5

**Contact**
Siddington, Macclesfield SK11 9JY

t 01625 861221
w capesthorne.com
e info@capesthorne.com

741 Macclesfield

# Gawsworth Hall

1 hr+   Apr–Oct

An ancient manor house that includes the Fitton family chapel, licensed in 1365. The original Norman house was rebuilt in 1480 and remodelled in 1701. A famous duel took place in 1712 between Lord Mohun and the Duke of Hamilton in which both duellists were killed.

* Samuel Johnson, the last professional jester, lived here
* Open-air theatre season Jun–Aug

**Location**
On A536 between Macclesfield & Congleton

**Opening**
Daily: mid-Jun–Aug 2pm–5pm; times may vary, please phone for details

**Admission**
Adult £5, Child £2.50

**Contact**
Church Lane, Macclesfield SK11 9RN

t 01260 223456
w gawsworthhall.com
e enquiries@gawsworthhall.com

## 742 Macclesfield

# Jodrell Bank Science Centre & Arboretum

2 hrs+    Mar–Oct

This is the visitor centre for the Lovell radio telescope. There is an observational pathway around the base of the telescope, a small exhibition area and a 3D theatre as well as the Space Café and shop.

\* 35-acre arboretum is a tree-lovers' paradise
\* Environmental discovery centre

| Location | Admission |
|---|---|
| Between Holmes Chapel & Chelford, on A535, 8 miles W of Macclesfield | Adult £1.50, Child £1. Car park £3 |
| Opening | Contact |
| Daily: Mar–Oct 10.30am–5.30pm | Lower Withington, Macclesfield SK11 9DL |
| The centre is under development so please phone for details | t  01477 571339 |
| | w  jb.man.ac.uk/scicen |
| | e  visitorcentre@jb.man.ac.uk |

## 743 Macclesfield

# Macclesfield Silk Museum

2 hrs    All year

This building was once the Macclesfield School of Art built in 1877 to train designers for the silk industry. It now houses exhibitions exploring the properties of silk, design education, Macclesfield's diverse textile industries, workers' lives and historic machinery.

\* Temporary exhibits
\* Try your hand at weaving & designing

| Location | Contact |
|---|---|
| In town centre | Roe Street, Macclesfield SK11 6UT |
| Opening | t  01625 613210 |
| Daily: Mon–Sat 11am–5pm | w  silk-macclesfield.org |
| Bank Hols 12noon–4pm | e  silkmuseum@tiscali.co.uk |
| Admission | |
| Adult £3.95, Concs £3.20 | |

## 744 Neston

# Ness Botanic Gardens

1 hr+    All year

When a Liverpool cotton merchant began to create a garden in 1898, he laid the foundations of one of the major botanic gardens in the UK. Now internationally renowned, the collection includes breathtaking rhododendrons and azaleas.

\* Adopt a tree scheme
\* Heather, herb & water gardens

| Location | Admission |
|---|---|
| 6 miles from exit of M53, 5 miles from Western End of M56, off A540 Chester Hoylake road | Adult £5, Child free, Concs £4.50 |
| Opening | Contact |
| Daily: Mar–Oct 9.30am–5pm; | Ness, Neston CH64 4AY |
| Nov–Feb 9.30am–4pm | t  0151 353 0123 |
| | w  nessgardens.org.uk |
| | e  nessgdns@liv.ac.uk |

## 745 Northwich

# Anderton Boat Lift

1 hr    Mar–Oct

Reopened in 2002 after a £7 million restoration, the Anderton Boat Lift is one of the greatest monuments to Britain's last canal age and is known as the 'Cathedral of the Canals'. Built in 1875, it was the world's first, and is currently England's only boat lift.

\* New operations centre open
\* Quality Assured Visitor Attraction

| Location | Admission |
|---|---|
| Follow A556 & then A559 to Northwich town centre, then follow signs | Adult £6.50, Child £4.50, Concs £5.25 |
| Opening | Contact |
| Daily: Mar–Oct 10am–5pm | Lift Lane, Anderton |
| Please visit the website or phone for boat & lift times | Northwich CW9 6FW |
| | t  01606 786777 |
| | w  andertonboatlift.co.uk |
| | e  info@andertonboatlift.co.uk |

## 746 Northwich

# Arley Hall & Gardens

2 hrs    Apr–Sep

These charming English gardens feature a double herbaceous border laid out in 1846, a pleached lime avenue, giant cylinders of *Quercus ilex*, topiary and collections of roses, rhododendrons and azaleas. The hall reveals fine panelling and plasterwork.

* Voted one of the top 50 gardens in Europe
* Gardens include rose & fallen timber gardens

| Location | Admission |
|---|---|
| Junction 19 or 20 of M6, or junction 9 or 10 of the M56 | *Hall* Adult £2.50, Child £1, Concs £2 *Hall & Gardens* £4.70, £2, £4.20 |
| Opening | Contact |
| *Hall* Apr–Sep Tue, Sun & Bank Hols 12noon–5pm | Arley, Northwich CW9 6NA |
| *Gardens* Apr–Sep Tue–Sun & Bank Hols 11am–5pm | t 01565 777353 w arleyhallandgardens.com e enquiries@arleyhallandgardens.com |

## 747 Northwich

# Lion Salt Works

1 hr    All year

The Lion Salt Works is a unique survival of the traditional inland salt works which once produced this essential commodity. The site illustrates the whole process of salt production and dates from the late C19/C20. It is the only surviving site in Cheshire.

* Cheshire once produced 86% of the nation's salt
* Building renovation in progress

| Location | Contact |
|---|---|
| Junction 19 from M6 via A556. Junction 10 from M56 via A559. | Ollershaw Lane, Marston Northwich CW9 6ES |
| Opening | t 01606 41823 |
| Sun–Thu 1.30pm–4.30pm | w lionsaltworkstrust.co.uk |
| Admission | e afielding@lionsalt.demon.co.uk |
| Adult £1, Child 50p | |

## 748 Runcorn

# Norton Priory Museum

1 hr    All year

This 38-acre site includes a museum, a magnificent 800-year-old vaulted storage range, a historic priory, remains excavated by archaeologists, and the unique St Christopher statue. The woodland gardens are the setting for a collection of contemporary sculpture.

* Four North West in Bloom awards
* The BBC2's programme *Hidden Gardens* filmed here

| Location | Admission |
|---|---|
| From junction 11 off M56. Turn for Warrington & follow signs | Adult £4.50, Concs £3.25 |
| Opening | Contact |
| Nov–Mar daily 12noon–4pm; Apr–Oct Mon–Fri 12noon–5pm , Sat–Sun 12noon–6pm | Tudor Road, Manor Park, Runcorn WA7 1SX |
| | t 01928 569895 w nortonpriory.org e info@nortonpriory.org |

## 749 Sandbach

# Sandbach Crosses

½ hr    All year

Rare Saxon stone crosses, carved with animals and biblical scenes, stand in the cobbled market square of Sandbach. The crosses are believed to date from the C9. Close inspection reveals the ancient carvings.

* One of the most photographed sights in Cheshire
* Restored in 1816 after destruction by iconoclasts

| Location | Contact |
|---|---|
| Market Square, Sandbach | English Heritage, Canada House, 3 Chepstow Street, Manchester M1 5FW |
| Opening | |
| Daily: any reasonable times | t 0161 242 1400 |
| Admission | w english-heritage.org.uk |
| Free | e northwest@english-heritage.org.uk |

## 750 Scholar Green

# Rode Hall

2 hrs+    Apr–Sep

The house was constructed in two stages, the earlier two-storey wing and stable block around 1705 and the main building in 1752. The house contains examples of furniture by Gillow of Lancaster, a collection of portraits and an important collection of English porcelain.

* Rode Hall stands in a Repton landscape
* Garden renowned for its snowdrops & kitchen garden

| Location | Admission |
|---|---|
| 5 miles SW of Congleton between A34 & A50 | House & Gardens Adult £5, Concs £4<br>Gardens Adult £3, Concs £2.50 |
| Opening | Contact |
| House Apr–Sep Wed & Bank Hols 2pm–5pm;<br>Feb Tue–Sun to view snowdrops | Scholar Green, Cheshire ST7 3QP<br>t 01270 873237<br>w rodehall.co.uk<br>e rodehall@scholargreen.fsnet.co.uk |

## 751 Stockport

# Bramall Hall

2 hrs    All year

This is a grand black and white timber-framed building. The hall was built in the traditional local style with an oak framework, joined using mortice and tenon joints and held in place with oak pegs. Wattle and daub or lath and plaster were used to fill the spaces in the timbers.

* Guided tours available on request
* Open woodland

| Location | Admission |
|---|---|
| Junction 1 or 27 of M60 | Adult £3.95, Child & Concs £2.50 |
| Opening | Contact |
| Easter–Sep daily 1pm–5pm.<br>Bank Hols 11am–5pm;<br>Oct–2 Jan Tue–Sun 1pm–4pm,<br>Bank Hols 11am–4pm;<br>3 Jan–Easter Sat–Sun only 1pm–4pm | Bramall Park, Stockport SK7 3NX<br>t 0161 485 3708<br>w bramallhall.org.uk<br>e bramall.hall@stockport.gov.uk |

## 752 Stockport

# Lyme Park

2 hrs+    Mar–Oct

Originally a Tudor house, Lyme was transformed by the Venetian architect Leoni into an Italianate palace. Some of the Elizabethan interiors survive and contrast dramatically with later rooms. The state rooms are adorned with Mortlake tapestries.

* Pemberley in BBC's adaptation of Pride & Prejudice
* Important collection of English clocks

| Location | Admission |
|---|---|
| On A6, 6 miles S of city centre.<br>Follow signs | House Adult £5, Child £2.50<br>Gardens £3.50, £2<br>House & Gardens £6.50, £3.30 |
| Opening | Contact |
| Daily: late Mar–Oct<br>House, Park & Gardens please phone for details | Disley, Stockport SK12 2NX<br>t 01663 762023/766492<br>w nationaltrust.org.uk<br>e lymepark@nationaltrust.org.uk |

## 753 Tabley

# Cuckoo Land

1 hr+   All year

The museum hosts one of the world's largest collections of cuckoo clocks with thousands of assorted exhibits. Most of the clocks are rare or unique, and they combine a number of ingenious methods of time keeping.

* Collection of Black Forest organs
* Display of vintage motorcycles

**Location**
Just off Junction 19 of M6

**Opening**
Daily: 10am–5pm

**Admission**
£5 per person includes guided tour

**Contact**
The Old School, Chester Road, Tabley WA16 0HL

t 01565 633039
w cuckoolanduk.net
e mpiekarski@btconnect.com

## 755 Tarporley

# Oulton Park Race Circuit

All day   Apr–Oct

Set in 320 acres of glorious Cheshire countryside, Oulton Park offers spectacular car and bike racing, including British superbikes, touring cars, Formula 3 and family-fun days. Experience the thrill for yourself with racing, rally and early-drive activities.

* Full racing programme
* Drive Like a Professional courses

**Location**
Take junction 18 off M6 & follow A54 to Chester for 12 miles. Turn left onto A49 to Whitchurch & follow signs

**Opening**
Apr–Oct open Sat for minor meetings, open Sun & Bank Hols for major meetings

**Admission**
Please phone for details

**Contact**
Motorsport Vision
Little Budworth, Tarporley
Cheshire CW6 9BW

t 01829 760301
w motorsportvision.co.uk

## 754 Tarporley

# Beeston Castle

1 hr+   All year

Standing majestically on sheer, rocky crags, Beeston has stunning views. Its history stretches back more than 4,000 years, to when it was a Bronze Age hill fort. The castle was built from 1226 and soon became a royal stronghold, only falling centuries later in the English Civil War.

* Exhibition outlines the history of this strategic site
* Panoramic views of the Cheshire Plain

**Location**
11 miles SE of Chester on a minor road off A49

**Opening**
Daily: Apr–Sep 10am–6pm;
Oct–Mar 10am–4pm

**Admission**
Adult £3.60, Child £1.80, Concs £2.70

**Contact**
Tarporley CW6 9TX

t 01829 260464
w english-heritage.org.uk

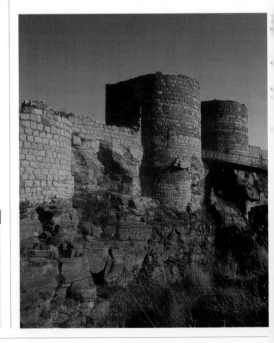

## 756 Warrington

# Warrington Museum & Art Gallery

1 hr+    All year

This museum houses exhibitions on Warrington and the surrounding area, together with exhibitions by renowned artists. Shows have included etchings by Picasso and fashions by the Warrington-born designer Ozzie Clark. There is also a gallery with a fossil-handling section.

* Temporary exhibition programme
* Education department for schools

| Location | Contact |
|---|---|
| In town centre | 3 Museum Street, Warrington WA1 1JB |
| **Opening** | t 01925 442392 |
| Mon–Fri 9am–5pm, | w warrington.gov.uk |
| Sat 9am-4.30pm | e museum@warrington.gov.uk |
| **Admission** | |
| Free | |

## 757 Whitchurch

# Hack Green Secret Nuclear Bunker

1 hr+    Jan–Nov

One of the nation's most secret defence sites, Hack Green has played a central role in the defence of Britain for almost 60 years. Once through the blast doors visitors are transported into the chilling world of the Cold War to learn what living conditions were like.

* Sounds & smells of a civil defence HQ
* Soviet Spy Mouse Trail for children

| Location | Contact |
|---|---|
| Off A530 Whitchurch road, outside Nantwich, 30 mins from Chester | PO Box 127, Nantwich CW5 8AQ |
| **Opening** | t 01270 623353 |
| Mar–Oct 10.30am–5.30pm; | w hackgreen.co.uk |
| Nov & Jan–Feb Sat–Sun 11am–4.30pm | e coldwar@hackgreen.co.uk |
| **Admission** | |
| Adult £5.80, Child £4, Concs £5.50 | |

## 758 Widnes

# Catalyst Science Discovery Centre

3 hrs+    All year

This is the only science centre solely devoted to chemistry and how the products of chemistry are used in everyday life – from medicines to Meccano. The centre aims to inform visitors about chemistry and its role in our lives – past, present and future.

* Four interactive galleries with 100+ exhibits
* Virtual-reality theatre & discovery lab new in Spring 2006

| Location | Contact |
|---|---|
| Junction 12 of M56 & junction 7 of M62 | Mersey Road, Widnes WA8 0DF |
| **Opening** | t 0151 420 1121 |
| Tue–Fri & Bank Hols 10am–5pm, | w catalyst.org.uk |
| Sat & Sun 11am–5pm | e info@catalyst.org.uk |
| **Admission** | |
| Adult £4.95, Child £3.50, Concs £3.95 | |

## 759 Wirral

# Port Sunlight Village & Heritage Centre

4 hrs+    All year

A picturesque C19 village founded by William Hesketh Lever for his soap factory workers and named after his famous Sunlight soap. The Heritage Centre explores the history of the village and community. The Lady Lever Art Gallery houses rich and varied collections.

* C18 furniture & Wedgwood china
* Gift shop & garden centre

| Location | Admission |
|---|---|
| 20 mins from Liverpool, junction 5 off M53 take A41 to Birkenhead. Follow signs | Adult £1, Child £0.60, Concs £0.80 |
| | **Contact** |
| **Opening** | 95 Greendale Road, Port Sunlight, Wirral CH62 4XE |
| Daily: Apr–Oct 10am–4pm | |
| Nov–Mar Mon–Fri 10am–4pm, | t 0151 644 6466 |
| Sat–Sun 11am–4pm | w portsunlightvillage.com |

760   Barrow-in-Furness

# Dock Museum

3 hrs     All year

A spectacular modern museum built over an original Victorian graving dock. Displays explore the history of Barrow-in-Furness and how it grew from a tiny C19 hamlet to become the biggest iron and steel centre in the world and a major shipbuilding force in just 40 years.

* Attractions include film shows & model ships
* New section on social history

| Location | Admission |
|---|---|
| Follow signs in Barrow-in-Furness | Free |
| **Opening** | **Contact** |
| Easter–Oct Tue–Fri 10am–5pm, | North Road, |
| Sat–Sun 11am–5pm; | Barrow-in-Furness LA14 2PW |
| Nov–Easter Wed–Fri 10.30am–4pm, | t  01229 894444 |
| Sat–Sun 11am–4.30pm | w  dockmuseum.org.uk |
| (last admission 45 mins before closing) | e  dockmuseum@barrowbc.gov.uk |

761   Barrow-in-Furness

# Furness Abbey

1 hr     All year

St Mary of Furness was founded in 1123 by Stephen, later king of England. It originally belonged to the small Order of Savigny but it passed to the Cistercians in 1147, becoming one of the richest monasteries in England, second only to Fountains Abbey in Yorkshire.

* Romantic building, often visited by Wordsworth
* Visitor centre with exhibition about the abbey

| Location | Contact |
|---|---|
| ½ mile NE of Barrow-in-Furness | North West Region, Canada House, |
|  | 3 Chepstow Street, Manchester M1 5FW |
| **Opening** |  |
| Apr–Sep daily 10am–6pm; | t  01229 823420 |
| Oct–Mar Thu–Mon 10am–4pm | w  english-heritage.org.uk |
|  | e  northwest@english-heritage.org.uk |
| **Admission** |  |
| Adult £3.30, Child £1.70, Concs £2.50 |  |

762   Brampton

# Lanercost Priory

1 hr     Easter–Oct

Situated near the Scottish border in Cumbria are the impressive remains of this C12 Augustinian priory. It boasts a rich history, from the tranquillity of life as a monastic house to its involvement in the turbulent Anglo-Scottish wars of the C14 and eventual dissolution.

* Hadrian's Wall is close by, audio guide available
* West front is fine example of C12 English architecture

| Location | Contact |
|---|---|
| Off minor road S of Lanercost, 2 miles | Lanercost, Brampton CA8 2HQ |
| NE of Brampton |  |
| **Opening** | t  01697 73030 |
| Daily: 10am–6pm | w  english-heritage.org.uk |
| **Admission** | e  northwest@english-heritage.org.uk |
| Adult £2.60, Child £1.30, Concs £2 |  |

763 Carlisle

# Carlisle Castle

1 hr    All year

This is a formidable border fortress with a rich and colourful history spanning more than 900 years. Once commanding the western end of the Anglo-Scottish border, Carlisle Castle has witnessed countless sieges over the centuries.

* Admission includes entrance to Roman exhibition
* See the legendary 'licking stones'

| Location | Contact |
|---|---|
| On N side of city, beyond cathedral | Carlisle CA3 8UR |
| Opening | t 01228 591922 |
| Daily: Apr–Sep 9.30am–6pm; | w english-heritage.org.uk |
| Oct–Mar 10am–4pm | e northwest@english-heritage.org.uk |
| Admission | |
| Adult £4, Child £2, Concs £3 | |

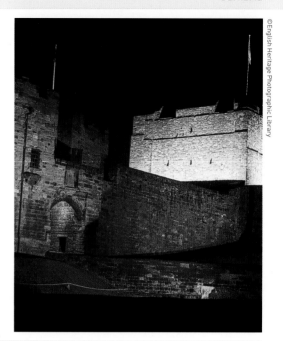

---

764 Carlisle

# Carlisle Cathedral

2 hrs    All year

Founded in 1122 and battered by centuries of warfare, the cathedral retains many items of interest, perhaps most notably the east window with its fine tracery containing C14 stained glass. Other items include the magnificent C16 Brougham triptych and notable medieval painted panels.

* Beautifully painted ceiling in the choir
* Display of cathedral & diocesan silver in the treasury

| Location | Contact |
|---|---|
| In city centre | 7 The Abbey, Castle Street, |
| | Carlisle CA3 8TZ |
| Opening | t 01228 535169 |
| Daily: Mon–Sat 7.30am–6.15pm, | w carlislecathedral.org.uk |
| Sun 7.30am–5pm | e office@carlislecathedral.org.uk |
| Admission | |
| Free, donations welcomed | |

---

765 Carlisle

# Tullie House

2 hrs    All year

Tullie House museum and art gallery offers visitors a multi-faceted experience, combining the features of a historic house with a modern museum. It has a superb collection of Roman artefacts and the displays include many hands-on exhibits that appeal to all ages.

* Underground space brings Carlisle's past to life
* Displays of key artworks by Pre-Raphaelites

| Location | Admission |
|---|---|
| Signed from junction 42, 43 & 44 of M6 | Adult £5.20, Child £2.60, Concs £3.60 |
| Opening | Contact |
| Daily: Apr–Jun & Sep–Oct Mon–Sat | Castle Street, Carlisle CA3 8TP |
| 10am–5pm, Sun 12noon–5pm ; | t 01228 534781 |
| Jul–Aug Mon–Sat 10am–5pm, | w tulliehouse.co.uk |
| Sun 11am–5pm; | e enquiries@tullie-house.co.uk |
| Nov–Mar Mon–Sat 10am–4pm, | |
| Sun 12noon–4pm | |

## 766 Cockermouth

# Lakeland Sheep & Wool Centre

2 hrs   All year

This centre offers visitors the opportunity to meet Cumbria's most famous residents – 19 different breeds of sheep. Discover interesting facts about each breed and be amazed by the great skills of the sheepdogs handling a flock.

* Show theatre holds up to 170 people
* Extensive retail outlet for woollen goods

| Location | Admission |
| --- | --- |
| On A66 at A5086 roundabout. | *Show* **Adult £4.50, Child £3.50** |
| **Opening** | **Contact** |
| Daily: 9.30–5pm | Egremount Road, |
| *Sheepdog shows* **Mar–Oct Sun–Thu** | Cockermouth CA13 0QX |
| 10.30am, 12noon, 2pm & 3.30pm | t 01900 822673 |
| | w sheep-woolcentre.co.uk |

## 767 Cockermouth

# Wordsworth House

2 hrs   Mar–Oct

Meet some of the Wordsworth household and find out what life was like for the maid, manservant and clerk. Enjoy the sights and sounds of a working C18 kitchen. There is a wonderful garden overlooking the banks of the River Derwent.

* William Wordsworth's childhood home
* Events & hands-on activities

| Location | Contact |
| --- | --- |
| Main street in Cockermouth | Cockermouth CA13 GRX |
| **Opening** | t 01900 820884 |
| Late Mar, Jun & Sep–Oct Tue–Sat | w nationaltrust.org.uk |
| 11am–4.30pm; | e rwordh@smtp.ntrust.org.uk |
| Jul–Aug Mon–Sat 11am–4.30pm | |
| **Admission** | |
| Adult £4.70, Child £2.60 | |

## 768 Coniston

# Brantwood

3 hrs   All year

As the home of John Ruskin, Brantwood became a great literary and artistic centre. The house is filled with Ruskin's work as well as his original furniture, books and personal items. Brantwood's attraction is increased by 250 acres of woodland and lakeside meadows.

* Gardens cover 30 acres
* Well-marked nature trail winds through the estate

| Location | Contact |
| --- | --- |
| E shore of Coniston Water on B5285 | Coniston LA21 8AD |
| **Opening** | t 01539 441396 |
| Mid–Mar–mid–Nov daily | w brantwood.org.uk |
| 11am–5.30pm; | e enquiries@brantwood.org.uk |
| winter Wed–Sun 11am–4.30pm | |
| **Admission** | |
| Adult £5.50, Child £1 | |

## 769 Dalton-in-Furness

# South Lakes Wild Animal Park

2 hrs+    All year

The Lake District's only zoological park is recognised as one of Europe's leading conservation zoos. Its 17 acres are home to some of the rarest animals on earth, saved from almost certain extinction in the wild, thanks to coordinated breeding programmes.

\* Penguins, hippos & many animals are free to roam
\* Home of the Sumatran Tiger Trust

**Location**
Follow signs from junction 36 of M6

**Opening**
*summer* 10am–5pm;
*winter* 10am–4.30pm

**Admission**
Adult £9.50, Child & Concs £6

**Contact**
South Lakes Wild Animal Park,
Dalton-in-Furness LA15 8JR

t  01229 466086
w  wildanimalpark.co.uk
e  office@wildanimalpark.co.uk

## 770 Grasmere

# Dove Cottage & Wordsworth Museum

1 hr    Feb–Dec

The home of William Wordsworth from December 1799 to May 1808, the years of his best work as a poet. The cottage remains much as it was during this time. The garden was a passion for Wordsworth and he spent many hours developing his 'domestic slip of mountainside'.

\* Museum includes original manuscripts & rare books
\* Also shows period images of Grasmere

**Location**
S of Grasmere on A591
Kendal–Keswick road

**Opening**
Daily: 7 Feb–Dec 9.30am–5.30pm

**Admission**
Adult £6, Child £3.75, Concs £5.40

**Contact**
Grasmere LA22 9SH

t  01539 435544
w  wordsworth.org.uk
e  enquiries@wordsworth.org.uk

## 771 Hawkshead

# Beatrix Potter Gallery

½ hr    Apr–Oct

This gallery houses annually changing exhibitions of original sketches and watercolours painted by Beatrix Potter for her children's stories. The C17 building was once the office of Beatrix's husband, William Heelis.

\* The interior remains substantially unaltered
\* 2006 exhibit Jeremy Fisher, Miss Moppett & The Story of the Fierce Bad Rabbit

**Location**
In town centre

**Opening**
Apr–Oct Sat–Wed 10.30am–4.30pm

**Admission**
Adult £3.50, Child £1.70

**Contact**
Main Street, Hawkshead LA22 0NS

t  01539 436355
w  nationaltrust.org.uk
e  beatrixpottergallery@nationaltrust.
org.uk

## 772 Kendal

# Kendal Museum

1 hr+    Feb–Dec

Founded in 1796, Kendal Museum houses one of the country's oldest collections of local archaeology, history and geology. There is also an international natural history collection, including lakeland flora and fauna from prehistory to the C20.

\* Wildlife garden simulates local habitats
\* Changing programme of temporary exhibitions

**Location**
10 mins from junction 36 of M6

**Opening**
Apr–Oct Mon–Sat 10.30am–5pm;
Feb–Mar & Nov–Dec Mon–Sat
10.30am–4pm

**Admission**
Adult £2.70, Child free, Concs £2.10

**Contact**
Station Road, Kendal LA9 6BT

t  01539 721374
w  kendalmuseum.org.uk
e  info@kendalmuseum.org.uk

773 Kendal

# Levens Hall

2 hrs    Apr–Oct

This world-famous C17 topiary garden was designed by Guillaume Beaumont, who also laid out the gardens at Hampton Court. The original designs have remained largely unchanged for 300 years. The house has lots of beautiful Elizabethan rooms with many notable paintings.

* Dining room has embossed leather wall-coverings

| Location | Contact |
|---|---|
| 5 miles S of Kendal on A6 | Kendal LA8 0PD |
| **Opening** | t 01539 560321 |
| Mid-Apr–mid Oct Sun–Thu | w levenshall.co.uk |
| *House* 12noon–5pm | e email@levenshall.fsnet.co.uk |
| *Gardens* from 10am | |
| **Admission** | |
| Adult £8, Child £3.80 | |

774 Kendal

# Museum of Lakeland Life

1 hr    All year

In 1973 the museum was the first winner of the coveted Museum of the Year Award. The permanent collections include displays linked to the Arts & Crafts Movement, *Swallows and Amazons* author Arthur Ransome and the Victorian period.

* Temporary displays largely from costume collection
* Large shop selling local crafts & toys

| Location | Admission |
|---|---|
| Next to Abbots Hall Gallery, junction 36 of M6 | Adult £3.75, Child £2.75 |
| **Opening** | **Contact** |
| Apr–Oct Mon–Sat 10.30am–5pm; | Kendal LA9 5AL |
| 20 Jan–Mar & Nov–Dec | t 01539 722464 |
| Mon–Sat 10.30am–4pm | w lakelandmuseum.org.uk |
| | e ws@lakelandmuseum.org.uk |

775 Keswick

# Derwent Water Marina

1 hr +    All year

This centre specialises in watersports with RYA sailing courses, windsurfing courses, and canoe, kayak and dinghy hire available. Other activities include ghyll scrambling, abseiling, climbing and walking. A great experience for families, friends and groups.

| Location | Contact |
|---|---|
| From Keswick take A66 & follow signs for Portinscale | Portinscale, Keswick, Cumbria CA12 5RF |
| **Opening** | t 01768 772912 |
| Daily: 9am–5pm; closed 20 Dec–12 Jan | w derwentwatermarina.co.uk |
| **Admission** | e info@derwentwatermarina.co.uk |
| Activities priced individually | |

776 Newby Bridge

# Aquarium of the Lakes

1 hr    All year

Explore a range of naturally themed Lake District habitats featuring the UK's largest collection of freshwater fish. See otters, British sharks and a variety of British mammals. Discover our underwater tunnel featuring giant carp and diving ducks.

* Midnight at the water's edge new in 2005
* Large number of nocturnal creatures

| Location | Admission |
|---|---|
| 15 mins from junction 36 of M6, take A590 to Newby Bridge & follow signs | Adult £6.25, Child £3.95, Concs £5.50 |
| **Opening** | **Contact** |
| Daily: Apr–Oct 9am–6pm; | Lakeside, Newby Bridge LA12 8AS |
| Nov–Mar 9am–5pm | t 01539 530153 |
| (last admission 1 hr before closing) | w aquariumofthelakes.co.uk |
| | e aquariumofthelakes@reallive.co.uk |

Newby Bridge

## Scott Park Bobbin Mill

1 hr  Apr–Oct

This gem of the Industrial Revolution has remained largely unchanged since it was built by John Harrison in 1835. Scott Park created the wooden bobbins vital to the spinning and weaving industries of Lancashire.

* Mill worked continuously until 1971
* Steam days (Mon, Tue, Wed & Thu) show engines working

**Location**
2 miles N of Newby Bridge, off A590

**Opening**
Daily: Apr–Sep 10am–6pm;
Oct, please phone for details

**Admission**
Adult £4, Child £2, Concs £3

**Contact**
Finsthwaite, nr Newby Bridge,
Ulverston LA12 8AX

t 01539 531087
w english-heritage.org.uk
e northwest@english-heritage.org.uk

---

Penrith

## Acorn Bank Garden & Watermill

2 hrs  Easter–Oct

Ancient oaks and the high enclosing walls keep out the extremes of the Cumbrian climate, resulting in a spectacular display of shrubs, roses and herbaceous borders. Sheltered orchards contain a variety of traditional fruit trees. The watermill is under restoration.

* Famed herb garden has huge collection of plants
* Watermill remains open to public during restoration

      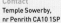

**Location**
N of Temple Sowerby, 6 miles E of Penrith on A66

**Opening**
Easter–Oct Wed–Sun 10am–5pm

**Admission**
Adult £3, Child £1.50

**Contact**
Temple Sowerby,
nr Penrith CA10 1SP

t 01768 361893
w nationaltrust.org.uk
e acornbank@nationaltrust.org.uk

## 779 Penrith

# Brougham Castle

1 hr     Apr–Oct

Brougham Castle was built by William Rufus in 1092 on the site of a Roman fort. The original castle was destroyed in 1172 but rebuilt by Henry II. His tower survives but later buildings were destroyed by fire in 1521. A stone curtain wall was added around 1300.

* Once home to Lady Anne Clifford
* Introductory exhibition includes Roman carved stone

| Location | Contact |
|---|---|
| ½ mile SE of Penrith off A66 | North West Region, Canada House, 3 Chepstow Street, Manchester M1 5FW |
| **Opening** | |
| Daily: Apr–Sep 10am–6pm; | t 01768 862488 |
| Oct Thu–Mon 10am–4pm | w english-heritage.org.uk |
| | e northwest@english-heritage.org.uk |
| **Admission** | |
| Adult £2.60, Child £1.30, Concs £2 | |

## 780 Penrith

# Dalemain Historic House & Gardens

2 hrs     Easter–Oct

A medieval, Tudor and early Georgian house that has been home to the Hasell family since 1679. The Tudor legacy is a series of winding passageways, unexpected rooms and oak panelling. A good example of the Georgian period is the breathtaking Chinese room.

* C15 medieval hall
* The estate includes many famous valleys & fells

| Location | Contact |
|---|---|
| On A592 Penrith–Ullswater road | Penrith CA11 0HB |
| **Opening** | |
| House 11am–4pm | t 01768 486450 |
| Gardens and tearoom 10.30am–5pm | w dalemain.com |
| Please phone for details | e admin@dalemain.com |
| **Admission** | |
| Adult £6.50, Child free | |

## 781 Ulverston

# Conishead Priory & Buddhist Temple

1 hr     Easter–Oct

A stunning example of early Georgian Gothic architecture. It is dominated by two 100 ft (30m) octagonal towers. Special features include decorative ceilings and a vaulted Great Hall with fine stained glass. The Buddhist Kadampa Temple was established at the priory in 1997.

* Anyone welcome to visit the temple by appointment
* Prayers for world peace every Sunday morning

| Location | Contact |
|---|---|
| On A5087, 2 miles S of Ulverston | Priory Road, Ulverston LA12 9QQ |
| **Opening** | |
| Please phone for details | t 01229 584029 |
| | w manjushri.org.uk |
| **Admission** | e info@manjushri.org.uk |
| Free | |

## 782 Ulverston

# Gleaston Water Mill

1 hr     All year

This imposing watermill has been part of the local landscape for more than 400 years. Located close to the ruins of Gleaston Castle, the present building dates from 1774. Visitors can see the 18ft (5½m) waterwheel and machinery operating most days.

* Thousands of piggy collectables
* Try our homemade food, all cooked in our tea rooms

| Location | Contact |
|---|---|
| Follow signs from A5087 Ulverston–Barrow-in-Furness coast road | Gleaston, nr Ulverston LA12 0QH |
| **Opening** | t 01229 869244 |
| Tue–Sun & Bank Hols 10.30am–5pm | w watermill.co.uk |
| **Admission** | |
| Adult £2.50, Child £1.50 | |

## 783 Ulverston

# Holker Hall & Gardens

3 hrs    Mar–Dec

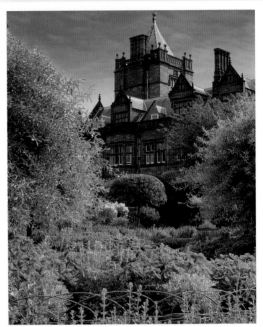

Only a short distance from the sea, Holker Hall is situated on the magnificent wooded slopes of the Cartmel Peninsula. The house exhibits all the grandeur and prosperity of the late Victorian era and is set in immaculate gardens.

* The Campbell Legend *Bluebird* exhibition

**Location**
Follow signs from A590 from Barrow-in-Furness M6 junction 36

**Opening**
*Hall & Gardens* 26 Mar–29 Oct Sun–Fri 10am–5.30pm
*Museum* Mar–Dec daily
Please phone for opening times or visit the website

**Admission**
Adult £10.50, Child £5.70

**Contact**
Cark-in-Cartmel,
Cumbria LA11 7PL
t 01539558328
w holker-hall.co.uk
e publicopening@holker.co.uk

---

## 784 Ulverston

# Laurel & Hardy Museum

1 hr    Feb–Dec

Visit the world-famous museum devoted to Laurel and Hardy in Ulverston, the town where Stan was born on 16 June 1890. Everything you ever wanted to know about them is here. The collection includes letters, photographs, personal items and furniture.

* Small cinema shows films & documentaries all day

**Location**
In town centre

**Opening**
Daily: Feb–Dec 10am–4.30pm

**Admission**
Adult £3, Child & Concs £2

**Contact**
4c Upper Brook Street,
Ulverston LA12 7BH
t 01229 582292
w laurel-and-hardy-museum.co.uk

---

## 785 Ulverston

# Lakeland Motor Museum

3 hrs    Mar–Dec

This unique collection includes more than 30,000 motoring exhibits. There are die-cast scale models of historical transport, rally cars and tractors, as well as classic, comical and curious cars, superb scooters, magnificent motorbikes and much more.

* More than 100 years of motoring history
* Recently voted Best Small Visitor Attraction in England

**Location**
At Holker Hall signed from junction 36 M6 via the A590

**Opening**
Daily: Mar–19 Dec from 10.30am

**Admission**
Adult £5, Child £3

**Contact**
Cark-in-Cartmel LA11 7PL
t 01539 558509
w lakelandmotormuseum.co.uk
e info@lakelandmotormuseum.co.uk

786 Windermere

# Lake District National Park

4 hrs    All year

Enjoy some of England's most dramatic mountain and lake scenery in one of the finest of the Britain's national parks. Get a better understanding of the area at the visitor centre at Brockhole on Lake Windermere.

* Exhibition, displays & gardens down to the lake
* Gardens designed by Mawson

**Location**
Visitor centre on A591 between Windermere & Ambleside

**Opening**
*Visitor centre* Daily: Mar–Oct 10am–5pm
*Gardens & Grounds* All year

**Admission**
Free. Car park pay & display

**Contact**
The Lake District Visitor Centre, Brockhole, Windermere LA23 1LJ
t 01539 446601
w lake-district.gov.uk

---

787 Windermere

# Windermere Lake Cruises

3 hrs    All year

Steamers and launches sail daily between Ambleside, Bowness and Lakeside with main season connections for the Lakeside & Haverthwaite Steam Railway, Wray Castle and the Lake District National Park (Brockhole). Or sail to the aquarium and the World of Beatrix Potter.

* 24-hour 'Freedom' tickets for unlimited travel
* Other links to lake's attractions – visit the website

**Location**
Take junction 36 off M6. Follow brown tourist signs along A590 to Lakeside or A591 to Windermere for Bowness & Ambleside

**Opening**
Daily: *summer* open during daylight hours; *winter* 9.45am–4.30pm

**Admission**
Adult from £5.25, Child from £2.60

**Contact**
Lakeside, Newby Bridge, Ulverston LA12 8AS
t 01539 531188
w windermere-lakecruises.co.uk
e mail@windermere-lakecruises.co.uk

---

788 Accrington

# Haworth Art Gallery

2 hrs    All year

This Edwardian house, set in parkland, houses the finest public collection of Tiffany art glass outside the USA. There is also an excellent collection of oil paintings from the C19.

* Regularly changing exhibitions

**Location**
Leave M65 at junction 7, M61, junction 9, M6 at junction 29

**Opening**
Wed–Fri 2pm–5pm, Sat–Sun 12noon–4.30pm

**Admission**
Free

**Contact**
Haworth Park, Manchester Road, Accrington BB5 2JS
t 01254 233782
w hyndburnbc.gov.uk

## 789 Blackburn

# Blackburn Museum & Art Gallery

2 hrs    All year

The museum is housed in a fine Arts & Crafts-style building that opened in 1872 as a museum and a library. Highlights include the Hart Collection of more than 10,000 rare coins, 500 books and illuminated manuscripts, and a superb collection of Victorian oils and watercolours.

* The Lewis Collection of more than 1,000 Japanese prints
* Award-winning South Asian Gallery & Egyptian Room

| Location | Contact |
|---|---|
| In town centre | Museum Street, Blackburn BB1 7AJ |
| **Opening** | t 01254 667130 |
| Tue–Sat 10am–4.45pm | w council.blackburn/services/ |
| | museum |
| **Admission** | e paul.flintoff@blackburn.gov.uk |
| Free | |

## 790 Blackburn

# Whalley Abbey Gatehouse

1 hr    All year

Situated beside the River Calder, this is the outer gate house of the nearby Cistercian abbey. There was originally a chapel on the first floor. The adjacent parish church has further remains including three pre-Norman Conquest cross shafts. The abbey has an exhibition centre.

* Vast display of remains

| Location | Contact |
|---|---|
| In Whalley, 6 miles NE of Blackburn on a minor road off A59 | Whalley, Clitheroe BB7 9SS |
| **Opening** | t 01793 414910 |
| Daily: any reasonable times | w english-heritage.org.uk |
| **Admission** | |
| Free | |

## 791 Blackpool

# Blackpool Illuminations

2 hrs    Sep–Nov

Experience Blackpool's annual spectacular event. Six miles of lights electrify this well-loved resort's promenade as the world-famous illuminations shine every night for 66 nights. Enjoy a grandstand seat aboard a cleverly disguised tram.

* View the giant clifftop tableaux
* Festival of Light throughout the town

| Location | Contact |
|---|---|
| Central Promenade | Blackpool Tourism, |
| | 1 Clifton Street FY1 1LY |
| **Opening** | |
| Daily: Sep–5 Nov | t 01253 478222 |
| | w visitblackpool.com |
| **Admission** | e tourism@blackpool.gov.uk |
| Free | |

## 792 Blackpool

# Blackpool Lifeboat Station & Visitor Centre

1 hr    Easter–Nov

This lifeboat station accommodates an Atlantic 75 B-class and 2 D-class lifeboats, launching vehicles and ancillary equipment. The visitor centre incorporates current and historic displays and sea-safety information. There is an accessible public viewing area.

* This station was established by the RNLI in 1864
* Nelson's flagship *Foudroyant* wrecked in gale near here in 1897

| Location | Contact |
|---|---|
| Central Promenade | Central Promenade, |
| | Blackpool FY1 5JA |
| **Opening** | |
| Daily: Easter–Nov 10am–4pm | t 01253 620424/290816 |
| | w rnli.org.uk |
| **Admission** | e blackpool@rnli.org.uk |
| Free | |

793 Blackpool

# The Blackpool Piers

4 hrs+    Easter–Nov

Blackpool's Piers are a fantastic place for all the family to be entertained, day and night throughout the season. Ride the rollercoaster, big wheel and dodgems. Visit one of our many Family Fun Bars for tempting food and drink and free entertainment.

\* Children's entertainer (all piers)
\* Fairground rides (South & Central Piers)

**Location**
North Pier on North Promenade;
South Pier on South Promenade;
Central Pier on Central Promenade

**Opening**
Daily: Easter–Nov from 10am

**Admission**
Free, except North Pier (50p toll)
Charges for individual rides

**Contact**
c/o Leisure Parks Ltd,
97 Church Street, Blackpool FY1 1HU

t 01253 629600
w blackpoollive.com

794 Blackpool

# Blackpool Tower & Circus

5 hrs+    Easter–Nov

Inside the tower visitors will find an award-winning circus and a world-famous ballroom. Explore the Charlie Cairoli exhibition, Under Sea World, the Hornpipe Gallery, the Tower Top ride and the Walk of Faith.

\* Please phone for details of venue for evening entertainment
\* Indoor adventure play area

**Location**
Take M55 for Blackpool & follow signs

**Opening**
Daily: Easter–May 10am–6pm;
Jun–Nov 10am–11pm

**Admission**
*Tower & Circus* Adult £14, Child £12,
Concs £10

**Contact**
Leisure Park Ltd, 97 Church Street,
Blackpool FY1 4BJ

t 01253 622242 /01253 292029
w blackpooltower.co.uk
e website@leisure-parcs.co.uk

795 Bolton

# Animal World & Butterfly House

1 hr    All year

Animal World provides a caring environment for a variety of animals and birds, from farm animals to chipmunks, from wildfowl to tropical birds. Butterfly House features free-flying butterflies and moths in a tropical environment, as well as insects, spiders and reptiles.

\* Collection of tropical plants

**Location**
In Bolton.Take A58 to Moss Bank Way

**Opening**
Daily: Apr–Sep 10am–4.30pm;
Oct–Mar Sat–Thu 10am–3.30pm,
Fri 10am–2.30pm

**Admission**
Free

**Contact**
Moss Bank Park, Moss Bank Way,
Bolton BL1 6NQ

t 01204 334050
w visit-bolton.com
e animal.world@bolton.gov.uk

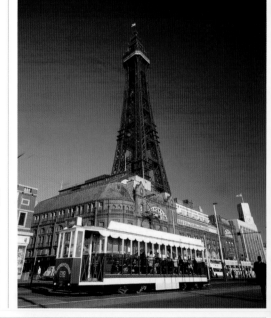

796 Bolton

# Bolton Aquarium

2 hrs   All year

If you're curious about catfish, partial to piranhas or want to be knowledgeable about knifefish, visit Bolton's Aquarium. Fish from around the world can be seen in an environment designed to offer an insight into their hidden lives. The aquarium is one of the oldest in the country.

* Notable collection of piranha fish
* Predatory blue-head knifefish from Venezuela

| Location | Contact |
|----------|---------|
| In town centre | Le Mans Crescent, Bolton BL1 1SE |
| **Opening** | t  01204 332211 |
| Mon–Sat 9am–5pm; | w  boltonmuseums.org.uk |
| Closed Bank Hols | e  aquarium@bolton.gov.uk |
| **Admission** | |
| Free | |

---

797 Bolton

# Bolton Museum & Art Gallery

2 hrs   All year

Bolton Museum and Art Gallery has something for the whole family, from the Ancient Egypt Gallery, Costume, Local History and the Story of Bolton to Natural History and Wildlife on Your Doorstep. There are also activities, talks and workshops.

* Varied programme of events & exhibitions
* Ancient Egyptian sculpture *The Princess*

| Location | Contact |
|----------|---------|
| In town centre | Le Mans Crescent, Bolton BL1 1SE |
| **Opening** | t  01204 332211 |
| Mon–Sat 9am–5pm; | w  boltonmuseums.org.uk |
| closed Bank Hols | e  museums@bolton.gov.uk |
| **Admission** | |
| Free | |

---

798 Bolton

# Bolton Wanderers Football Club

2 hrs   All year

Look behind the scenes at the Reebok Stadium, home of Bolton Wanderers. Begin at the interactive museum where the history of the club is brought to life. Visit the players' dressing and warm-up rooms, the officials' changing rooms and the manager's dug-out.

| Location | Contact |
|----------|---------|
| Junction 6 off M61 | Burnden Way, Bolton BL6 6JW |
| **Opening** | t  01204 673670 |
| Daily: Mon–Fri 9am–5pm, | w  bwfc.premiumtv.co.uk |
| Sat 9am–4pm, Sun 11am–4pm | e  sparker@bwfc.co.uk |
| **Admission** | |
| Adult £2.50, Child & Concs £1.50 | |

---

799 Bolton

# Hall i' th' Wood Museum

1 hr   All year

This half-timbered hall, built in the C15, was owned by wealthy yeomen and merchants. After 1697 it was rented out to various tenants. During this period a young Samuel Crompton lived here with his parents. He invented the spinning mule, which revolutionised the cotton industry.

* Activities ongoing all year
* Experience life in Tudor & Stuart times by dressing in period costumes

| Location | Contact |
|----------|---------|
| In town centre | Green Way, Bolton BL1 8UA |
| **Opening** | t  01204 332370 |
| 23 Mar–Oct Wed–Sun 11am–5pm; | w  boltonmuseums.org.uk |
| Nov–Mar Sat–Sun 11am–5pm | e  hallithwood@bolton.gov.uk |
| **Admission** | |
| Adult £2, Child & Concs £1 | |

## 800 Bolton

# Smithills Hall

1 hr    All year

This is one of the earliest examples of a Lancashire manor house, which has recently had additional rooms restored to their full splendour. It has been developed by generations of owners, and mirrors changes in fashion and living conditions from the late C14 to the C19.

* Gift shop & various events throughtout the year
* Stained-glass windows in the chapel

| Location | Admission |
|---|---|
| Take M62 for Bolton | Adult £3, Child & Concs £1.75 |
| **Opening** | **Contact** |
| Apr–Sep Tue–Sat 11am–5pm, Sun 2pm–5pm; Oct–Mar Tue & Sat 1pm–5pm, Sun 2pm–5pm (last tour 4.15pm) | Smithills Dean Road, Bolton BL1 7NP<br>t 01204 332377<br>w smithills.org<br>e office@smithills.org |

## 801 Bolton

# Turton Tower

2 hrs    Feb–Nov

Turton Tower was originally built by the Orrell family to defend their land and later became a luxurious home. The house was lavishly furnished and extended in the Tudor and early Stuart periods. Today Turton displays a rich, extensive collection of paintings and furniture.

* Experience the relaxing woodland gardens
* Victorian follies & tennis court

| Location | Contact |
|---|---|
| Take A66 & A676 & follow signs | Turton, Bolton BL7 0HG |
| **Opening** | t 01204 852203 |
| Mar–Apr & Oct Sat–Wed 1pm–5pm; Nov–Feb Sun 1pm–4pm | w lancashire.gov.uk<br>e turton.tower@muslancscc.gov.uk |
| **Admission** | |
| Adult £3, Child free, Concs £1.50 | |

## 802 Burnley

# Gawthorpe Hall

2 hrs    Easter–Oct

An Elizabethan gem, Gawthorpe resembles the great Hardwick Hall and is probably by the same architect, Robert Smythson. In the mid-C19 Sir Charles Barry was commissioned to restore the house. Charlotte Brontë was a frequent visitor.

* Many notable paintings & C17–C19 furniture
* Unparalleled collection of British C19–C20 needlework

| Location | Contact |
|---|---|
| On E outskirts of Padiham, N of A671 | Padiham, Burnley BB12 8UA |
| **Opening** | t 01282 771004 |
| Easter–Oct Tue–Thu & Sat–Sun 1pm–5pm | w Lancsmuseum.gov.uk<br>e gawthorpehall@ntrust.org.uk |
| **Admission** | |
| Adult £3, Child free, Concs £1.50 | |

## 803 Burnley

# Queen Street Mill

1 hr    Mar–Nov

A unique survivor of the textile industry, Queen Street Mill is the last commercial steam-powered textile mill in Europe. The actual mill closed in 1982 but it is preserved as a museum that recreates the days when steam ran the world.

* Smell the oil, see the steam & breathe the atmosphere
* 300 Lancashire looms

| Location | Admission |
|---|---|
| Corner of Queen Street and Harrison street, Harle Syke | Adult £2.50, Child free, Concs £1.25 |
| **Opening** | **Contact** |
| Mar & Nov Tue–Thu 12noon–4pm; Apr & Oct Tue–Fri 12noon–5pm; May–Sep Tue–Sat 12noon–5pm | Harle Syke, Burnley BB10 2HX<br>t 01282 412555<br>w lancashire.gov.uk |

## 804 Carnforth

# Leighton Hall

2 hrs    May–Sep

Leighton Hall is the home of the famous furniture-making Gillow dynasty. Learn about the past of this ancient Lancashire family, wander through the grounds and pretty gardens and witness displays by trained birds of prey.

* C19 walled garden, landscaped parkland & woodland
* Entertaining guides reveal the family's history

**Location**
Take junction 35A of M6, to North Carnforth

**Opening**
May–Sep Tue–Fri & Sun 2pm–5pm;
Aug Tue–Fri & Sun 12.30pm–5pm

**Admission**
Adult £5.50, Child £4, Concs £5

**Contact**
Carnforth LA5 9ST

t 01524 734474
w leightonhall.co.uk
e info@leightonhall.co.uk

## 805 Chorley

# Astley Hall Museum & Art Gallery

1 hr    Easter–Sep

This hall dates back to Elizabethan times but changes have been made over the centuries. The collections range from C18 creamware and glass to the first Rugby League Cup and C16 shovelboard table.

* Programme of special exhibitions, events & activities
* C17 plaster ceilings

**Location**
W of Chorley town centre off A581 Chorley–Southport road

**Opening**
Easter–Sep Sat–Sun & Bank Hols 12noon–5pm

**Admission**
Free

**Contact**
Astley Park, Chorley PR7 1NP

t 01257 515927
w astleyhall.co.uk
e astleyhall@lineone.net

## 806 Clitheroe

# Clitheroe Castle Museum

½ hr    Feb–Dec

Set on a prominent limestone mound close to the ruined Norman keep of Clitheroe Castle, this museum houses collections of local history and geology. Displays cover the history of the Ribble Valley, the Hacking ferryboat, witchcraft, local birds and roadside geology.

* Reconstructed lead mine & clogger's shop
* Edwardian kitchen

**Location**
In town centre on Castle Hill

**Opening**
Easter–Oct Mon–Sat 11.15am–4.30pm,
Sun 1pm–4.30pm;
Mar–Apr Sat–Wed 11.15am–4pm;
Nov–Dec & Feb Sat 11.15am–4pm,
Sun 1pm–4pm

**Admission**
Adult £2, Child 50p, Concs £1

**Contact**
Castle Hill, Clitheroe BB7 1BA

t 01200 424635/01200 425566
  (Tourist Information Centre)
w ribblevalley.gov.uk
e museum@ribblevalley.gov.uk

## 807 Colne

# British in India Museum

1 hr   Apr–Sep

The museum was opened in 1972 and contains a fascinating collection of material relating to the British in India, including model soldiers, dioramas, postage stamps, picture postcards, paintings and military uniforms.

* Shows British & Indian military artefacts
* Learn about the people behind the Raj

| Location | Contact |
|---|---|
| Take A56–A6068 between Burnley & Keighley | Newtown Street, Colne BB8 0JJ |
| | t 01282 613129 |
| Opening | |
| Apr-Sep Wed & Sat 2pm–5pm | |
| Admission | |
| Adult £3, Child 50p | |

## 808 Fleetwood

# Fleetwood Museum

1 hr   Apr–Nov

Built in 1838 and occupying the old Customs House designed by architect Decimus Burton, this fascinating museum brings the story of Fleetwood and the surrounding coast to life. Trace Fleetwood's past, its cargo trade and famous fishing industry.

* Understand a fisherman's life & the harsh working conditions
* See the *Harriet*, the last surviving fishing smack in the North West

| Location | Contact |
|---|---|
| Follow M55 to Fleetwood, then A585 | Queen's Terrace, Fleetwood FY7 6BT |
| Opening | t 01253 876621 |
| Daily: Mon–Sat 10am–4pm, | w nettingthebay.org.uk |
| Sun 1pm–4pm | e fleetwood.museum@muslancscc. gov.uk |
| Admission | |
| Adult £2, Child free, Concs £1 | |

## 809 Horwich

# Horwich Heritage Centre

1 hr   All year

This centre aims to preserve and present the rich history and heritage of Horwich by featuring specific aspects of Horwich life over the centuries, using videos, displays, artefacts and exhibits. There is a guest speaker on the second Tuesday of every month.

* Exhibition of local historic works
* Full range of publications on Horwich available

| Location | Contact |
|---|---|
| Junction 6 of M61 & A673 | Longworth Road, Horwich BL6 7BG |
| Opening | t 01204 847797 |
| Wed 2pm–4pm, Sat 10am–12noon, | w horwichheritage.co.uk |
| 2nd Tue every month 7.30pm–9pm | |
| Admission | |
| Free | |

## 810 Lancaster

# Judges' Lodgings

1 hr   Easter–Oct

This is Lancaster's oldest town house, home to Thomas Cavell, keeper of the castle during Lancashire's witch trials of 1612. Later used as a residence for judges visiting Lancaster Castle, it is now a museum displaying a wealth of furniture, porcelain, silver and paintings.

* Collection of Gillow furniture in period rooms
* Collection of dolls, toys & games from C18 to today

| Admission | |
|---|---|
| Near train station, on cobbled roads just down from castle | Adult £2, Child free, Concs £1 |
| Opening | Contact |
| Easter–Jun & Oct Mon–Fri 1pm–4pm, | Church Street, Lancaster LA1 1YS |
| Sat–Sun 12noon–4pm; | t 01524 32808 |
| Jul–Sep Mon–Fri 10am–4pm, | w lancsmuseums.gov.uk |
| Sat–Sun 12noon–4pm | e judgeslodgings@mus.lancsscc.gov.uk |

811 Lancaster

# Lancaster Castle

1 hr+    All year

One of the best-preserved and hardest-working castles in the country and still used today as a court and prison. Visitors can see where the Lancashire Witches were tried and condemned to die, the Hanging Corner where prisoners were hanged, dungeons and the Drop Room.

\* Display of heraldic shields in the Shire Hall
\* Beautiful Gillow furniture in jury room

**Location**
Castle is off St Georges Quay in the city, at the end of Vicarage Lane

**Opening**
Daily: 10am–5pm
Admission by guided tour only

**Admission**
Adult £4, Child & Concs £2.50

**Contact**
Castle Parade, Lancaster LA1 1YJ
t 01524 64998
w lancastercastle.com
e christine.goodier@mus.lancscc.gov.uk

---

812 Lancaster

# Lancaster Maritime Museum

2 hrs    All year

Lancaster Maritime Museum occupies two historic buildings on St George's Quay, the main C18 harbour. The former Customs House of 1764, designed by Richard Gillow, contains displays on the history of the port of Lancaster and the local fishing industry.

\* Lancaster Canal & Morecambe Bay ecology displays
\* *Sir William Priestley* & *Coronation Rose* ships

**Location**
St George's Quay

**Opening**
Easter–Oct 11am–5pm;
Nov–Easter 12.30pm–4pm

**Admission**
Adult £2, Child free, Concs £1

**Contact**
St George's Quay, Lancaster LA1 1RB
t 01524 64637
w lancsmuseums.gov.uk
e sarah.riddle@mus.lancscc.gov.uk

---

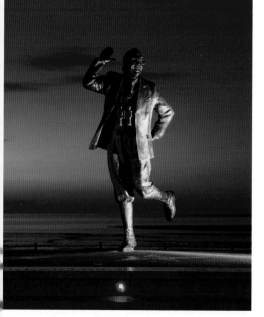

813 Morecambe

# Eric Morecambe statue

1 hr    All year

Unveiled by the Queen in 1999, the larger-than-life statue depicts Eric Morecambe in a characteristic pose with a pair of binoculars around his neck (he was a keen ornithologist). The statue is set against the backdrop of Morecambe Bay and the Lake District hills.

\* People queue to have their photograph taken here

**Location**
Leave M6 at junction 34 or 35 & follow signs for Morecambe. Statue is on Central Promenade area

**Opening**
All reasonable times

**Admission**
Free

**Contact**
Central Promenade, Morecambe, or Tourist Information Centre
t 01524 582808
w visitmorecambe.co.uk

## 814 Ormskirk

# Rufford Old Hall

2 hrs+    Mar–Oct

This is a fine C16 building, famed for its Great Hall which has an intricately carved 'moveable' wooden screen and hammerbeam roof. It is rumoured that Shakespeare performed in this hall for the owner, Sir Thomas Hesketh.

* Fine collections of C16–C17 oak furniture
* Arms, armour & tapestries

| Location | Admission |
|---|---|
| 7 miles N of Ormskirk in Rufford village on E side of A59 | *House & Gardens* Adult £4.90, Child £2.50 |
| | *Gardens* £2.80, £1.30 |
| Opening | Contact |
| 25 Mar–29 Oct Sat–Wed 1pm–5pm Please phone to check opening hours before visiting | Rufford, Ormskirk L40 1SG |
| | t  01704 821254 |
| | w  nationaltrust.org.uk |
| | e  ruffordoldhall@ntrust.org.uk |

## 815 Preston

# British Commercial Vehicle Museum

2 hrs    Apr–Oct

This is one of Britain's most important heritage collections. It contains a unique line-up of historic commercial vehicles and buses representing a century of truck and bus building. It is located in the heart of Leyland.

* Sound & light show on WWII
* Pope mobile

| Location | Contact |
|---|---|
| M6 Junction 28 off M6. Follow signs | King Street, Leyland, Preston PR25 2LE |
| Opening | t  01772 451011 |
| Apr–Sep Sun, Tue–Thu & Bank Hol Mon 10am–5pm; Oct Sun only | w  commercialvehiclemuseum.co.uk |
| Admission | |
| Adult £4, Child £2 | |

## 816 Preston

# Harris Museum & Art Gallery

2 hrs    All year

Discover the best of Preston's heritage in a beautiful Grade I listed building. The Harris has large collections of paintings, sculpture, textiles, costume, glass and ceramics, as well as the Story of Preston gallery that brings the history of the town to life.

* Exciting programme of exhibitions
* National reputation for contemporary art shows

| Location | Contact |
|---|---|
| In city centre | Market Square, Preston PR1 2PP |
| Opening | t  01772 258248 |
| Daily: Mon–Sat 10am–5pm, Sun 11am–4pm | e  harris.museum@preston.gov.uk |
| Admission | |
| Free | |

## 817 Preston

# Museum of Lancashire

2 hrs    All year

Located in the Old Sessions' House, which was built in 1825, this museum traces the history of the county and its people, from the Middle Ages through to recent times. It houses a collection of military objects and memorabilia, from three Lancashire regiments.

* Colourful uniforms & splendid swords displayed
* Reconstruction of a WWI trench

| Location | Contact |
|---|---|
| On A6, Stanley Street, Preston | Stanley Street, Preston PR1 4YP |
| Opening | t  01772 534075 |
| Mon–Wed, Fri & Sat 10.30am–5pm | w  lancsmuseums.gov.uk |
| Admission | e  museums.enquiries@mus.lancscc.gov.uk |
| Adult £2, Child free, Concs £1 | |

818 Preston

# National Football Museum

2 hrs   All year

Travel on a journey through football's history. Learn how the game was invented, how it has developed over the past 150 years, and what the future will hold for players and supporters. Discover the individuals and teams who have helped to shape the game we know today.

* Football Hall of Fame
* Enjoy our new penalty shoot-out game

| Location | Contact |
|---|---|
| 2 miles from junction 31, 31A or 32 on M6. Follow signs | Sir Tom Finney Way, Deepdale, Preston PR1 6RU |
| **Opening** | t 01772 908403/442 |
| Tue–Sat 10am–5pm, Sun 11am–5pm | w nationalfootballmuseum.com |
| **Admission** | e enquiries@nationalfootballmuseum.com |
| Free | |

819 Rivington

# Lever Park

3 hrs+   All year

Sited on the West Pennine moors, this park has good facilities for fishing, walking and refreshments as well as an arboretum and pinetum. Other interesting features include the remains of Lord Leverhulme's gardens and two cruck barns.

* Ruined replica of Liverpool Castle & Rivington Pike
* Reservoir

| Location | Contact |
|---|---|
| Off A673 north of Horwich. On Rivington Lane | Great House Information Centre, Rivington Lane, Horwich BL6 7SB |
| **Opening** | t 01204 691549 |
| Wed–Sun & Bank Hols 10.30am–4.30pm | w unitedutilities.com |
| **Admission** | |
| Free | |

## 820 Rossendale

# Helmshore Textile Museums

2 hrs   Easter–Oct

Experience two original textile mills, a waterwheel and textile machines from the Industrial Revolution. At Whitaker's Mill, a C19 cotton-spinning mill, visitors can see working spinning mules.

\* Watch live demonstrations by skilled workers

**Location**
Holcombe Road in the centre of Helmshore

**Opening**
Please phone for details

**Admission**
Adult £3, Child free, Concs £1.50

**Contact**
Holcombe Road, Helmshore, Rossendale BB4 4NP
t 01706 226459/218838
w lancashire.gov.uk
e helmshoremuseum@muslancscc.gov.uk

## 822 Manchester

# Castlefield Urban Heritage Park

1 hr+   All year

See evidence of Manchester's great industrial past, including railway viaducts and canal systems. Visit the remains of the Roman fort of Mamucium, go for a pleasant walk or boat trip and enjoy many events in the outdoor arena.

\* Britain's first urban heritage park

**Location**
In city centre, follow signs for Museum of Science & Industry

**Opening**
Park Daily: All reasonable times

**Admission**
Free

**Contact**
Castlefield, Manchester
t 0161 2343 157
w visitmanchester.com

## 821 Wigan

# Haigh Country Park

5 hrs+   All year

This park includes an art and craft gallery with exhibitions of pottery, embroidery and paintings. The model village features a railway, helipad, pub and castle. The walled garden originally supplied the hall with fruit and vegetables and now provides a peaceful retreat.

\* Ranger-guided walks around the park
\* 9 & 18 hole golf complex

**Location**
Near B5238 & B5239

**Opening**
Park Daily: dawn–dusk
Visitor centre Mon–Sun 9am–5pm

**Admission**
Free

**Contact**
Haigh, Wigan WN2 1PE
t 01942 832895
w haighhall.net
e hhgen@wict.org

## 823 Manchester

# Chinese Arts Centre

1 hr   All year

This modern building offers changing contemporary art exhibitions, workshops, education programmes and information about Chinese art and culture, with a particular emphasis on supporting Sino-British artistic expression.

\* State-of-the-art education suite
\* Traditional Chinese tea rooms

**Location**
In city centre, Market Buildings, Thomas Street

**Opening**
Mon–Sat 10am–6pm,
Sun 11am–5pm

**Admission**
Free

**Contact**
Thomas Street, Manchester M4 1 EU
t 0161 832 7271
w chinese-arts-centre.org
e info@chinese-arts-centre.org

## 824 Manchester

# Heaton Hall & Park

2 hrs     Easter–Sep

Heaton Hall has beautifully restored interiors housing a collection of furniture and musical instruments. In the park there is a range of facilities for all tastes including cafés, an Animal Centre, Tram Museum, bowling greens, golf course, horse-riding and a boating lake.

* Architect James Wyatt re modelled the house in 1772
* One of the finest neo classical houses in the country

**Location**
In middle of Heaton Park off Middleton Road in East Manchester

**Opening**
Easter–Sep Wed–Sun & Bank Hols
10am–5.30pm
*Park* Daily: All reasonable times

**Admission**
Free

**Contact**
Heaton Park, Prestwich,
Manchester M25 5SW

t 0161 235 8888
w manchestergalleries.org

## 825 Manchester

# Jewish Museum of Manchester

2 hrs     All year

Manchester's Jewish Museum is unique as it is housed in a former Spanish and Portuguese synagogue. The former Ladies Gallery tells the history of Manchester Jewry using pictures, documents, room settings and handsets with testimonies from people of the past.

* Lavish Moorish décor & stained glass

**Location**
On A665, 1 mile from city centre

**Opening**
Mon–Thu 10.30am–4pm'
Sun 10.30am–5pm;
closed Sat & Jewish holidays

**Admission**
Adult £3.95, Child & Concs £2.95

**Contact**
190 Cheetham Hill Road,
Manchester M8 8LW

t 0161 834 9879
w manchesterjewishmuseum.com
e info@manchesterjewishmuseum.com

## 826 Manchester

# Imperial War Museum North

1 hr+     All year

The museum, situated on the banks of the Manchester Ship Canal, offers people of all ages thought-provoking displays and direct access to its evocative collections. It gives valuable insights into the enormous impact of war in the C20 and C21.

**Location**
Junction 9 of M60, then follow the signs to quays

**Opening**
Daily: Mar–Oct 10am–6pm;
Nov–Feb 10am–5pm

**Admission**
Free

**Contact**
Trafford Wharf Road, The Quays,
Trafford Park M17 1TZ

t 0161 836 4000
w iwm.org.uk
e info@iwm.org.uk

©Tom Pollock

## 827 Manchester

# Manchester Art Gallery

4 hrs+    All year

Manchester Art Gallery houses one of the country's finest art collections in spectacular surroundings. Highlights include outstanding Pre-Raphaelite paintings, craft and design and early C20 British art. It also has a lively new space with hands-on activities for families.

\* Collection spans six centuries of fine & decorative art
\* Exceptional for C19 British paintings

**Location**
In city centre

**Opening**
Tue–Sun 10am–5pm;
closed Mon except Bank Hols

**Admission**
Free

**Contact**
Mosley Street, Manchester M2 3JL

t 0161 235 8888
w manchestergalleries.org

## 828 Manchester

# Manchester Museum

1 hr    All year

This museum, with its four floors of displays and exhibitions in 15 galleries, houses collections from all over the world. Visit the famous Egyptology galleries, the new Science for Life gallery and the zoology gallery containing mammals, birds and live animals.

\* Ethnology collections from South America
\* Collections of fossils & minerals

**Location**
In Oxford Road to S of city centre

**Opening**
Daily: Tue–Sat 10am–5pm,
Sun–Mon & Bank Hols 11am–4pm

**Admission**
Free. Special events may charge

**Contact**
The University of Manchester,
Oxford Road,
Manchester M13 9PL

t 0161 275 2634
w museum.manchester.ac.uk
e michael.rooney@manchester.ac.uk

## 829 Manchester

# Museum of Science & Industry

4 hrs+    All year

Situated in the oldest-surviving passenger railway buildings in the world, the museum tells the story of the history, science and industry of Manchester – the world's first industrial city. Stimulate the senses in Xperiment, an interactive science gallery.

\* Demonstrators operate thunderous cotton machinery

**Location**
On Liverpool Road in Castlefield,
signed from city centre

**Opening**
Daily: 10am–5pm

**Admission**
Free. Exhibitions may charge

**Contact**
Liverpool Road, Castlefield,
Manchester M3 4FP

t 0161 832 2244
w msim.org.uk
e marketing@msim.org.uk

## 830 Manchester

# Museum of Transport

2 hrs    All year

Housed in a former bus depot, this wonderfully quirky museum is packed with vintage vehicles, including buses, fire engines and lorries, some 100 years old. The vehicles are lovingly maintained and restored in workshops on the premises.

\* Biggest collection of vintage buses in the UK

**Location**
1 mile N of city centre at N end of
Boyle Street, next to Queen's Road bus
garage

**Opening**
Mar–Oct Wed, Sat–Sun & Bank Hols
10am–5pm; Nov–Feb 10am–4pm;
closed Christmas & New Year

**Admission**
Adult £4, Child & Concs £2

**Contact**
Boyle Street, Cheetham,
Manchester M8 8UW

t 0161 205 2122
w gmts.co.uk
e email@gmts.co.uk

## 831 Manchester

# Old Trafford Museum & Tour

2 hrs    All year

Britain's first purpose-built football museum covers the history of Manchester United from 1878 to the present day. There are frequently updated exhibits and guided tours of the stadium. Picture yourself with the players, using the latest digital imaging technology.

* Play your own commentary on United games
* Multi-award winner

WC ¶¶

**Location**
From Chester Road (A56), turn into Sir Matt Busby Way, or use Old Trafford Metrolink station

**Opening**
Daily: 9.30am–5pm
Museum closes 30 mins before kick-off. Please phone for details of times & to book tours

**Admission** *Museum only* Adult £5.50, Child & Concs £3.75

**Contact**
Sir Matt Busby Way, Old Trafford, Manchester M16 0RA

t 0870 442 1994
w manutd.com

## 832 Manchester

# Trafford Ecology Park

2 hrs+   All year

Once an industrial wasteland, Trafford Ecology Park has now been transformed into a thriving activity centre and haven for wildlife. Visitors can see the displays, take part in the events, or simply discover the wealth of wild flowers, trees, birds and animals that flourish there.

* Centred on a reclaimed boating lake
* Based in Europe's largest industrial estate

**Location**
From M602 take A576. From M60 Junction 9 take A5081

**Opening**
Mon–Fri 9am–5pm;
closed weekends & Bank Hols

**Admission**
Free

**Contact**
Lake Road, Trafford Park, Manchester M17 1TU

t 0161 873 7182
w trafford.gov.uk
e ecology.reception@groundworks.gov.uk

## 833 Manchester

# Urbis

2 hrs    All year

Urbis explores urban culture and the cities of today and tomorrow. Make your own ID cards; keep one and stick one on the wall for all to see. Select your crime, choose your city and receive your sentence from the world's only automatic law dispenser.

* A visit begins with a sky glide in the glass elevator
* Combination of audio, visual & sensory environments

WC ¶¶

**Location**
In city centre

**Opening**
Tue–Sun 10am–6pm

**Admission**
Free. Charge may apply to Level 1 gallery

**Contact**
Cathedral Gardens, Manchester M4 3BG

t 0161 605 8200
w urbis.org.uk
e info@urbis.org.uk

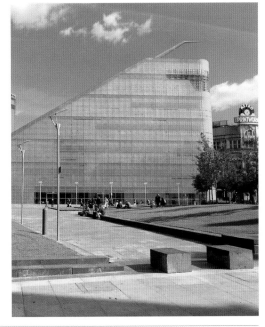

834 Manchester

# The Whitworth Art Gallery

1 hr   All year

This gallery houses an impressive range of watercolours, prints, drawings, modern art and sculpture, as well as the largest collection of textiles and wallpapers outside London. The Whitworth uses its collections to create changing exhibitions exploring different themes.

* Programme of innovative touring exhibitions
* Specialist centre for works on paper & textiles

**Location**
Follow Oxford Road to S of Manchester city centre & to S of University of Manchester campus

**Opening**
Mon–Sat 10am–5pm, Sun 2pm–5pm
Sat afternoon free eye-opener tour at 2pm

**Admission**
Free

**Contact**
The University of Manchester, Oxford Road, Manchester M15 6ER
t  0161 275 7450
w  manchester.ac.uk/whitworth
e  whitworth@manchester.ac.uk

835 Birkenhead

# Birkenhead Priory & St Mary's Tower

1 hr   All year

This Benedictine monastery, established in around 1150, is the oldest standing building on Merseyside. There is a memorial to those who lost their lives aboard the submarine *Thetis*. Enjoy the magnificent views up, down and across the River Mersey to Liverpool.

* Views of Birkenhead, Oxton Ridge, Bidston & the Wirral
* Concerts on Sundays in August

**Location**
M53 on to A41, follow signs to Birkenhead

**Opening**
Easter–Oct Wed–Fri 1pm–5pm'
Sat–Sun 10am–5pm;
Nov–Easter Wed–Fri 12noon–4pm,
Sat–Sun 10am–4pm

**Admission**
Free

**Contact**
Priory Street, Birkenhead CH41 5JH
t  0151 666 1249
w  wirral.gov.uk
e  comments@wirral.gov.uk

## 836   Birkenhead

# Birkenhead Tramway & Wirral Transport Museum

1 hr       All year

Birkenhead is the home of the first street tramway in Europe. Take the tramway from Woodside visitor centre to the Old Colonial pub at the Taylor Street terminus. From there visit the Heritage Centre, which houses a collection of restored and part-restored local buses and trams.

\* Open-topped 1901 Birkenhead tram 20
\* Day-to-day service operated by two Hong Kong trams

**Location**
Signed to Taylor Street from Woodside ferry terminal

**Opening**
*summer* Sat–Sun 1pm–5pm
*winter* Nov–Mar 12noon–4pm; school hols, Easter, spring half-term & summer, Wed–Sun 1pm–5pm

**Admission**
Adult £1, Child 50p

**Contact**
1 Taylor Street, Birkenhead CH41 1BG

t 0151 647 2128

## 837   Birkenhead

# Historic Warships at Birkenhead

3 hrs      All year

This is the largest collection of C20 fighting vessels in the UK. Among them are the submarine *Onyx* and the anti submarine frigate HMS *Plymouth*. On the quayside explore the Bofors Gun and the LCVP which used to be HMS *Intrepid*, as well as the minehunter HMS *Bronington*.

\* U534, the last U-boat to leave Germany in WWII
\* LCT 7074, last surviving LCT of D-Day landings

**Location**
Leave M53 at junction 1, & follow signs to All Docks. Signed from there

**Opening**
Apr–Sep 10am–5pm
Oct–Mar 10am–4pm

**Admission**
Adult £6, Child £4, Concs £5

**Contact**
East Float, Dock Road, Birkenhead CH41 1DJ

t 0151 650 1573
w historicwarships.org

## 838   Birkenhead

# Williamson Art Gallery & Museum

1 hr       All year

The Williamson houses a superb art collection, with Cammell Laird's and other ship models illustrate local and maritime history. On display are Victorian oil paintings, Della Robbia Pottery and Liverpool porcelain, tapestries by Arthur Lee & Sons and British watercolours.

\* Part of the Merseyside embroidery trail
\* Varied programme of temporary exhibitions

**Location**
In town centre on Slatey Road

**Opening**
Tue–Sun & Bank Hols 10am–5pm

**Admission**
Free

**Contact**
Slatey Road, Birkenhead CH 43 4UE

t 0151 652 4177
w wirral.gov.uk
e williamsonartgallery@wirral.gov.uk

## 839   Knowsley

# National Wildflower Centre

2 hrs      Apr–Sep

The National Wildflower Centre is set in a Victorian park within 35 acres of parkland. It has an innovative visitor centre where visitors can learn all about wild flowers. It places an emphasis on creative conservation and preserving and reintroducing wildflowers in Britain.

\* Seasonal wildflower demonstration areas
\* Working garden nursery & shop

**Location**
In Knowsley's Court Hey Park, off junction 5 of M62

**Opening**
Daily: Apr–Sep 10am–5pm

**Admission**
Adult £3, Child free, Concs £1.50

**Contact**
Court Hey Park, Knowsley L16 3NA

t 0151 738 1913/722 8292
w nwc.org.uk
e info@nwc.org.uk

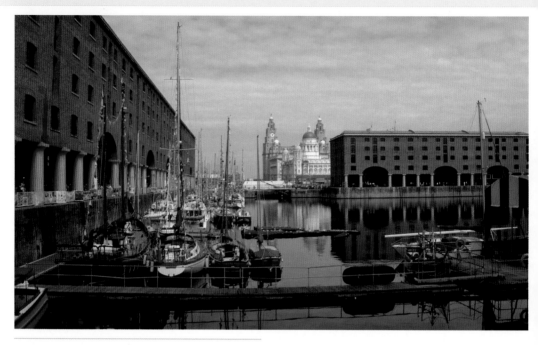

# Aintree Racecourse & Visitor Centre

2 hrs +    June–Sept

Discover the history of a race once believed to be suitable only for scoundrels. There is a museum and picture gallery plus the chance to explore the weighing room, stables and parade ring before browsing through the memorabilia and papers in the Reading Room.

| Location | Contact |
|---|---|
| 5 miles from Liverpool city centre, well signed | Ormskirk Road, Aintree, Liverpool L9 5AS |
| **Opening** | t 0151 523 2600 |
| Group visits only, please phone for details | w aintree.co.uk |
| **Admission** | |
| Adult £7, Child & Concs £4 | |

# Albert Dock

4 hrs+    All year

The Albert Dock is an architectural triumph. Opened in 1846, it became a treasure house of precious cargoes from all over the world. Today redevelopment has transformed it into a busy and cosmopolitan centre as well as a top heritage attraction.

\* Converted C19 warehouse buildings
\* Visit albertdock.com for a web cam view of the attraction

| Location | Contact |
|---|---|
| On Liverpool's waterfront, adjacent to Pier Head | Edward Pavilion, Albert Dock, Liverpool L3 4AF |
| **Opening** | t 0151 708 7334 |
| Daily: any reasonable times | w albertdock.com |
| **Admission** | e enquiries@albertdock.com |
| Free | |

## 842 Liverpool

# Beatles Story

2 hrs    All year

Imagine reliving the greatest story the pop world has ever known – in the city where it all began! Take a nostalgic trip through the multi-award-winning Beatles Story experience, on Liverpool's historic Albert Dock.

\* New living history audio tour
\* Personal insights from those who really knew the Fab Four

| Location | Contact |
|---|---|
| Follow signposts to Albert Dock | Albert Dock, Britannia Vaults, Liverpool L3 4AD |
| **Opening** | t 0151 709 1963 |
| Daily: 10am–6pm (last admission 5pm) | w beatlesstory.com |
| **Admission** | |
| Adult £8.99, Child £4.99, Concs £5.99 | |

## 843 Liverpool

# Cains Brewery

1 hr+    All year

Cains has always been renowned for producing award-winning cask ales. Incorporating the Brewery Tap, now one of Liverpool's drinking landmarks, Robert Cains's original Mersey brewery stands today as a fine example of Victorian brewhouse architecture.

\* Tours include buffet & 2 pints in the Brewery Tap pub

| Location | Contact |
|---|---|
| In West Parliament Street, near Albert Dock | Stanhope Street, Liverpool L8 5XJ |
| **Opening** | t 0151 7098734 |
| Tours: Mon–Thu at 6.30pm | w ainsbeer.com |
| **Admission** | e brewerytour@cainsbeers.com |
| Adult (over18's only) £3.75 | |
| Pre booking essential | |

## 844 Liverpool

# The Cavern Club

4 hrs+    All year

Visit the most famous club in the world and learn all there is to know about the Cavern Club, from its early days as a jazz club in the cellar of a fruit warehouse, to the live music venue of today. This is a carbon copy of the original club where the Beatles found fame.

\* Paul McCartney played his last gig of the century here
\* Wall of Fame

| Location | Contact |
|---|---|
| In city centre | Mathew Street, Liverpool L2 6RE |
| **Opening** | t 0151 236 1965 |
| Mon–Wed 11am–6pm, Thu 11am–2am, | w caverncitytours.com |
| Fri–Sat 11am–2.45am, | e office@thecavernliverpool.com |
| Sun 12noon–12.30am | |
| **Admission** | |
| Adult £2 | |

## 845 Liverpool

# Conservation Centre

1 hr    All year

This Conservation Centre is housed in the former Midland Railway goods depot, which was built in the 1870s. The centre cares for all of the National Museums of Liverpool collections. There are more than a million objects, ranging from tiny natural history specimens to space rockets.

\* Conservation science section
\* Many world-famous masterpieces cared for here

| Location | Contact |
|---|---|
| Near Queen's Square bus station | Whitechapel, Liverpool L1 6HZ |
| **Opening** | t 0151 478 4999 |
| Please phone for details | w liverpoolmuseums.org |
| **Admission** | e conservation@liverpoolmuseums. org.uk |
| Free | |

846 Liverpool

# Everton Football Club

2 hrs    All year

A tour of Goodison Park will include a behind-the-scenes look at what it's like to play for the Toffees. Walk down the tunnel and imagine the roar of 40,000 fans, explore the dressing room and see where the players relax and celebrate or commiserate after a game.

| Location | Contact |
|---|---|
| 3 miles N of city centre | Goodison Park, Liverpool L4 4EL |
| **Opening** | t 0870 442 1878 |
| Daily, except on match days | w evertonfc.com |
| **Admission** | e boxoffice@evertonfc.com |
| Adult £8.50, Child & Concs £5 | |
| Pre booking essential | |

847 Liverpool

# Liverpool Cathedral

2 hrs    All year

This is the largest Anglican cathedral in Europe and one of the great buildings of the C20. It boasts the highest Gothic arches, the largest working organ and the heaviest ring of bells in the world and throughout the year hosts exhibitions, concerts and recitals.

* New visitor centre in June 2006
* The grand organ has 9,765 pipes

| Location | Contact |
|---|---|
| Half a mile from city centre | St James' Mount, Liverpool L1 7AZ |
| **Opening** | t 0151 709 6271 |
| 8am–6pm (subject to services) | w liverpoolcathedral.org.uk |
| **Admission** | e info@liverpoolcathedral.org.uk |
| Free, donations welcomed | |

# Liverpool Football Club Museum & Tour Centre

1 hr     All year

A tour of Anfield includes a walk down the players' tunnel and the opportunity to touch the famous sign that proclaims 'This is Anfield'. Experience the dressing room where the manager delivers his team talks. The museum is packed with things to do, see and listen to.

* Film takes visitors through the life of the club
* Hillsborough memorial tribute to 96 fans who died in 1989

| Location | Admission |
|---|---|
| 3 miles from city centre, 4 miles from M62, 7 miles from end of M57 & M58 | Adult £9, Child & Concs £5.50 |
| | **Contact** |
| **Opening** | Anfield Road, Liverpool L4 0TH |
| Daily: 10am–5pm | |
| Last admissions 4pm | t 0151 260 6677 |
| (closes 1 hr before kick-off) | w liverpoolfc.tv |
| | e events@liverpoolfc.tv |

# Liverpool Museum

2 hrs     All year

This is the largest of the National Museums of Liverpool venues. The fascinating and varied collections cover archaeology, ethnology and the natural and physical sciences. Special attractions include the award-winning natural history centre and the planetarium.

* Exhibition galleries include Egypt & the Near East
* Space & Time Gallery

| Location | Contact |
|---|---|
| Opposite entrance to Birkenhead tunnel, 5 min walk from Tourist Information Centre in Queen's Square | William Brown Street, Liverpool L3 8EN |
| | t 0151 478 4399 |
| **Opening** | w worldmuseumliverpool.org.uk |
| Daily: 10am–5pm | e worldmuseum@liverpool.org.uk |
| **Admission** | |
| Free | |

## 850 Liverpool

# Sefton Park Palm House

1 hr    All year

Sefton Park Palm House is a Grade II listed Victorian glasshouse. It is an octagonal three-tiered structure, showcasing the Liverpool botanical collection that was created from specimens brought to the city from all over the world during its maritime heyday.

* One of the largest municipal collections in the country
* Four sculptures by Leon-Joseph Chavailiaur

**Location**
Take M62 on to the A5058 towards Queen's Drive & Alliton Road

**Opening**
Nov–Mar 10.30am–4pm;
Apr–Oct 10.30am–5pm
Restricted opening during events, please phone for details

**Admission**
Free

**Contact**
Sefton Park, Liverpool L17 1AP
t  0151 726 2415
w  palmhouse.org.uk
e  info@palmhouse.org.uk

## 851 Liverpool

# Mendips & 20 Forthlin Road

2 hrs    Mar–Oct

This is a joint tour of Mendips, the childhood home of John Lennon, and Forthlin Road, the home of the McCartney family, where the Beatles met, rehearsed and wrote many of their earliest songs. Displays include contemporary photographs and Beatles memorabilia.

* Audio tour features Sir Paul McCartney
* Evocative photographs of life at 20 Forthlin Road

**Location**
Morning tours leave from Conservation Centre in city centre, afternoon tours leave from Speke Hall

**Opening**
Tours depart 10.30am & 11.20am from Albert Dock, 2.15pm & 3.55pm from Speke Hall

**Admission**
Adult £12, Child £1

**Contact**
20 Forthlin Road, Allerton, Liverpool L24 1YP
t  0151 708 8574/427 7231
w  nationaltrust.org.uk
e  spekehall@nationaltrust.org.uk

©Tony Stuchbury www.ajsphotos.co.uk

## 852 Liverpool

# Speke Hall, Garden & Estate

2 hrs    Mar–Dec

Behind the black and white half-timbered façade of this hall are interiors that represent many centuries. The Great Hall and priest's holes evoke Tudor times, while the oak parlour and smaller rooms show the Victorian desire for privacy and comfort.

* Fine Jacobean plasterwork & carved furniture
* Fully equipped Victorian kitchen & servants' hall

**Location**
8 miles SE of central Liverpool, next to Liverpool airport, signed

**Opening**
Mar–Oct Wed–Sun 1pm–5.30pm;
Nov–Dec Sat–Sun 1pm–4.30pm

**Admission**
Adult £6.25, Child £3.50

**Contact**
The Walk, Speke, Liverpool L24 1XD

t  0151 427 7231
w  nationaltrust.org.uk
e  spekehall@nationaltrust.org.uk

## 853 Liverpool

# Tate Liverpool

2 hrs    All year

Tate Liverpool is one of the largest galleries of modern art outside London and displays special exhibitions that bring together artworks from around the world. The exhibitions show art from 1900 to the present day which include photography, video and installation.

* Photography, printmaking, painting & sculpture
* Daily talks, shops & café

**Location**
Walking distance from Liverpool Lime Street station, signposted from city centre

**Opening**
Tue–Sun 10am–5.50pm

**Admission**
*Tate Liverpool* Free
*Exhibition* Adult £4, Child free, Concs £3

**Contact**
The Colonnades, Albert Dock,
Liverpool L3 4BB

t  0151 702 7400
w  tate.org.uk/liverpool
e  liverpoolinfo@tate.org.uk

## 854 Liverpool

# The Walker

1 hr    All year

The Walker holds one of the finest collections of fine and decorative art in Europe. The gallery has recently undergone a major £4.3m refurbishment programme. These improvements include special exhibition galleries that display important touring shows.

* Children's gallery
* Craft & design gallery of decorative arts

| Location | Contact |
| --- | --- |
| Opposite entrance to Birkenhead tunnel, 5 mins from Tourist Information Centre | William Brown Street, Liverpool L3 8EL |
| **Opening** | t 0151 478 4199 |
| Daily: 10am–5pm | w thewalker.org.uk |
| **Admission** | e thewalker@liverpoolmuseums.org.uk |
| Free | |

## 855 Prescot

# Knowsley Safari Park

3 hrs+    All year

During the 5-mile-long drive visitors can see a wide range of wild animals, including camels, buffalo, white rhino, emu, wallabies, elephants, giraffes and lions. A separate reptile house is home to snakes, iguanas, lizards, scorpions and stick insects.

* 500 acres of rolling countryside

| Location | Admission |
| --- | --- |
| Leave M62 at junction 6, the M57 at junction 2, & follow signs | Adult £9.50, Child & Concs £6.50 |
| **Opening** | **Contact** |
| Daily: Mar–Oct 10am–4pm; Nov–Feb 10.30am–3pm | Prescot, Merseyside L34 4AN |
| | t 0151 430 9009 |
| | w knowsley.com |
| | e safari.park@knowsley.com |

## 856 Southport

# Formby

2 hrs    All year

This nature reserve is home to one of Britain's last thriving colonies of red squirrels. These can be seen in the pine trees, while the shoreline attracts waders such as oyster-catchers and sanderlings. As well as the beautiful beach, there are miles of walks across the sand dunes.

| Location | Contact |
| --- | --- |
| 15 miles N of Liverpool, 2 miles W of Formby, 2 miles off A565 & 6 miles S of Southport | Blundell Avenue, Formby L37 1PH |
| **Opening** | t 01704 878591 |
| All year. Dawn–dusk | w nationaltrust.org.uk |
| **Admission** | e formby@nationaltrust.org.uk |
| Free. Car park £3.30 | |

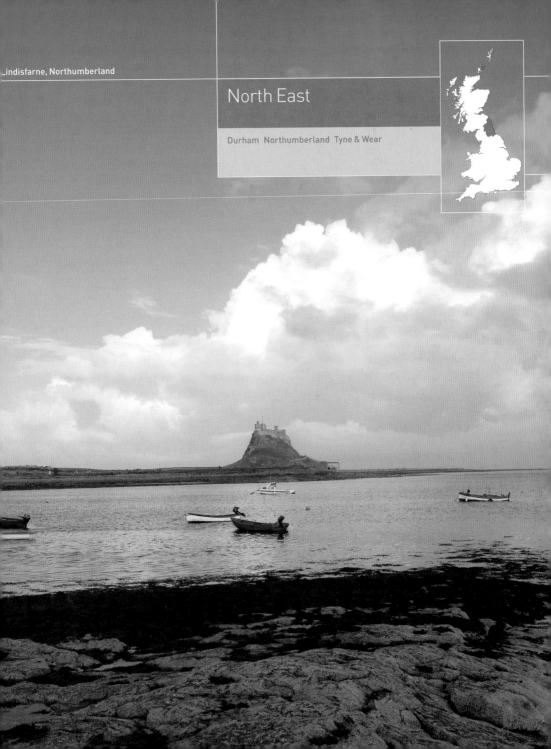

# North East

Durham Northumberland Tyne & Wear

## 857 Barnard Castle

# Barnard Castle

1 hr+   All year

This imposing English Heritage property sits high above the River Tees. The C12 stone castle was once one of the largest castles in northern England, the principal residence of the Baliol family, and a major power base in the many conflicts between England and Scotland.

* Beautiful views of River Tees
* Home to Richard III & Henry VII

**Location**
In Barnard Castle town, off Galgate on A688

**Opening**
Daily: Apr–Sep 10am–6pm; Oct 10am–4pm; Nov–Mar Thu–Mon 10am–4pm

**Admission**
Adult £3, Child £1.50, Concs £2.30

**Contact**
Barnard Castle
t  01833 638212
w  english-heritage.org.uk

## 858 Barnard Castle

# Bowes Museum

3 hrs   All year

Founded by local businessman John Bowes and his French wife, Josephine, this magnificent museum, which opened in 1892, houses one of Britain's finest collections of paintings, ceramics, furniture and textiles. There are special outdoor events and family fun days.

* Set in 23 acres of parkland, with parterre garden
* Outstanding temporary art exhibition programme

**Location**
Just off A66, 20 mins from Scotch Corner (A1)

**Opening**
Daily: 11am–5pm

**Admission**
Adult £7, Child free, Concs £6

**Contact**
Barnard Castle DL12 8NP
t  01833 690606
w  bowesmuseum.org.uk
e  info@bowesmuseum.org.uk

## 859 Beamish

# Beamish, The North of England Open Air Museum

4 hrs+   All year

Beamish is a unique living, working experience of life as it was in the north of England in both the early C18 and C19 and C19 to C20. It shows how the region was transformed in that time from its thinly populated rural roots to being a site of heavy industrialisation.

* Costumed guides explain each attraction
* Former European Museum of the Year

**Location**
Follow signs from junction 63 of A1(M)

**Opening**
Apr–Oct daily 10am–5pm;
Nov–Apr Tue–Thu & Sat–Sun 10am–4pm

**Admission**
Adult £15, Child £9, Concs £12
Nov–Mar £6 per person

**Contact**
Beamish DH9 0RG
t  0191 370 4000
w  beamish.org.uk
e  museum@beamish.org.uk

## 860 Bishop Auckland

# Hamsterley Forest

2–4 hrs   All year

Covering some 2,000 hectares, Hamsterley Forest has something for everyone – play and picnic areas, several walks and cycle routes ranging from a 1½-mile easy-access footpath to a 7-mile black cycle route and downhill descent course for the more adventurous.

* Largest forest in County Durham
* New cycle routes

**Location**
From A68 at Witton-le-Wear follow brown tourist signs

**Opening**
*Forest* Daily: 7.30am–sunset
*Visitor centre* Apr–Oct Mon–Fri 10am–4pm, Sat–Sun 11am–5pm
Please phone for details of Nov–Dec

**Admission**
Free. Toll for forest drive & car park charge (£2 per car)

**Contact**
Redford, Bishop Auckland DL13 3NL
t  01388 488312
w  forestry.gov.uk

# 861 Bishop Auckland

## Harperley POW Camp

1 hr    All year

Harperley was one of the few purpose-built POW camps in Britain. It housed low-risk prisoners, first from Italy and then from Germany. At its height it had 1,500 prisoners. In addition to the museum, there is a garden centre and a farm shop.

* Children's outdoor play area
* Featured in the BBC programme *Restoration*

**Location**
Approximately 250m from junction of A68 & A689 near village of Crook

**Opening**
Daily: 10am–5pm

**Admission**
Free

**Contact**
Firtree, Crook,
County Durham DL15 8DX

t 01388 767098
w powcamp.com
e info@powcamp.com

# 862 Darlington

## Darlington Railway Centre & Museum

2 hrs    All year

The museum celebrates nearly 180 years of railway history in the town and in the North East. Of greatest significance is Stephenson's locomotive which hauled the inaugural multicarriage train on the Stockton and Darlington Railway.

* Including an 1840s Darlington-built locomotive
* Museum is in the 1842 railway station

**Location**
1 mile from town centre on A167

**Opening**
Daily: 10am–5pm

**Admission**
Adult £2.50, Child & Concs £1.50

**Contact**
North Road Station,
Darlington DL3 6ST

t 01325 460532
w drcm.org.uk
e museum@darlington.gov.uk

# 863 Darlington

## Raby Castle

3 hrs+    Easter–Sep

Built in the C14, Raby Castle is one of the largest and most impressive of English medieval castles, with towers, turrets, interiors and artworks from the medieval, Regency and Victorian periods. Enjoy walled gardens, a deer park and a children's adventure playground.

* Great kitchen little altered in 600 years
* Paintings by Reynolds & other Old Masters

**Location**
1 mile N of Staindrop on A688

**Opening**
Easter weekend 11am–5.30pm;
May & Sep Wed & Sun 11am–5.30pm;
Jun–Aug Sun–Fri 11am–5.30pm

**Admission**
Adult £9, Child £4, Concs £8

**Contact**
PO Box 50, Staindrop,
Darlington DL2 3AH

t 01833 660202
w rabycastle.com
e admin@rabycastle.com

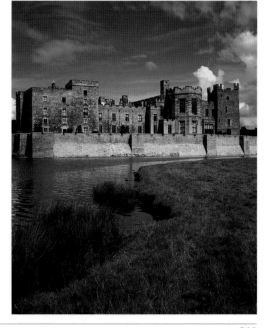

## 864 Durham

# Crook Hall Gardens

1 hr+          Easter–Sep

On the banks of the River Wear with views of Durham cathedral and castle, Crook Hall is a Grade I listed medieval manor house with C13 hall. There are various beautiful gardens with traditional and modern planting schemes and an established maze.

* Fruit trees wreathed in rambling roses
* 'A tapestry of colourful blooms' according to Alan Titchmarsh

**Location**
Short walk from Durham's Millburngate shopping centre, opposite Gala Theatre

**Opening**
Easter–Jul & Sep Sun only 1pm–5pm; Aug Sat–Thu & Bank Hols 1pm–5pm

**Admission**
Adult £4, Concs £3.50

**Contact**
Frankland Lane, Sidegate, Durham DH1 5SZ

t 0191 384 8028
w crookhallgardens.co.uk
e info@crookhallgardens.co.uk

## 865 Durham

# Durham Castle

1 hr           Mar–Sep

Dating from 1072, this is one of the largest Norman castles and one of the grandest Romanesque palaces to survive in England. It was the seat of the Prince Bishops until 1832 and is now a residential college for the University of Durham.

* World Heritage Site
* Entrance by guided tour only

**Location**
In city centre. Uphill walk or no. 40 bus to Palace Green

**Opening**
Daily: mid-Mar–mid-Apr & Jul–Sep 10am–12.30pm & 2pm–4.30pm. Other times usually Mon, Wed, Sat–Sun afternoons but please phone to confirm

**Admission**
Adult £5, Child & Concs £2.50

**Contact**
Durham DH1 3RW

t 0191 334 3800
w durhamcastle.com
e university-college.www@durham.ac.uk

## 866 Durham
# Old Fulling Museum of Archaeology

1 hr  All year

This former mill has become one of the most photographed buildings in the North East. It now houses the Museum of Archaeology among whose striking exhibits is a major collection of Roman inscriptions from the north of England and an outstanding collection of Samianware.

* Artefacts from ancient Greece and Rome
* Medieval finds from Durham city centre

**Location**
Just below cathedral in city centre

**Opening**
Apr–Oct 11am–4pm;
Nov–Mar Fri–Mon 11.30am–3.30pm

**Admission**
Adult £1, Child & Concs 50p

**Contact**
The Banks, Durham DH1 3EB
t 0191 334 1823
e fulling.mill@dur.ac.uk
w dur.ac.uk/fulling.mill

## 867 Durham
# Oriental Museum

1 hr  All year

The only museum of its kind in the UK, entirely devoted to art and archaeology from cultures throughout the Orient. The collections range from prehistoric Egypt and China to the work of living artists. The museum is part of Durham University.

* Used as a resource by researchers around the world
* Students of higher education enter free

**Location**
S side of Durham, signed from A177

**Opening**
Daily: Mon–Fri 10am–5pm,
Sat–Sun 12noon–5pm

**Admission**
Adult £1.50, Concs 75p

**Contact**
Elvet Hill, off South Road, Durham DH1 3TH
t 0191 334 5694
w dur.ac.uk/oriental.museum
e oriental.museum@durham.ac.uk

## 868 Durham
# *Prince Bishop* River Cruiser

1 hr  All year

The 150-seater cruiser sails regularly from Durham city centre. The one-hour trip offers spectacular views of the cathedral, the castle and other tourist attractions. There is wheelchair access to the open-air upper deck and saloons.

* Sun deck & onboard barbecue
* 1-hour Santa Cruises in Dec

**Location**
Cruiser is found below Prince Bishop shopping centre in Durham

**Opening**
Please phone for details

**Admission**
Adult £4.50, Child £2, Concs £4

**Contact**
The Boathouse, Elvet Bridge, Durham DH1 3AH
t 0191 386 9525

## 869 Durham
# University of Durham Botanic Garden

2 hrs  All year

The garden features a large glasshouse that is split between the tropical house and the cactus house. Outside there are more than 20 collections featuring plants from around the world including a mutant bed highlighting some of nature's weirder creations.

* Exhibitions of local art
* Different trails for children to follow

**Location**
Signed from city centre

**Opening**
Mar–Oct 10am–5pm;
Nov–Feb 10am–4pm

**Admission**
Adult £2, Child £1, Concs £1.50

**Contact**
Hollingside Lane, South Road, Durham DH1 3TN
t 0191 3345521
w dur.ac.uk/botanic.garden
e botanic.garden@durham.ac.uk

## 870 Hartlepool

# Hartlepool's Maritime Experience

4–6 hrs     All year

Step back in time and visit a superb recreation of an C18 seaport including HMS *Trincomalee*, the oldest warship afloat in the UK. The historic quayside, children's adventure centre, costumed guides and Museum of Hartlepool together make a great day out for all ages.

\* Excellent disabled access to most decks
\* One of several attractions around Historic Quay

| Location | Contact |
|---|---|
| Follow signs for Hartlepool Historic Quay | HMS *Trincomalee* Trust, Jackson Dock, Hartlepool TS24 0XZ |
| **Opening** Daily: 10am–5pm | t 01429 860077 w hartlepoolmaritimeexperience.com e info@hartlepoolmaritimeexperience .com |
| **Admission** Adult £6.25, Child £3.75, Concs £4.75 | |

## 871 Middlesbrough

# Dorman Museum

1 hr     All year

The Dorman recently reopened after a major construction programme that has created a diverse range of galleries and exhibitions. The museum, first opened in 1904, now houses hands-on science sections such as $H_2O$ and Earth in Space as well as local history displays.

\* See the story of Linthorpe Pottery
\* Constantly changing art exhibitions

| Location | Contact |
|---|---|
| In centre of Middlesbrough, at junction of Ayresome Street & Linthorpe Road | Linthorpe Road, Middlesbrough TS5 6LA |
| **Opening** Apr–Oct Tue–Sun 10am–5.30pm Nov–Mar Tue–Sun 9am–4.30pm | t 01642 813781 w dormanmuseum.co.uk e dormanmuseum@middlesbrough. gov.uk |
| **Admission** Free | |

## 872 Stockton on Tees

# Four Seasons White Water Rafting

2 hrs     Feb–Nov

A nationally recognised centre for canoeing, kayaking and white-water rafting. The tidal River Tees guarantees white water all year with fast-flowing rapids carrying you down the course on an exhilarating and adrenalin-fuelled trip. Equipment hire available.

\* Customisable difficulty for beginners and experts
\* Training for all levels

| Location | Admission |
|---|---|
| On N bank of River Tees near Tees Barrage Bridge, Stockton on Tees | From £15 |
| **Opening** All year – booking advised Please phone for details | **Contact** Tees Barrage, Stockton on Tees TS18 2QW t 01642 678000 w 4seasons.co.uk e kanu@4seasons.co.uk |

## 873 Upper Weardale

# Killhope Lead Mining Museum

4 hrs     Easter–Oct

This fully restored lead mine explores the lives of Victorian mining families. Guided tours take visitors along the original tunnels (wellingtons, hard hat and cap-lamp provided). A woodland walk gives access to further reminders of lead mining.

\* Warm clothes required even during summer
\* Winner of Family Friendly Museum 2004

| Location | Contact |
|---|---|
| Off A689 between Stanhope & Alston | The North of England Lead Mining Museum, nr Cowshill, Upper Weardale DL13 1AR |
| **Opening** Daily: Easter–Oct 10.30am–5pm | t 01388 537505 w durham.gov.uk/killhope e killhope@durham.gov.uk |
| **Admission** Adult £6, Child £3, Concs £5.50 No under-4s allowed in mine | |

## 874 Alnwick

# Alnwick Castle

2 hrs+    Apr–Oct

This foreboding medieval castle, known as the Windsor of the North, has stunning state rooms, fine furniture and paintings by Canaletto, Van Dyck and Titian. Home to the Percy family for 700 years, it has also been a *Harry Potter* film location.

* Knight school & superb gift shop
* Museum of Royal Northumberland Fusiliers

| Location | Contact |
|---|---|
| Alnwick, 35 miles N of Newcastle upon Tyne, 1 mile from A1 | Alnwick NE66 1NQ |
| | t 01665 510777 |
| Opening | w alnwickcastle.com |
| Daily: Apr–Oct 11am–5pm | e enquiries@alnwickcastle.com |
| Admission | |
| Adult £7.95, Child £2.95, Concs £7.50 | |

## 875 Amble

# Warkworth Castle

1 hr+    All year

The magnificent eight-towered keep stands high on a hill overlooking the River Coquet. Home to the Percy family who at times wielded more power in the north than the King. Sir Henry Percy (Harry Hotspur) was immortalised in Shakespeare's *Henry IV*.

* Opening scenes of *Henry IV* were set in Warkworth
* Duke's Rooms first opened in 2003

| Location | Admission |
|---|---|
| 8 miles SE of Alnwick, on A1068 | Adult £3.30, Child £1.70, Concs £2.50 |
| Opening | Contact |
| Daily: Apr–Sep 10am–6pm; Oct 10am–4pm; Nov–Mar Sat–Mon 10am–4pm | nr Amble, Morpeth NE65 0UJ |
| | t 01665 711423 |
| | w english-heritage.org.uk |

## 876 Ashington

# Wansbeck Riverside Park

2–5 hrs    All year

Stretching along the banks of the River Wansbeck, the park provides miles of pleasant walks and trails right down to the sea at Sandy Bay. There are picnic areas for families and play facilities for children. The river can be used for fishing for a small fee.

* Picnic & play areas
* 4-mile riverside walk

| Location | Contact |
|---|---|
| Take A1068. Park is located between Ashington & Bedlington | Green Lane, Ashington NE63 8TX |
| Opening | t 01670 843444 |
| Daily: 8am–dusk | |
| Admission | |
| Free | |

## 877  Bamburgh

# Bamburgh Castle

2 hrs   Mar–Oct

One of the finest castles in England. Perched on a basalt outcrop on the very edge of the North Sea it was restored in 1750 and again extensively by the C19 industrialist Lord Armstrong. Tour the magnificent King's Hall, Cross Hall, reception rooms and armoury.

* Still home to the Armstrong family
* Exhibits include fine furniture, tapestries & arms

| Location | Contact |
|---|---|
| 20 miles S of Berwick-upon-Tweed by B1342 | Bamburgh NE69 7DF |
| | t  01668 214515 |
| Opening | w  bamburghcastle.com |
| Daily: mid-Mar–Oct 11am–4.30pm | e  bamburghcastle@aol.com |
| Admission | |
| Adult £6, Child £2.50, Concs £5 | |

## 878  Berwick-upon-Tweed

# Berwick Barracks Museum & Art Gallery

All year

The barracks are home to a number of attractions, including 'By Beat of Drum', showing what life was like for British infantry soldiers until Queen Victoria's reign. The regimental museum tells the history of the King's Own Scottish Borderers.

* One of the first purpose-built barracks
* Walk on ramparts affords great views of River Tweed

| Location | Contact |
|---|---|
| Off Church Street in town centre | The Parade, Berwick-upon-Tweed PD15 1DF |
| Opening | t  01289 304493 |
| Daily: Easter–Sep 10am–6pm (5pm in Oct); Nov–Mar Wed–Sun 10am–4pm | w  english-heritage.org.uk |
| Admission | |
| Adult £3.30, Child £1.70, Concs £2.50 | |

## 879  Carlisle-Newcastle

# Hadrian's Wall

1 hr+   All year

One of the most important monuments built by the Romans in Britain. It is the best-known frontier in the entire Roman Empire and is designated a World Heritage site. Various attractions along the wall include Roman forts and several museums.

* Museum brings Roman history to life
* 84-mile coast-to-coast walk along Wall now open

| Location | Contact |
|---|---|
| A69 between Newcastle & Carlisle runs parallel to Hadrian's Wall (approximately 2–5 miles S) | Hadrian's Wall Tourism Partnership, 14b Gilesgate, Hexham NE46 3NJ |
| Opening | t  01434 322002 |
| Times vary, please phone for details | w  hadrians-wall.org |
| Admission | e  info@hadrians-wall.org |
| Prices vary, please phone for details | |

Chillingham

# Chillingham Castle

1 hr+  May–Sep

This remarkable castle with alarming dungeons and torture chamber has been in the family of the Earls Grey and their relations since the C13. See active restoration of complex masonry, metalwork and ornamental plaster in a wide diversity of rooms and styles.

\* Beautiful grounds with commanding views
\* Formal gardens & woodland walks open to the public

| Location | Contact |
|---|---|
| Signed from A1 & A697 | Chillingham NE66 5NJ |
| **Opening** | t 01668 215359 |
| May–Sep Sun–Fri 12noon–5pm; | w chillingham-castle.com |
| Oct–Apr by appointment | e enquiries@chillingham-castle.com |
| **Admission** | |
| Adult £6, Child (under 5s) £1, Child (over 5s) £3, Concs £5.50 | |

Hexham

# Cherryburn

1 hr  Mar–Oct

This C19 farmhouse was the birthplace of Thomas Bewick who pioneered wood-engraving. Bewick was an outstanding artist and naturalist and drew on his passion to produce beautiful engravings of wildlife. The cottage contains an exhibition on his life and works.

\* Occasional demonstration of printing
\* Stunning views of valley of the River Tyne from garden

| Location | Contact |
|---|---|
| Take A695 to Mickley Square & follow signs, 11 miles from Hexham | Station Bank, Mickley, nr Stocksfield NE43 7DD |
| **Opening** | t 01661 843276 |
| 18 Mar–29 Oct Thu–Tue 11am–5pm (last admission 4.30pm) | w nationaltrust.org.uk |
| | e cherryburn@nationaltrust.org.uk |
| **Admission** | |
| Adult £3.50, Child £1.75 | |

Hexham

# Vindolanda

2½ hrs  Feb–Nov

A fascinating Roman fort and settlement lying just to the south of Hadrian's Wall. On the site itself stands a full-size replica of a section of Hadrian's Wall in both stone and timber, giving the visitor a true idea of the impressive might of the monument.

\* Full-sized reconstructions of Roman temple and shop
\* Rare & fascinating personal documents to be read

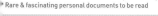

| Location | Contact |
|---|---|
| Take A69 and B6318 near village of Bardon Mill, then follow signs | Chesterholm Museum, Bardon Mill Hexham, Northumberland NE47 7JN |
| **Opening** | t 01434 344277 |
| Apr–Sep 10am–6pm; | w vindolanda.com |
| Feb–Mar & Oct–Nov 10am–5pm | e info@vindolanda.com |
| **Admission** | |
| Adult £4.95, Child £3, Concs £4.10 | |

Holy Island–Lindisfarne

# Lindisfarne Castle

½ hr  Feb–Oct

Perched on top of a rocky crag and accessible only across a causeway at low tide. The castle, originally a Tudor fort, was converted into a private house in 1903 by the young Edwin Lutyens. The small rooms are full of intimate decoration and design.

\* Charming walled garden planned by Gertrude Jekyll
\* Check crossing times before making a long journey

| Location | Admission |
|---|---|
| Holy Island, 6 miles E of A1, across causeway | Adult £5, Child £2.50 |
| **Opening** | **Contact** |
| 2 Feb–20 Feb daily; 12 Mar–30 Oct Tue–Sun; | Holy Island, Berwick-upon-Tweed TD15 2SH |
| Times vary depending upon tides, usually 10.30am–3pm or 12noon–4pm | t 01289 389244 |
| | w nationaltrust.org.uk |

## 884 Holy Island–Lindisfarne

# Lindisfarne Priory

1 hr+    All year

A holy site since being founded by St Aidan in AD635, Lindisfarne remains a place of pilgrimage today. Lindisfarne Priory was the site of one of the most important early centres of Christianity in Anglo-Saxon England. Check the tides before visiting.

* Anglo-Saxon carvings in museum
* Refurbished museum

**Location**
Holy Island, 6 miles E of A1, across causeway

**Opening**
Daily: Apr–Sep 10am–6pm; Mar & Oct 10am–4pm; Nov–Mar Sat–Mon 10am–2pm Times vary depending on tides

**Admission**
Adult £3.60, Child £1.80, Concs £2.70

**Contact**
Holy Island,
Berwick-upon-Tweed TD15 2RX

t 01289 389200
w english-heritage.org.uk

## 885 Morpeth

# Belsay Hall, Castle & Gardens

3 hrs    All year

A dramatic, well-preserved medieval tower house, to which a Jacobean manor house was added in 1614. Belsay Hall (1807), designed by Sir Charles Monck in Greek Revival style after the Temple of Theseus in Athens, has great architectural importance within Europe.

* 2 acres of rhododendrons at their best May–Jun
* Formal terraces & winter garden, original planting

**Location**
In Belsay, 14 miles NW of Newcastle upon Tyne on A696

**Opening**
Apr–Sep daily 10am–6pm
Oct daily 10am–4pm
Nov–Mar Thu–Mon 10am–4pm

**Admission**
Adult £5.30, Child £2.70, Concs £4

**Contact**
Belsay NE20 0DX

t 01661 881636
w english-heritage.org.uk

## 886 Morpeth

# Carlisle Park

1–3 hrs    All year

In the heart of historic Morpeth lies Carlisle Park with ancient woodland walks, a C12 castle and an C11 motte. The formal gardens display immaculate annual and carpet bedding, and link to the William Turner Garden, a modern version of a Tudor knot and physic garden.

* Green Flag award & Quality Assured Visitor Attraction
* Boating, bowls, paddling pool, walks & beautiful gardens

**Location**
Follow signs to Morpeth town centre, then Carlisle Park is within walking distance of many car parks, as well as bus station & train station

**Opening**
Daily: All reasonable times
*Turner Garden* Daily: 7.30am–dusk
*Sporting Facilities* Apr–Oct 10am–9pm

**Admission**
Free

**Contact**
Castle Morpeth Borough Council, Coopies Lane Depot, Coopies Lane Industrial Estate, Morpeth NE61 6JT

t 01670 500777
w castlemorpeth.gov.uk
e firstcall@castlemorpeth.gov.uk

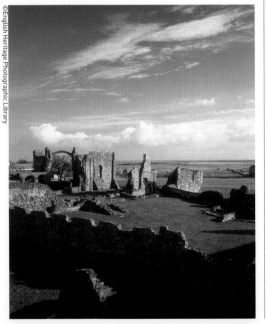

## 887 Morpeth

# Cragside Estate

3 hrs+    Apr–Dec

Cragside estate was the revolutionary home of Lord Armstrong, Victorian inventor and landscape genius. Surrounding the house is one of the largest handmade, rock gardens in Europe. In the Pinetum below, England's tallest Douglas fir soars above other woodland giants.

* Used to impress important armaments customers
* 3-acre rock garden, fruit house & Italian garden

| Location | Contact |
|---|---|
| 1 mile N of Rothbury on B6341 | Rothbury, Morpeth NE65 7PX |
| **Opening** | t 01669 620333 |
| *Estate* Apr–Oct 10.30am–7pm; | w nationaltrust.org.uk |
| 1 Nov–17 Dec 11am–4pm | e cragside@nationaltrust.org.uk |
| **Admission** | |
| Adult £5.70, Child £2.60 | |

## 888 Morpeth

# Wallington

3 hrs+    Easter–Oct

Wallington House reopened in 2004 after extensive renovation. The Wallington estate was laid out in the C18 by Sir Walter Blackett. The original formality underlies the natural landscape in which walks offer a variety of lawns, shrubberies, lakeland and woodland.

* Stone griffin heads on the lawn
* Set in evocative Northumberland moorland

| Location | Admission |
|---|---|
| 12 miles W of Morpeth on B6343 | Adult £7.30, Child £3.65 |
| **Opening** | **Contact** |
| *House* Easter–Oct Wed–Mon | Cambo, Morpeth NE61 4AR |
| 1pm–5pm | t 01670 773600 |
| *Grounds* All year: daily 10am–dusk | w nationaltrust.org.uk |
| | e wallington@nationaltrust.org.uk |

## 889 Rothbury

# Brinkburn Priory

1 hr    Apr–Sep

Founded in 1135 as a house for the Augustinian canons, the church is the only complete surviving building of the monastery. In the summer season a number of choral events can be attended at this functioning church.

* Adjacent manor house has open ground floor
* Lovely setting beside River Coquet

| Location | Contact |
|---|---|
| 4½ miles SE of Rothbury off B6344 | Longframlinton, |
| **Opening** | Morpeth NE65 8AR |
| Daily: Apr–Sep 10am–6pm | t 01665 570628 |
| **Admission** | w english–heritage.org.uk |
| Adult £2.30, Child £1.20, Concs £1.70 | |

## 890 Seahouses

# Farne Islands

2½ hrs    Varies

Lying 2–3 miles off the Northumberland coast, the islands are home to a large colony of Atlantic or grey seals and the most famous seabird sanctuary in Britain. Visitors can see 20 different species, including puffins, eider ducks and tern.

* Views of Bamburgh Castle
* Regular ferry services for a small charge

| Location | Admission |
|---|---|
| Islands are 2–3 miles off N | May–Jul Adult £5, Child £2.50 |
| Northumberland coast. Take B1340, | All other times £4, £2 |
| then a boat from Seahouses harbour | **Contact** |
| **Opening** | The Sheiling, 8 St Adams, |
| Please phone for details | Seahouses NE68 7SR |
| | t 01665 721099 |
| | w nationaltrust.org.uk |

891 Dunston

# Whickham Thorns Outdoor Activity Centre

1 hr+    All year

This centre offers a wide range of activities, including climbing, skiing, snow boarding, mountain biking, orienteering and archery. There are snowboarding and skiing courses for beginners, activity days and mountain bikes for hire.

* High-ropes aerial assault course new in 2005
* First boulder park in the North East

| Location | Admission |
|----------|-----------|
| Off A1 on opposite side of motorway from MetroCentre | Free. Please phone for activity prices |
| **Opening** | **Contact** |
| Daily: Mon–Fri 11am–10pm, Sat 11am–6.30pm, Sun 12noon–3pm; closed Bank Hols Please phone for details | Market Lane, Dunston, Gateshead NE11 9NX t 0191 433 5767 w gateshead.gov.uk |

892 Gateshead

# BALTIC

1 hr+    All year

A major new international centre for contemporary art, situated on the south bank of the River Tyne. Housed in a 1950s grain warehouse (part of the former Baltic Flour Mills), BALTIC is a site for the production, presentation and experience of contemporary art.

* Constantly changing programme of exhibitions
* Displays of work by artists in residence

| Location | Contact |
|----------|---------|
| Gateshead Quayside, 10 min walk from town centre | South Shore Road, Gateshead NE8 3BA |
| **Opening** | t 0191 478 1810 |
| Times vary, please phone for details or visit the website | w balticmill.com e info@balticmill.com |
| **Admission** | |
| Free | |

893 Jarrow

# Bede's World & St Paul's Church

3 hrs    All year

The extraordinary life of the Venerable Bede (AD 673–735) left a rich legacy that is celebrated today at Bede's World, where Bede lived and worked 1,300 years ago. Visitors can explore the site of the Anglo-Saxon monastery of St Paul and medieval monastic ruins.

* Herb garden based on Anglo-Saxon & medieval plants
* Anglo-Saxon demo farm, complete with animals

| Location | Admission |
|----------|-----------|
| Near S end of Tyne tunnel, off A185 | Adult £4.50, Child & Concs £3 |
| **Opening** | **Contact** |
| Apr–Oct Mon–Sat 10am–5.30pm, Sun 12noon–5.30pm, (4.30pm in Nov–Mar) Church closed during services | Church Bank NE32 3DY t 0191 489 2106 w bedesworld.co.uk e visitorinfo@bedesworld.co.uk |

894 Newcastle upon Tyne

# Discovery Museum

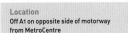
3 hrs    All year

Discovery is the region's biggest free museum and the gateway to fun and facts about life on Tyneside. Explore Newcastle's past from Roman times to the present day, Tyneside's inventions that changed the world, and a fun approach to science, and take a walk through fashion.

* See Roman, Norman & medieval Newcastle upon Tyne
* Find out about life along the River Tyne

| Location | Contact |
|----------|---------|
| Short walk from Newcastle Central station | Blandford Square, Newcastle upon Tyne NE1 4JA |
| **Opening** | t 0191 232 6789 |
| Daily: Mon–Sat 10am–5pm, Sun 2pm–5pm | w twmuseums.org.uk/discovery e discovery@twmuseums.org.uk |
| **Admission** | |
| Free | |

895   Newcastle upon Tyne

# Life Science Centre

2 hrs+   All year

Discover amazing facts about life and understand how DNA spells out instructions for every species. Explore where life comes from and how it works. Meet your 4-billion-year-old family, find out what makes you unique and test your brainpower.

* Open-air ice rink in winter (separate charge)
* Enjoy the thrill of the motion simulator

| Location | Contact |
|---|---|
| Near Central Station | Times Square, Newcastle upon Tyne NE1 4EP |
| **Opening** | t 0191 243 8223 / 243 8210 |
| Daily: Mon–Sat 10am–6pm, Sun 11am–6pm | w lifesciencecentre.org.uk |
| | e bookings@life.org.uk |
| **Admission** | |
| Adult £6.95, Child £4.50, Concs £5.50 | |

896   North Shields

# Stephenson Railway Museum

1 hr   May–Sep

Relive the glorious days of the steam railway at the Stephenson Railway Museum. The museum is home to George Stephenson's *Billy* (a forerunner to the world-famous *Rocket*) and many other engines from the age of steam. Rides on a steam train can be taken.

* Many activities throughtout the year
* Please phone for details of days & times of steam train rides

| Location | Contact |
|---|---|
| Well signed from junction of A19/A1058 | Middle Engine Lane, North Shields NE29 8DX |
| **Opening** | t 01912 007 146 |
| May–Sep Tue–Thu 11am–3pm Sat, Sun & Bank Hols 11am–4pm | w twmuseums.org.uk/stephenson |
| | e stephenson@twmuseums.org.uk |
| **Admission** | |
| Free | |

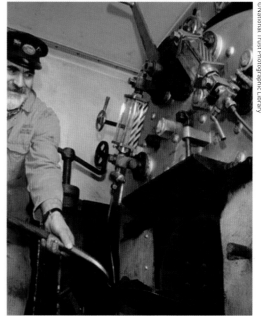

## 897 Rowlands Gill

# Gibside

3 hrs    All year

One of the North's finest landscapes, much of which is a Site of Special Scientific Interest. A forest garden is currently under restoration, embracing many miles of riverside and forest walks. Deer, kingfishers, herons and even badgers may be spotted.

* Outstanding buildings, including a Palladian chapel
* Newly restored greenhouse & stables

**Location**
6 miles SW of Gateshead on B6314

**Opening**
*Grounds* Mar–Oct Tue–Sun & Bank Hols 10am–6pm;
Nov–Feb 10am–4pm
*Chapel* Apr–Oct Tue–Sun
11am–4.30pm

**Admission**
Adult £3.50, Child £2

**Contact**
nr Rowlands Gill,
Burnopfield NE16 6BG

t 01207 541820
w nationaltrust.org.uk
e gibside@nationaltrust.org.uk

## 898 South Shields

# Arbeia Roman Fort

2 hrs    All year

Arbeia was an essential part of a mighty frontier system. Built in approximately AD160, it guarded the entrance to the River Tyne. See excavated remains, stunning reconstructions of original buildings and displays of finds discovered at the site.

* 3 reconstructed buildings on their original sites
* Time Quest archaeological dig

**Location**
10 min walk from South Shields Metro & bus station; signed from Ocean Road

**Opening**
Easter–Sep Mon–Sat 10am–5.30pm,
Sun 1pm–5pm; Oct–Easter Mon–Sat
10am–3.30pm

**Admission**
Free

**Contact**
Baring Street,
South Shields NE33 2BB

t 0191 456 1369
w twmuseums.org.uk

## 899 Sunderland

# Souter Lighthouse

1 hr+    Feb–Nov

When it first shone its light in 1871, Souter was the most advanced lighthouse in the world, and the first purpose-built lighthouse to utilise electricity. Explore the compass room, Victorian keeper's cottage, engine room and huge optic, and enjoy the stunning views.

* When operational, light could be seen from 26 miles
* See the engine room & cramped living quarters

**Location**
2½ miles S of South Shields on A183

**Opening**
Daily: Feb–local half-term 11am–5pm;
Easter–6 Nov Sat–Thu 11am–5pm
(last admission 4.30pm)

**Admission**
Adult £3.80, Child £2.20

**Contact**
Coast Road, Whitburn,
Sunderland SR6 7NH

t 0191 529 3161
w nationaltrust.org.uk
e souter@nationaltrust.org.uk

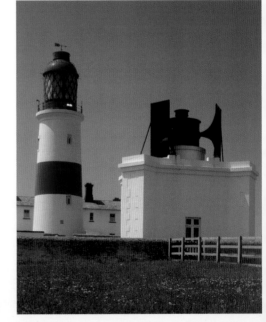

# 900 Sunderland

## Sunderland Museum & Winter Gardens

  4 hrs  All year

Hands-on exhibits and interactive displays tell the story of Sunderland from its prehistoric past through to the present day. The art gallery features paintings by L S Lowry alongside Victorian masterpieces. The Winter Gardens contain more than 1,500 flowers and plants.

* Good facilities for disabled visitors
* Many educational exhibits

**Location**
In centre on Burdon Road

**Opening**
Daily: Mon–Sat 10am–5pm, Sun 2pm–5pm

**Admission**
Free

**Contact**
Burdon Road,
Sunderland SR1 1PP
t  0191 553 2323
w  twmuseums.org.uk/sunderland
e  sunderland@twmuseums.org.uk

# 901 Tynemouth

## Blue Reef Aquarium

  1 hr+    All year

Overlooking the North Sea, the aquarium has a gigantic ocean display complete with underwater tunnel and is home to hundreds of tropical marine species. There's a nursery with newborn creatures, frogs, predators and an octopus that can unscrew jam-jar lids.

* See Asian short-clawed otters

**Location**
From A19 take A1058 to town centre & follow brown tourist signs

**Opening**
Daily: Mar–Oct 10am–5pm;
Nov–Feb 10am–4pm

**Admission**
Adult £5.50, Child £3.75, Concs £4.95

**Contact**
Grand Parade,
Tynemouth NE30 4JF
t  0191 258 1031
w  bluereefaquarium.co.uk
e  tynemouth@bluereefaquarium.
   co.uk

# 902 Tynemouth

## Tynemouth Priory & Castle

  1 hr  All year

A burial place of saints and kings, this commanding castle has provided defence against the Vikings, medieval Scotland, Napoleon and C20 Germany. The Benedictine priory was founded in 1090 on the site of an ancient Anglian monastery.

* Restored magazines of a coastal defence gun battery on view at weekends

**Location**
In Tynemouth, near North Pier

**Opening**
Daily: Apr–Sep 10am–6pm; Oct 10am–4pm; Nov–Mar Thu–Mon 10am–4pm

**Admission**
Adult £3.30, Child £1.70, Concs £2.50

**Contact**
Tynemouth
t  0191 257 1090
w  english-heritage.org.uk

# 903 Wallsend

## Segedunum Roman Fort, Baths & Museum

  2 hrs+  All year

For almost 300 years Segedunum, which means 'strong fort', was home to 600 Roman soldiers and was the last outpost of Hadrian's Wall. Today the complex combines the excavated remains with reconstructions and hands-on museum displays of life in Roman Britain.

* The most extensively excavated site in Britain
* 100ft-high viewing tower plus audio guide

**Location**
1 min walk from Wallsend Metro & bus station

**Opening**
Apr–Aug 9.30am–5.30pm;
Sep–Oct 10am–5pm;
Nov–Mar 10am–3.30pm

**Admission**
Adult £3.50, Child & Concs £1.95

**Contact**
Buddle Street, Wallsend NE28 6HR
t  0191 236 9347
w  twmuseums.org.uk

904 Washington

# Washington Old Hall

2 hrs   Apr–Oct

From 1183 this house was the family home of George Washington's direct ancestors, who took their surname from the village of Washington. The manor remained in the family until 1613. Mementoes of the American connection and the War of Independence are on display.

\* Fine collection of blue & white Delftware
\* Jacobean-style garden

**Location**
5 miles W of Sunderland, well signed

**Opening**
*House* Apr–Oct Sun–Wed 11am–5pm;
open Good Fri

**Admission**
Adult £3.80, Child £2.30

**Contact**
The Avenue,
Washington Village NE38 7LE
t  0191 416 6879
w  nationaltrust.org

905 Washington

# Wildfowl & Wetlands Trust Washington

3 hrs   All year

Ideally placed to provide a stopover and wintering habitat for migratory waterbirds after their passage over the North Sea, this recreated wetland provides large flocks of curlew and redshank with a safe place to roost and herons with a place to breed.

\* Nuthatch sighted in 2003 for first time in 10 years
\* See waders, kingfishers, snipe, shovelers & flamingoes

**Location**
E of Washington, 4 miles from A1(M)

**Opening**
Daily: *summer* 9.30am–5.30pm;
*winter* 9.30am–4pm

**Admission**
Adult £5.95, Child £3.75, Concs £4.75

**Contact**
Pattinson, Washington NE38 8LE
t  0191 416 5454
w  wwt.org.uk
e  info.washington@wwt.org.uk

Ring of Brodgar, Orkney

# Scotland

Central Scotland  Grampian
Highlands & Islands  Southern Scotland

Outer Hebrides

Pabbay
Berneray

Taransay
Harris
Scalpay

Shiant
Islands

Rudha
Hallagro
Ronay

BERNERAY

Rudha Maddadh
(Lochmaddy)

Huishinish
Point

Gallan
Head

Leitam
(Tarbert)
Island

WESTERN ISLES

Stearnabhagh
(Stornoway)

Isle of
Lewis

Rudha Rhobhanais
(Butt of Lewis)

Port Nis
(Port of Ness)

Cellar Head

Eye Peninsula

976

983

981

Poolewe

deg

Uig

Portree

Raasay

Rona

Rudha
Reidh

Greenstone
Point

Lochcarron

Strome Ferry

Shieldaig

Kinlochewe

Torridon

Gairloch

Aultbea

Ullapool

Lochinver

Oykel Bridge

Cape Wrath

Durness

Whiten
Head

st Highlands

Achnasheen

Garve

Dingwall

Alness

Invergordon

Bonar Bridge

Inverness

969

Nairn

Cromarty

Dornoch

Tain

984

Lairg

Altnaharra

Tongue

Bettyhill

Kinbrace

Strathy
Point

Melvich

Scrabster

Thurso

Torbat
Ness

Helmsdale

Latheron

Dunnet
Head

Castletown

Mainland

Kirkwall

Island of Stroma

Duncansby Head

John O'Groats

Ness Head

Wick

Forres

963

MORAY

Elgin

Lossiemouth

Buckie

Cullen

Dufftown

962

Keith

Banff

Huntly

Turriff

Macduff

Fraserburgh

964

965

Peterhead

Ellon

Aberlour

Grantow-

## 906 Aberfeldy

# Aberfeldy Watermill

1 hr    All year

The mill, built in 1825 and renovated in the early 1980s, has had further renovations to open it in this present form. The original machinery has been retained and the huge 5m waterwheel can usually be seen in operation generating electricity to power its lighting.

\* Book shop & gallery
\* Booked events throughout the year

**Location**
Aberfeldy is on A827 between Loch Tay and Pitlochry

**Opening**
Daily: Mon–Sat 9.30am–5.30pm
Sun 12noon–5pm

**Admission**
Free

**Contact**
Mill Street, Aberfeldy PH15 2BG

t 01887 822896
w aberfeldymill.com
e info@aberfeldymill.com

## 907 Aberfeldy

# Highland Adventure Safaris

2 hrs    All year

An exciting way to experience the exhilaration and freedom of this beautiful part of the Highlands. Visitors can bring the great outdoors a little closer by trying out Land Rovers on Ecotours, wildlife-watching trips or an exciting off-road driving experience.

\* Families, groups or individuals catered for
\* Skills courses available

**Location**
From A827 at Aberfeldy, follow B846 for 2 miles past Castle Menzies until you see the signs

**Opening**
Daily: 9am–5pm
Please phone for details

**Admission**
Prices vary, please phone for details

**Contact**
Drumdewan, Aberfeldy,
Perthshire PH15 2JQ

t 01887 820071
w highlandadventuresafaris.co.uk
e info@highlandadventuresafaris.
co.uk

## 908 Aberfoyle

# Forest Hills Watersports

½–1 day    All year

Based on the banks of Loch Ard and accessible by motor-boat, canoe, kayak and sailing boat, the centre offers a multitude of activities for all ages and abilities. Sailing, canoeing, fishing, quad biking and off-road driving are just some of the courses on offer.

\* Equipment available for hire
\* Courses taught by qualified instructors

**Location**
Off junction 10 of M9 & junction 16 of M8. Follow signs for Aberfoyle, then to Forest Hills Watersports, 4 miles along B829

**Opening**
Daily: summer 9.30am–7pm
winter 10.30am–5pm

**Admission**
Activities priced individually

**Contact**
Kinlochard, Aberfoyle,
Stirlingshire FK8 3TL

t 01877 387775
w goforth.co.uk
e info@goforth.co.uk

## 909 Arbroath

# Arbroath Abbey

2 hrs+    All year

This was the site of the signing of the Declaration of Arbroath in 1320, when Scotland's nobles affirmed their allegiance to Robert the Bruce as their king. The recent addition of a visitor centre has reinforced its reputation as one of Scotland's most important historical places.

\* Audio-visual facilities
\* Displays on abbey life

**Location**
On A92, in town centre

**Opening**
Daily: Apr–Sep 9.30am–6.30pm;
Oct–Mar 9.30am–4.30pm

**Admission**
Adult £3.30, Child £1, Concs £2.50

**Contact**
Arbroath, Angus DD11 1EG

t 01241 878756
w historic-scotland.gov.uk
e hs.explorer@scotland.gsi.gov.uk

## 910 Crieff

# Auchingarrich Wildlife Centre

2 hrs+    All year

This award-winning centre features the Highland Cattle Centre. You can see these majestic beasts, stroke them and feed them. Other animals include wallabies, raccoons, otters, chipmunks, porcupines and Scotland's largest collection of waterfowl and ornamental birds.

* More than 150 species of animals & birds
* Hatchings every day Easter–October

| Location | Contact |
|---|---|
| On B827, 2 miles N of Comrie | Glascorrie Road, Crieff, Perthshire PH6 2JS |
| Opening | |
| Daily: 10am–5pm | t 01764 679469 |
| | e auchingarrich@wilton.sol.co.uk |
| Admission | |
| Adult £5.50, Child & Concs £4 | |

## 911 Crieff

# Drummond Castle Gardens

1 hr    May–Oct

Drummond Castle Gardens are thought to be Scotland's most important formal gardens and are certainly among the finest in Europe. The magnificent Italianate parterre was first laid in the C17 by John Drummond and it was renewed in the 1950s.

* Charles I's sundial
* Gardens featured in the film *Rob Roy*

| Location | Admission |
|---|---|
| Off A822, 2 miles S of Crieff | Adult £4, Child £1.50, Concs £3 |
| Opening | Contact |
| Daily: May–Oct 1pm–5pm; | Muthill, nr Crieff, Perthshire PH5 2AA |
| Also open at Easter | t 01764 681257 |
| | w drummondcastlegardens.co.uk |
| | e info@drummondcastle.sol.co.uk |

## 912 Crieff

# The Famous Grouse Experience at Glenturret Distillery

1 hr+    All year

Scotland's only five-star, Bafta award-winning interactive whisky attraction is fun for young and old alike. Crack some ice, splash in the water and do a jigsaw puzzle with your feet or 'fly' over the wondrous beauty of Scotland on the back of a grouse.

* Audio-visual presentation
* Award-winning famous restaurant

| Location | Contact |
|---|---|
| Off A85, 1 mile from Crieff | Glenturret Distillery, The Hosh, Crieff, Perthshire PH7 4HA |
| Opening | |
| Daily: 10am–6pm (last tours at 4.30pm) | t 01764 656565 |
| | w famousgrouse.com |
| Admission | e enquiries@famousgrouse.com |
| *Tours* Adult £3.95–£6.95 depending on tour, Child £2.50 | |

© National Trust Scotland

## 913 Crieff

# Stuart Crystal Factory Shop

½ hr    All year

Come and see the wonderful craft of making crystalware. Be tempted by a large display of Stuart Crystal, Waterford Crystal and Wedgwood china, with factory seconds. There is also an engraving service for that personalised special gift or memento.

* Souvenir gift shop
* Chip repair service

| Location | Admission |
|----------|-----------|
| Signed from town centre | Free |
| **Opening** | **Contact** |
| Jun–Sep daily 10am–6pm; | Muthill Road, Crieff, |
| Oct–May Mon–Sat 10am–5pm, | Perthshire PH7 4HQ |
| Sun 11am–5pm | t 01764 654004 |

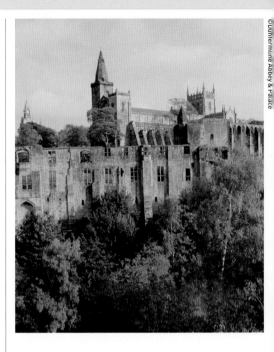

©Dunfermline Abbey & Palace

## 914 Cupar

# Hill of Tarvit Mansion House & Garden

2 hrs    Easter–Oct

A fascinating mansion house, built in 1906, reflects the period 1870–1920, when Scotland was the industrial workshop of the world. It is a showcase for Flemish tapestries, Chinese porcelain and bronzes, French and English furniture and paintings by many eminent artists.

* Edwardian-style interior
* Set in beautiful gardens

| Location | Contact |
|----------|---------|
| Off A916, 2 miles S of Cupar | Cupar, Fife KY15 5PB |
| **Opening** | t 01334 653127 |
| Easter Sat & Sun 1pm–5pm; | w nts.org.uk |
| May–Sep daily 1pm–5pm | e hilloftarvit@nts.org.uk |
| **Admission** | |
| Please phone for details | |

## 915 Dunfermline

# Dunfermline Abbey & Palace

1 hr    All year

The elegant ruins of Dunfermline Abbey are what is left of a great Benedictine abbey founded by Queen Margaret in the C11. Robert the Bruce was buried in the choir and the royal palace next door, also partially ruined, was the birthplace of Charles I.

* Substantial parts of the abbey nave remain
* Next to the ruin of the royal palace

| Location | Contact |
|----------|---------|
| Off M90, in town centre | St Margaret Street, Dunfermline, |
| **Opening** | Fife KY12 7PE |
| Apr–Sep daily 9.30am–6.30pm; | t 01383 739026 |
| Oct–Mar Mon–Wed & Sat | w historic-scotland.gov.uk |
| 9.30am–4.30pm, Sun 2pm–4.30pm | |
| **Admission** | |
| Adult £2.50, Child £1, Concs £1.90 | |

916 Dunfermline

# Knockhill Racing Circuit

3 hrs      All year

Scotland's national motorsport centre features major international and national motorsport events for both cars and bikes. It's also a major venue for corporate entertainment, as visitors can drive race and rally cars, go off-road on a 4 × 4 course and do many other activities.

* Hands-on driving experiences
* Relaxing hospitality at race events

| Location | Contact |
|---|---|
| Signed from M90 junction 4 | Dunfermline, Fife KY12 9TF |
| **Opening** | t  01383 723337 |
| Daily: 9am–6pm | w  knockhill.co.uk |
| **Admission** | e  enquiries@knockhill.co.uk |
| Prices vary depending on the event, please phone for details | |

917 Dundee

# Atholl Country Life Museum

1 hr      May–Sep

This museum of local life has exhibitions on rural trades and agricultural and domestic life. Displays cover a wide variety of subjects – road, rail and postal services, the kirk and school, and photographs of the local way of life.

* Gamekeeper's corner
* Display of stuffed wild animals

| Location | Admission |
|---|---|
| Turn off A9 for Blair Atholl, 7 miles N of Pitlochry | Adult £3, Child £1, Concs £2.50 |
| **Opening** | **Contact** |
| Daily: Easter & May–Sep 1.30pm–5pm; Jul–Aug from 10am on weekdays | Blair Atholl, Pitlochry, Perthshire PH18 5SP |
| | t  01796 481232 |
| | w  blairatholl.org.uk |
| | e  janet.cam@virgin.net |

918 Dundee

# Discovery Point

1 hr+      All year

Climb aboard Captain Scott's royal research ship, *Discovery*, which was originally built in Dundee to sail to the Antarctic and is now berthed on the River Tay and open to visitors. The ship represents the city's shipbuilders' greatest achievement.

* State-of-the-art multimedia exhibitions
* Voted Scottish Family Attraction of the Year 2004

| Location | Admission |
|---|---|
| City centre, opposite train station | Adult £6.45, Child £3.85, Concs £4.90 |
| **Opening** | **Contact** |
| Daily: Apr–Oct Mon–Sat 10am–6pm, Sun 11am–6pm; Nov–Mar Mon–Sat 10am–5pm, Sun 11am–5pm | Discovery Quay, Dundee DD1 4XA |
| | t  01382 201245 |
| | w  rrsdiscovery.com |
| | e  info@dundeeheritage.co.uk |

## 919 East Fortune
# Museum of Flight

2 hrs+     All year

Man's fascination with flight is celebrated at this protected WWI and WWII airfield. Experience the highs and lows of the supersonic Concorde. See the R34 airship which took off from East Fortune in 1919 on a record-breaking transatlantic flight.

* Newest display, a Britten-Norman Islander, an aircraft described as the most versatile in the world

 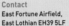

| Location | Contact |
|---|---|
| Off A1, 20m E of Edinburgh | East Fortune Airfield, East Lothian EH39 5LF |
| Opening | |
| 16 Mar–Oct daily 10am–5pm; Nov–Mar Sat–Sun 10am–4pm | t 01620 880308 w nms.ac.uk/flight/ |
| Admission | |
| Adult £5, Child free, Concs £4 | |

## 920 Edinburgh
# Edinburgh Castle

1 hr+     All year

A majestic landmark that dominates the city's skyline, Edinburgh Castle is the top visitor attraction in Scotland. Perched on an extinct volcano and offering stunning views, this fortress is a powerful national symbol and part of Edinburgh's World Heritage site.

* Guided & audio tours
* The Scottish Crown Jewels & the Stone of Destiny

| Location | Admission |
|---|---|
| In city centre, at top of Royal Mile | Adult £9.80, Child £3.50, Concs £7.50 |
| Opening | Contact |
| Daily: Apr–Sep 9am–6pm; Oct–Mar 9am–5pm | Castle Hill, Edinburgh EH1 2NG t 0131 225 9846 w historic-scotland.gov.uk |

## 921 Edinburgh

# Edinburgh Dungeon

1 hr  All year

A unique combination of real history, horror and humour bring gruesome goings-on back to life in the C21. Live actors, special effects and boat rides transport you back to those black bleak times. Are you brave enough to delve into the darkest chapters of history?

\* Opened in 2005 – Haunted Labyrinth
\* Horror rides

| Location | Contact |
|---|---|
| In city centre | 31 Market Street, Edinburgh EH1 1QB |
| **Opening** | t 0131 240 1000 |
| Daily: Sep–Oct 10am–7pm; | w thedungeons.com |
| Nov–Feb Mon–Fri 11am–4pm, | e edinburghdungeon@ |
| Sat–Sun 11am–4.30pm | merlinentertainments.biz |
| **Admission** | |
| Adult £8.95, Child (10–14) £6.95, Child (4–9) £4.95, Child (under 4) free | |

## 922 Edinburgh

# Edinburgh Zoo

4 hrs  All year

This is Scotland's most popular wildlife attraction, with more than 1,000 animals, including meerkats, pygmy hippos, tigers, a red panda and blue poison arrow frogs. Set in beautiful parkland, it has the world's biggest penguin pool, home to Europe's largest colony of penguins.

\* African Plains Experience & Magic Forest
\* Hilltop safari, tour & maze

| Location | Contact |
|---|---|
| 10 mins from city centre | 134 Corstorphine Road, Edinburgh EH12 6TS |
| **Opening** | t 0131 334 9171 |
| Daily: Apr–Sep 9am–6pm; | w edinburghzoo.org.uk |
| Oct & Mar 9am–5pm; | e info@edinburghzoo.org.uk |
| Nov–Feb 9am–4.30pm | |
| **Admission** | \*Adult (over 17) must accompany |
| Adult £9, Child\* £6, Concs £6.50 | children under 14 at all times |

## 923 Edinburgh

# Museum of Scotland

2 hrs+  All year

This museum presents, for the first time, the history of Scotland – its land, its people and their achievements – through the rich national collections. The stunning series of galleries takes you from Scotland's geological beginnings through time right up to the C20.

\* More than 10,000 artefacts
\* Same site as Royal Museum of Scotland

| Location | Contact |
|---|---|
| Off A7 South Bridge, in city centre | Chambers Street, Edinburgh EH1 1JF |
| **Opening** | t 0131 247 4422 |
| Daily: Mon–Sat 10am–5pm, | w nms.ac.uk |
| Tue 10am–8pm, Sun 12noon–5pm | e info@nms.ac.uk |
| **Admission** | |
| Free | |

## 924 Edinburgh

# National Portrait Gallery

2 hrs  All year

The gallery provides a visual history of Scotland, told through portraits of those who shaped it: royals and rebels, poets and philosophers, heroes and villains. All the portraits of Scots are by well-known masters, including Kokoschka and Van Dyck.

\* Works by Gainsborough, Copley & Rodin
\* Unparalleled collection of Scottish portraits

| Location | Contact |
|---|---|
| E end of Queen Street, in city centre | 1 Queen Street, Edinburgh EH2 1JD |
| **Opening** | t 0131 624 6200 |
| Daily: 10am–5pm, Thu 10am–7pm; | w nationalgalleries.org |
| 1 Jan 12noon–5pm | e enquiries@nationalgalleries.org |
| **Admission** | |
| Free | |

# National Gallery of Scotland

½–2 hrs    All year

The gallery is home to Scotland's greatest collection of European paintings and sculpture, ranging from the Renaissance to Post-Impressionism. One of Edinburgh's major attractions, it is also one of the finest galleries of its size in the world.

\* Includes masterpieces by Van Dyck & Tiepolo
\* Comprehensive collection of Scottish paintings

| Location | Contact |
|---|---|
| Off Princes Street, in city centre | The Mound, Edinburgh EH2 2EL |
| **Opening** | t 0131 624 6200 |
| Daily: Mon–Wed Fri–Sun 10am–5pm, | w nationalgalleries.org |
| Thu 10am–7pm | e enquiries@nationalgalleries.org |
| **Admission** | |
| Free, charges for some exhibitions | |

# Our Dynamic Earth

2 hrs    All year

See how Earth works! Take a walk through Scotland's geological history and travel back in time to follow the creation of planet Earth.  Be shaken by a volcano, feel the chill of polar ice and get caught in a tropical rainstorm. Look to the future – you decide what could happen!

\* Live 4,500 million years in a day

| Location | Admission |
|---|---|
| At foot of Arthur's Seat, adjacent to new Scottish Parliament | Adult £8.95, Child &Concs £5.45 |
| | **Contact** |
| **Opening** | 112 Holyrood Road, |
| Apr–Oct daily 10am–5pm; | Edinburgh EH8 8AS |
| Jul–Aug daily 10am–6pm; | |
| Nov–Mar Wed–Sun 10am–5pm | t 0131 550 7800 |
| (last admission 70mins before closing) | w dynamicearth.co.uk |
| | e enquiries@dynamicearth.co.uk |

# Palace of Holyroodhouse

1 hr    All year

Originally founded in 1128 as a monastery, the Palace of Holyroodhouse in Edinburgh is the Queen's official residence in Scotland, and is no stranger to royalty, as Mary, Queen of Scots, among others, lived here. In fact, the palace has many associations with Scottish history.

\* New Queen's Gallery
\* One of the finest art collections in the world

| Location | Contact |
|---|---|
| At bottom of Royal Mile | Royal Mile, Edinburgh  EH8 8DX |
| **Opening** | t 0131 556 5100 |
| Daily: Apr–Oct 9.30am–6pm; Nov–Mar | w royal.gov.uk |
| 9.30am–4.30pm | e information@royalcollection.org.uk |
| **Admission** | |
| Adult £8.50, Child £4.50, Concs £7 | |
| (by timed ticket slots) | |

## 928 Edinburgh

# Royal Botanic Garden Edinburgh

2 hrs   All year

Founded in the C17 as a 'physic garden', growing medicinal plants, the Royal Botanic Garden is now acknowledged as one of the finest gardens in the world. It's a place to rest and relax, away from the city's hustle and bustle, and is home to unusual and beautiful plants.

\* Guided & themed tours
\* Refurbished Victorian palm house

| Location | Contact |
|---|---|
| Off A902, 1 mile N of city centre | 20A Inverleith Row, Edinburgh EH3 5LR |
| Opening · | t 0131 552 7171 |
| Daily: Apr–Sep 10am–7pm; | w rbge.org.uk |
| Mar Oct 10am–6pm; | e info@rbge.org.uk |
| Nov–Feb 10am–4pm | |
| Admission | |
| Free, charges apply to glasshouses | |

## 929 Edinburgh

# The Spirit of the Tattoo

1 hr   All year

Many visitors to Edinburgh may never have the chance to see the Tattoo in August, so this year-round attraction, which presents the Tattoo's colourful story, will provide visitors with a comprehensive review of Scotland's matchless spectacle of music, dance and display.

\* Interactive exhibition and film theatre
\* Rooftop café

| Location | Contact |
|---|---|
| In city centre, on Royal Mile just below castle | 555 Castlehill, The Royal Mile, Edinburgh EH1 2ND |
| Opening | t 0131 225 9661 |
| Daily: Mon–Sat 10am–5pm, | w edinburgh-tattoo.co.uk |
| Sun 11am–5pm | e administration@edintattoo.co.uk |
| Admission | |
| Free | |

## 930 Edinburgh

# St Giles' Cathedral

½ hr+   All year

This is the High Kirk of Edinburgh and it has been at the heart of the city's spiritual life for at least 900 years. A living church with an active congregation, it also welcomes visitors who come to experience the unique atmosphere of continuing worship and ages-old history.

\* Mother church of Presbyterianism
\* One of Scotland's most historically important buildings

| Location | Admission |
|---|---|
| On Royal Mile, in city centre | Free, recommended donation of £1 per person |
| Opening | |
| Daily: May–Sep Mon–Fri 9am–7pm, | Contact |
| Sat 9am–5pm, Sun 1–5pm; | High Street, Edinburgh EH1 1RE |
| Oct–Apr Mon–Sat 9am–5pm, | |
| Sun 1pm–5pm | t 0131 225 9442 |
| | w stgilescathedral.org.uk |
| | e info@stgilescathedral.org.uk |

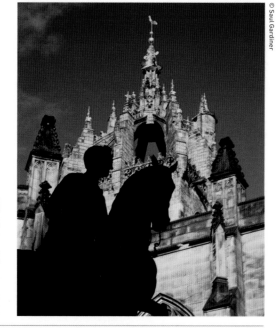

## 931 Fife

# Scottish Deer Centre

2 hrs + | All year

This 55-acre park is home to more than 140 deer representing 9 species. Other attractions include ranger tours, dramatic birds of prey demonstrations, a treetop walkway, viewing platforms, scenic pathways, and indoor and outdoor adventure play areas for children.

* Falconry displays
* Wolf wood

| Location | Contact |
|----------|---------|
| On the outskirts of Cupar, 12 miles from St Andrews on A91 | Bow-of-Fife, Cupar, Fife KY15 4NQ |
| Opening | |
| Please phone for details | t 01337 810391 |
| Admission | w tsdc.co.uk |
| Adult £5.10, Child £3.55, Concs £4.05 Under 3's are free | e info@tsdc.co.uk |

## 932 Glamis by Forfar

# Glamis Castle

2 hrs+ | Mar–Dec

Glamis Castle has a long and colourful history. It has a legendary association, at least according to Shakespeare, with the C11 Macbeth and has a place in C20 history as the childhood home of HM The Queen Mother.

* Rich variety of furnishings, tapestries & art
* Extensive estate & formal gardens

| Location | Contact |
|----------|---------|
| On A94, between Aberdeen & Perth | The Castle Administrator, Estates Office, Glamis by Forfar, Angus DD8 1RJ |
| Opening | |
| Daily: Mar–Oct 10am–6pm; Nov–23 Dec 11am–3pm | t 01307 840393 |
| Admission | w glamis-castle.co.uk |
| Adult £7, Child £3.80, Concs £5.70 | e enquiries@glamis-castle.co.uk |

## 933 Glasgow

# Burrell Collection

½ hr+ | All year

When Sir William Burrell gifted his collection of more than 9,000 works of art to Glasgow, the city acquired one of its greatest collections. He had been an art collector since his teens and the collection constitutes a vast array of works of all periods, from all over the world.

* Medieval art, tapestries, alabasters & stained glass
* Paintings by Degas & Cézanne

| Location | Contact |
|----------|---------|
| 5 miles S of city centre | Pollok Country Park, 2060 Pollokshaws Road, Glasgow G43 1AT |
| Opening | |
| Daily: Mon–Thu & Sat 10am–5pm, Fri & Sun 11am–5pm | t 0141 287 2550 |
| Admission | w glasgowmuseums.com |
| Free | e cls.glasgow.gov.uk |

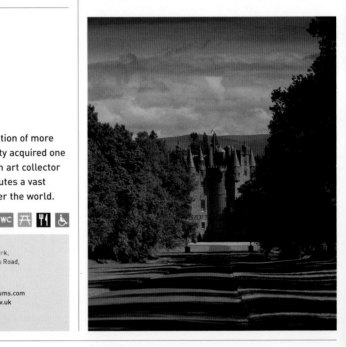

934 Glasgow

# Gallery of Modern Art

½ hr   All year

GoMA is the second most visited contemporary art gallery outside London, offering a thought-provoking programme of temporary exhibitions and workshops. The focus of the gallery is on contemporary social issues, often featuring groups marginalised in today's society.

\* Includes work by Bridget Riley & Scottish artists John Byrne
& Christine Borland & photographer Sebastio Salgado

| Location | Admission |
|---|---|
| In city centre, off Buchanan Street, close to Queen Street & central station | Free |
| Opening | Contact |
| Mon–Tue & Sat 10am–5pm Thu 10am–8pm, Fri & Sun 11am–5pm | Royal Exchange Square, Glasgow G1 3AH |
| | t 0141 229 1996 |
| | w glasgowmuseums.com |

935 Glasgow

# Glasgow Science Centre

2 hrs+   All year

Shake hands with yourself, make a 3D image of your face and see how you will look in years to come. Enjoy more than 300 hands-on and interactive exhibits, take in a live science show, see the latest IMAX® fim, visit the Scottishpower planetarium and observe the stars.

\* IMAX® cinema
\* Several new exhibitions for 2006

| Location | Contact |
|---|---|
| Opposite Scottish Exhibition Centre and the Moat House Hotel on River Clyde | 50 Pacific Quay Glasgow G51 1EA |
| Opening | t 0141 420 5000 |
| Daily: 10am–6pm | w glasgowsciencecentre.org |
| Admission | e admin@gsc.org.uk |
| Adult £6.95, Child & Concs £4.95 | |

936 Glasgow

# Necropolis

1 hr+   All year

The Necropolis stands on a hill to the east of Glasgow Cathedral, just a short walk across the Bridge of Sighs. The monument to John Knox, which was erected in 1825, dominates the hill. This Victorian cemetery was modelled on Père-Lachaise in Paris.

\* Glasgow's great architects are buried here, including
Thomson, Wilson, Baird, Bryce & Hamilton

| Location | Contact |
|---|---|
| Near Glasgow Cathedral | Cemeteries and Crematoria, 1st Floor, 20 Trongate, Glasgow G1 5ES |
| Opening | t 0141 287 3961 |
| Daily: 8am–4.30pm | |
| Admission | |
| Free | |

## 937 Glasgow
# People's Palace

2 hrs+    All year

The People's Palace is Glasgow's social history museum and tells the story of the people and city of Glasgow from 1760 to the present. There are paintings, prints and photographs displayed alongside a wealth of historic artefacts, film and computer interactives.

* Discover how a family lived in a typical single-end Glasgow tenement

| Location | Admission |
|---|---|
| Short walk from city centre | Free |
| Opening | Contact |
| Daily: Mon–Thu & Sat 10am–5pm, Fri & Sun 11am–5pm | Glasgow Green, Glasgow G40 1AT |
| | t 0141 271 2951 |
| | w glasgowmuseums.com |

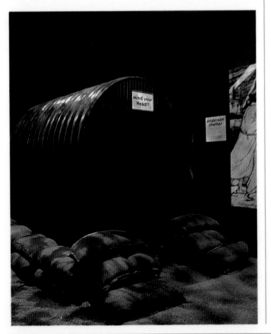

## 938 Glasgow
# The Piping Centre

½ hr    All year

Nothing makes a Scotsman feel more patriotic than the sound of a pipe band. This is the sound of Scotland, a haunting melody or a noise fit to lift the soul. At the Museum of Piping you can witness hundreds of years of Scottish heritage, played out before your eyes and ears.

* Outstanding collection of piping artefacts
* Study the history & origins of bagpiping

| Location | Contact |
|---|---|
| In Glasgow, off junction 16 of M8 & along A804 towards the E | 30–34 McPhater Street, Glasgow G4 0HW |
| Opening | t 0141 353 0220 |
| Daily: 9am–9pm; closed Sun in winter | w thepipingcentre.co.uk |
| Admission | e reception@thepipingcentre.co.uk |
| Adult £3, Child & Concs £2 | |

## 939 Glasgow
# Scottish Football Museum

2 hrs+    All year

The world's first national football museum is housed at Hampden Park, the oldest continuously used international ground in the world. It is owned by Queen's Park FC, the oldest association team in Scotland (founded 1867) and one with an unrivalled history.

* World's most impressive collection of football memorabilia, covering 140 years of football history

| Location | Admission |
|---|---|
| Take junction 1 off M77, on to B768 (Titwood Road), right on to B766 (Battlefield Road), then Kings Park Road and left into Kinghorn Drive | Adult £5, Child & Concs £2.50 |
| | Contact |
| | Hampden Park, Glasgow G42 9BA |
| Opening | t 0141 616 6139 |
| Mon–Sat 10am–5pm, Sun 11am–5pm | w scottishfootballmuseum.org.uk |
| | e museumInfo@scottishfootball museum.org.uk |

## 940 Glasgow

# Tall Ship in Glasgow Harbour

1 hr+    All year

Explore the tall ship *Glenlee*, one of only five Clyde-built sailing ships that remain afloat. Built in 1896, she operated as a long-haul cargo vessel before being bought by the Spanish Navy as a training ship. She has circumnavigated the globe four times.

\* Exhibition tells the *Glenlee* story
\* Visitor centre

**Location**
Off M8 junction 19, follow brown thistle signs

**Opening**
Daily: Mar–Nov 10am–5pm
Dec–Feb 11am–4pm

**Admission**
Adult £4.95, Child £2.50, Concs £3.75
(Adult price includes 1 child)

**Contact**
100 Stobe Cross Road, Glasgow G3 8QQ

t  0141 222 2513
w  thetallship.com
e  info@thetallship.com

## 941 Kinross

# Loch Leven Castle

2 hrs    Apr–Oct

The dramatic ruins of this castle stand on an island in Loch Leven. This late C14 or early C15 tower is infamous as the place where Mary, Queen of Scots, was imprisoned in 1567. She escaped the following year, but her ghost is alleged to haunt the castle to this day.

\* The Loch is now a National Nature Reserve

**Location**
Accessible by boat from Scottish Angling Academy in Kinross, signposted from A922

**Opening**
Daily: Apr–Sep 9.30am–5.15pm;
Oct Mon, Wed–Thu, Sat–Sun
9.30am–3.15pm

**Admission**
Adult £3.50, Child £1.30, Concs £2.50

**Contact**
Kinross, Perthshire KY13 7AR

t  07778 040483
w  historic-scotland.gov.uk

## 942 Kircaldy

# Craigencalt Ecology Centre

1 hr    All year

The Ecology Centre provides environmental education and information across a wide range of subjects. It is the home of the UK's first 'Earthship', a building created from waste and natural materials to be self-sufficient in energy and water.

\* Community woodland & organic garden

**Location**
Take B923 off A921 between Burntisland & Kirkcaldy. Located beside Kinghorn Loch

**Opening**
Daily: 10am–5pm
Earthship by arrangement

**Admission**
Free

**Contact**
Craigencalt Farm, Kinghorn
Fife KY3 9YG

t  01592 891567
w  cfec.org.uk
e  cfec@freeuk.com

## 943 Kirriemuir

# Barrie's Birthplace

½ hr    Apr–Sep

J M Barrie, the creator of the eternal magic of *Peter Pan*, was born here in 1860. The upper floor is furnished as it was when Barrie lived here. The adjacent house, number 11, houses an exhibition about Barrie's literary and theatrical works.

\* Audio programme
\* Near Kirriemuir Camera Obscura

**Location**
A901/A926 in Kirriemuir, 6 miles NW of Forfar

**Opening**
Jul–Aug daily 11am–5pm;
Apr–Jun & Sep Sat–Wed 12noon–5pm;
Sun all year 1pm–5pm

**Admission**
Adult £5, Child & Concs £4

**Contact**
9 Brechin Road, Kirriemuir,
Angus DD8 4BX

t  01575 572646
w  nts.org.uk/barrie.html
e  barriesbirthplace@nts.org.uk

## 944 Lanark

# New Lanark World Heritage Site

2 hrs+    All year

The cotton mills of New Lanark were founded more than 200 years ago and the village became famous for the work of mill-owner Robert Owen, who provided a decent life for the villagers. Today New Lanark has been restored and visitors can explore this fascinating village.

* Award-winning visitor centre
* Accommodation available at New Lanark Mill Hotel

| Location | Contact |
|---|---|
| Off M74 junction 13, signed off all routes | New Lanark Mills, South Lanarkshire ML11 9DB |
| **Opening** | t  01555 661345 |
| Daily: Jun–Aug 10.30am–5pm; Sep–May 11am–5pm | w  newlanark.org |
| | e  trust@newlanark.org |
| **Admission** | |
| Adult £5.95, Child & Concs £3.95 | |

## 945 Leith

# The Royal Yacht *Britannia*

1 hr+    All year

Now permanently moored in Edinburgh's historic port of Leith, *Britannia* welcomes you to its visitor centre, located in Ocean Terminal, Edinburgh's stylish waterfront shopping and leisure development. Then step on board for a self-led audio tour of five decks.

* See royal apartments & crews' quarters
* Children's audio tour

| Location | Admission |
|---|---|
| At Leith Docks, signed from city outskirts | Adult £9, Child £5, Concs £7 |
| **Opening** | **Contact** |
| Daily: Apr–Sep 9.30am–4.30pm; Oct–Mar 10am–3.30pm | Ocean Terminal, Leith Edinburgh EH6 6JJ |
| Pre-booking is advised in Aug | t  0131 555 5566 |
| | w  royalyachtbritannia.co.uk |
| | e  enquiries@tryb.co.uk |

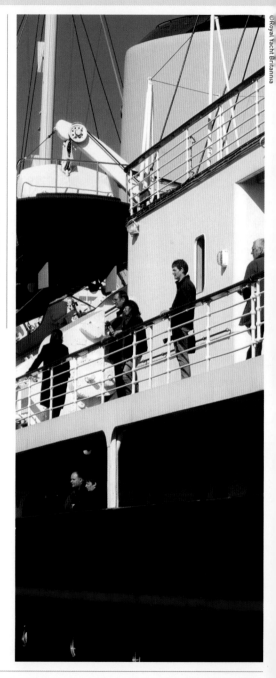

## 946 Linlithgow

# Linlithgow Palace

1 hr · All year

This magnificent ruin of a great royal palace is set in its own park, beside Linlithgow Loch. It was a favoured home of the Stuart kings and queens, from James I (1406–37) onward, and building work from the eras of James I, III, IV, V and VI can be seen, including the Great Hall and chapel.

* Birthplace of James V & Mary, Queen of Scots
* Oldest working fountain in Britain

**Location**
On A803/M9, in town centre

**Opening**
Apr–Sep daily 9.30am–6.30pm;
Oct–Mar Mon–Sat 9.30am–4.30pm,
Sun 2pm–4.30pm

**Admission**
Adult £4, Child £1.60, Concs £3

**Contact**
Kirkgate, Linlithgow, West Lothian
EH49 7AL

t  01506 842896
w  historic-scotland.gov.uk

## 947 Newtongrange

# Scottish Mining Museum

2 hrs · All year

This museum is based at one of the finest surviving examples of a Victorian colliery in Europe, the Lady Victoria Colliery at Newtongrange. A fully accessible, three-storey visitor centre allows everyone to experience the atmosphere and noise of a working pit.

* 2 major exhibitions: The Story of Coal & A Race Apart
* Audio tour with 'magic helmets'

**Location**
On A7, 9 miles S of Edinburgh

**Opening**
Daily: Mar–Oct 10am–5pm;
Nov–Feb 10am–4pm

**Admission**
Adult £4.95 ,Child & Concs £3.30

**Contact**
Lady Victoria Colliery, Newtongrange,
Midlothian EH22 4QN

t  0131 663 7519
w  scottishminingmuseum.com
e  enquiries@scottishminingmuseum
   .com

## 948 North Queensferry

# Deep Sea World

2 hrs+ · All year

Explore the undersea world at the triple award-winning National Aquarium of Scotland. Situated on the banks of the Firth of Forth, below the Forth Railway Bridge, this fascinating attraction ensures a perfect day out for the whole family.

* Seal sanctuary dedicated to orphan & sick seal pups

**Location**
1 mile from M90 on N side of
Forth Road Bridge

**Opening**
Daily: Apr–Aug 10am–6pm;
Sep–Mar Mon–Fri 10am–5pm,
Sat–Sun 10am–6pm
last admission 1 hr before closing

**Admission**
Adult £8.55, Child £6.30, Concs £6.75

**Contact**
North Queensferry, Fife KY11 1JR

t  01383 411411
w  deepseaworld.com
e  info@deepseaworld.co.uk

## 949 Perth

# Scone Palace

1 hr+ · Apr–Oct

In a spectacular setting above the River Tay, Scone Palace has been the seat of parliaments and the crowning place of kings. It has housed the Stone of Destiny and been immortalised in Shakespeare's *Macbeth*, and is regarded by many as the heart of Scottish history.

* One of the finest private collections of furniture in Britain
* Beautiful gardens, including Moot Hill

**Location**
Signed from M90/A9, between
Edinburgh & the Highlands

**Opening**
Daily: Apr–Oct 9.30am–5.30pm

**Admission**
Adult £6.95, Child £4, Concs £5.95

**Contact**
The Administrator, Scone Palace,
Perth, Perthshire PH2 6BD

t  01738 552300
w  scone-palace.co.uk
e  visits@scone-palace.co.uk

## 950 Pittenweem

# Kellie Castle & Garden

2 hrs    All year

Now in the care of the National Trust for Scotland, Kellie Castle contains magnificent plaster ceilings, painted panelling and furniture by Sir Robert Lorimer. A special exhibition commemorates Hew Lorimer's life and work. Take audio tour of the lovely garden.

* Fine example of domestic architecture
* Beautiful walled garden

| Location | Admission |
|---|---|
| On B9171, 3 miles from Pittenweem | *Castle* Adult £8, Child & Concs £5 |
| **Opening** | *Gardens* £3, £2 |
| *Castle* Daily: Easter & May–Sep | **Contact** |
| 1pm–5pm | Pittenweem, Fife KY10 2RF |
| *Gardens* Daily: 9.30am–5.30pm | t 01333 720271 |
| | w nts.org.uk |
| | e info@1001daysout.com |

© National Trust for Scotland

## 951 Pitlochry

# Blair Castle

1 hr+    All year

More than 700 years of Scottish history await you at Blair Castle. See displays of beautiful furniture, fine paintings, arms and armour, china, costumes, lace and embroidery, masonic regalia and Jacobite relics – all of which provide a colourful picture of Scottish life from the C16 to today.

* Spectacular setting in the Strath of Garry
* Guided tours available for parties of more than 12

| Location | Contact |
|---|---|
| At Blair Atholl, N of Pitlochry | Blair Atholl, Pitlochry, |
| **Opening** | Perthshire PH18 5TL |
| Daily: Mar–Oct 9.30am–4.30pm; | t 01796 481207 |
| Nov–Feb Tue & Sat 9.30am–12.30pm | w blair-castle.co.uk |
| **Admission** | e office@blair-castle.co.uk |
| Adult £7.20, Child £4.50, Concs £6.20 | |

## 952 Pitlochry

# Killiecrankie Visitor Centre

½ hr+    Apr–Oct

In 1689 the Pass of Killiecrankie echoed with the sounds of battle, when a Jacobite army defeated the government forces. The spectacular gorge is tranquil now and a fine example of mixed deciduous woodland. The visitor centre explains the battle, natural history and ranger services.

* Site of Special Scientific Interest
* Visitors can watch birds nesting via a remote camera

| Location | Contact |
|---|---|
| On B8079, 3 miles N of Pitlochry | nr Pitlochry, Tayside PH16 5LG |
| **Opening** | t 01796 473233 |
| Daily: Apr–Oct 10am–5.30pm | w nts.org.uk |
| **Admission** | |
| Free. Car park £2 | |

## 953 St Andrews

# British Golf Museum

½ hr+   All year

Come to St Andrews to see the history of golf unfold before your eyes. Imaginative displays are enhanced by stunning interactives that add to the exciting and varied ways of looking at golf's past. A visit to the British Golf Museum is the perfect break from playing golf.

* Regular calendar of events
* Guided walks on the Old Course (summer only)

| Location | Contact |
|---|---|
| Signed from town centre | Bruce Embankment, St Andrews, Fife KY16 9AB |
| **Opening** | |
| Apr–Oct Mon–Sat 9.30am–5.30pm, Sun 10am–5pm; Nov–Mar daily 10am–4pm | t 01334 460046 |
| | w britishgolfmuseum.co.uk |
| | e alisonwood@randagc.org |
| **Admission** | |
| Adult £5, Child £2.75, Concs £4 | |

## 954 St Andrews

# Scotland's Secret Bunker

1 hr+   Apr–Oct

Discover the twilight world of the government's Cold War headquarters. Hidden for more than 40 years beneath a Scottish farmhouse, a tunnel leads to Scotland's Secret Bunker – 24,000 square feet of secret accommodation on two levels, 100 feet underground.

* Built in complete secrecy in the 1950s
* Discover how they would have survived & you wouldn't

| Location | Contact |
|---|---|
| On B940, between St Andrews & Anstruther | Crown Buildings, Troywood, nr St Andrews, Fife KY16 8QH |
| **Opening** | |
| Daily: Apr–Oct 10am–6pm (last admission 5pm) | t 01333 310301 |
| | w secretbunker.co.uk |
| | e mod@secretbunker.co.uk |
| **Admission** | |
| Adult £7.20, Child £4.50, Concs £5.95 | |

## 955 Stirling

# Argyll's Lodging

½ hr   All year

A superb mansion built around an earlier core in about 1630 and further extended by the Earl of Argyll in the 1670s. It is the most impressive town house of its period in Scotland. The principal rooms are now restored to their 1680 state.

* Beautiful furniture & furnishings
* Magnificent restoration

| Location | Contact |
|---|---|
| Near town centre | Castle Wynd, Stirling, Stirlingshire FK8 1EG |
| **Opening** | |
| Daily: Apr–Oct 9.30am–6pm Nov–Mar 9.30am–5pm | t 01786 431319 |
| | w historic-scotland.gov.uk |
| **Admission** | |
| Adult £3.30, Child £1.30, Concs £2.50 | |

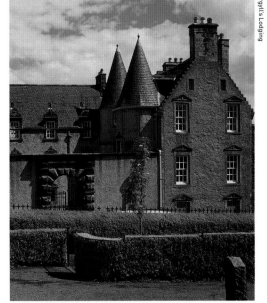

## 956 Stirling

# Bannockburn Heritage Centre

½ hr+    Feb–Dec

Located at one of the most important historical sites in Scotland, this centre offers great insights into the Battle of Bannockburn, Robert the Bruce and William Wallace. Learn about the legendary battle in which Bruce and his army defeated Edward II of England.

\* Wars of independence exhibition
\* Audio-visual presentation of the famous battle

| Location | Admission |
|---|---|
| Off M80/M9 junction 9, 2 miles S of Stirling | Adult £5, Child & Concs £4 |
| Opening | Contact |
| Daily: Feb–Mar & Nov–Dec 10.30am–4pm; Apr–Oct 10am–5.30pm | Glasgow Road, Whins of Milton, Stirling, Stirlingshire FK7 OLJ |
| | t 01786 812664 |
| | w nts.org.uk |

## 957 Stirling

# Stirling Castle

1 hr+    All year

Without doubt one of the grandest of all Scottish castles, both in its architecture and in its situation on a rocky outcrop. The Great Hall and gatehouse of James IV, the marvellous palace of James V, the Chapel Royal and the artillery fortifications are all of outstanding interest.

\* Audio guides in 6 languages
\* Regimental Museum of the Highlanders

| Location | Admission |
|---|---|
| Off M9, in old town | Adult £8, Child £3, Concs £6 |
| Opening | Contact |
| Daily: Apr–Sep 9.30am–6pm; Oct–Mar 9.30am–5pm (last admission 45 mins before closing) | Esplanade, Stirling, Stirlingshire FK8 1EJ |
| | t 01786 450000 |
| | w historic-scotland.gov.uk |

## 958 Stirling

# Wallace Monument

1 hr    All year

This is a chance to renew your acquaintance with Scotland's national hero and the Hollywood legend, Sir William Wallace, popularly known as Braveheart, at the spectacular 220ft (67m) National Wallace Monument, completed in 1869.

\* See the mighty two-handed broadsword
\* Exhibition of the building of the Monument

| Location | Admission |
|---|---|
| Off M9 junction 10, 1 mile NE of Stirling town centre | Adult £6, Child & Concs £4 |
| Opening | Contact |
| Daily: Mar–May & Oct 10am–5pm; Jun 10am–6pm; Jul–Aug 9.30am–6pm; Sep 9.30am–5pm; Nov–Feb 10.30am–4pm | Abbey Craig, Stirling, Stirlingshire FK9 5LF |
| | t 01786 472140 |
| | w nationalwallacemonument.com |
| | e nwm@aillst.ossian.net |

959 Aberdeen

# Aberdeen Maritime Museum

1 hr+   All year

This museum tells the story of Aberdeen's long, close relationship with the sea. It houses a unique collection, covering shipbuilding, fast sailing ships, fishing and port history, and is the only place in the UK where you can see displays about the North Sea oil industry.

\* Incorporates Provost Ross's House, built in 1593
\* Offers a spectacular viewpoint over busy harbour

**Location**
On the harbour

**Opening**
Daily: Mon–Sat 10am–5pm,
Sun 12noon–3pm

**Admission**
Free

**Contact**
Shiprow, Aberdeen AB11 5BY

t  01224 337700
w  aagm.co.uk
e  info@aagm.co.uk

960 Aberdeen

# Beach Leisure Centre

4 hrs+   All year

This remarkable centre has a leisure pool with many water features, including waves, a fountain and rapids. There is a well-equipped fitness studio, saunas, a steam room and a double-sized sports hall, equipped for virtually every indoor game.

\* Free crèche
\* Ice arena

**Location**
Next to the beach at Aberdeen

**Opening**
Please phone for details

**Admission**
Facilities individually priced

**Contact**
Beach Promenade,
Aberdeen AB24 5NR

t  01224 647647
w  www.aberdeencity.gov.uk
e  info@aberdeencity.gov.uk

961 Ballater

# Balmoral Castle & Estate

1 hr+   Apr–Jul

The Queen's favourite home is still a thriving estate. A visit provides a marvellous insight into royal heritage and the life of a large estate, which provides employment and housing as well as working to conserve and regenerate the natural environment.

\* Access to grounds, gardens, exhibitions, shops, tea
  room & ballroom

**Location**
Off A93, between Ballater & Braemar

**Opening**
Daily: Apr–Jul 10am–5pm
(last admission 4pm)

**Admission**
Adult £6, Child £1, Concs £5

**Contact**
Estates Office, Balmoral Estates,
Ballater, Aberdeenshire AB35 5TB

t  01339 742534
w  balmoralcastle.com
e  info@balmoralcastle.com

© Britain on View

## 962 Dufftown

# Glenfiddich Distillery

2 hrs    All year

Visit the home of the only Highland single malt Scotch whisky that is distilled, matured and bottled at its distillery. Whisky has flowed from the stills at this site since 1887. A must for all whisky connoisseurs.

\* Distillery tours & shop
\* Visitor centre

**Location**
On A941, ½ mile N of Dufftown

**Opening**
Daily: Easter–mid Oct Mon–Sat
9.30am–4.30pm, Sun 12noon–4.30pm;
mid Oct–Easter Mon–Fri
9.30am–4.30pm;
closed 2 weeks at Christmas

**Admission**
Free

**Contact**
Dufftown, Banffshire AB55 4DH

t  01340 820373
w  glenfiddich.com

## 963 Forres

# Findhorn Heritage Icehouse

1 hr    May–Sep

Explore underground arched chambers built 150 years ago to store ice for packing salmon on the way to London. The chambers are now used to display all aspects of the salmon fishing industry. Visit the Heritage Centre where the history and ecology are graphically displayed.

\* Junior quiz to complete
\* See the unique Findhorn class yacht

**Location**
From Forres take B9089 to Kinloss,
then the B9011 to Findhorn & follow
signs

**Opening**
Jun–Aug daily 2pm–5pm;
May & Sep Sat–Sun 2pm–5pm

**Admission**
Free, donations welcomed

**Contact**
North Shore, Findhorn
Forres, Moray IV36 3YL

t  01309 690659
w  findhornbay.net
e  s.eibbor@tesco.net

## 964 Fraserburgh

# The Museum of Scottish Lighthouses

2 hrs+    All year

Located in Scotland's oldest lighthouse, the museum tells the history of Scotland's lighthouses. There are multi screen audio-visual presentations and a guided tour to the top of the fully restored lighthouse where visitors can enjoy panoramic views of the Buchan coast.

\* Largest collection of lighthouse equipment in the UK
\* First lighthouse built on top of a fortified castle

**Location**
In Fraserburgh

**Opening**
Daily: Apr–Oct, Mon–Sat, 11am–5pm,
Sun, 12 noon–5pm; Jul–Aug, Mon–Sat,
10am–6pm, Sun, 11am–6pm; Nov–Mar,
Mon–Sat, 11am–4pm, Sun 12 noon–4pm

**Admission**
Adult £5, Child £2, Concs £4

**Contact**
Kinnaird Head, Stevenson Road,
Fraserburgh AB43 9DU

t  01346 511022
w  lighthousemuseum.co.uk

## 965 Peterhead

# Peterhead Maritime Heritage

1 hr+    Jun–Aug

This heritage centre, housed in an award-winning building, offers an historic look back at the Peterhead experience in sea-based industries. There are Interactive displays on fishing, whaling, navigation and a brief insight into the oil industry.

\* Audio-visual displays on maritime life
\* 3 Star Speciality Attraction

**Location**
Overlooking Peterhead Bay &
beside beach and marina. Reached via
A90 or A950

**Opening**
Daily: Jun–Aug 10.30am–5pm, Sun
11.30am–5pm

**Admission**
Free

**Contact**
South Road, Peterhead,
Aberdeenshire AB42 2YP

t  01779 473000
w  aberdeenshire.gov.uk

## 966 Aviemore

# Cairngorm Reindeer Centre

½ hr    Feb–Dec

See Britain's only reindeer herd roaming free in the Cairngorm mountains. These extremely tame and friendly animals are a joy to all who come and meet them. Under supervision, visitors can feed and stroke the animals in this herd of about 50.

* Guided tours on the hills (weather permitting)
* Learn more about these fascinating creatures

**Location**
6 miles E of Aviemore

**Opening**
Daily: Feb half-term, Apr & Oct–Dec 11am; May–Sep 11am & 2.30pm

**Admission**
Adult £8, Child & Concs £4

**Contact**
Glenmore, Aviemore, Invernessshire PH22 1QU

t 01479 861228
w reindeer-company.demon.co.uk
e info@reindeer-company.demon.co.uk

## 967 Balmaha

# Loch Lomond National Nature Reserve

3 hrs    All year

Inchailloch, one of the most accessible of Loch Lomond's 38 islands, has a long association with Christianity. It is cloaked in oak woodland, with a wealth of bird life and flora, and there are several woodland trails giving fantastic views of the loch.

* Wonderful camp & picnic site
* Remains of a C13 parish church

**Location**
Inchailloch is reached by ferry from Balmaha boatyard

**Opening**
Daily: wardens present Apr–Sep

**Admission**
Free

**Contact**
Loch Lomond & Trossachs National Park, Balmaha Visitor Centre

t 01389 722600
w lochlomond-trossachs.org
e info@lochlomond-trossachs.org

## 968 Broadford

# *Family's Pride II* Glassbottom Boat Trips

1 hr    Mar–Oct

Frequent daily sailings provide an opportunity to see the stunning coastal scenery of Skye and marine wildlife (which may include dolphins, whales and seals), both above and below the waves through unique undersea windows, enhanced by an aquatic floodlight system.

* Trips on *SkyeJet*, a water-jet propelled Rigid Inflatable Boat (RIB) also available

**Location**
In Broadford, Isle of Skye, 8 miles from Skye Bridge

**Opening**
Daily: Mar–Oct 10.30am–4.45pm

**Admission**
Adult £9.50, Child (under 12) £4.75

**Contact**
5 Scullamus, Breakish, Isle of Skye IV42 8QB

t 0800 783 2175
w glassbottomboat.co.uk

969 Culloden Moor

# Culloden Battlefield

1 hr+          Feb–Dec

Few names in Scottish history evoke more emotion than Culloden, the bleak moor where, in 1746, Bonnie Prince Charlie's hopes were crushed and the Jacobite Rising was put down. The prince's forces were greatly outnumbered, but nevertheless went into battle with legendary courage.

\* Permanent exhibition of weapons used in the battle
\* Audio-visual programme

**Location**
On B9006, 5 miles E of Inverness

**Opening**
Daily: Apr–Oct 9am–6pm;
Nov–Dec & Feb–Mar 11am–4pm

**Admission**
Adult £5, Child & Concs £4

**Contact**
The National Trust for Scotland,
Culloden Moor, Inverness IV2 5EU

t 01463 790607
w nts.org.uk/culloden

970 Drumnadrochit

# Loch Ness Monster Exhibition Centre

1 hr+          All Year

Through photographs, descriptions and film footage, this exhibition presents the evidence about the existence of the Loch Ness Monster. It also highlights the efforts of various search expeditions, by both individuals and respected institutions, such as Operation Deepscan.

\* Travel round the loch, view places & meet locals
\* Exhibition cinema in 8 languages

**Location**
On A82, W of Inverness

**Opening**
Daily: Apr–Oct 9am–9pm
Nov–Mar 9am–5pm

**Admission**
Adult £5, Child £3.50, Concs £3.95

**Contact**
Drumnadrochit, Invernessshire
IV63 6TU

t 01456 450342
w lochness-centre.com
e donald@lochness-centre.com

## 971 Fort William

# The Jacobite Steam Train

6 hrs    Jun–Oct

Described as one of the great railway journeys of the world, the Jacobite Steam Train leaves Fort William and travels on an 84-mile round trip. It passes Ben Nevis, then crosses the Glenfinnan Viaduct used in the *Harry Potter* films and arrives by the Atlantic Ocean in Mallaig.

* Leaves Fort William at 10.20am & returns at 4pm
* 1½ hour stopover in Mallaig

| Location | Contact |
|---|---|
| Fort William station, in town centre | West Coast Railway Company, Warton Road, Carnforth, Lancashire LA5 9HX |
| **Opening** | |
| 29 May–22 Jul Mon–Fri 10.20am; | t 01463 239026 |
| 23 Jul–27 Aug Sun–Fri 10.20am; | w steamtrain.info |
| 28 Aug–13 Oct Mon–Fri 10.20am | e jacobite@wcrc.co.uk |
| **Admission** | |
| *Return tickets* Adult £27, Child £16 | |
| *First class* £40, £20 | |

## 972 Fort William

# Treasures of the Earth

1hr    Feb–Dec

A unique collection of minerals, fossils and precious stones from all around the world, displayed in simulated caves and caverns. There are casts of Tyrannosaurus Rex and a sabre-toothed tiger, together with fossil fish and dinosaur bones.

| Location | Contact |
|---|---|
| In Corpach by Fort William | Corpach, Fort William, Invernessshire PH33 7JL |
| **Opening** | |
| Daily: *summer* 9.30am–7pm; | t 01397 772283 |
| *winter* 10am–5pm; closed Jan | |
| **Admission** | |
| Adult £3.50, Child £2, Concs £3 | |

## 973 Fort William

# Vertical Descents

3 hrs+    All year

Located at Inchree Falls, this is Scotland's first and longest canyoning descent. Canyoning involves a combination of abseiling, swimming and sliding through water flumes, plus jumping into giant rock pools, as you make your way downstream. Try abseiling and fun yakking, too.

* Other activities include paintballing & white-water rafting
* All necessary clothing & equipment provided

| Location | Contact |
|---|---|
| Off A82, 7 miles S of Fort William | Inchree Falls, Inchree, Onich, nr Fort William PH33 6SE |
| **Opening** | |
| All year: closed Christmas hols | t 01855 821593 |
| | w activities-scotland.com |
| **Admission** | e verticaldescents@yahoo.com |
| £35 per person (half-day canyoning) | |
| Activities individually priced | |

974 Glencoe

# Glencoe Visitor Centre

1 hr    All year

Some of the finest climbing and walking country in the Highlands is to be found within this area of dramatic landscapes and historical fact and legend. The infamous massacre of 1692 took place throughout the glen, one of the main locations being near the new visitor centre.

* Summer events programme
* Display on the history of mountaineering in the glen

**Location**
On A82, between Glasgow
& Fort William

**Opening**
Mar daily 10am–4pm;
Apr–Aug daily 9.30am–5.30pm;
Sep–Oct daily 10am–5pm;
Nov–Feb Thu–Sun 10am–4pm

**Admission**
Adult £5, Child & Concs £4

**Contact**
Ballachulish, Argyll PH49 4LA
t  01855 811307
w nts.org.uk
e sborland@nts.org.uk

---

975 Inverary

# Inverary Castle

1 hr    Apr–Oct

Also known as the 'Fairy Tale Castle', it's easy to see why this is one of Scotland's hidden treasures. Originally the home of the Campbell clan, the castle now boasts a selection of magnificent rooms through which the visitor can trace its fascinating history.

* History of the clan Campbell
* Remains the home of the Duke & Duchess of Argyll

**Location**
On A83, on shores of Loch Fyne

**Opening**
Daily: Jun–Sep Mon–Sat
10am–5.45pm, Sun 1pm–5.45pm;
Apr–May & Oct Mon–Thu & Sat
10am–1pm & 2pm–5.45pm, Sun
1pm–5.45pm

**Admission**
Adult £6.30, Child £4.10, Concs £5.20

**Contact**
The Factor, Argyll Estates Office,
Inverary, Argyll PA32 8XE
t  01499 302203
w inverary-castle.com
e enquiries@inveraray-castle.com

---

976 Lewis

# Calanais Standing Stones

1 hr    All year

This is a cross-shaped setting of 50 standing stones. The site dates back to 3,000BC and the configuration, reminiscent of the larger formations of Carnac in Brittany, is unique in Scotland. The audio-visual presentation in the visitor centre tells their fascinating story.

* Visitor centre
* Story of the Stones exhibition

**Location**
Off A859, 12 miles W of Stornoway

**Opening**
*Site* Daily
*Visitor centre* Apr–Sep Mon–Sat
10am–6pm; Oct–Mar Wed–Sat
10am–4pm

**Admission**
*Exhibition* Adult £1.85, Child 85p,
Concs £1.35

**Contact**
Visitor Centre, Calanais, Isle of Lewis,
Western Isles HS2 9DY
t  01851 621422
w historic-scotland.gov.uk

977 Kyle of Lochalsh

# Eilean Donan Castle

1 hr    Mar–Nov

Eilean Donan is located on a small island near Dornie, Rossshire. In a superbly romantic setting amid silent, tree-clad hills, it possesses a rare and dreamlike quality, but, in reality, is a fortress of solid stone and formidable defences. The Isle of Skye can be seen across the water.

\* Visitor centre & gift shop
\* Most photographed castle in Scotland

**Location**
On A87, 8 miles from Kyle of Lochalsh

**Opening**
Apr–Oct 10am–5.30pm;
Mar–Nov 10am–3.30pm

**Admission**
Adult £4.75, Child & Concs £3.75

**Contact**
Dornie, Kyle of Lochalsh IV40 8DX

t 01599 555202
w eileandonancastle.com
e info@donan.f9.co.uk

978 Mull

# Hebridean Whale & Dolphin Trust

½ hr    All year

Mull has a greater variety and abundance of wildlife than any other Hebridean island. Go to the HWDT visitor centre in Tobermory for information on whale and dolphin-watching trips, as well as a whole range of other wildlife 'safaris'.

\* Huge variety of Scottish wildlife in its natural habitat
\* Land & sea 'safaris'

**Location**
To reach Mull take ferry from Oban to Craignure. Trust is opposite clock tower in Tobermory

**Opening**
Daily: Apr–Oct 10am–5.30pm;
Nov–Mar 11am–5pm

**Admission**
Free

**Contact**
28 Main Street, Tobermory,
Isle of Mull, Argyll PA75 6NU

t 01688 302620
w hwdt.org
e info@hwdt.org

## 979 Oban

# McCaig's Tower

1 hr    All year

Undoubtedly Oban's most outstanding feature, McCaig's Tower was built in 1897 by local banker John Stuart McCaig to provide work for local stonemasons and a lasting monument to his family. The steep climb from the town centre is well worth the effort.

* Breathtaking views over Oban Bay to the Atlantic islands
* Peaceful gardens inside the tower

| Location | Contact |
|---|---|
| Short, steep walk from town centre | Oban Tourist Information Centre, Argyll Square, Oban, Argyll |
| Opening | |
| Daily | t 01631 563122 |
| | w oban.org.uk |
| Admission | e info@oban.org.uk |
| Free | |

## 981 Skye

# Dunvegan Castle

2 hrs    All year

Northern Scotland's oldest inhabited castle is also Skye's most famous landmark, having been the seat and home of the MacLeod chiefs for 800 years. Dunvegan Castle is a fortress stronghold in an idyllic lochside setting, surrounded by dramatic scenery.

* Many fine oil paintings & great clan treasures
* Picturesque woodland garden

| Location | Contact |
|---|---|
| 1 mile N of Dunvegan | Isle of Skye IV55 8WF |
| Opening | |
| Daily: Mar–Oct 10am–5.30pm | t 01470 521206 |
| Nov–Feb 11am–4pm | w dunvegancastle.com |
| | e infp@dunvegancastle.com |
| Admission | |
| Summer Adult £6.80, Child £3.80, Concs £5.80 | |
| Winter £5, £2.50, £3.50 | |

## 980 Oban

# Scottish Sealife & Marine Sanctuary

2½ hrs    All year

Located on the shores of beautiful Loch Creran, the sanctuary is home to more than 30 fascinating natural marine habitats containing everything from shrimps and starfish to sharks and stingrays. The sanctuary cares for many sick and injured seal pups every year.

* 3-Star Marine Attraction
* New displays added regularly

| Location | Contact |
|---|---|
| 10 miles N of Oban on A828 | Sanctuary, Barcaldine By Oban, Argyll PA37 1SE |
| Opening | |
| Daily: Feb–Nov 10am–6pm (last admission 5pm); Dec–Jan weekends & hols | t 01631 720386 |
| | w sealsanctuary.co.uk |
| | e oban@sealife.fsbusiness.co.uk |
| Admission | |
| Please phone for details | |

© Arnol Blackhouse

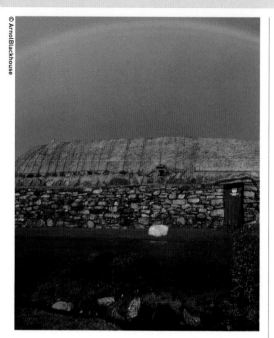

## 982 Spean Bridge

# Monster Activities

2 hrs    All year

From its base in the Scottish Highlands, this sports centre offers outdoor activities of all kinds, including the country's most exciting white-water rafting. Not only does it offer instruction, hire, courses and short breaks, it also guarantees fun for the whole family.

\* All kinds of outdoor activities on land & water
\* All necessary equipment available for hire

| Location | Contact |
|---|---|
| On A82, between Fort William & Inverness | Great Glen Water Park, South Laggan, Spean Bridge, Invernessshire PH34 4EA |
| Opening | |
| Daily: 9.30am–5.30pm | t 01809 501340 |
| | w monsteractivities.com |
| Admission | e info@monsteractivities.com |
| Depends on activity, please phone for details | |

## 983 Stornoway

# The Black House Museum

½ hr+    All year

The site includes a traditional Lewis thatched crofter's cottage, or black house, with byre and stackyard, complete with a peat fire burning in the central hearth. There is also a restored 1920s white house and a visitor centre with fascinating information about Hebridean life.

\* Green Gold Tourism Award winner
\* 5-Star Scottish Tourism Award

| Location | Admission |
|---|---|
| Off A858 | Adult £3, Child £1, Concs £2.30 |
| Opening | Contact |
| Apr–Sep Mon–Sat 9.30am–6pm; Oct–Mar Mon–Sat 9.30am–4pm | Arnol, Isle of Lewis HS2 9DB |
| | t 01851 710395 |
| | w historic-scotland.gov.uk |

## 984 Tain

# Glenmorangie Distillery Centre

1 hr    All year

Tour the distillery in the company of one of the guides, who will explain the whisky-making process from beginning to end and introduce you to the Sixteen Men of Tain who make it, before a visit to the tasting room to sample the results of their industry and skill.

\* Located in the Glen of Tranquillity
\* Regular distillery tours

| Location | Admission |
|---|---|
| On A9, 1 hour N of Inverness | Adult £2.50 |
| Opening | Contact |
| Shop Daily: Mon–Fri 9am–5pm, Sat 10am–4pm, Sun 12noon–4pm | Tain, Rossshire IV19 1PZ |
| Tours Daily: 10.30am, 11.30am, 2.30pm & 3.30pm (prebooking advised) | t 01862 892477 |
| | w glenmorangie.com |
| | e visitors@glenmorangieplc.co.uk |

## 985 Alloway

# Burns National Heritage Park

2 hrs    All year

Now fully restored to its original state, Burns's cottage forms the heart of this attraction, offering a unique encounter with Scotland's most exceptional man. Set among the delightful scenery of historic Alloway, this is an opportunity to experience Scotland's national poet.

* Unique authentic locations & artefacts
* World's most important Robert Burns collection

**Location**
On A719, S of Ayr

**Opening**
Daily: Apr–Oct 10am–5.30pm;
Nov–Mar 10am–5pm

**Admission**
Adult £4, Child £1.60, Concs £3

**Contact**
Murdoch's Lone, Alloway,
Ayr KA7 4PQ

t  01292 443700
w  burnsheritagepark.com
e  info@burnsheritagepark.com

© Tony Stuchbury www.ajsphotos.co.uk

---

## 986 Annan

# Devil's Porridge Exhibition

1 hr    May–Oct

In 1915 the greatest munitions factory on earth was built in Gretna; 30,000 people were employed in the factory, which stretched for 9 miles and was 2 miles wide. The exhibition tells the story of this remarkable venture and the secret cities that were created to accommodate its workers.

* Learn about Britain's worst rail disaster
* Hear stories from WWII evacuees

**Location**
Follow A75 from Gretna, take
Eastriggs turn off & follow signs

**Opening**
May–Oct Mon–Sat 10am–4pm,
Sun 12noon–4pm

**Admission**
Adults £1.50, Child & Concs £1

**Contact**
Dunedin Road, Eastriggs,
nr Annan DG12 6QE

t  01461 700021
e  devils-porridge@tiscali.net
w  devilsporridge.co.uk

---

## 987 Ayr

# The Electric Brae

½ hr    All year

A hill with a difference. While the views are spectacular, try placing a round object, like a ball, on the ground. In which direction do you think it will roll? Thanks to an optical illusion, the ball will roll upwards; let off the handbrake for a second and the car will move uphill!

**Location**
A719 9 miles S of Ayr, 2 miles S of
Dunure, 1 mile N of the A719–B7023
junction, NW edge of the hamlet of
Knoweside

**Opening**
Daily: at any reasonable time

**Admission**
Free

**Contact**
t  01292 678100
w  south-ayrshire.gov.uk/tourism/
around_dunure.htm

988 Caerlaverock

# WWT Caerlaverock Wetlands Centre

½ day    All year

This 1,400-acre wild nature reserve is a must for bird lovers. The site has hides and observation towers linked by a network of screened approaches. The number of barnacle geese that fly from Norway to the Solway Firth each year is testament to the quality of the wetlands.

* Self-catering accommodation available
* Badger-watching & summer nature trail

**Location**
Located 9 miles SE of Dumfries along Solway Coast Heritage Trail

**Opening**
Daily: 10am–5pm

**Admission**
Adult £4.40, Child (under 4s) free, (over 4s) £2.70, Concs £3.60

**Contact**
Eastpark Farm, Caerlaverock, Dumfriesshire DG1 4RS

t 01387 770200
w wwt.org.uk
e info.caerlaverock@wwt.org.uk

---

989 Dumfries

# Dumfries Museum & Camera Obscura

1 hr    Mar–Oct

A treasure house of the history of south-west Scotland, the museum is centred on the C18 windmill tower that stands above the town. On the top floor there is a camera obscura and on the tabletop screen visitors can see panoramic views of Dumfries and the surrounding countryside.

* Prehistoric reptile footprints
* Tools & weapons from the area's oldest people

**Location**
In town centre

**Opening**
Daily: Apr–Sep Mon–Sat 10am–5pm, Sun 2pm–5pm;
Mar & Oct Tue–Sat 10am–1pm & 2pm–5pm

**Admission**
*Museum* Free
*Camera Obscura* Adult £1.80, Child & Concs 90p

**Contact**
Rotchell Road, Dumfries DG2 7SW

t 01387 253374
w dumfal.gov.uk/museums
e dumfriesmuseum2dumfal.gov.uk

---

990 Dumfries

# Gretna Green World Famous Blacksmith's Shop

1 hr+    All year

Runaway marriages began in 1753, when it became illegal to marry under 21. However, in Scotland it was, and still is, possible to marry at 16. Gretna Green is the first village across the border that many 'elopers' reached and the Blacksmith's Shop was the centre of the marriage trade.

* Old coach collection
* Juicy stories of romance, intrigue & scandal

**Location**
On A74, just N of border

**Opening**
Daily: Apr–Sep 9am–early evening;
Oct–Mar 9am–5pm

**Admission**
*Exhibition* Adult £3, Child & Concs £2.50

**Contact**
Gretna Green Group Ltd,
Headless Cross, Gretna Green,
Dumfriesshire DG16 5EA

t 01461 338441
w gretnagreen.com
e info@gretnagreen.com

991 Eyemouth

# Eyemouth Museum

1 hr    Apr–Oct

This museum has a magnificent 15ft x 4ft tapestry that commemorates the East coast fishing disaster of 1881 in which 189 local fishermen were drowned. It also has exhibitions on fishing, farming, milling, wheelwrighting, and blacksmithing.

* 3-Star Attraction
* Newly refurbished

**Location**
In centre of town

**Opening**
Daily: Apr–Jun & Sep Mon–Sat 10am–5pm, Sun 12noon–3pm; Jul–Aug Mon–Sat 10am–5pm, Sun 12noon–4pm; Oct Mon–Sat 10am–4pm

**Admission**
Adult £2.50, Child free, Concs £2

**Contact**
Auld Kirk, Manse Road, Eyemouth
t 01890750678

992 Hawick

# Drumlanrig's Tower

1 hr    Mar–Oct

The Black Tower of Drumlanrig is an imposing landmark in the Scottish Border town of Hawick. The tower has borne silent witness to the savage cross-border warfare and bitter interfamily feuding that marked the town's turbulent past.

* Exhibition tells the story of the house
* Display of watercolours by the artist Tom Scott

**Location**
Hawick in high street

**Opening**
Daily: Apr–Jun & Sep–Oct Mon–Sat 10am–5pm, Sun 1pm–5pm; Jul–Aug Mon–Sat 10am–6pm, Sun 1pm–5pm; winter times vary, please phone for details

**Admission**
Adult £2.50, Child free, Concs £1.50

**Contact**
1 Towerknowe, Hawick TD9 9EN
t 01450 373457
w discovertheborders.co.uk/places/41.html

993 Heathhall

# Dumfries & Galloway Aviation Museum

3hrs    Easter–Oct

Founded in 1977 by a group of aviation enthusiasts and based on a former WWII airfield, the museum is located in and around the original 3-storey-high control tower. It is now home to engines, memorabilia and records of personal histories.

* 3-Star Visitor Attraction
* Huge collection of artefacts

**Location**
On Heathhall Industrial Estate, easily accessed from A75 Dumfries bypass. From town centre follow A701 Edinburgh road

**Opening**
Easter–Oct Sat–Sun 10am–5pm; Jul–Aug Wed–Fri 11am–4pm

**Admission**
Adult £2.50, Child & Concs £1.50

**Contact**
Heathhall Industrial Estate, Heathhall, Dumfries DG13PH
t 01387 251623
w dumfriesaviationmuseum.com
e alammin@hotmail.com

994 Isle of Arran

# King's Cave

2 hrs    All year

This is said to be the legendary spot where Robert the Bruce, dejected and battle weary, was inspired by the tenacity of a small spider as it painstakingly spun its web. He went on to win many battles after this episode. On the cave wall are rare writings by Picts.

**Location**
Off A841, near Blackwaterfoot, Isle of Arran, access by coastal path only

**Opening**
Daily: All reasonable times

**Admission**
Free

**Contact**
Blackwaterfoot, Isle of Arran
t 0845 225 5121
w showcaves.com

995 Kelso

# 995 Kelso

## Floors Castle

2 hrs    Apr–Oct

Boasting fine views over the River Tweed to the Cheviot Hills, the castle has been home to the Roxburghe family since it was built by WIlliam Adam in 1721. It houses superb collections of art, tapestries and antiques and is set in parkland that abounds with flora and fauna.

* Various sporting activities (golf, shooting) on offer
* Works by well-known artists, including Matisse

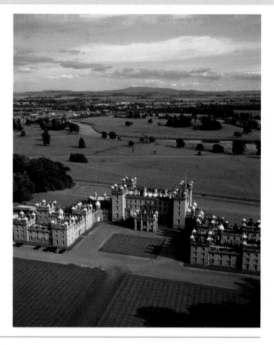

| Location | Contact |
|---|---|
| On edge of Kelso | Kelso, Roxburghshire TD5 7SF |
| **Opening** | t 01573 223333 |
| Daily: Apr–Oct 10am–4.30pm | w floorscastle.com |
| | e marketing@floorscastle.com |
| **Admission** | |
| Adult £6, Child £3.25, Concs £5 | |

# 996 Largs

## The Viking Experience

1 hr    Feb–Nov

This multimedia journey recounts the saga of the Vikings in Scotland, from invasion to defeat at the Battle of Largs. Meet the Gods and Valkyries in Valhalla, come face to face with Odin, the Viking god of war, and walk with him into the Viking world of 700 years ago.

* Shows begin regularly
* Leisure facilities, soft play centre & theatre

| Location | Admission |
|---|---|
| On Largs seafront | Adult £4, Child & Concs £3 |
| **Opening** | **Contact** |
| Daily: Apr–Sep 10.30am–5.30pm; | Vikingar, Greenock Road, |
| Mar & Oct 10.30am–3.30pm; | Largs, Ayrshire KA30 8QL |
| Feb & Nov Sat 12.30pm–3.30pm; | |
| Sun 10.30am–3.30pm | t 01475 689777 |
| | w vikingar.co.uk |
| | e info@vikingar.co.uk |

# 997 Lockerbie

## Carlyle's Birthplace

½ hr    May–Sep

The Arched House, in which Thomas Carlyle was born in 1795, was built by his father and uncle in 1791. Carlyle was a great writer and historian and one of the most powerful influences on C19 British thought. The house is now furnished to reflect Victorian domestic life.

* Collection of portraits
* Carlyle's belongings

| Location | Contact |
|---|---|
| Off M74, on A74, in Ecclefechan, | The Arched House, Ecclefechan, |
| 5½ miles SE of Lockerbie | Lockerbie, Dumfries & Galloway |
| | DG11 3DG |
| **Opening** | |
| Please phone for details | t 01576 300666 |
| | w nts.org.uk |
| **Admission** | |
| Adult £5, Child & Concs £4 | |

## 998 Melrose

# Abbotsford

1 hr+     Mar–Oct

Abbotsford is the house built and lived in by Sir Walter Scott, the C19 novelist and author of timeless classics such as *Waverley*, *Rob Roy* and *Ivanhoe*. Situated on the banks of the River Tweed, the house contains an impressive collection of relics, weapons and armour.

\* Rob Roy's gun & Montrose's sword
\* Extensive grounds & walled garden

**Location**
On B6360, 2 miles W of Melrose

**Opening**
20 Mar–30 Oct Mon–Sat 9.30am–5pm;
Mar–May & Oct Sun 2pm–5pm;
Jun–Sep Sun 9.30am–5pm

**Admission**
Adult £5, Child £2.50

**Contact**
Melrose, Borders TD6 9BQ

t  01896 752043
w  scottisabbotsford.co.uk
e  enquiries@scottisabbotsford.co.uk

## 999 Melrose

# Melrose Abbey

½ hr     All year

Arguably the finest of Scotland's border abbeys, Melrose is a magnificent ruin on a grand scale with lavishly decorated masonry. It is thought to be the burial place of Robert the Bruce's heart, marked with a commemorative carved stone plaque within the grounds.

\* Large collection of objects found during excavation
\* Museum with local artefacts found in abbey grounds

**Location**
Off A7 / A68, in Melrose

**Opening**
Apr–Sep daily 9.30am–6.30pm;
Oct–Mar Mon–Sat 9.30am–4.30pm,
Sun 2pm–4.30pm

**Admission**
Adult £4, Child £1.60, Concs £3

**Contact**
Abbey Street, Melrose,
Roxburghshire TD6 9LG

t  01896 822562
w  historic-scotland.gov.uk

## 1000 Melrose

# Three Hills Roman Centre & Fort

4 hrs+        All year

The most important Roman military complex between Hadrian's Wall and the Antonine Wall guarded and secured the crossing of the River Tweed at Newstead in the C1 and C2 AD. Excavations have revealed much of what went on there. See finds from 1905–1910.

\* See millennium milestone & timber tower
\* Viewing platforms & information boards

**Location**
Market Square in Melrose

**Opening**
Daily: Apr–Oct 10.30am–4.30pm
Nov–Mar please phone for details

**Admission**
*Walks* Adult £3, Child free, Concs £2.50
*Exhibition* £1.50, £1, £1

**Contact**
t 01896 822651
w trimontium.net

## 1001 Newton Stewart

# Galloway Red Deer Range

2 hrs        Jun–Sep

This attraction has a viewpoint near the road from which beautiful red deer can be observed in their natural habitat. Visitors to the range can also walk among the deer, photograph them and even touch them, under supervision – a memorable experience.

\* Guided tours in summer
\* See & hear roaring stags during the rutting season

**Location**
On A712, 3 miles SW of Clatteringshaws Loch

**Opening**
End of Jun–mid-Sep Tue & Thu 11am–2pm, Sun 11am–2.30pm
*Tours* Tue & Thu 11am & 2.30pm, Sun 2.30pm

**Admission**
Adult £3.50, Child £1.25, Concs £2.50

**Contact**
Red Deer Range Car Park,
nr Clatteringshaws, Newton Stewart,
Dumfries & Galloway DG7 3SQ

t 01671 402420
w forestry.gov.uk/gallowayforestpark
e galloway@forestry.gsi.gov.uk

# Index

# Acknowledgements & Picture Credits

The Publishers would like to acknowledge the important contribution the British Tourist Authority made to this publication through the use of images from its website, *www.britainonview.com*.

The publishers would like to thank The National Trust, The National Trust for Scotland and English Heritage who kindly supplied photographs for use with their entries.

The publishers would also like to thank all contributors who provided information, and particularly all those who kindly supplied photographs. Particular thanks go to Tony Stuchbury (www.ajsphotos.co.uk).

Compiled, edited and designed by Butler and Tanner. Edited by Libby Willis. Design and layout by Lyn Davies and Carole McDonald. Project Manager Nick Heal. Special thanks to Carl Luke and Jennie Golding.